CALIFORNIA CIVIL PROCEDURE

Fifth Edition

David I. Levine
Raymond L. Sullivan Professor of Law
University of California
College of the Law, San Francisco

Rochelle J. Shapell
Adjunct Professor of Law (Retired)
University of California
College of the Law, San Francisco

QUICK REVIEW SERIES

WEST ACADEMIC

Sum & Substance Quick Review Series is a publication of West Academic Publishing.

860 Blue Gentian Road, Suite 350
Eagan, MN 55121
1-877-888-1330

Published in the United States of America

ISBN: 979-8-31770-424-7

In Memory of Our Parents

PREFACE

As students go through law school, they sometimes wonder whether they should know more about the differences in civil practice in state and federal courts. Failing to act on this concern is risky. Students who start their professional careers assuming that civil procedure in California's state courts fully mirrors the federal system they encountered in their first civil procedure course are in for an unpleasant surprise. It is especially perilous to presume that the two systems operate the same way because state civil procedure is eligible for testing on the California Bar Examination.

Readers who find their way to this Quick Review will probably fall into one of four groups. Some law students will have chosen to take an advanced course in California Civil Procedure and are now looking for a study guide. Other students will have neglected or elected not to take a state procedure course, but they are nevertheless interested in learning about the differences between the two systems. Graduating students looking toward the California Bar Examination may find this outline a helpful supplemental study aid. New (or not so new) lawyers may also find this Quick Review to be a handy guide if they are about to be cast into the unfamiliar territory of state court. Whichever category describes you best, we hope that this Quick Review will meet your needs.

This Quick Review provides a tour through the most important aspects of California civil procedure. The book addresses topics not usually covered in the standard first-year course in procedure where California has taken a road not followed in federal practice. It also features topics where California procedural law has solved problems in somewhat different fashion than in the federal courts. Throughout the book you will find sections entitled "Compare Federal Procedure," which expressly highlight the state/federal differences that are so crucial to this field of study. Finally, each chapter contains illustrations and chapters 2–9 include sample examination questions, placed in California state courts, so you can test your understanding of the topics. (All characters appearing in illustrations and sample examination questions are fictitious. Any resemblance to real persons, living or dead, is coincidental.)

Nearly all of the state and federal statutes and rules cited in the Quick Review can be found in David I. Levine, Civil Procedure in California: State and Federal. West Academic publishes this paperback of supplemental materials annually. In Chapter 1 of the Quick Review, we cite to useful secondary sources for further understanding of, or research in, California Civil Procedure. We have eliminated internal quotation marks when necessary to reduce clutter and increase clarity.

PREFACE

We express our profound thanks to Stefano G. Moscato and William R. Slomanson, our coauthors on Cases and Materials in California Civil Procedure (West Academic, 7th ed. 2026). Through our collaboration on that project, they have contributed enormously to our understanding of this challenging field.

D.I.L.
R.J.S.

May 2026

TABLE OF CONTENTS

CALIFORNIA CIVIL PROCEDURE

Fifth Edition

CHAPTER 1

INTRODUCTION

I. SOURCES OF CALIFORNIA PROCEDURAL LAW

A. Primary Authorities

"Primary authorities" constitute "the law." See CCP §§ 1895–1899. All primary authorities have binding force in their respective jurisdictions.

1. Constitutions

a. Constitution of California

California's Constitution contains many procedural provisions. For example, the Constitution sets out the structure and hierarchy of the state's trial and appellate courts (art. VI), and it secures the right to a jury trial in civil and criminal cases (art. I, § 16). In contrast to the U.S. Constitution, the state Constitution explicitly provides an inalienable right to privacy (art. I, § 1), which affects such procedural matters as the scope of discovery (see Chapter 4).

b. Constitution of the United States

The federal Constitution impacts California procedure to the extent its provisions apply to the states. For example, the Due Process Clause of the Fourteenth Amendment is applicable to the exercise of personal jurisdiction in California. See Chapter 2(II). However, the Seventh Amendment's right to a jury trial in civil cases does not apply to the states. Minneapolis & St. Louis Railroad Co. v. Bombolis, 241 U.S. 211, 36 S.Ct. 595, 60 L.Ed. 961 (1916). See Chapter 6(II).

2. Statutes

The California Code of Civil Procedure (CCP) is the repository for numerous provisions enacted by the California Legislature that govern state civil procedure. In addition to the CCP, several other California codes contain important procedural statutes, including the Civil, Evidence, and Government Codes.

3. Case Law

California appellate courts develop a body of legal precedent that is constantly evolving. Often, the courts interpret and apply constitutional provisions, statutory enactments, and rules of court. Sometimes, in keeping with the common law tradition, the appellate courts "make" law.

a. Structure of California Courts

California has three levels of courts:

1) Superior Court

Each of California's 58 counties has a trial court called the superior court. In civil matters, the superior courts are empowered to hear unlimited civil cases, limited civil cases, and small claims matters. See Chapter 2(I). In addition to conducting pretrial proceedings and trials, the superior courts are also authorized to review certain matters designated for hearing within the courts' appellate division. CCP § 77.

2) Court of Appeal

The California Court of Appeal hears appeals in panels of three justices. The Court of Appeal is divided into six geographic districts. The larger appellate districts are organized into divisions.

3) Supreme Court

The highest court of the state is the California Supreme Court. It has one Chief Justice and six Associate Justices.

The following chart describes the jurisdiction of each level of California court:

CALIFORNIA COURT SYSTEM

CALIFORNIA SUPREME COURT

One Chief Justice and Six Associate Justices

Jurisdiction

Discretion to hear appeals from Court of Appeal.
Must hear appeals directly from superior courts in death penalty matters.
Original jurisdiction in mandamus, certiorari, prohibition, and habeas corpus proceedings.
Hears appeals directly from decisions of Public Utilities Commission, recommendations of State Bar on attorney admission and discipline, and recommendations of Commission on Judicial Performance on discipline of judges.

CALIFORNIA COURT OF APPEAL

106 Justices in Six Districts (19 Divisions)
First District: San Francisco
Second District: Los Angeles, Ventura
Third District: Sacramento
Fourth District: San Diego, Riverside, Santa Ana
Fifth District: Fresno
Sixth District: San Jose

Jurisdiction

Hears appeals and writ petitions from decisions of superior courts within appellate district.
Original jurisdiction in mandamus, certiorari, prohibition, and habeas corpus proceedings.
Hears appeals and writ proceedings from decisions of Workers' Compensation Appeals Board, Agricultural Labor Relations Board, and Public Employment Relations Board.

CALIFORNIA SUPERIOR COURT

1,781 Judgeships, 257 authorized Commissioners and Referees
58 Counties, 450+ court locations

Jurisdiction

Trial Department: conducts pretrial and trial proceedings in civil (unlimited and limited) and criminal (felony and misdemeanor) cases.
Small Claims Division: conducts civil proceedings within jurisdictional limit.
Appellate Division: hears appeals from limited civil cases and criminal misdemeanor cases.

Source: David I. Levine, Stefano G. Moscato, Rochelle J. Shapell & William R. Slomanson, Cases and Materials on California Civil Procedure (West Academic, 7th ed. 2026).

b. Publication and Citation of Judicial Decisions

All California Supreme Court opinions are officially published. No superior court decisions at the trial level are officially published. Decisions of the Court of Appeal or the appellate division of the superior court are officially published according to criteria contained in Rule 8.1105 of the California Rules of Court (CRC) and implemented by the California Supreme Court. The California Supreme Court may order a published Court of Appeal opinion to be depublished. CRC 8.1125. If the California Supreme Court grants review of a published Court of Appeal decision, that decision may be cited only for its persuasive value or to show a conflict in the law. CRC 8.1105(e)(1) & 8.1115(e)(1).

1) Certification for Publication

Certification of a Court of Appeal or superior court appellate division decision for publication requires consideration of several factors, such as whether the opinion establishes a new rule of law or involves an issue of public interest. CRC 8.1105(b)–(c).

2) Citation to Unpublished Cases

With limited exceptions, citation to unpublished or depublished California Court of Appeal or superior court appellate division decisions is prohibited. CRC 8.1115. However, a party may cite unpublished decisions from other courts. See, e.g., Farm Raised Salmon Cases, 42 Cal.4th 1077, 72 Cal.Rptr.3d 112, 175 P.3d 1170 (2008) (unpublished federal court opinions), cert. denied, sub nom. Albertson's, Inc. v. Kanter, 555 U.S. 1097, 129 S.Ct. 896, 173 L.Ed.2d 106 (2009); and Bushansky v. Soon-Shiong, 23 Cal.App.5th 1000, 234 Cal.Rptr.3d 54 (2018) (unpublished opinions from other state courts).

3) *Compare Federal Procedure*

Federal Rule of Appellate Procedure (FRAP) 32.1 permits citation of all federal opinions and dispositions issued after January 1, 2007, including those that have been designated as "unpublished" or "non-precedential." Ninth Circuit Rule 36–3 prohibits citation of most pre-2007 unpublished dispositions issued by courts within the circuit. Unpublished rulings are specifically deemed "not precedent" under the Ninth Circuit rule.

4) Illustration

Defendant Demi filed a motion for summary judgment against Plaintiff Park in an action pending in San Benito County Superior Court. In her memorandum of points and authorities in support of the motion, Demi included a citation to a California Court of Appeal decision that she believed was the ideal precedent for her argument. Unfortunately for Demi, the case had not been certified for publication pursuant to CRC 8.1105. Under CRC 8.1115, Demi may not include the citation in her memorandum, and the court may not rely upon the unpublished decision when ruling on the motion. Schmier v. Supreme Court of California, 78 Cal.App.4th 703, 93 Cal.Rptr.2d 580, cert. denied, 531 U.S. 958, 121 S.Ct. 382, 148 L.Ed.2d 294 (2000).

4. California Rules of Court

The Judicial Council of California is authorized by the California Constitution (art. VI, § 6) and statutes (e.g., CCP §§ 575 & 901) to adopt the California Rules of Court (CRC), which govern many aspects of civil procedure and practice in the state's trial and appellate courts. The state Constitution (art. VI, § 6) requires that the CRC "not be inconsistent with statute." The main purposes of the CRC are to achieve statewide uniformity and to supplement statutory provisions contained in the CCP and other codes.

5. Local Rules

The superior courts are empowered by CCP § 575.1 and Cal. Gov't Code § 68070 to adopt written rules applicable to an individual county superior court. The six districts of the Court of Appeal also are authorized to publish local rules. CRC 10.1030. Local rules are invalid if they are inconsistent with the California Constitution, statutes, or the statewide CRC. Elkins v. Superior Court, 41 Cal.4th 1337, 63 Cal.Rptr.3d 483, 163 P.3d 160 (2007).

6. Local Policies and Practices

Sometimes, courts adopt procedures that apply only within a single branch or district of a court, or even a particular judicial department or courtroom. Such local practices or policies are grounded in the inherent authority of courts to supervise and manage litigation, which is derived from the California

Constitution (art. VI, § 1). Huang v. Hanks, 23 Cal.App.5th 179, 232 Cal.Rptr.3d 609 (2018). In addition, judges possess statutory power to control judicial proceedings. CCP §§ 128(a)(3) & 187. Although local policies and practices are considered less formal, they must be published so litigants are on notice of their existence and requirements. CCP § 575.1(c). Local practices and policies must be consistent with the U.S. and California Constitutions, state statutes, rules of court, and applicable case law. Jameson v. Desta, 5 Cal.5th 594, 234 Cal.Rptr.3d 831, 420 P.3d 746 (2018).

7. California Code of Regulations

Administrative agencies (which are part of the state's executive branch) are empowered to adopt regulations to aid in the implementation of statutory law. The California Code of Regulations (formerly called the California Administrative Code) is the compilation that contains California's regulatory law.

B. Secondary Authorities

Several secondary authorities exist to aid a California practitioner in interpreting and understanding civil procedural laws and practices contained in the primary authorities discussed above. Secondary authorities are not "the law" itself, but they can be very influential in gap-filling where primary authorities do not provide answers. Secondary authorities include legislative histories, opinions of the California Attorney General, scholarly publications, practice guides, and California Civil Instructions (CACI). Publications that are periodically updated include: Bernard E. Witkin, California Procedure; Rutter Group's California Practice Guides; Eileen C. Moore & Michael P. Thomas, California Civil Practice: Procedure; and David I. Levine, O'Connor's California Practice: Civil Pretrial.

II. CHOICE BETWEEN CALIFORNIA AND FEDERAL COURT

A. How Choice Arises

The many procedural distinctions that exist between the California and federal courts (noted throughout this Quick Review) give rise to a key litigation question: Should an action be filed in state or federal court? The choice arises when subject matter jurisdiction in the federal and state courts is concurrent. However, subject matter jurisdiction considerations may dictate that an action involving exclusive federal jurisdiction must be filed in federal district court, or that a federal forum is not available for cases not invoking diversity or federal question jurisdiction. In addition, a party might have standing in a particular forum but not in another. (See Chapter 3(I)(A).) But once those "givens" are taken into account, several tactical and practical reasons may sway a litigant toward one court system over the other when a choice is available.

B. State/Federal Distinctions

Some areas in which state/federal distinctions are particularly noteworthy include:

- subject matter jurisdiction (Chapter 2)
- venue and choice of forum (Chapter 2)
- pleading and joinder (Chapter 3)
- discovery (Chapter 4)
- alternative dispute resolution (Chapter 5)
- disposition without trial (Chapter 5)
- jury trials (Chapter 6)
- right to costs and attorney's fees (Chapter 7)
- appellate review (Chapter 8)
- claim preclusion (Chapter 9)

CHAPTER 2

JURISDICTION, VENUE AND CONFLICT OF LAWS

I. SUBJECT MATTER JURISDICTION IN THE SUPERIOR COURT

Subject matter jurisdiction refers to the fundamental power of a trial court to hear or determine a cause of action or to act in a particular way. A judgment entered by a court lacking subject matter jurisdiction is void. Quigley v. Garden Valley Fire Protection District, 7 Cal.5th 798, 249 Cal.Rptr.3d 548, 444 P.3d 688 (2019). The subject matter jurisdiction of the California superior courts is broader than the limited subject matter jurisdiction governing the federal district courts. Federal subject matter jurisdiction may be exclusive, or it may be concurrent with that of state courts. Haywood v. Drown, 556 U.S. 729, 129 S.Ct. 2108, 173 L.Ed.2d 920 (2009).

A. Superior Courts as Courts of General Jurisdiction

The superior courts are trial courts of general jurisdiction. Cal. Const., art. VI, § 10. Unless jurisdiction resides exclusively in another court or tribunal, the superior courts have the power to decide any matter, whether it involves California law, federal law, or the law of other states or nations.

B. Structure of Superior Courts

1. Former Structure

Until 1998, the trial courts of California were divided into superior and municipal courts, with separate jurisdictional requirements, procedures, and administration.

2. Current Structure

With the passage of Proposition 220 by California voters in 1998, the two trial court systems began the process of consolidation or unification. Since 2001, each of California's 58 counties has had a unified superior court and has eliminated the municipal court. The distinctions between the former superior and municipal court systems are reflected in the current classifications of civil cases in the unified superior court. Before trial court unification, cases that are now classified as unlimited civil cases were those within the jurisdiction of the superior court, and those now classified as limited civil cases were within the jurisdiction of the municipal court. These classifications do not affect the exercise of subject matter jurisdiction, as both unlimited and limited civil cases are within the subject matter jurisdiction of the unified superior court.

C. Classification of Actions

1. Unlimited Civil Cases

A civil action other than a limited civil case (see below) is classified as an unlimited civil case. CCP § 88. Unlimited civil cases are primarily those in which the amount in controversy exceeds $35,000. The full range of equitable relief is also encompassed in the subject matter jurisdiction over unlimited civil cases.

2. Limited Civil Cases

a. Criteria for Classification

CCP §§ 85–86 set out the "narrowly and precisely delineated and defined" boundaries of limited civil cases. Stratton v. Beck, 9 Cal.App.5th 483, 492, 215 Cal.Rptr.3d 150, 156 (2017). Most commonly, a limited civil case is one in which the amount in controversy is $35,000 or less. CCP § 86(a)(1). The court hearing a limited civil case also has restricted equitable and declaratory jurisdiction. (Generally, a complaint praying for an equitable remedy must be classified as an unlimited civil case.)

b. Economic Litigation Procedures

Limited civil cases are subject to Economic Litigation Procedures that restrict the number and types of pleadings, motions, and discovery requests permitted in that category of actions. CCP §§ 90–100; and Meza v. Portfolio Recovery Associates, LLC, 6 Cal.5th 844, 243 Cal.Rptr.3d 569, 434 P.3d 564 (2019). The pleadings allowed in a limited civil case are complaints, answers, cross-complaints and general demurrers. No special demurrers are allowed, and motions to strike must be based only on the ground that the allegations of the complaint do not support the relief sought. Anti-SLAPP motions to strike are not permitted. An answer to a limited civil case complaint need not be verified, even if the complaint is verified. CCP § 92. Written discovery and depositions are restricted in number. CCP § 94. These Economic Litigation restrictions do not apply to unlimited civil cases.

3. Compare: Small Claims Cases

Small claims matters are limited civil cases that are adjudicated within the small claims division of the superior court. If the amount in controversy is within the limits of a small claims action, a litigant may choose whether to maintain the action as a limited civil case or as a small claims case. The small claims division has jurisdiction over cases in which the amount in controversy does not exceed $12,500 for a natural person and $6250 for most other types of plaintiffs. CCP §§ 116.221 & 116.220(a)(1). Small claims cases are subject to several important restrictions. For example, discovery is not available, and generally attorneys are not permitted to appear on behalf of parties. CCP §§ 116.310 & 116.530. A small claims plaintiff may not appeal the judgment rendered, but a small claims defendant may appeal the judgment to the superior court and obtain a trial de novo. CCP § 116.710.

4. Cost Consequences of Incorrect Classification

Plaintiffs who exaggerate the value of their cases may be subject to cost consequences. These consequences are intended to encourage plaintiffs to classify their actions appropriately. If the plaintiff files the action as an unlimited civil case but recovers a judgment within the boundary of a limited civil case, the superior court in its discretion may deny an award of costs to the plaintiff. CCP § 1033(a); and Chavez v. City of Los Angeles, 47 Cal.4th 970, 104 Cal.Rptr.3d 710, 224 P.3d 41 (2010). Similar cost consequences hold true for a plaintiff in a limited civil case that could have been filed as a small claims case. CCP § 1033(b)(1).

5. Amount in Controversy

a. Calculating the Amount

"Amount in controversy" refers to "the amount of the demand, or the recovery sought, or the value of the property, * * * that is in controversy in the action, exclusive of attorneys' fees, interest, and costs." CCP § 85(a). Generally, the amount demanded in the prayer of the complaint determines the amount in controversy—and thus the classification—of the case, unless the prayer is fraudulent or fictitious on its face. A party may waive any portion of a demand that is in excess of $35,000 in order to retain limited civil case status. CCP § 403.040(f).

b. Aggregation of Claims

The amount in controversy may be influenced by the aggregation of claims:

- One Plaintiff v. One Defendant: All of the plaintiff's claims against a single defendant will be aggregated in determining the amount in controversy.
- One Plaintiff v. Multiple Defendants: All of the plaintiff's claims against any one defendant will be aggregated. Claims against multiple defendants will not be aggregated if they involve separate causes of action or obligations. If the claims against the defendants involve a joint obligation, they will be aggregated. If the plaintiff's claim against at least one of the defendants exceeds $35,000, the entire action may be treated as an unlimited civil case if the claims against the other defendants can be joined under CCP § 379 (i.e., they arise from the same transaction and occurrence and share a common question of law or fact).
- Multiple Plaintiffs v. One or More Defendants: Where the plaintiffs have suffered an indivisible harm or where their claims are otherwise necessarily joint, the claims of the plaintiffs will be aggregated. However, each separate claim—where each plaintiff will recover individually—will be assessed separately when determining the amount in controversy. If one plaintiff's separate claims exceed $35,000, all claims by the other plaintiffs also may be heard as unlimited civil cases as long as they satisfy the requirements for joinder under CCP § 378 (same transaction or occurrence and common question of law or fact).

6. *Compare Federal Procedure*

While the California superior courts are courts of general jurisdiction, federal district courts have limited jurisdiction. (If there is subject matter jurisdiction in federal court, usually there is concurrent jurisdiction in state court.) Federal courts can hear only those cases permitted by the U.S. Constitution and by statutes, such as those involving a federal question or where diversity of citizenship exists. 28 USC §§ 1331 & 1332. The amount in controversy for most diversity cases must exceed $75,000. In calculating the amount in controversy in a diversity action, the district court will aggregate the claims of plaintiffs against defendants under the same aggregation rules as apply in a California state court. There is no amount in controversy requirement for federal question actions.

7. Illustration

Pajaro Water Agency (PWA) filed an action in Monterey County Superior Court against Doon to collect charges of $17,500 related to Doon's extraction of well water on his property in the town of Pajaro. The complaint classified the action as a limited civil case. The court entered judgment against Doon for $2000. When PWA brought a subsequent action to collect on the judgment, Doon argued that the judgment was void because the court did not have subject matter jurisdiction over the first action. CCP § 86(a)(1) requires that matters involving the legality of a tax, impost, assessment, toll, or municipal fine be treated as unlimited civil cases, even if the amount in controversy is $35,000 or less. Doon argued that the superior court acted without subject matter jurisdiction when it entered judgment, rendering the judgment void. However, the superior court is California's court of general jurisdiction, and it possesses the power to adjudicate this matter. The fact that the first action was treated as a limited civil case does not affect the fundamental jurisdiction of the court; it affects only the manner in which the case is adjudicated and the available remedies. Doon could have moved to reclassify the first action as an unlimited civil case. In the absence of that motion, the lawsuit could properly proceed as a limited civil case. A judgment rendered by a court acting in excess of its jurisdiction is merely voidable, whereas one entered by a court lacking fundamental jurisdiction is void. Pajaro Valley Water Management Agency v. McGrath, 128 Cal.App.4th 1093, 27 Cal.Rptr.3d 741 (2005).

D. Reclassification of Actions

Prior to trial court unification, a case lodged in a court (superior or municipal) lacking subject matter jurisdiction had to be formally transferred to a court possessing jurisdiction. CCP § 396. Now that the superior court has general subject matter jurisdiction over both limited and unlimited civil cases, an action that has been erroneously classified may simply be reclassified.

1. Motion for Reclassification

A party or the court may move to reclassify an action. CCP § 403.040. Notice and opportunity to be heard are required. If, before trial, it becomes clear that the verdict or judgment in an unlimited civil case will "necessarily" fall below the $35,000 jurisdictional dividing line, the court will reclassify the action as a limited civil case. Hiona v. Superior Court, 48 Cal.App.5th 866, 262 Cal.Rptr.3d 371 (2020). If a party seeks reclassification from a limited civil case to an unlimited civil case, the court will order reclassification if there is a "possibility" that the damages will exceed $35,000. Ytuarte v. Superior Court, 129 Cal.App.4th 266, 28 Cal.Rptr.3d 474 (2005). In evaluating the amount in controversy, the court may consider the prayer of the complaint, as well as evidence such as settlement or case management conference statements, and arbitration awards.

2. Reclassification by Amended Complaint or by Cross-Complaint

A matter may be reclassified if the plaintiff files an amended complaint that alters the amount in controversy or the type of relief sought, and she pays the reclassification fee to the court. No motion for reclassification is required. CCP § 403.020; and Leonard v. Superior Court, 237 Cal.App.4th 34, 187 Cal.Rptr.3d 565 (2015). In a limited civil case, if a defendant files a cross-complaint for an amount over $35,000, the filing will be sufficient to reclassify the entire action as an unlimited civil case. CCP § 403.030. In an unlimited civil case, a cross-complaint for an amount of $35,000 or less will not cause the case to be reclassified as limited—the court will have jurisdiction to dispose of the limited cross-complaint as part of the unlimited civil action. CCP § 403.040(e).

3. Compare: Challenge Based on Lack of Subject Matter Jurisdiction

In contrast to reclassification, a defendant who contends that the superior court lacks fundamental subject matter jurisdiction over the action (i.e., is without power to adjudicate) may file a demurrer (CCP § 430.10(a)) or motion for judgment on the pleadings (CCP § 438(c)(1)(B)) on that ground. See Chapter 3(VI).

4. *Compare Federal Procedure*

There is no federal equivalent to California's reclassification procedures. If a federal district court finds, from the face of the complaint, that there is a "legal certainty" that the plaintiff cannot meet amount in controversy for diversity jurisdiction, it will dismiss the action for lack of subject matter jurisdiction. St. Paul Mercury Indemnity Co. v. Red Cab Co., 303 U.S. 283, 288–289, 58 S.Ct. 586, 590, 82 L.Ed.2d 845 (1938).

5. Illustration

Pluto discovered that his accountant, Denzel, had falsely represented that he was a licensed certified public accountant. Pluto sued Denzel in Stanislaus County Superior Court for fraud and unfair business practices. Pluto's unlimited civil complaint prayed for $36,000 in damages. The court conducted a case management conference and referred the action to judicial arbitration, which resulted in an award for Pluto of $18,000. Upon receiving Pluto's request for a trial de novo in the superior court, Denzel filed a motion to reclassify the action as a limited civil case on the ground that Pluto will not be able to obtain a verdict at trial above the minimum amount of an unlimited civil case. The court will reclassify the action as a limited civil case only if it determines that the verdict will necessarily fall below the $35,001 required for an unlimited classification. In making its determination, the court may consider the prayer of the complaint, the case management conference statements, and the judicial arbitration results. Stern v. Superior Court, 105 Cal.App.4th 223, 129 Cal.Rptr.2d 275 (2003).

II. JURISDICTION OVER PERSONS

In addition to possessing subject matter jurisdiction over the action, a state court must have personal jurisdiction over the defendant to enter a binding judgment. The exercise of personal jurisdiction in California state courts is subject to the Due Process Clause of the Fourteenth Amendment of the U.S. Constitution and the state's "long arm" statute. California's broad long arm statute permits the exercise of personal jurisdiction on any "basis not inconsistent with the Constitution of this state or of the United States." CCP § 410.10.

A. Traditional Bases of Personal Jurisdiction

California, like other states, routinely exercises personal jurisdiction over defendants in a number of traditional situations:

- The defendant is *domiciled* in California;
- The defendant is served while *physically present* in the state, even if the defendant's presence is transient;
- The defendant has *consented* to jurisdiction (e.g., appointment of agent for service of process, execution of contract containing a forum-selection clause); or

- The defendant has made a *general appearance* before the California court by participating in the action in a way that recognizes the authority of the court to adjudicate the merits. Typically, a defendant generally appears in an action by filing an answer, but other motions and litigation conduct also may constitute a general appearance. See CCP § 1014 (filing motion to strike, to transfer venue, or to reclassify action considered general appearance). See also section IV(A), below.

B. Constitutional Limitations: Minimum Contacts

1. Background

To be subject to the personal jurisdiction of a state court, the Due Process Clause requires that a defendant who is not present in the state or has not consented to jurisdiction must "have certain minimum contacts with [the forum state] such that the maintenance of the suit does not offend 'traditional notions of fair play and substantial justice.' " International Shoe Co. v. Washington, 326 U.S. 310, 316, 66 S.Ct. 154, 158, 90 L.Ed. 95 (1945). California recognizes two categories of personal jurisdiction under the minimum contacts analysis: general (all-purpose) jurisdiction and specific (case-linked) jurisdiction.

a. General Jurisdiction

California state courts may exercise general jurisdiction over a nonresident defendant if the defendant's "affiliations with the State are so 'continuous and systematic' as to render [it] essentially at home in the forum State." Goodyear Dunlop Tires Operations, S.A. v. Brown, 564 U.S. 915, 919, 131 S.Ct. 2846, 2851, 180 L.Ed.2d 796 (2011). Accordingly, the inquiry under *Goodyear* is not whether a foreign corporation's in-forum contacts can be said to be in some sense "continuous and systematic"; it is whether, by virtue of those continuous and systematic contacts, the defendant is "essentially at home in the forum State." Id., 131 S.Ct. at 2851, 180 L.Ed.2d 796. If general jurisdiction exists, the court has personal jurisdiction over the defendant for all causes of action against it, including those unrelated to the defendant's contacts with the forum state. General jurisdiction is applied most frequently to corporations or other business entities.

b. Specific Jurisdiction

When a court has specific jurisdiction over a defendant, the court may exercise personal jurisdiction only for causes of action arising out of or related to the defendant's activities in the forum state. California courts have recognized three requirements for specific jurisdiction:

- The defendant must have purposefully availed itself of the benefits of the forum or purposefully directed its activities to California;
- The controversy must arise from or be related to the defendant's California contacts; and
- California's exercise of personal jurisdiction must comport with traditional notions of fair play and substantial justice.

See Pavlovich v. Superior Court, 29 Cal.4th 262, 127 Cal.Rptr.3d 329, 58 P.3d 2 (2002); and Bristol-Myers Squibb Co. v. Superior Court, 582 U.S. 255, 137 S.Ct. 1773, 198 L.Ed.2d 395 (2017).

1) Purposeful Availment

" 'The purposeful availment inquiry . . . focuses on the defendant's intentionality. This prong is only satisfied when the defendant purposefully and voluntarily directs [its] activities toward the forum so that [it] should expect, by virtue of the benefit [it] receives, to be subject to the court's jurisdiction based on' [its] contacts with the forum." *Pavlovich*, 29 Cal.4th at 269, 127 Cal.Rptr.3d at 335, 58 P.3d. 2.

2) Arising from or Related to

The "arising from or related to" prong requires a sufficient connection between the defendant's contacts with the forum state and the underlying controversy. "The first half of that standard ['arising from'] asks about causation; but the back half, after the 'or,' contemplates that some relationships will support jurisdiction without a causal showing." Ford Motor Co. v. Montana Eighth Judicial District Court, 592 U.S. 351, 362, 141 S.Ct. 1017, 1026, 209 L.Ed.2d 225 (2021). The required relationship for the "related to" segment is more in the nature of "substantial connection" rather than a "but for" or "proximate cause" standard. But exactly what the "related to" standard requires has not yet been fully fleshed out by either the U.S. or the California Supreme Court.

2. *Compare Federal Procedure*

Federal law under the Due Process Clause generally recognizes the same traditional bases for and constitutional limitations on the exercise of personal jurisdiction as do the California courts. See Bristol-Myers Squibb Co. v. Superior Court, 582 U.S. 255, 137 S.Ct. 1773, 198 L.Ed.2d 395 (2017) (specific jurisdiction); and Daimler AG v. Bauman, 571 U.S. 117, 134 S.Ct. 746, 187 L.Ed.2d 624 (2014) (general jurisdiction).

3. Illustration

Pam frequented her favorite Ojai vaping shop, Vape Vault, several times a week to pick up supplies and try out new varieties of e-cigarette flavorings. On one visit, she purchased a new lithium-ion battery for her "electronic nicotine delivery system." Upon leaving Vape Vault, Pam put the battery in the front pocket of her jeans. As she reached her car, the battery exploded, causing severe burns to Pam's leg, hand and abdomen. Pam was hospitalized for a week and missed two months of work. When she was sufficiently recovered, Pam filed a lawsuit for personal injury and product liability in Ventura County Superior Court against Vape Vault and Daredevil Electronics, the manufacturer of the battery she had purchased. Daredevil is a South Korea corporation that sells its batteries directly to only three California companies, all of them in the electric vehicle industry. Daredevil has never distributed its batteries to Vape Vault or any other vaping business, nor had it authorized anyone else to do so. Daredevil filed a motion to quash service of summons, contending that the superior court could not exercise specific jurisdiction over it. In evaluating the first two prongs of the specific jurisdiction analysis (which are separate inquiries where the burden of proof is on plaintiff Pam), the court will find that Daredevil purposefully availed itself of the benefits of doing business in California because of its battery sales to the three California companies for use in California electric vehicles. In this first prong, there is no requirement to establish that the sale of Daredevil's products is connected to Pam's causes of action against it. In the second "relatedness" prong, however, the court will find an insufficient relationship between Pam's claims and Daredevil's forum activities. Although Daredevil sold its products to California companies, it "deliberately limited its sales to a narrow range of businesses and tailored these transactions to avoid a consumer market." As a result, Daredevil's forum activities cannot be said to arise from or relate to Pam's causes of action regarding Vape Vault's specific sale of a battery to her. Because Pam did not meet her burden to establish both the first and second prongs of the specific jurisdiction analysis, the court will not consider the third prong: whether Daredevil can show that the exercise of jurisdiction would not comport with notions of fair play and substantial justice. LG Chem, Ltd. v. Superior Court, 80 Cal.App.5th 348, 368, 295 Cal.Rptr.3d 661, 677 (2022).

C. Compare: In Rem and Quasi In Rem Jurisdiction

A civil in rem action is an action against property located in the state, frequently involving adjudication of the rights to the property. In rem jurisdiction arises in actions for quiet title, condemnation, civil forfeiture, probate, and marital dissolution, among others. See, e.g., Capra v. Capra, 58 Cal.App.5th 1072, 273 Cal.Rptr.3d 402 (2020) (probate). Quasi in rem jurisdiction type I arises in disputes over property located in the state when there is no attempt to obtain personal jurisdiction over the defendant. Quasi in rem type II involves disputes that do not relate to the property, so jurisdiction over the defendant cannot be based merely on the presence of his property in the state. The distinction between in personam, in rem and quasi in rem jurisdiction is no longer sharply delineated because due process and minimum contacts are required for all exercises of jurisdiction by the court. Shaffer v. Heitner, 433 U.S. 186, 97 S.Ct. 2569, 53 L.Ed.2d 683 (1977).

III. SERVICE OF PROCESS

Upon commencing an action by filing a complaint with the court, the plaintiff must then notify the defendant of the lawsuit through service of process (also called service of summons). Service of process on a defendant within California establishes personal jurisdiction over that defendant. Service on a defendant outside of California does not in itself create personal jurisdiction. The defendant must also have had sufficient minimum contacts with California or be subject to jurisdiction under one of the traditional bases. (See section II(A)–(B), above.) The plaintiff must use a proper method of service of process (CCP §§ 415.10–415.95) that accomplishes service on the appropriate "person to be served" (CCP §§ 416.10–416.90). California courts interpret the statutory requirements for service of process liberally in order to uphold service. If the defendant received actual notice of the lawsuit, defective service will likely be considered valid as long as the plaintiff substantially complied with the service statutes.

A. Summons

1. Purposes of Summons

The court clerk issues a summons to the plaintiff. The summons serves several purposes, including:

- providing notice to the defendant in English and Spanish of the filing of the lawsuit;
- warning that the defendant must respond to the lawsuit within 30 days or be subject to entry of default judgment; and
- suggesting that the defendant might wish to seek advice of counsel before the response is due.

CCP § 412.20.

2. Who May Serve Summons

The summons may be served by "any person who is at least 18 years of age and not a party to the action." CCP § 414.10.

B. Manner of Service

California statutes authorize several methods of service of process, depending on the status and whereabouts of the "person to be served." The person to be served may be the named defendant or may be a person statutorily authorized to receive process on behalf of the named defendant. (See section III(C), below.)

1. Service of Process Within California

a. Personal Delivery

Personal delivery of a copy of the summons and complaint is the most reliable method of service. CCP § 415.10. As long as the process server informs the person to be served that they are being served with process and leaves the papers in close proximity to that person, service will be deemed valid (even if the person to be served refuses the papers). Service is complete upon delivery.

b. Substituted Service

Substituted service involves serving the person to be served by leaving a copy of the summons and complaint with an authorized person in an authorized location, followed by mailing copies of the papers to the person to be served at the location where the papers were left. Service is complete on the tenth day after the date of mailing. CCP § 415.20.

1) Substituted Service on Individual

If the person to be served is an individual (or a representative of an individual, such as a conservator), the plaintiff must make a reasonably diligent effort to serve that person by personal delivery before using substituted service. CCP § 415.20(b); and Kremerman v. White, 71 Cal.App.5th 358, 286 Cal.Rptr.3d 283 (2021). "[A] party shows reasonable diligence by attempting personal delivery of the summons and complaint, in good faith, on at least three occasions on three different days at three different times." CCP § 415.20(b)(2) (effective Jan. 1, 2027). Substituted service on an individual may be made by leaving the papers with a person at least 18 years old who is a "competent member of the household," or with a person "apparently in charge of [the] office, place of business, or usual mailing address" of the person to be served.

2) Substituted Service on Entity

No prior attempt at personal delivery is required before substituted service may be made on a corporation or other entity. CCP § 415.20(a). Substituted service on an entity is accomplished by leaving the papers—"during usual office hours" in the office of the person to be served on behalf of the entity—with a "person apparently in charge" of the office. If the physical office address is unknown, the papers are left with a person apparently in charge of the usual mailing address of the person to be served.

c. Service by Mail: Notice and Acknowledgement

This method involves mailing a copy of the summons and complaint to the person to be served, accompanied by two copies of a notice and acknowledgement of receipt of summons. CCP § 415.30. On the acknowledgement, the person to be served merely notes the date and location of receipt of the summons and complaint. The notice informs the person to be served that if they fail to return the acknowledgement to the plaintiff within 20 days, they may be liable for the expenses the plaintiff subsequently incurs in attempting service in another manner. Service by this method is deemed complete on the date the person to be served executes the acknowledgement, as long as it is returned to the plaintiff.

d. Service by Publication

Service by publication is the method least likely to result in actual notice. For that reason, this method can be utilized only with leave of court. It is used when the address or whereabouts of the person to be served are unknown or if that person has evaded service. The plaintiff must demonstrate that they used reasonable diligence to locate the person to be served and that attempts to accomplish service by other methods were unsuccessful. The court orders the summons to be published once a week for four successive weeks in a newspaper "most likely to give actual notice" to the person to be served. Service is deemed complete on the 28th day following the first day of publication. CCP § 415.50; Cal. Gov't Code § 6064.

2. Service of Process Outside of California

a. Interstate Service

A defendant outside California may be served by any of the methods available for in-state defendants or by a method permitted by the state in which the defendant is served. CCP § 413.10(b). In addition, out-of-state defendants may be served by mail. Dill v. Berquist Construction Co., 24 Cal.App.4th 1426, 29 Cal.Rptr.2d 746 (1994). This manner of service requires mailing (by first-class mail, postage prepaid, return receipt) a copy of the summons and complaint to the person to be served. It does not require sending a notice and acknowledgement of receipt of summons. Service by mail is complete on the tenth day after the mailing. CCP § 415.40.

b. International Service

To serve a foreign defendant, a plaintiff may use any of the methods of service authorized under the CCP, as well as any method of service authorized by the place of service as long as that method is reasonably calculated to give actual notice. CCP § 413.10(c). Parties who are citizens of signatories to certain service treaties, such as The Hague Service Convention or the Inter-American Convention on Letters Rogatory, generally must use the methods of service described in those treaties.

3. Electronic Service of Process

Electronic service and filing of certain motion and litigation documents are permitted and commonplace (see Chapter 3(VI)(B)(1)). California also allows courts to authorize service of a summons by email, social media, or other electronic means, if the plaintiff demonstrates that, despite reasonable diligence, it has been unsuccessful at serving the defendant by each of the other methods allowed by statute. The court-approved method of electronic service must be reasonably calculated to give actual notice to the person to be served. CCP § 413.30(a).

C. Person to Be Served

As noted in section III(B), above, in addition to utilizing a proper method of service, a plaintiff must accomplish service of process on a proper "person to be served." CCP §§ 416.10–416.90 describe the types of persons who may be served with process. For example, for parties that are corporations or unincorporated associations (including partnerships), the proper persons to be served include several specified categories of officers or employees (such as president, vice president, secretary, treasurer, or general manager), the person designated as agent for service of process, or a person authorized by the entity to receive service of process. CCP §§ 416.10–416.40. Individual defendants may be served personally, or through an authorized representative (such as a parent, guardian, or other fiduciary). CCP §§ 416.60–416.90.

D. Proof of Service

Unless a defendant has already made a general appearance, proof of service of a summons must be filed with the court after completion of service. CCP § 417.30. Specific proof of service requirements apply depending on the manner of service and whether service occurred inside or outside of California. See CCP §§ 413.30(a) & 417.10–417.20. The filing of proof of service showing compliance with statutory requirements gives rise to a rebuttable presumption that service has been properly executed.

E. Abrogation of Immunity from Service of Process

California does not grant immunity from service of process to those nonresidents temporarily present in the state to participate in litigation. Silverman v. Superior Court, 203 Cal.App.3d 145, 249 Cal.Rptr. 724 (1988).

F. *Compare Federal Procedure*

The methods of service of process under FRCP 4 are largely similar to those authorized by the California statutes. Moreover, FRCP 4(e)(1) permits service of process to be implemented pursuant to the law of the state in which the federal district court sits. The Ninth Circuit has permitted service of process on a foreign defendant by email. Rio Properties, Inc. v. Rio International Interlink, 284 F.3d 1007 (9th Cir.2002). A few district courts have allowed service via social media. Compare St. Francis Assisi v. Kuwait Finance House, 2016 WL 5725002 (N.D.Cal.2016) (Twitter); and Elson v. Black, 2019 WL 4673211 (C.D.Cal.2019) (Facebook) with Republic of Nicaragua v. Hills Exploration Corp., 2025 WL 360653 (N.D.Cal.2024) (rejecting service via WhatsApp). In contrast to California courts, the federal courts generally continue to recognize common law immunity from service of process for witnesses and parties participating in state court proceedings.

G. Illustration

Leo Bloom owned a snazzy vacation house in Clearlake, which he rented to Roger DeBris. The original one-year lease had been extended several times. Roger decided that he could no longer afford the rent increases for the luxurious residence, and he purchased a more modest house in Middletown, about 20 miles away. Roger moved out of Leo's property three months before the lease had expired, and he gave Leo his new address. Leo's assistant, Ulla, calculated three months of unpaid rent that Leo contended Roger owed. When Roger refused to pay, Leo sued Roger in Lake County Superior Court for breach of the lease agreement. Ulla was tasked with serving process on Roger. She made several attempts to serve Roger at his new house. Not only was there no answer at the door, but Ulla had brought with her an incorrect version of the complaint. Ulla subsequently attempted service with the correct complaint, but she did so at the Clearlake house that Roger had vacated. Ulla then provided proof of substituted service, stating that she left a copy of the correct summons and complaint for Roger "with a competent member of the household at the dwelling house or usual place of abode," but the person she identified as a "member of the household" was actually an employee of a commercial mailbox facility in Clearlake where Roger maintains a mailbox. Roger did not respond to the complaint, and Leo sought a default judgment. Leo will not be successful because there was no substantial compliance with the service of process statutes in several respects, rendering the default judgment void. First, Leo did not make a reasonably diligent effort to serve Roger by personal delivery of the correct complaint at the correct location before resorting to substituted service. Second, the mailbox facility employee was not a "competent member of the household," and the postal facility is not Roger's household or place of abode. Third, substituted service was not properly executed at the commercial mailbox facility because it was not "the only address reasonably known" for Roger. CCP § 415.20(c). Because Roger was not properly served with process, the court will set aside the default judgment entered against him.

Kremerman v. White, 71 Cal.App.5th 358, 286 Cal.Rptr.3d 283 (2021).

IV. CHALLENGING PERSONAL JURISDICTION AND SERVICE OF PROCESS

Several procedures are available to a defendant who wishes to challenge the propriety of service of process and the exercise of personal jurisdiction.

A. Special Appearance

A defendant may make a special appearance in the superior court to challenge service of process and personal jurisdiction without otherwise submitting to the court's jurisdiction.

1. Motion to Quash Service of Summons

A defendant may specially appear by moving to quash service of summons on the ground of lack of jurisdiction. CCP § 418.10(a)(1). The defendant must file this motion on or before the last day to respond to the complaint. CCP § 418.10(a).

a. Protection from General Appearance

The defendant may move to quash and "simultaneously answer, demur, or move to strike the complaint or cross-complaint" without making a general appearance. CCP § 418.10(e). In fact, no litigation act by a defendant who has filed a motion to quash will constitute a general appearance, until the court denies the motion. CCP § 418.10(e)(1); and Air Machine Com SRL v. Superior Court, 186 Cal.App.4th 414, 112 Cal.Rptr.3d 482 (2010). Failure to move to quash service at the same time as filing a separate answer, demurrer or motion to strike will be deemed a waiver of the jurisdiction objection. Roy v. Superior Court, 127 Cal.App.4th 337, 25 Cal.Rptr.3d 488 (2005).

b. General Appearance if Motion Denied

If the motion to quash is denied, the defendant will be deemed to have made a general appearance unless the defendant seeks immediate appellate court review via a writ petition. CCP § 418.10(c) & (e)(2).

c. Burden on Motion

The burden on a motion to quash is on the plaintiff to demonstrate proper service and a valid basis for personal jurisdiction. If the plaintiff meets this burden, it then shifts to the defendant to show that the exercise of jurisdiction would be unreasonable.

d. *Compare Federal Procedure*

Unlike California practice, a federal defendant may preserve the right to challenge the exercise of personal jurisdiction by including the objection as an affirmative defense in its responsive pleading. The defendant may also object to personal jurisdiction by a motion to dismiss under FRCP 12(b)(2). In contrast to California procedure, if a federal judge denies a defendant's challenge to personal jurisdiction, the defendant may defend the case on the merits and still raise the jurisdictional objection on appeal because the denial of a challenge to personal jurisdiction is not considered an immediately appealable order. InfoSpan, Inc. v. Emirates NBD Bank PJSC, 903 F.3d 896 (9th Cir.2018).

e. Illustration

Party Central, a national chain of stores for every type of celebratory need, brought an action for unfair competition in Riverside County Superior Court against its largest competitor, Delights, Inc., headquartered in Philadelphia, Pennsylvania. Before filing its answer, Delights, Inc. moved to quash service of summons under CCP § 418.10 on the ground that it lacked minimum contacts with California sufficient for the exercise of personal jurisdiction over it. While the motion was pending, Delights, Inc. served Party Central with a settlement offer. Party Central rejected the offer. Party Central then argued that Delights, Inc.'s motion to quash should be denied because it had made a general appearance via the settlement offer and thus had waived its objection to personal jurisdiction. Because Delights, Inc. made its settlement offer while the motion to quash was pending, the offer does not constitute a waiver or a general appearance. Under CCP § 418.10(e)(1), no act of a defendant will result in a general appearance as long as the defendant previously or simultaneously filed a motion to quash service of summons. Air Machine Com SRL v.

Superior Court, 186 Cal.App.4th 414, 112 Cal.Rptr.3d 482 (2010).

2. Motion to Dismiss for Failure to Serve Summons

A defendant may make a special appearance to file a motion to dismiss an action where service of process has not been completed within two years (discretionary dismissal) or three years (mandatory dismissal) from the filing of the complaint. CCP §§ 418.10(a)(3); 583.210–.250 & 583.410–.420. See Chapter 5(III)(A).

3. Motion to Set Aside Default Judgment for Lack of Actual Notice

If service of process was defective and did not result in actual notice to the defendant, and the plaintiff obtained a default judgment, the defendant may make a special appearance to set aside the default judgment. CCP § 473.5. Generally, the defendant must bring a concurrent motion to quash service of summons so the court can simultaneously rule on the defendant's jurisdictional objections.

B. Other Challenges

A defendant may decline to make an appearance in an action involving objections to service or personal jurisdiction. Instead, the defendant may appeal from any default judgment entered against him and challenge defective service and lack of jurisdiction at that time. Alternatively, the defendant may bring a separate superior court lawsuit in equity to attack the entry of default judgment for lack of jurisdiction.

V. VENUE

Venue in California refers to the county for the "trial of the action." CCP §§ 392(a) & 395(a). The purpose of California's venue statutes is to ensure that a defendant is not compelled to defend in an unreasonably distant county within the state. A defendant may move the court to transfer or change venue based on several grounds set out in CCP § 397.

A. Proper Court: Classification of Actions

Based on the allegations of the complaint, actions are classified for venue purposes as local or transitory. Each classification has its own set of rules governing the proper location of trial.

1. Local Actions

Local actions relate to real property. Examples include actions seeking recovery of real property, adjudication of the rights of the parties to real property, or recovery for injuries to real property. Venue in local actions is proper in the county or counties in which the real property or any part of it is located. CCP § 392(a).

2. Transitory Actions

Actions not classified as local are transitory. Under the general rule for transitory actions, venue is proper in the county in which "the defendants or some of them reside at the commencement of the action." CCP § 395(a).

a. Expanded Venue Choices in Particular Actions

In addition to the general transitory venue rule, venue may be proper in other counties in certain types of actions:

- Personal injury or wrongful death actions: in the county in which the injury occurred.
- Contract actions: in the county in which the obligation is to be performed or the contract was entered.

CCP § 395(a).

b. Actions Against Corporations

In an action against a corporation, venue is proper in the county in which the contract was made or was to be performed, the obligation or liability arose, the breach occurred, or the corporation has its principal place of business. CCP § 395.5.

3. Mixed Actions

a. Application of General Transitory Venue Rule

In a mixed action, defendants and/or causes of action might be subject to different venue rules. For example, a complaint may contain a local and a transitory cause of action, or it may include a cause of action or defendant subject to a special venue rule outside of the general transitory venue provisions contained in CCP § 395. Generally, venue in a mixed action is proper in a county in which any defendant resides. If a defendant is entitled to a change of venue to his or her residence county on one cause of action in a mixed action, the court must grant a change of venue on all causes of action in the complaint. Gallin v.

Superior Court, 230 Cal.App.3d 541, 281 Cal.Rptr. 304 (1991).

b. Effect of Special Venue Rules

While the general transitory venue rule may apply to some causes of action, public policy or other compelling considerations may supersede the general rule, favoring venue in a location other than in the defendant's county of residence. See Brown v. Superior Court, 37 Cal.3d 477, 208 Cal.Rptr. 724, 691 P.2d 272 (1984) (special venue rule under Fair Employment and Housing Act supplants transitory venue rule governing mixed actions).

4. Main Relief Rule

If the complaint contains one cause of action but seeks both local and transitory forms of relief, proper venue is determined by the main relief rule. Massae v. Superior Court, 118 Cal.App.3d 527, 173 Cal.Rptr. 527 (1981). For example, if a complaint seeks relief in the form of an adjudication of the rights to land (local) as well as specific performance of a land purchase contract (transitory), venue is proper according to the rule governing the main relief sought.

5. *Compare Federal Procedure*

For federal actions, 28 USC § 1390 defines venue as "the geographic specification of the proper court." More specifically, 28 USC § 1391 sets out three alternative districts where a federal action may be brought: where all defendants reside; where a substantial part of the claim arose; or (if neither of the first two alternatives is satisfied) where any defendant is subject to personal jurisdiction. In contrast to California's categorization of actions as either local or transitory, the federal statutes make no distinction between local actions and transitory actions; all federal actions are treated under the rules governing transitory actions.

6. Illustration

Phoebe was a rabid fan of the rock group Broken Chain. Much to her distress, Phoebe learned that the members of the group did not actually sing the lyrics. Rather, other singers performed without credit on Broken Chain's recordings. In concerts, members of Broken Chain "lip-synched" the words to recorded lyrics. Phoebe sued the members of Broken Chain and their manager, Dodge, for fraud and for causes of action under the California Consumers Legal Remedies Act. Phoebe alleged that she had attended two Broken Chain concerts in Martinez, where she bought Broken Chain merchandise under the impression that the band members performed their own songs. Phoebe filed the complaint in Contra Costa County Superior Court, where she resides. Dodge brought a motion to transfer venue to Marin County, the county of his residence, arguing that no defendant resides in Contra Costa County. Phoebe contended that the Consumers Legal Remedies Act provided for additional venue choices, including the county in which a substantial portion of the transaction occurred. Phoebe argued that the special venue rule for the Consumers Legal Remedies Act should govern all of her causes of action, making venue in Contra Costa County proper. Dodge asserted that in a mixed action such as this one, the defendant is entitled to transfer the entire action to the county of his residence. The court will likely agree with Dodge's position and order transfer to Marin County. The Consumers Legal Remedies Act does not provide an exclusive statutory remedy for Phoebe's claims, and there has been no violation of a fundamental right. Thus, there are no compelling policy reasons to supersede the general venue rule for a mixed action. Gallin v. Superior Court, 230 Cal.App.3d 541, 281 Cal.Rptr. 304 (1991).

B. Grounds for Transfer or Change of Venue

1. Improper Court

If the plaintiff has filed the complaint in an "improper" court according to the statutes and principles discussed in section V(A), above, any defendant may move for a transfer of venue to a proper court. CCP §§ 396b & 397(a). If no defendant objects to improper venue, the original court has the power to conduct the trial and enter a valid judgment. Capra v. Capra, 58 Cal.App.5th 1072, 273 Cal.Rptr.3d 402 (2020) (venue distinguished from jurisdiction). A motion to transfer venue based on the ground of improper court must be brought within the time to responsively plead to the complaint. CCP § 396b(a).

a. *Compare Federal Procedure*

A federal party may challenge improper venue via either an affirmative defense or a motion. FRCP 12(b)(3). A challenge based on improper venue is waived unless timely raised. In addition, if venue is improper in the original district, the court may transfer venue in "the interest of justice" to a district or division where the action could have been brought, as an alternative to dismissal. 28 USC § 1406(a).

The transferee court must have subject matter jurisdiction, personal jurisdiction, and proper venue.

b. Illustration

Peet sued his supervisor Dylan for wrongful termination and intentional infliction of emotional distress in Shasta County Superior Court, the county where Peet lived and worked. Dylan moved to transfer venue to Trinity County, where she resided. Peet opposed the motion on the ground that the emotional distress claim constitutes a "personal injury" cause of action under CCP § 395, making Shasta County a proper venue. However, Peet's intentional infliction of emotional distress claim resulting from a wrongful termination is not considered a personal injury action within the statutory language of section 395. "Personal injury," in the context of the venue statutes, encompasses only physical injury. Therefore, Shasta County, based on the sole fact that it was the place of harm, is not a proper venue, and Dylan is entitled to a transfer of venue to Trinity County. Cubic Corp. v. Superior Court, 186 Cal.App.3d 622, 231 Cal.Rptr. 18 (1986).

2. Convenience of Witnesses and Ends of Justice

Even if venue is in a "proper" court, a defendant may move for a change of venue on the ground that "the convenience of witnesses and the ends of justice would be promoted by the change." CCP § 397(c). Additionally, convenience of witness and the ends of justice may be raised by a party in opposition to a motion to transfer to a proper venue. CCP § 396b(d). Generally, the court evaluates the convenience of nonparty witnesses only. The convenience of parties or attorneys is not considered. In addition to demonstrating how a change of venue would enhance witness convenience, the moving defendant must show how the ends of justice will be promoted (e.g., that material evidence is available only in the transferee county). A motion for, or in opposition to, a change of venue on this ground will not be considered until the answers of all defendants are filed. Cholokian & Associates v. Superior Court, 236 Cal.App.4th 361, 186 Cal.Rptr.3d 525 (2015).

a. *Compare Federal Procedure*

The district court may transfer venue to a district or division where the action might have been brought for "the convenience of parties and witnesses, in the interest of justice." 28 USC § 1404(a).

b. Illustration

Leigh, a student at University of California, Santa Barbara, attended a party in Summerland, where she became severely intoxicated. A friend summoned a rideshare car from Dent, Inc., to take Leigh back to her dormitory a few miles away on campus in Goleta. On a freeway offramp, Leigh demanded that the Dent, Inc. driver, Drake, slow down, and Leigh jumped out of the car. She ran down the offramp, and Drake lost sight of her. About a half hour later, eyewitnesses observed Leigh walking on the freeway, where she was struck by two cars and killed. Leigh's mother, Page, brought an action in Santa Cruz County Superior Court against Dent, Inc. and Drake. Santa Cruz County is the location of Dent, Inc.'s headquarters. After the defendants had answered the complaint, Drake moved the court for a transfer of venue to Santa Barbara County on the ground that the convenience of witnesses and ends of justice will be promoted by the change. Drake argued that Santa Barbara County was the location of virtually every material nonparty witness with the ability to testify to key facts, including Leigh's condition at the party at which she became intoxicated, the actions or omissions of Dent, Inc. and its driver, the police investigations and medical interventions, and the observations of the eyewitnesses who saw Leigh get struck and killed. Dent, Inc. opposed the motion, contending that any nonparty witnesses who cannot provide testimony in person in Santa Cruz County may do so remotely, pursuant to CRC 3.672. Even though the trial court may order remote testimony to foster access to the courts, judges retain discretion to require in-person appearances when appropriate. Given the large number of key witnesses whose testimony will be required in this lawsuit, and given that the vast majority of material witnesses reside in Santa Barbara County, the convenience of witnesses and ends of justice will be promoted by transferring venue to Santa Barbara County. Rycz v. Superior Court, 81 Cal.App.5th 824, 297 Cal.Rptr.3d 487 (2022).

3. Additional Grounds

A defendant may move to change the place of trial "[w]hen there is reason to believe that an impartial trial cannot be had therein" (CCP § 397(b)), or "[w]hen from any cause there is no judge of the court qualified to act" (CCP § 397(d)). In addition, CCP § 394 authorizes transfer of venue to a "neutral" county in actions involving certain governmental plaintiffs and defendants.

C. Venue Selection Agreements

Traditionally, California courts have not permitted parties to contractually designate venue because venue is fixed by statute. Alexander v. Superior Court, 114 Cal.App.4th 723, 8 Cal.Rptr.3d 111 (2003). However, if a venue selection clause designates venue in a county otherwise permitted by an applicable venue statute, the clause is valid. Battaglia Enterprises, Inc. v. Superior Court, 215 Cal.App.4th 309, 154 Cal.Rptr.3d 907 (2013). See section VI(D), below, to compare the enforceability of forum selection agreements.

VI. FORUM NON CONVENIENS

A. Nature of Doctrine

Even if jurisdiction and venue are proper, a court may exercise its discretion to stay or dismiss an action under the doctrine of forum non conveniens. Originally a common law doctrine, forum non conveniens has been codified in state law. CCP §§ 410.30 & 418.10. Under section 410.30(a), upon motion of any party or the court, the court shall stay or dismiss an action when it "finds that in the interest of substantial justice an action should be heard in a forum outside this state" (either another state or a foreign nation). CCP § 418.10 sets out the procedure for a defendant's forum non conveniens motion. Forum non conveniens does not effect a transfer of the action to another forum. It is "an equitable doctrine invoking the discretionary power of a court to decline to exercise the jurisdiction it has over a transitory cause of action when it believes that the action may be more appropriately and justly tried elsewhere." Stangvik v. Shiley, Inc., 54 Cal.3d 744, 751, 1 Cal.Rptr.2d 556, 559, 819 P.2d 14 (1991).

B. Timing

Like a motion to quash service of summons, CCP § 418.10(a) authorizes a defendant's motion based on "inconvenient forum" to be brought within the time to file a responsive pleading to the complaint if the defendant has not already generally appeared in the action. If a defendant files a demurrer or motion to strike, she will be deemed to have made a general appearance unless she simultaneously brings a forum non conveniens motion. CCP § 418.10(e)(1) & (e)(3). In contrast to the motion to quash, a defendant who has made a general appearance may still bring a subsequent forum non conveniens motion within a reasonable time, as authorized by CCP § 410.30(b). Global Financial Distributors, Inc. v. Superior Court, 35 Cal.App.5th 179, 247 Cal.Rptr.3d 48 (2019). However, the court may not grant the motion if the defendant has taken advantage of discovery unrelated to forum non conveniens before filing the motion. Martinez v. Ford Motor Co., 185 Cal.App.4th 9, 109 Cal.Rptr.3d 873 (2010).

C. Court's Analysis

1. Two-Step Approach

The court applies a two-step analysis to decide a forum non conveniens motion:

Step 1: Suitability of Alternative Forum

This step involves no exercise of discretion. The court determines whether:

- the defendant is subject to personal jurisdiction in the alternative forum;
- a statute of limitations would bar the action in the alternative forum; and
- the alternative forum will provide basic due process, an impartial tribunal, and some form of remedy.

Chong v. Superior Court, 58 Cal.App.4th 1032, 68 Cal.Rptr.2d 427 (1997). "[A] forum is suitable where an action 'can be brought,' although not necessarily won." Kiely v. HYPH (USA), Inc., 113 Cal.App.5th 95, 106, 335 Cal.Rptr.3d 201, 210 (2025). The defendant may agree to waive personal jurisdiction and statute of limitations defenses in order to render the alternative forum suitable. The fact that the law of the alternative forum may disadvantage a party or provide a less favorable remedy does not make that forum unsuitable. However, an alternative forum will be found unsuitable if it provides no remedy at all or lacks fundamental due process protections. Aghaian v. Minassian, 234 Cal.App.4th 427, 183 Cal.Rptr.3d 822 (2015) (Iran unsuitable forum).

Step 2: Balancing of Private and Public Interest Factors

If the alternative forum is suitable, the court exercises its discretion in balancing a number of private and public interest factors. No one of these factors is in itself dispositive:

- Private interests of the litigants: These factors include: residence of the parties; ease of access to evidence and witnesses; the availability of procedures to compel attendance of unwilling witnesses; and expense.
- Public interest in retaining the action: These factors include: the burden on the local court system, jurors and taxpayers; the difficulty of the application of foreign law in California courts; and a comparison of the interest of the alternative forum with California's interest.

2. Discretion to Dismiss or Stay Action

If the forum non conveniens motion survives the two-step analysis, the court determines whether to stay or dismiss the litigation. If the court stays the action, the court retains jurisdiction and can order the action tried in California if the plaintiff's rights turn out to be seriously compromised in the alternative forum. Stays are more commonly granted than dismissals. A dismissal is likely only if the balance of all factors clearly points to the superiority of the proposed forum over the California forum. If the court orders dismissal, the California court no longer has jurisdiction over the matter. If the plaintiff is a California resident, great deference is given to its choice of forum. In that case, the court will likely not dismiss the action—it will only consider a stay. If the plaintiff is not a California resident, less deference is given to its choice of a California forum.

3. *Compare Federal Procedure*

The federal common law forum non conveniens doctrine and analysis are substantially similar. The common law doctrine is applied in federal court where the alternative forum is a foreign country. Piper Aircraft Co. v. Reyno, 454 U.S. 235, 102 S.Ct. 252, 70 L.Ed.2d 419 (1981). Where another federal district is a more appropriate forum, the original federal court will instead transfer the action under 28 USC § 1404(a). In either context, the plaintiff's choice of forum will not be disturbed unless the defendant makes a strong showing of public and private interest factors favoring litigation in another country or district. A distinction between the common law and statutory doctrines is that in a transfer under section 1404(a), the substantive law of the transferor district will apply in the transferee district, whereas under the forum non conveniens doctrine, the law of the original forum will not carry over to the alternative forum.

4. Illustration

Dawn Airlines flight XY5478 crashed into a lake near Shanghai, China, shortly after takeoff, killing 60 passengers and crew members. Pang and other relatives of the crash victims, all residents of Shanghai, filed wrongful death and product liability actions against Dawn Airlines in San Diego County Superior Court. San Diego County was where key mechanical parts of the plane were manufactured. Dawn Airlines' headquarters and maintenance facilities were located in China. Dawn Airlines filed a motion to dismiss, or alternatively to stay, the California action on the ground of forum non conveniens, contending that China provided a more appropriate forum. Pang objected to the motion, arguing that China's judiciary would not provide basic due process protections and a full range of remedies. The superior court must conduct a two-step analysis. In the first step, the court must determine whether China is a suitable alternative forum by assessing whether China would lack personal jurisdiction over Dawn Airlines and whether there would be a statute of limitations bar. Because of the objections raised by Pang, the court must also examine in the first step whether the Chinese courts would fail to provide a sufficiently fair and independent forum, and whether Chinese law would provide "no remedy at all" to Pang. If the court finds China to be a suitable forum, the second step requires the court to balance the private interests of the parties against the public interest in adjudicating the case in California. If the court is inclined to grant the motion, it will likely stay the action rather than dismiss it so that it can retain jurisdiction while monitoring the Chinese judiciary issues. Because Pang is not a California resident, the court would give limited deference to her choice of a California forum. Guimei v. General Electric Co., 172 Cal.App.4th 689, 91 Cal.Rptr.3d 178 (2009).

D. Forum Selection Agreements

1. Enforceability

Parties may include a forum selection agreement in a contract. Generally, a mandatory forum selection agreement is presumed valid; the court will uphold the agreed choice of forum unless the opponent of the agreement shows that enforcement would be unreasonable or would violate a strong California public policy.

EpicentRx, Inc. v. Superior Court, 18 Cal.5th 58, 334 Cal.Rptr.3d 702, 572 P.3d 1 (2025). When the underlying dispute involves unwaivable statutory rights, the burden is placed on the proponent of the agreement to show that enforcement would not diminish these rights. Lathrop v. Thor Motor Coach, Inc., 105 Cal.App.5th 808, 326 Cal.Rptr.3d 159 (2024), rev. granted, 328 Cal.Rptr.3d 697, 561 P.3d 847 (2025). If a forum selection clause is permissive, providing only for submission to jurisdiction and not requiring litigation in a particular forum, the court will perform a traditional forum non conveniens analysis to determine enforceability. See section VI(C), above.

2. *Compare Federal Procedure*

Federal courts presume forum selection clauses to be enforceable. If a forum selection agreement designates a federal district other than that in which an action is filed, a party may seek to enforce the agreement via a motion under 28 USC § 1404(a). The action will be transferred unless extraordinary circumstances not related to the convenience of the parties clearly make transfer inappropriate. The court will evaluate only public interest factors, not private interest factors. Atlantic Marine Construction Co. v. United States District Court, 571 U.S. 49, 134 S.Ct. 568, 187 L.Ed.2d 487 (2013). If the forum selection agreement designates a state or a foreign country, a party must bring a forum non conveniens motion to enforce the agreement.

3. Illustration

Premier Podcasting, LLC, and Digitech Media, Inc. entered into a contract for Premier to create an audio and video podcast interview series with chefs and restaurant owners, entitled "OnlyPans." Digitech agreed to advance money for Premier's expenses and to stream the new series on its distribution platform. The project disintegrated when Premier's principals, Carmy and Sydney, experienced "creative differences" with Digitech's owners, Jimmy and Natalie. Premier sued Digitech for breach of contract in Los Angeles County Superior Court. The contract contained a clause providing that "the parties consent and submit to the jurisdiction of the state courts of New York." Digitech brought a motion for forum non conveniens, arguing that the forum selection clause is mandatory, requiring Premier to file the action in New York. Mandatory clauses are typically phrased unambiguously, stating that the chosen state has "exclusive jurisdiction" over the dispute or that the matter "shall" be litigated there. In contrast, a permissive forum selection agreement provides that the parties submit to the jurisdiction of the chosen state, but it does not require the action to be filed there. The language of the Premier-Digitech forum selection clause is permissive. Thus, the court must perform a traditional forum non conveniens analysis (see section VI(C), above) to determine whether the action should be stayed or dismissed in favor of litigation in New York. Animal Film, LLC v. D.E.J. Productions, Inc., 193 Cal.App.4th 466, 123 Cal.Rptr.3d 72 (2011).

VII. CONFLICT OF LAWS

Ordinarily, California courts apply the substantive law of California to the causes of action being litigated. However, a party may raise a conflict of laws issue when the law of another state or country potentially also applies to the causes of action. California once followed the "lex loci" approach to conflict of laws, applying the law of the place of the wrong. Since 1967, a California court's approach to resolving conflict of laws issues has involved a broader set of considerations. See, e.g., Reich v. Purcell, 67 Cal.2d 551, 63 Cal.Rptr. 31, 432 P.2d 727 (1967); and Bernhard v. Harrah's Club, 16 Cal.3d 313, 128 Cal.Rptr. 215, 546 P.2d 719 (1976).

A. Governmental Interest Approach in Tort Actions

1. Test

In tort actions, the court uses a three-part analysis to choose the law of the state whose interest will be more significantly impaired if its law is not applied:

- The court first determines whether the laws of each state are materially different.
- If they are materially different, the court assesses whether each state has an interest in the application of its law. If only one state has such an interest, there is a "false conflict," and the law of the only interested state is applied. If each state has such an interest, a "true conflict" exists.
- In a true conflict, the court evaluates the "comparative impairment" to each state's interest if a different state's law is applied, and it chooses the law of the state whose interest would be more impaired.

Kearney v. Salomon Smith Barney, Inc., 39 Cal.4th 95, 45 Cal.Rptr.3d 730, 137 P.3d 914 (2006).

2. Illustration

Pablo, a resident of El Centro, California, was injured on a highway in New Mexico when his car was struck by a truck driven by intoxicated Ivan, a resident of Roswell, New Mexico. Ivan had borrowed the truck from its owner, Daniel, a California resident who had driven the truck to New Mexico. Pablo sued Daniel and Ivan for negligence in Imperial County Superior Court. Daniel argued that New Mexico's substantive law should apply to this litigation. Assume that under New Mexico law, the registered owner of a vehicle is not liable for the negligence of a permissive user of the vehicle. Assume further that California's law holds the owner of a vehicle liable for a limited amount of damages for the negligence of a permissive user. Under the governmental interest test, the court would apply the law of New Mexico. While the laws of the two states are different, New Mexico has a greater interest in this case in the application of its long-standing law, which imposes liability on the vehicle's negligent permissive user rather than on its owner in order to control the conduct of drivers on its roads. New Mexico's interest would be seriously impaired if New Mexico vehicle owners were subject to the application of different standards of liability depending on the state of residence of the plaintiff. California has a legitimate interest in applying its law to more fully compensate California resident Pablo. However, California's law appears designed to protect California drivers from injury by permissive users on California roads. Because New Mexico's interest in regulating the liability of vehicle owners and deterring negligent driving by permissive users would be more impaired if California law were applied than would California's interest if New Mexico law were applied, New Mexico law would govern. Castro v. Budget Rent-A-Car System, Inc., 154 Cal.App.4th 1162, 65 Cal.Rptr.3d 430 (2007).

B. Choice of Law Approaches in Contract Actions

1. Enforceable Choice of Law Clause in Contract

In contract actions, the court analyzes whether a choice of law clause in a contract is enforceable by applying the approach set forth in Nedlloyd Lines B.V. v. Superior Court, 3 Cal.4th 459, 11

Cal.Rptr.2d 330, 834 P.2d 1148 (1992) and Restatement (Second) of Conflict of Laws § 187 (1971)[1]:

- The court first ascertains whether the choice of law clause encompasses all of the causes of action of the complaint.
- If so, the court determines whether the clause is enforceable by applying the test in section 187(2) of the Restatement (Second) of Conflict of Laws (1971):
  - Does the chosen state have a substantial relationship with the parties or their transaction; or
  - Is there any other reasonable basis for the parties' choice of law?
- If either Restatement test is met, the court will enforce the parties' choice of law unless:
  - The chosen state's law is contrary to a fundamental California policy; and
  - California has a materially greater interest than the chosen state in the determination of the specific issue.

Washington Mutual Bank, FA v. Superior Court, 24 Cal.4th 906, 103 Cal.Rptr.2d 320, 15 P.3d 1071 (2001).

2. No Enforceable Choice of Law Clause in Contract

If a choice of law clause in a contract is unenforceable, or if the parties' contract does not contain such a clause, a party might still raise a choice of law issue. In such a case, the court generally applies the governmental interest approach (see section VII(A)(1), above) to determine which state's law will apply to the causes of action.

3. Other Approaches

The court might employ the factors set forth in Restatement (Second) of Conflict of Laws § 188 (1971) to determine which state's law would apply, examining where the contract was negotiated, entered, and performed. Expansion Pointe Properties Ltd. Partnership v. Procopio, Cory, Hargreaves & Savitch, LLP, 152 Cal.App.4th 42, 61 Cal.Rptr.3d 166 (2007). Sometimes, the choice of law rule is supplied by a statute. For contract interpretation issues, for example, Cal. Civ. Code § 1646 identifies the governing law as the place of performance

---

[1] The American Law Institute is preparing the Restatement (Third) of Conflicts of Laws.

or the place where the contract was made. Frontier Oil Corp. v. RLI Insurance Co., 153 Cal.App.4th 1436, 63 Cal.Rptr.3d 816 (2007).

4. Illustration

Palmer works as a delivery truck driver out of the Petaluma, California facility of Dinky Donuts, a Texas corporation with its headquarters in Waco, Texas. At the time Palmer was hired, Palmer and Dinky Donuts signed an employment agreement in Petaluma, which provided that Texas law must be applied to any dispute arising under the agreement. The agreement also contained a contractual jury trial waiver, requiring all disputes between Palmer and Dinky Donuts to be adjudicated by the court. When Dinky Donuts repeatedly refused to pay Palmer overtime, Palmer sued Dinky Donuts in Sonoma County Superior Court. Palmer made a demand for a jury trial. Dinky Donuts objected to the demand pursuant to the parties' waiver agreement, arguing for the application of Texas law to the agreement. Under Texas law, predispute contractual jury trial waivers are enforceable, while under California law they are not. (See Chapter 6(II)(A)(2); and Grafton Partners L.P. v. Superior Court, 36 Cal.4th 944, 32 Cal.Rptr.3d 5, 116 P.3d 479 (2005).) Under the *Nedlloyd*/Restatement analysis, the court will find that California law applies to the jury trial waiver issue for several reasons: (a) California has a substantial relationship to the action because it is the location of Palmer's employment and where the parties signed the agreement; (b) California's Constitution (art. I, § 16) and statute (CCP § 631(a)) hold the right to jury trial to be inviolate and provide for a waiver of that right only in accordance with statute. CCP § 631(f) identifies the sole methods by which a party may waive its fundamental right to a jury trial, and predispute contractual jury trial waivers are not among the statutory grounds. Thus, application of Texas law on this issue would violate a fundamental policy under California law; and (c) California has a materially greater interest in the application and enforcement of its jury waiver law in its courts than Texas has in enforcing the waiver provision in the agreement. The key interest of California in the context of this dispute is the enforcement of "its policy that only the Legislature can determine the permissible methods for waiving the right to jury trial when parties submit their civil disputes to a court in this state for resolution." California, not Texas, has the "paramount" interest here. Under California law, the waiver provision in the agreement is not enforceable. Rincon EV

Realty LLC v. CP III Rincon Towers, Inc., 8 Cal.App.5th 1, 14–15, 18, 213 Cal.Rptr.3d 410, 421, 424 (2017).

C. *Compare Federal Procedure*

Choice of law rules are considered substantive under *Erie* principles. Klaxon Co. v. Stentor Electric Manufacturing Co., 313 U.S. 487, 61 S.Ct. 1020, 85 L.Ed. 1477 (1941). Thus, a federal court sitting in diversity will apply the choice of law rules of the state in which the federal court sits.

SAMPLE EXAM QUESTIONS

OBJECTIVE QUESTIONS

The questions in this section are based on the following hypothetical:

Joe filed a complaint in San Mateo County Superior Court for injuries he sustained when he slipped on the shiny marble floor of his friend Omar's Foster City home during a Super Bowl party. Joe is a resident of Pescadero, also located in San Mateo County. The defendants are Omar and his co-owner Lily, who bought the house with Omar as an investment. Lily resides permanently in Scottsdale (Maricopa County), Arizona.

---

(1) The total demand in Joe's complaint is $9000, which is within the jurisdictional limit of the small claims division of the superior court. If Joe brings his case in the small claims division:

a. Joe may appeal the small claims judgment to the superior court for a trial de novo, but Omar and Lily may not;

b. Omar and Lily may appeal the small claims judgment to the superior court for a trial de novo, but Joe may not;

c. No lawyers are permitted to appear;

d. Both b and c.

(2) Assume that the total amount of damages demanded in Joe's complaint is $36,000, making it an unlimited civil case. The action might be reclassified from an unlimited civil case to a limited civil case:

a. At any time by the court on its own motion without a hearing;

b. During the pretrial stage, if it is clear that the matter will necessarily result in a verdict below the amount required for classification as an unlimited civil case;

c. If, at a jurisdictional hearing, clear and convincing evidence establishes that the action was classified as unlimited due to mistake or inadvertence;

d. During the pretrial stage, when there is a possibility that the matter will result in a verdict below the amount required for classification as an unlimited civil case.

(3) True or False: Joe's unlimited civil case must be reclassified as a limited civil case if Omar files a cross-complaint against Joe for $15,000 in damages.

(4) Joe hired a process server to serve Omar with a copy of the summons and complaint. The process server tried unsuccessfully to personally deliver the papers to Omar at Omar's Redwood City (San Mateo County)

office three times and at Omar's Foster City home once. Finally, the process server delivered a copy of the summons and complaint to Omar's office, leaving the documents with the administrative assistant of the Vice President of Omar's company, with instructions to give the documents to Omar. If Omar files a timely motion to quash service of summons, the court will likely rule that service is improper because:

a. The process server did not mail a copy of the summons and complaint to Omar after leaving the documents at Omar's office;

b. The process server did not exercise reasonable diligence to deliver the papers to Omar before leaving them at his office;

c. Substituted service may be effected only at Omar's dwelling place, not at his office;

d. The process server should have attempted service by mail before leaving the papers at Omar's office.

(5) If Lily wishes to challenge the San Mateo County Superior Court's exercise of personal jurisdiction over her, she may:

a. File a motion to strike the complaint for lack of personal jurisdiction;

b. File a separate motion to quash service of summons before or at the same time she files her answer;

c. Assert lack of personal jurisdiction as a defense in her answer and bring a motion to dismiss the action at a later time;

d. File a general demurrer on the ground of lack of personal jurisdiction.

(6) True or False: Omar may not challenge the exercise of personal jurisdiction over him after Joe has obtained a default judgment against him.

(7) San Mateo County is a proper venue for Joe's action because it is the county:

a. Where Joe, the plaintiff, resides;

b. Where Omar, one of the defendants, resides;

c. Where the injury occurred;

d. Both b and c.

(8) After Lily answered the complaint, she decided that she would like a change of venue to Santa Clara County because that county would be more convenient for her, her architect, and her contractor (who designed and installed the marble floor, respectively, but are not parties to the action) to attend trial as witnesses. Lily's motion for change of venue:

a. Is untimely because she has already filed her answer;

b. Will be granted based on Lily's showing of greater convenience to her, the architect and the contractor by conducting the trial in Santa Clara County;

c. Will be granted based on Lily's showing of greater convenience to the architect and the contractor of conducting the trial in Santa Clara County;

d. Will be granted based on Lily's showing that the interests of justice will be promoted by the greater availability of evidence located in Santa Clara County;

e. Both c and d.

(9) Assume that Lily believes that the trial should proceed in Maricopa County, Arizona, instead of San Mateo County. Lily's most appropriate alternative is to make a motion before the San Mateo County Superior Court to:

a. Transfer venue to Maricopa County;

b. Transfer the action to Maricopa County on the ground of inconvenient forum;

c. Stay the California action in favor of the action proceeding in Maricopa County;

d. Dismiss the California action in favor of the action proceeding in Maricopa County.

(10) Assume that Joe has also sued Marvelous Marble, Inc. (MM), the supplier of the marble floor at Omar's house, for his injuries and medical expenses. MM's principal place of business is in Columbus, Ohio, where the marble for Omar's house was fabricated and from where it was shipped. MM believes that the law of Ohio should apply to Joe's suit against it. Assume that Ohio's law limits liability of suppliers of household materials to $50,000, while California's law has no limit. In analyzing MM's request to apply the law of Ohio, the California court will:

a. Apply the test set out in section 187 of the Restatement (Second) of Conflict of Laws (1971);

b. Apply the governmental interest test;

c. Apply the lex loci test;

d. Conclude that the law of California automatically applies because it is the forum state.

(11) Assume that Omar and MM have executed a written contract for the installation of the marble floor at Omar's home. The contract contains a clause stating: "The parties expressly submit to the jurisdiction of the

state courts of Ohio." Omar has filed a breach of contract action against MM in California. The court likely will find the clause to be:

a. Mandatory and will enforce it if it is reasonable;

b. Mandatory and will decide whether to enforce it after performing a forum non conveniens analysis;

c. Permissive and will decide whether to enforce it after performing a forum non conveniens analysis;

d. Permissive and will enforce it if it is reasonable.

Answers to Objective Questions

(1) **d.** Both (b) and (c) are correct. Only defendants may appeal a small claims judgment to the superior court. No attorneys are permitted to appear in a proceeding in the small claims division.

(2) **b.** The court applies the preunification standard to reclassify the action to a limited civil case.

(3) **False.** A limited civil cross-complaint filed in an unlimited action does not reclassify the action as a limited civil case. Joe's action will remain an unlimited civil case.

(4) **a.** Substituted service at Omar's place of business is not complete unless the process server mails a copy of the summons and complaint to Omar at the same address where he left the documents.

(5) **b.** Lily must file a separate motion to quash service of summons before or at the same time as she files her answer in order to preserve her jurisdictional objection. CCP § 418.10. Lily may not merely include an affirmative defense in her answer, proceed to litigate, and subsequently raise the lack of personal jurisdiction. Lack of personal jurisdiction is not a ground for a motion to strike or a general demurrer.

(6) **False.** Omar may permit a default judgment to be entered against him, and then challenge personal jurisdiction in a special appearance via a simultaneous motion to set aside the default judgment and motion to quash service of summons. He may also raise the jurisdiction issue on an appeal from the entry of the default judgment.

(7) **d.** Both (b) and (c) are correct. The general venue rule for transitory actions is that venue is proper in the county of residence of at least one of the defendants. An additional venue choice in personal injury actions such as this one is the county where the injury occurred.

(8) **e.** Both (c) and (d) are correct. Change of venue is permitted on the ground that the convenience of witnesses (not parties or attorneys) *and* the ends of justice will be promoted by the change. CCP § 397(c). The motion to change venue on this ground is brought after the answer has been filed.

(9) **c.** The doctrine of forum non conveniens applies to these facts. The court does not transfer the action to the alternative forum. It either stays or dismisses the California action to permit the plaintiff to refile it in the other jurisdiction. Because Joe is a California plaintiff, the court will stay the action rather than dismiss it.

(10) **b.** California applies the governmental interest test in tort actions.

(11) **c.** The forum selection clause is permissive because it does not require the action to be litigated only in Ohio. The court determines whether to enforce a permissive clause by performing a forum non conveniens analysis. It considers the suitability of the alternative forum and the balance of the public and private interest factors.

ESSAY QUESTIONS

A. Dennis Drinker was at the weekly "Beer on the Beach" party with his friends one Thursday afternoon on the volleyball courts at California State University, Chico. Dennis had too much to drink, but he decided to drive home anyway. Dennis reached for his phone to check a text message while he was driving. The car swerved to the right and jumped onto the sidewalk, running into three pedestrians—Athena, Blake and Carlo.

Athena sustained the most serious injuries. She spent nearly a month in the hospital, after which she underwent extensive rehabilitation. She has incurred $175,000 in hospital and medical bills. She has sustained $40,000 in lost wages and has experienced significant pain and suffering.

Blake escaped with only scrapes and bruises. He spent $700 on medical bills to cover his brief trip to the emergency room.

Carlo sustained a sprained ankle and a concussion. He recovered quickly and missed only a few days of work. Carlo incurred $15,000 in medical bills.

Athena, Blake and Carlo have each filed separate lawsuits against Dennis Drinker in Butte County Superior Court.

(1) Discuss the classification of each plaintiff's action.

(2) Assess how these classifications might be affected should the plaintiffs join together to file a single action against Dennis.

(3) Discuss whether and how Carlo's case might be reclassified if he amends his complaint to seek $43,000 due to additional medical expenses and pain and suffering damages.

B. Adelaide is a graphic designer. She worked at Shosh Green Stationery Corporation (SGSC), located in Seattle, Washington. As part of her employment contract, Adelaide agreed not to disclose SGSC's confidential information, including its trade secrets. After working at SGSC for nearly ten years, Adelaide resigned. Two years later, she began working at the Seattle office of Rainbow Papers, one of SGSC's competitors.

During Adelaide's unemployment, Mira, a former SGSC employee, relocated to join Rainbow Papers' San Francisco office. Since Adelaide began working at Rainbow Papers in Seattle, she has exchanged emails and video calls with Mira two to three times a month. Adelaide has also made at least two telephone calls to Rainbow Papers' distribution warehouse located in San Francisco.

Shortly after she began working for Rainbow Papers, Adelaide attended two one-day business-related meetings in California. Other than those meetings, she had been in California one additional time, on a layover at the San Francisco International Airport on her way to her sister's wedding in Hawaii.

SGSC filed suit against Adelaide in San Francisco County Superior Court, alleging breach of her contractual nondisclosure duty and misappropriation of SGSC's trade secrets. Adelaide was served with process by Federal Express delivery at her office address in Seattle.

Adelaide's attorney has filed a timely motion to quash service of summons based on lack of personal jurisdiction and invalid service of process. Assess the strengths and weaknesses of Adelaide's position regarding personal jurisdiction and the validity of service of process.

C. Brainy Consulting, Inc. (Brainy) specializes in consulting with companies wishing to expand their operations into additional geographical markets. Brainy is incorporated in Delaware, with its headquarters in Connecticut. It has recently opened an office in Carmichael (Sacramento County), California.

Presidential Publications, Inc. (Presidential) hired Brainy to assist it in expanding its production facilities to several California counties. Presidential is incorporated in Delaware, with its headquarters in Missouri.

Presidential and Brainy signed a contract for Brainy's services. Under the terms of the contract, Brainy was supposed to help Presidential with all stages of its industrial expansion into Alameda and San Joaquin counties, including overseeing the actual construction of the new plants. The contract was negotiated by telephone and email by the vice presidents of operations for each company from their respective company headquarters in Connecticut and Missouri. After the vice presidents had reached agreement on terms, they had a final face-to-face meeting in San Joaquin County to sign the contract.

Unfortunately, Brainy was unable to provide the level of service required by the contract, and Presidential filed suit against Brainy in Alameda County Superior Court for breach of contract. Brainy has filed a motion to transfer venue, arguing that Sacramento County is the proper venue.

(1) Discuss whether Alameda County is a proper venue for this action.

(2) Assess whether there are grounds to transfer the action to a different California county or counties.

D. Fit & Fab, a gym in Mendocino, California, had a long-term contract with ShapeUp, Inc., for the purchase of exercise equipment and the replacement of machines as new models became available. Fit & Fab purchased 12 treadmills from ShapeUp, all of the same design. ShapeUp is incorporated and located in Illinois. About one third of its clients are gyms in Illinois and another one third are gyms in California. The remaining gym clients are located throughout the United States. The contract was executed by Fit & Fab and ShapeUp in California. It contains a clause stating: "This Agreement is governed by the laws of the State of Illinois."

Fit & Fab experienced three incidents where customers were injured using the ShapeUp treadmills when the speed suddenly increased, causing the customers to lose their balance. Fit & Fab filed a lawsuit against ShapeUp in Mendocino County Superior Court, alleging negligence, breach of contract, and breach of warranty. Fit & Fab sought both compensatory damages and an unspecified amount of punitive damages for ShapeUp's "egregious" conduct in selling dangerous equipment for use by the public. Assume that California law permits an award of punitive damages for actions involving the sale of dangerous consumer goods, but Illinois law does not.

ShapeUp filed a motion to strike Fit & Fab's punitive damages claim on the ground that under the parties' choice of law (Illinois), there is no entitlement to punitive damages. Describe the analysis you would use to determine whether Illinois or California law applies to Fit & Fab's punitive damages demand, and reach a conclusion as to which state's law should govern.

<u>Essay Answers</u>

<u>Essay A</u>

(1) <u>Classification of Actions</u>

- Athena v. Dennis:
  - This case will be classified as an unlimited civil case because the amount in controversy exceeds $35,000 ($175,000 in hospital bills + $40,000 in lost wages + general damages for pain and suffering).
  - Advantages of unlimited classification include access to full discovery, motions, pleadings and relief.

- Blake v. Dennis:
    - This case arguably is classified as a limited civil case to be litigated as a small claims proceeding because Blake sustained only $700 in damages for his bodily injuries. The jurisdictional limit for a small claims action brought by an individual plaintiff seeking damages for bodily injury from an automobile accident is a maximum of $12,500. Blake may pursue his case either in the Small Claims Division or as a limited civil case. If Blake chooses to maintain his action as a limited civil case instead of bringing it in the Small Claims Division, the court may deny Blake recovery of his costs even if he is the prevailing party, if he recovers less than $12,500.
    - If Blake files his action in the Small Claims Division, Blake and Dennis will not be allowed to have attorneys appear on their behalf, and they will not be entitled to discovery. If Blake loses his case, he is not permitted to appeal.
- Carlo v. Dennis:
    - If Carlo stated in the caption of his complaint that the action is a limited civil case, this case should be classified as a limited civil case because the amount in controversy does not exceed $35,000 and it exceeds the small claims maximum. Carlo's case will be subject to the Economic Litigation procedures.

(2) Aggregation

- If Athena, Blake and Carlo file a single lawsuit against Dennis, they may not aggregate their claims because they are not suing for indivisible harm. However, because Athena's case qualifies as an unlimited civil case, Blake and Carlo's cases also may be heard as unlimited civil cases if the requirements for joinder (CCP § 378) are satisfied.

(3) Amended Complaint

- If Carlo amends his complaint to seek damages within the classification of an unlimited civil case, Carlo would pay a reclassification fee at the time of filing the amended complaint, and the clerk of the court will reclassify the action as an unlimited civil case. No motion or hearing is required. CCP § 403.020(a).

Essay B

- California's long arm statute, CCP § 410.10, provides that California courts may exercise personal jurisdiction to the extent consistent with the U.S. and California Constitutions.

    - Thus, the only significant restrictions placed on California courts' exercise of personal jurisdiction are constitutional in nature.
- Personal jurisdiction over Adelaide in California:
    - No general jurisdiction exists because Adelaide's contacts with California are not pervasive and systematic such that she is essentially at home in the forum.
    - Specific jurisdiction via minimum contacts with California: the analysis should focus on the three-pronged test for specific jurisdiction.
        - Factors in favor of the exercise of specific jurisdiction:
            - Adelaide works for a company with offices and a warehouse in California.
            - Adelaide exchanged emails and video calls with Mira, her coworker located in the California office, two to three times per month.
            - Adelaide made at least two phone calls to the California warehouse.
            - Adelaide attended two work-related meetings in California.
            - On her way to her sister's Hawaii wedding, Adelaide had a layover in a California airport.
        - Factors weighing against the exercise of specific jurisdiction:
            - Adelaide's sporadic contacts with California do not compel the conclusion that she purposefully availed herself of the benefits of the California forum.
            - SGSC's causes of action against Adelaide arguably do not arise out of or relate to her limited contacts with California.
            - Adelaide's physical presence in California has been limited and only tangentially related to the lawsuit. Her contacts with California have mostly been by phone and email from Seattle.
            - Adelaide was present in California for only one day at a time (at most).
            - Adelaide's layover at the airport for the wedding trip was unrelated to SGSC's claims.

- While there are arguments for and against exercising personal jurisdiction in this case, the court is likely to conclude that Adelaide's motion to quash the service of summons should be granted due to lack of personal jurisdiction.

- Service of Process:
  - Adelaide may be served with process in the State of Washington by any of the methods of service available under California or Washington law. CCP § 413.10(b).
  - Alternatively, she may be served by first-class mail, postage prepaid, requiring a return receipt. CCP § 415.40.
  - The California statutes make no provision for service by Federal Express or other private mail service. Even if SGSC argues that the Federal Express delivery is an acceptable form of substituted service (if the summons and complaint had been left with a person apparently in charge of Adelaide's office), the requirements of that method of service have not been satisfied. See CCP § 415.20(b). Service via a private express mail service will be valid if permitted under Washington law.
  - Getting court permission to use electronic service does not seem likely here. It does not appear that SGSC will be able to demonstrate reasonable diligence in its failure to serve Adelaide by the methods allowed under California or Washington law.
  - Adelaide's motion to quash based on invalid service of process will probably be granted.

<u>Essay C</u>

(1) <u>Alameda County as Proper Court</u>

- This is a transitory action. CCP § 395.5 provides several venue alternatives for suits against a corporation like Brainy: the county where the contract is made or is to be performed; where the obligation or liability arises; where the breach occurs; or where the corporation's principal place of business is located.
- Is Alameda County a proper venue?
  - The parties intended to perform the contract partially in Alameda County, so Alameda County may be a proper venue on this basis.
  - Alameda County may also be where the contractual liability partially arises or where the breach partially occurs.

  - The contract was not made in Alameda County, so this basis for venue does not apply.
  - Alameda County is not the principal place of business of Brainy, so this ground for venue does not apply.
  - Brainy's choice of venue, Sacramento County, would not be a proper venue under any of the provisions of CCP § 395.5.

(2) <u>Grounds for Transfer or Change of Venue</u>

- Improper court:
  - The court may transfer the action to another county that meets the requirements of CCP § 395.5 if Brainy shows that Alameda County is not a proper venue. CCP § 397(a).
  - Brainy must bring a motion to transfer on this ground within the time to respond to the complaint.
- Convenience of witnesses and ends of justice:
  - The court may change venue in the action if Brainy can show that the change will promote the convenience of witnesses and the ends of justice. CCP § 397(c).
  - Brainy must have already filed its answer in order to bring a motion to change venue on this ground.
  - Brainy must provide:

    Names of witnesses;

    Nature of testimony expected from each witness;

    Reasons why attendance of each witness would be inconvenient; and

    Reasons why the ends of justice would be promoted by the change.
  - The facts in this case do not indicate that Brainy will be able to make this showing, so the motion will be denied.

<u>Essay D</u>

- The applicable conflict of laws test for this contractual matter is from *Nedlloyd* and the Restatement (Second) of Conflict of Laws (1971).
  - The court first ascertains whether the choice of law clause encompasses all of the causes of action of the complaint.

  - If so, the court determines whether the clause is enforceable by applying the test in section 187(2) of the Restatement (Second) of Conflict of Laws (1971):
    - Does the chosen state have a substantial relationship to the parties or their transaction; or
    - Is there any other reasonable basis for the parties' choice of law?
  - If either test is met, the court will enforce the parties' choice of law unless:
    - The chosen state's law is contrary to a fundamental California policy; and
    - California has a materially greater interest than the chosen state in the determination of the specific issue.
- Application:
  - The choice of law clause encompasses all of the causes of action in the complaint.
  - The clause is enforceable because Illinois has a substantial relationship to the parties and their transaction. It is the state of ShapeUp's incorporation and the location of the manufacture and distribution of the equipment.
  - The court will enforce the clause unless Fit & Fab can establish that the punitive damages limitations under Illinois law is contrary to a fundamental California policy to punish out-of-state companies and deter them from sending defective consumer goods into the state.
  - If California has a materially greater interest than Illinois in the application of its law on this issue, the court will apply California law despite the parties' choice of law clause.
- If the choice of law clause is found to be unenforceable, the court would likely apply the governmental interest test to determine which state's law to apply. Alternatively, the court might apply the factors in Restatement (Second) of Conflict of Laws § 188 (1971), examining where the contract was negotiated, entered, and performed.

CHAPTER 3

PARTIES, PLEADINGS AND JOINDER

I. PARTIES (WHO MAY SUE AND BE SUED)

The ability to sue or be sued is a central procedural requirement. A plaintiff must have both standing *and* the capacity to sue, and a defendant must have the capacity to be sued.

A. Standing

1. Real Party in Interest

"Every action must be prosecuted in the name of the real party in interest * * *." CCP § 367. "[A]nyone other than a real party in interest lacks standing." City of Brentwood v. Campbell, 237 Cal.App.5th 488, 504, 188 Cal.Rptr.3d 88, 102 (2015). The standing doctrine is intended to "ensure that the courts will decide only actual controversies between parties with a sufficient interest in the subject matter of the dispute to press their case with vigor." Common Cause v. Board of Supervisors, 49 Cal.3d 432, 439, 261 Cal.Rptr. 574, 577, 777 P.2d 610 (1989). If standing is not granted by a specific statutory provision, the real party in interest is usually considered to be the person to whom the substantive law grants the right to sue for relief. Statutory standing "analysis is grounded in the statutory text," but the text alone may not adequately "capture the other prudential and separation of powers considerations that have traditionally informed the outer limits of standing." Weatherford v. City of San Rafael, 2 Cal.5th 1241, 1247–1249, 218 Cal.Rptr.3d 394, 398–399, 395 P.3d 274 (2017). Lack of standing is a jurisdictional defect and may be raised at any time during the proceedings. The issue is not waived even if the opposing party fails to object.

2. *Compare Federal Procedure*

FRCP 17(a) also requires that an action be prosecuted in the name of the real party in interest. Principles of standing in federal court are based in the U.S. Constitution. Article III's "case or controversy" language has been interpreted to require that a party bringing suit in federal court must have suffered or "is under threat of suffering 'injury in fact' that is concrete and particularized; the threat must be actual and imminent, not conjectural or hypothetical; it must be fairly traceable to the challenged action of the defendant; and it must be likely that a favorable judicial decision will prevent or redress the injury." Summers v. Earth Island Institute, 555 U.S. 488, 493, 129 S.Ct. 1142, 1149, 173 L.Ed.2d 1 (2009). In addition, federal courts have traditionally relied on "prudential considerations" in examining standing. Those considerations have included whether the plaintiff's claims fall within the "zone of interests" sought to be protected, and whether the injury is reasonably confined to an individual or small group as opposed to constituting a "generalized grievance." Elk Grove Unified School District v. Newdow, 542 U.S. 1, 12, 124 S.Ct. 2301, 2309, 159 L.Ed.2d 98 (2004), abrogated on other grounds by Lexmark International, Inc. v. Static Control Components, Inc., 572 U.S. 118, 134 S.Ct. 1377, 188 L.Ed.2d 392 (2014). A party who has standing under California law does not necessarily have standing under federal law. Hollingsworth v. Perry, 570 U.S. 693, 133 S.Ct. 2652, 186 L.Ed.2d 768 (2013).

3. Illustration

In the past, Phil had been a victim of his wife's domestic abuse. Phil decided that if his wife ever physically harmed him again, he would seek help from a domestic violence shelter. Phil phoned two state-funded shelters in the Arcata area to initially find out if they accepted men. He was told that they did not. Phil sued both shelters in Humboldt County Superior Court under a California civil rights statute on the ground of sex discrimination. Phil does not have standing to sue the shelters. His complaint did not allege an actual injury because it did not state that Phil was a victim of domestic violence at the time he made his phone calls. Blumhorst v. Jewish Family Services of Los Angeles, 126 Cal.App.4th 993, 24 Cal.Rptr.3d 474 (2005).

B. Capacity

1. To Sue or Be Sued

Capacity to sue (or to be sued) is a separate concept from that of standing. For plaintiffs, both components are required: a person with standing (a right to relief) must also have capacity (the right to come to court). Defendants must have capacity to defend. Persons and entities generally have capacity to sue or be sued. Typical exceptions are minors and incompetent persons (who must appear in court through a guardian), and corporations whose powers have been suspended under the California tax laws for failure to pay state franchise (income) taxes. In contrast to standing, capacity is not a jurisdictional requirement. An objection based on capacity is waived if not timely asserted. A defendant's objection based on the plaintiff's lack of capacity to sue is usually raised via an affirmative defense in the answer, or by special demurrer. See CCP § 430.10(b); and section VI(A)(1)(b), below.

2. ***Compare Federal Procedure***

Capacity of an individual to sue or be sued in federal court is determined by the law of the individual's domicile. A corporation's capacity is determined by the law of the state of its incorporation. FRCP 17(b)(2).

3. **Illustration**

Polo Corp. sued Dolores in Lassen County Superior Court for failure to pay for the delivery of building materials to a home undergoing renovation in Susanville. Dolores answered the complaint. Dolores then discovered that a month before filing its complaint, Polo Corp.'s corporate powers had been suspended by the state for failure to pay franchise taxes. Dolores sought leave of court to amend her answer to include an affirmative defense based on Polo Corp.'s lack of capacity. The motion probably will be granted. Although Polo Corp. had standing to sue, it lacked capacity to sue because of its suspension for nonpayment of franchise taxes. Color-Vue, Inc. v. Abrams, 44 Cal.App.4th 1599, 52 Cal.Rptr.2d 443 (1996).

II. INITIATING A LAWSUIT

An action usually commences with the filing of the complaint. CCP § 411.10. Sometimes, a petition, rather than a complaint, is the document that initiates an action (e.g., petition to compel arbitration under CCP § 1281.2). Under some circumstances, a party must take additional steps before filing an action.

A. Prior Notice of Lawsuit

In some cases, a plaintiff must provide early notice of a claim. For example, a plaintiff who intends to sue a public entity must present a timely written claim to the appropriate public office within six months or one year of the accrual of the claim, depending on the nature of the claim. Cal. Gov't Code § 911.2. The plaintiff may bring a court action only after the claim is denied or deemed denied. Cal. Gov't Code § 945.4; and McCurdy v. County of Riverside, 106 Cal.App.5th 1103, 327 Cal.Rptr.3d 489 (2024). A plaintiff who seeks to sue a health care provider for professional negligence must first serve that provider with a notice at least 90 days prior to commencement of the litigation. CCP § 364 (MICRA). Where multiple statutes require prefiling notice of a plaintiff's claims, the plaintiff must be careful to satisfy the requirements of each statute. Wurts v. County of Fresno, 44 Cal.App.4th 380, 51 Cal.Rptr.2d 689 (1996) (notice of claim filed with a governmental agency pursuant to Cal. Gov't Code § 945.4 does not also constitute a notice of intent to sue under CCP § 364).

B. Certificate of Merit

Certain actions require a plaintiff to obtain, file and serve a certificate of merit in connection with a lawsuit. Failure to do so when required subjects the complaint to attack by demurrer or motion to strike. See, e.g., CCP § 411.35 (action for malpractice of architect, engineer or land surveyor); and Cal. Health & Safety Code § 25249.7(d) (private action to enforce Safe Drinking Water and Toxic Enforcement Act).

C. Court Order

To discourage certain lawsuits, some statutes require a court order before the plaintiff may file an action or a particular claim. Examples include claims for punitive damages against health care providers (CCP § 425.13) and religious organizations (CCP § 425.14), claims against attorneys for conspiracy with a client (Cal. Civ. Code § 1714.10), and actions filed by parties designated as vexatious litigants (see section VIII(B), below).

D. *Compare Federal Procedure*

Some federal statutes have prefiling requirements. For example, a plaintiff who intends to sue an employer for employment discrimination under federal antidiscrimination statutes, such as Title VII of the Civil Rights Act of 1964, must first file the claim with the Equal Employment Opportunity Commission (EEOC) and obtain a "right to sue" letter. See, e.g., 42 USC §§ 2000e–5(f)(1) & 2000e–16(c); compare Cal. Gov't Code § 12960 et seq. Claims under the Federal Tort Claims Act are also subject to prelawsuit claims requirements. 28 USC § 2675. The U.S. Supreme Court has held that a state law requiring that an affidavit of merit from an expert must accompany the complaint in medical malpractice cases does not apply in diversity actions in federal court. Such a state procedural requirement conflicts with FRCP 8(a)(2)'s pleading requirement of "a short and plain statement of the claim." Berk v. Choy, 607 U.S. ___, 146 S.Ct. 546, ___ L.Ed.2d ___ (2026).

E. Illustration

Pierce was incarcerated at Pelican Bay State Prison. Officials of the prison failed to diagnose and treat Pierce's lung cancer. After Pierce was eventually diagnosed, he sued the California Department of Corrections in Del Norte County Superior Court for violation of a federal civil rights statute (42 USC § 1983) and for state common law negligence. Because Pierce's attorney failed to comply with the prefiling requirements of California's Government Claims Act, Cal. Gov't Code § 945.4, the Department of Corrections filed a general demurrer. While a claim arising under federal law is not subject to the prefiling notice requirement of Cal. Gov't Code § 945.4, the state negligence claim is. Since Pierce failed to allege facts sufficient to establish compliance with Cal. Gov't Code § 945.4 or show why noncompliance should be excused, the negligence cause of action is subject to a general demurrer for failure to state facts sufficient to constitute a cause of action. State v. Superior Court (Bodde), 32 Cal.4th 1234, 13 Cal.Rptr.3d 534, 90 P.3d 116 (2004). If, however, the case had been filed as a diversity action in federal court, neither the federal claim nor (in all likelihood) the state negligence claim would be subject to the state statute's prefiling notice requirement. Berk v. Choy, 607 U.S. ___, 146 S.Ct. 546, ___ L.Ed.2d ___ (2026).

III. INITIAL PLEADING: COMPLAINT

The complaint is one of four documents characterized as "pleadings" in California civil actions. CCP § 422.10. (The others are the answer, cross-complaint, and demurrer, all discussed later in this chapter.) The complaint contains two principal components: factual allegations constituting the cause or causes of action; and a demand for judgment (also known as the prayer for relief).

A. Pleading Factual Allegations

A complaint (or cross-complaint) filed in a California court must contain a "statement of the facts constituting the cause of action, in ordinary and concise language." CCP § 425.10(a)(1). The standard in California for pleading factual allegations is called "fact" or "code" pleading. In examining the factual allegations of a complaint (or other pleading), the court must liberally construe the allegations "with a view to substantial justice between the parties." CCP § 452.

1. Cause of Action

"Cause of action" is a slippery concept in California procedure. The term has taken on varied meanings depending on the context in which it is used. In the pleading context, cause of action is often inaccurately used to mean a legal theory or claim for relief. It has a different meaning in the context of compulsory cross-complaints (arising out of the same transaction or occurrence; see section V(A), below). The correct definition of "cause of action" in California is the one arising in the context of claim preclusion: a single invasion of a primary right. See Chapter 9(II)(A). Multiple invasions of primary rights can give rise to multiple causes of action.

2. Fact Pleading

a. Ultimate Facts

Fact pleading requires that the plaintiff plead ultimate facts in the complaint. Ultimate facts are those upon which the defendant's liability or the plaintiff's right to recovery depends. They address each element of each cause of action included in the complaint. Neither evidentiary details nor bare legal conclusions are to be pleaded, but a court may disregard their inclusion as long as each cause of action contains sufficient allegations of ultimate facts. The liberal availability of discovery makes more detailed pleading less essential than in the past. E.g., Thomas v. Regents of the University of California, 97 Cal.App.5th 587, 315 Cal.Rptr.3d 623 (2023).

b. Stating Factual Allegations

Ultimate facts may be pleaded directly (based on the plaintiff's personal knowledge of the facts) or on information and belief ("Plaintiff is informed and believes, and based on that information and belief alleges, that X occurred."). In addition, documents attached to the complaint are considered a part of the pleading if they are properly incorporated by reference. Plaintiffs may plead facts or legal theories inconsistently or in the alternative. (Exception: inconsistent facts may not be pleaded in a verified complaint; see section III(D)(2), below.) Factual allegations "must be liberally construed with a view to substantial justice between the parties." Zakk v. Diesel, 33 Cal.App.5th 431, 447, 245 Cal.Rptr.3d 215, 228 (2019).

c. Heightened Pleading Standard

Certain causes of action must be pleaded with greater particularity than is required under normal fact pleading. Typical examples of this heightened pleading requirement are causes of action for fraud and for certain statutory violations (such as those under the Government Claims Act). The complaint must contain detailed factual allegations supporting each element of these causes of action. E.g., Rattagan v. Uber Technologies, Inc., 17 Cal.5th 1, 324 Cal.Rptr.3d 433, 553 P.3d 1213 (2024).

3. *Compare Federal Procedure*

In contrast to California's fact pleading standard, the federal rules use the notice pleading standard. FRCP 8(a)(2) requires a "short and plain statement of the claim showing that the pleader is entitled to relief." Although federal notice pleading is generally considered to not require the detailed allegations that state fact pleading requires, "a complaint must contain sufficient factual matter, accepted as true, to 'state a claim to relief that is plausible on its face.' A claim has facial plausibility when the plaintiff pleads factual content that allows the court to draw the reasonable inference that the defendant is liable for the misconduct alleged." Ashcroft v. Iqbal, 556 U.S. 662, 678, 129 S.Ct. 1937, 1949, 173 L.Ed.2d 868 (2009). Greater particularity is required in federal court in only limited circumstances, such as pleading fraud under FRCP 9(b), or for certain statutory claims.

4. Illustration

After a double mastectomy, Petra underwent a surgical procedure in Hanford to insert breast implants. Almost immediately, she experienced extreme pain and other troubling symptoms. She consulted several specialists, all of whom recommended that she have the implants removed. Over the year following the removal, she had three reconstructive surgeries. Petra then sued Dabney, Inc., the manufacturer of the implants, in Kings County Superior Court for product liability and fraud. In the fraud cause of action, Petra pleaded that Dabney, Inc. had falsely represented that its product was safe for use by the public, that it posed no dangerous risk, and that it would not require removal. These allegations are insufficient to meet the heightened pleading requirement for fraud. Petra failed to plead every element of the cause of action for fraud with specificity. She did not plead "what was said or

> to whom or in what manner." Petra may not merely recast her product liability cause of action as one for fraud without providing additional supporting facts. Goldrich v. Natural Y Surgical Specialties, Inc., 25 Cal.App.4th 772, 783, 31 Cal.Rptr.2d 162, 169 (1994).

B. Demand for Judgment (Prayer for Relief)

A complaint must contain a "demand for judgment for the relief to which the pleader claims to be entitled." CCP § 425.10(a)(2).

1. Damages

If the plaintiff seeks damages or other monetary relief, the general rule is that "the amount demanded shall be stated" in the complaint. CCP § 425.10(a)(2). There are several exceptions to this requirement:

a. Exception: Personal Injury and Wrongful Death Actions

In a personal injury or wrongful death action, the plaintiff may not state the amount of actual or punitive damages in the complaint. CCP § 425.10(b); and Schwab v. Rondel Homes, Inc., 53 Cal.3d 428, 280 Cal.Rptr.3d 83, 808 P.2d 226 (1991). In order to reveal the amount the plaintiff seeks, the plaintiff may serve on the defendant, or the defendant may request from the plaintiff, a separate "statement setting forth the nature and amount of damages being sought." CCP § 425.11(b). No default judgment may be entered against the defendant unless the plaintiff has served a statement of damages.

b. Exception: Claims for Punitive Damages

A plaintiff is prohibited from including in any complaint the amount of punitive damages sought. Cal. Civ. Code § 3295(e). If the plaintiff intends to seek an award of punitive damages, she preserves that right by serving on the defendant a statement of punitive damages under CCP § 425.115. The plaintiff must serve the defendant with this statement if she seeks a default judgment that includes an award of punitive damages. CCP § 425.115(f). If a personal injury or wrongful death plaintiff seeks punitive damages, she must also serve a statement of punitive damages, either as a separate document or as a part of the CCP § 425.11 statement of damages. CCP § 425.115(e).

2. *Compare Federal Procedure*

A federal complaint must contain "a demand for the relief sought." FRCP 8(a)(3). The rule does not explicitly require a party to state the actual amount of monetary damages in the complaint. As a matter of practice, however, federal plaintiffs in diversity actions typically demand a particular amount or at least plead that the amount in controversy exceeds the $75,000 minimum for diversity jurisdiction. In contrast to California law, there are no special federal rules regarding the pleading of damages in particular kinds of actions or for demanding punitive damages.

3. Illustration

The exclusive Rutherford winery, Prosper Cellars, sued neighboring Dharma Vineyards in Napa County Superior Court for misappropriation of trade secrets, requesting damages in the complaint "in excess of $50,000." Prosper subsequently served a statement of damages on Dharma claiming $8 million in compensatory damages. Dharma did not answer the complaint. The trial court entered a default judgment against Dharma and awarded Prosper $8 million in compensatory damages. The court may not enter judgment for this amount. Because Prosper's action is not one for personal injury or wrongful death, it was required to state the amount of damages in the complaint and not in the purported statement of damages. Consequently, Prosper is entitled to only up to $50,000 in compensatory damages, the amount stated in the complaint. Rodriguez v. Cho, 236 Cal.App.4th 742, 187 Cal.Rptr.3d 227 (2015).

C. Subscription

Every pleading must be "subscribed" (i.e., signed) by an attorney or unrepresented party. CCP § 446(a). The signature serves as a representation to the court that the pleading is warranted under law and fact and is not submitted for an improper purpose. CCP § 128.7 (see section VIII(A)(1), below). Absence of a signature does not render the complaint a nullity; the subscription defect may be cured by an amendment. Board of Trustees of Leland Stanford Jr. University v. Superior Court, 149 Cal.App.4th 1154, 57 Cal.Rptr.3d 755 (2007).

D. Types of Complaints

1. Form Complaints

Instead of filing a custom-drafted complaint, a plaintiff may use an official form complaint developed by the Judicial Council of California for certain types of actions (including personal injury, breach of contract, and fraud). CCP § 425.12. The form complaint must still allege ultimate facts sufficient to state a cause of action or it will be subject to attack by demurrer. People ex rel. Department of Transportation v. Superior Court, 5 Cal.App.4th 1480, 7 Cal.Rptr.2d 498 (1992).

2. Verified Complaints

a. Verification by Party

A verified complaint contains a declaration signed by the plaintiff under penalty of perjury attesting that the facts alleged in the complaint are true of the plaintiff's personal knowledge, except as to those facts stated on information and belief, and as to those matters the plaintiff believes them to be true. CCP § 446(a). Most of the time, the plaintiff has the option of filing either a verified or an unverified complaint. In some situations, however, a verified complaint is required (e.g., quiet title actions, Family Code pleadings, petition for writ of mandate). A pleading verified by the plaintiff has heightened evidentiary value because it is considered a sworn affidavit and can be cited as such when the plaintiff files a motion with the court. Except in limited civil cases and cases involving governmental defendants, an answer to a verified complaint must itself be verified by the defendant, and it must include specific denials instead of a general denial (see section IV(A), below).

b. Verification by Attorney

The plaintiff's attorney may verify the pleading if the plaintiff is absent from the county where the attorney has his office, or if the facts in the complaint are within the attorney's personal knowledge. CCP § 446(a).

c. Verification by Corporation or Governmental Party

Any corporate officer may verify a complaint filed by a corporation. The complaint of a governmental plaintiff is deemed to be verified. A nongovernmental defendant must file a verified answer in response to a governmental complaint. A governmental defendant need not file a verified answer, even if the complaint was verified. CCP § 446(a).

3. *Compare Federal Procedure*

Forms containing examples of pleadings for a variety of claims were included for many years in the Appendix to the Federal Rules. Effective December 1, 2015, the Appendix was abrogated. A few forms have been incorporated within the Federal Rules of Civil Procedure. See, e.g., FRCP 4. Other federal forms may be found on the website of the Administrative Office of the Courts.

A federal complaint must be signed by the attorney, but it is generally not required to be verified. FRCP 11(a). Even if a complaint is verified, the defendant is not obligated to file a verified answer.

4. **Illustration**

Prawn filed a complaint in Amador County Superior Court that included a verification stating that he is "familiar with the matters alleged in the complaint and based thereon knows that the allegations of said complaint are meritorious." The verification falls unacceptably short of the language of CCP § 446, which requires that the verification must state that the allegations are true of the plaintiff's own knowledge, except as to the matters which are stated on his information or belief, and as to those matters he believes them to be true. "Meritorious" is not synonymous with "true." The verification must state the truthfulness of the allegations so that sanctions for perjury may properly be imposed if the facts stated to be true actually are not. Ancora-Citronelle Corp. v. Green, 41 Cal.App.3d 146, 115 Cal.Rptr. 879 (1974).

IV. RESPONSIVE PLEADING: ANSWER

The answer is the defendant's substantive pleading in response to the factual allegations of the complaint. The filing of an answer places all unadmitted material facts in the complaint "at issue." The defendant may not request affirmative relief in the answer; it must file a cross-complaint for that purpose. Unless the defendant chooses to file a motion or demurrer attacking the complaint, or the court orders or the parties stipulate to an extension, an answer must be filed within 30 days after service of the summons and complaint on the defendant. CCP

§ 412.20(a)(3). An answer normally contains two components: denials and affirmative defenses.

A. Denials

Denials dispute the truth of the factual allegations of the complaint. Any material allegation that the defendant does not adequately deny in the answer will be deemed admitted. CCP § 431.20(a). A material allegation admitted by the defendant does not need to be proven by the plaintiff. A "material allegation" is "one essential to the claim or defense and which could not be stricken from the pleading without leaving it insufficient as to that claim or defense." CCP § 431.10(a). Denials may be either general or specific. CCP § 431.30(b)(1).

1. General Denials

A general denial is a blanket statement that the defendant denies each and every allegation of the complaint. The general denial is effective to deny all material allegations of an unverified complaint. A general denial is not permitted if the complaint is verified or deemed to be verified. CCP § 431.30(d).

2. Specific Denials

Specific denials take several forms. A defendant may deny certain paragraphs or parts of the complaint, or she may admit certain allegations and deny the remainder. The defendant may specifically deny an allegation: (a) directly, based on her personal knowledge; (b) based on information and belief; or (c) based on a lack of information or belief sufficient to enable the defendant to answer. CCP § 431.30(c)–(f).

3. Subscription

The defendant's attorney must sign the answer. CCP § 446(a). If the defendant is not represented by counsel, the defendant may sign.

4. Verification

A defendant must respond to a verified complaint with a verified answer containing specific denials. Exceptions include answers filed in limited civil cases (CCP § 92), and answers filed by a governmental entity (CCP § 446(a)).

5. *Compare Federal Procedure*

FRCP 8(b)(3) allows both general and specific denials. A general denial denies all allegations, including those on jurisdictional grounds, and must be made in good faith. All allegations, not only material allegations, are admitted by failure to deny. The only exception is for allegations relating to the amount of damages. FRCP 8(b)(6). A defendant may deny based on a lack of information sufficient to form a belief about the truth of an allegation. FRCP 8(b)(5).

6. Illustration

Pew filed suit in Alpine County Superior Court against Daw for specific performance of a real estate contract. Pew's complaint alleged that the consideration stated in the contract was the fair market value of the property. Daw's answer, consisting of many specific denials, did not deny Pew's allegation about the consideration. Pew's allegation constituted a material fact that will be deemed admitted and taken as true if not denied. Consequently, the admission relieves Pew of proving the reasonableness of the consideration at trial and precludes Daw from introducing contrary evidence. Hennefer v. Butcher, 182 Cal.App.3d 492, 227 Cal.Rptr. 318 (1986).

B. Affirmative Defenses

1. New Matter

Affirmative defenses do not respond directly to the elements of the plaintiff's prima facie case, as denials do. Nor do they seek affirmative relief. Instead, affirmative defenses raise new independent matter that would prevent the plaintiff from recovering, even if all allegations of the complaint were proven true. The defendant has the burden of proof on all affirmative defenses, which must be pleaded according to the standards of fact pleading applicable to complaints. Department of Finance v. City of Merced, 33 Cal.App.5th 286, 244 Cal.Rptr.3d 831 (2019). Some of the most commonly pleaded affirmative defenses are the statute of limitations, comparative negligence, fraud, waiver, estoppel, assumption of risk, and release. Most affirmative defenses will be deemed waived if the defendant fails to plead them in the answer.

2. *Compare Federal Procedure*

In contrast to the more detailed pleading standard in California courts, FRCP 8(b) and (c) requires only that affirmative defenses in federal answers be "stated." FRCP 8(c)(1) sets out a nonexclusive list of 18 potential affirmative defenses. A defendant must affirmatively assert these or any other applicable affirmative defenses in response to the complaint or they will be waived.

3. Illustration

When Pia's Plumbing, a plumbing contractor, did not receive payment for its work on a San Andreas apartment building, it brought a breach of contract action in Calaveras County Superior Court against Dwell, Inc., the developer of the building. In its complaint, Pia's Plumbing alleged that it "is a licensed plumbing contractor performing work under the laws of the State of California." Under Cal. Bus. & Prof. Code § 7031, a contractor suing for compensation for work that required a contractor's license must allege that it "was a duly licensed contractor at all times during the performance of that * * * contract." In its answer, Dwell, Inc. generally denied "each and every allegation" of the complaint, including the allegation of licensure. Pia's Plumbing contended that Dwell, Inc. was required to respond to the allegation of licensure via an affirmative defense, not merely as part of its general denial. Dwell, Inc.'s general denial of all of the material allegations of Pia's Plumbing's complaint, however, was sufficient to controvert the allegation of licensure and to compel Pia's Plumbing to prove its licensure by producing a verified certificate. Dwell, Inc. was not required to raise the matter as an affirmative defense for which it would have the burden of proof. Advantec Group, Inc. v. Edwin's Plumbing Co., 153 Cal.App.4th 621, 63 Cal.Rptr.3d 195 (2007).

C. Example of Common Affirmative Defense: Statute of Limitations

The statute of limitations is a frequently asserted affirmative defense in answers filed in civil actions. Alternatively, the matter might arise earlier in the pleading stage if the plaintiff pleads allegations on the face of the complaint revealing a statute of limitations issue. In that case, a defendant might file a demurrer or motion to strike. A plaintiff who has filed an untimely complaint under the applicable statute of limitations is barred from recovery, regardless of the truth of the allegations or the plaintiff's ability to prove them.

1. Accrual of Cause of Action

Statutes of limitations set out time limits that require a complaint to be filed within a statutorily prescribed period, starting from the date of the "accrual" of the cause of action pleaded in the complaint. CCP § 312. The point of accrual is determined according to two main principles: the general rule; and the discovery exception.

a. **General Accrual Rule**

Generally, a cause of action accrues when a plaintiff suffers "actual and appreciable harm." The moment of accrual is often stated to be when the "last element essential to the cause of action" has occurred. Norgart v. Upjohn Co., 21 Cal.4th 383, 397, 87 Cal.Rptr.2d 453, 463, 981 P.2d 79 (1999). The CCP contains a collection of statutes setting out time limits for bringing certain actions once the cause of action has accrued: e.g., two years for a personal injury or wrongful death action (CCP § 335.1); three years for a fraud action (CCP § 338); and four years for an action based on a written contract (CCP § 337).

b. **Delayed Accrual: Discovery of Injury**

Accrual of a cause of action may be delayed when a party has not discovered that she has been injured. Under these circumstances, the statute of limitations starts to run "when the plaintiff suspects or should suspect that her injury was caused by wrongdoing." Jolly v. Eli Lilly & Co., 44 Cal.3d 1103, 1110, 245 Cal.Rptr. 658, 662, 751 P.2d 923 (1988). The plaintiff may discover the cause of action even if she does not know the identity of the defendant. In this situation, the plaintiff may file a complaint containing fictitious "Doe" defendants and subsequently amend the complaint when the defendants' identities become known. (See section VII(B)(3), below.)

2. **Tolling**

The running of the statute of limitations may be tolled (halted) for a variety of reasons.

a. **Statutory Tolling**

The statute of limitations is tolled, for example, during the time the plaintiff is affected by war (CCP § 354), the plaintiff is a minor or is "lacking the legal capacity to make decisions" (CCP § 352(a)), or the plaintiff is incarcerated (CCP § 352.1(a)).

b. **Equitable Tolling**

Equitable tolling is a judge-made doctrine that suspends the running of a statute of limitations in the interests of practicality and fairness, as long as the suspension would not prejudice the defendant. Lantzy v. Centex Homes, 31 Cal.4th 363, 2 Cal.Rptr.3d 655, 73 P.3d 517 (2003). The doctrine requires the court to balance the injustice to the plaintiff from the imposition of the limitations period against the public interest or policy embodied in the limitations statute.

3. Compare: Laches

In actions for equitable relief, the judicial doctrine of laches may apply. A defendant must prove "unreasonable delay plus either acquiescence in the act about which plaintiff complains or prejudice to the defendant resulting from the delay." Johnson v. City of Loma Linda, 24 Cal.4th 61, 68, 99 Cal.Rptr.2d 316, 321, 5 P.3d 874 (2000). If the defendant prevails, the plaintiff will be prevented from recovering equitable relief even if the applicable statutory period has not expired.

4. Compare: Statutes of Repose

Unlike statutes of limitation, which are calculated under concepts of accrual based on the date of injury or its discovery, statutes of repose are calculated from when a specific event occurs. It does not matter whether a cause of action has accrued or whether any injury has resulted in that time period. A statute of repose simply extinguishes any potential right of action after the time period has elapsed. As a result, statutes of repose typically are not subject to equitable tolling. MACH-1 RSMH, LLC v. Darras, 103 Cal.App.5th 1288, 324 Cal.Rptr.3d 160 (2024). For example, CCP § 337.15, which sets out a ten-year period after substantial completion of construction projects during which a plaintiff may sue for damages for latent defects, is considered a statute of repose. It contains an absolute deadline to bring the action, regardless of when the injury was or could have been discovered. Lantzy v. Centex Homes, 31 Cal.4th 363, 2 Cal.Rptr.3d 655, 73 P.3d 517 (2003).

5. Compare: Revival Statutes

The Legislature occasionally enacts statutes that temporarily revive certain civil causes of action barred by the applicable statute of limitations. For example, CCP § 340.9 provided for a one-year revival in 2001 of time-barred claims against insurers arising out of the Northridge, California earthquake. CCP § 340.1 provided a one-year revival of certain causes of action based on childhood sexual abuse. Safechuck v. MJJ Productions, Inc., 43 Cal.App.5th 1094, 257 Cal.Rptr.3d 229 (2020).

6. *Compare Federal Procedure*

Civil actions arising under any federal statute enacted or amended after December 1, 1990, are subject to a four-year statute of limitations, unless otherwise provided in the federal statute in question. 28 USC § 1658(a). For suits arising under federal statutes containing no express limitation period and which were enacted prior to December 1, 1990, federal courts "borrow" comparable state law for the applicable statute of limitations. The accrual of a cause of action for statute of limitations purposes in diversity actions is considered "substantive" under *Erie* principles and thus directly subject to the applicable state law.

7. Illustration

Equine veterinarian Daria performed surgery in Benicia on Presto's horse, Rusty. Two weeks after the surgery, Rusty died from an infection acquired as a result of the procedure. Fourteen months after Rusty's death, Presto filed a professional negligence suit against Daria in Solano County Superior Court. Before filing the suit, Presto had sent Daria a letter of intent to sue, which, he argued, extended the running of the statute of limitations by 90 days under CCP § 364(d). That statute applies to actions against health care providers for personal injury and wrongful death. Daria's answer contained an affirmative defense that Presto's action was barred by the one-year statute of limitations contained in CCP § 340(c), which governs veterinary malpractice actions. Daria also filed a motion for judgment on the pleadings on that ground. Daria will prevail on the motion because Presto's action is barred by the one-year veterinary malpractice statute of limitations. The letter of intent to sue did not extend the statute of limitations because Presto's lawsuit was not one for personal injury or wrongful death. Animals are considered a form of property under California law. Thus, section 364(d) does not apply to Presto's action. Consequently, the lawsuit is untimely under section 340(c). Scharer v. San Luis Rey Equine Hospital, Inc., 204 Cal.App.4th 421, 138 Cal.Rptr.3d 758 (2012).

D. Pleas in Abatement

Certain categories of objections to the complaint must be specifically pleaded at the earliest opportunity or they are waived. These "pleas in abatement" (which are also called dilatory pleas to reflect their disfavored status) may be raised via an affirmative defense in the answer, or via a special demurrer if the defect appears on the face of the complaint. CCP §§ 430.30 & 430.80. Examples include: (1) lack of capacity to sue; (2) nonjoinder or misjoinder of parties; and (3) another pending action. See CCP § 430.10(b)–(d).

V. RESPONSIVE PLEADING: CROSS-COMPLAINT

The cross-complaint is a pleading that allows a defendant to assert a cause of action against the plaintiff, a codefendant, or one not yet a party to the suit. (Since the defendant may not seek affirmative relief in the answer, a cross-complaint against the plaintiff is the appropriate vehicle.) For most purposes, the cross-complaint is treated as an independent action severable from the original complaint. Cross-complaints serve the policy of judicial economy by resolving all disputes among the parties in one proceeding.

A. By Defendant Against Plaintiff

A cross-complaint filed by the defendant against the plaintiff is either compulsory or permissive.

1. Compulsory Cross-Complaint

A cross-complaint is compulsory when it alleges a cause of action that is related to the plaintiff's cause(s) of action. "Related" means that the cross-complainant's cause of action arises from the "same transaction, occurrence, or series of transactions or occurrences" as pleaded in the plaintiff's complaint. CCP § 426.10(c); and Align Technology, Inc. v. Tran, 179 Cal.App.4th 949, 120 Cal.Rptr.3d 343 (2009). (Some exceptions may apply. For example, a cross-complaint containing a related cause of action that arises after the defendant has answered the complaint is treated as permissive.) Failure to plead a compulsory cross-complaint when required will bar any assertion of the related cause of action in a later suit. CCP § 426.30(a). Because of this bar, the court liberally grants leave to file a compulsory cross-complaint at any time during the action.

2. Permissive Cross-Complaint

All other cross-complaints against the plaintiff are considered permissive, including those alleging any causes of action unrelated to the plaintiff's complaint. CCP § 428.10(a).

B. By Defendant Against Codefendant or Third Party

Cross-complaints filed by a defendant against any party other than the plaintiff are always permissive, never compulsory. A common use of a permissive cross-complaint is to seek indemnity from a codefendant or third party. The cause of action in the cross-complaint must arise out of the same transaction, occurrence, or series of transactions or occurrences, or relate to the same property or controversy, that is the subject of the cause of action brought by the plaintiff against the cross-complaining defendant. CCP § 428.10(b).

If those requirements are satisfied, that party may also bring unrelated causes of action, and even join new parties. If a cross-complaint involving third parties or unrelated causes of action unduly complicates the action, CCP § 1048(b) permits the court to order a separate trial of the cross-complaint. (See section IX(D)(1), below.)

C. Timing and Statute of Limitations

A defendant's cross-complaint against the plaintiff may be filed as a matter of right before or at the time of filing the answer to the complaint. Similarly, no leave of court is required to file a complaint for indemnity against a cross-defendant or third party before a trial date is set. In all other circumstances, leave of court is required, which is liberally granted in the interest of justice. CCP § 428.50. Because it is an independent action, a permissive cross-complaint is subject to its own applicable statute of limitations. A compulsory cross-complaint, however, will "relate back" to the date plaintiff filed the original complaint. (See section VII(C), below.)

D. *Compare Federal Procedure*

California uses the single term "cross-complaint" to refer to three devices that are kept distinct in federal court:

1. Counterclaims

The counterclaim is a claim for relief asserted by a defendant against the plaintiff. FRCP 13(a)–(e). Counterclaims may be either compulsory or permissive, and the tests for determining the nature of the counterclaim are nearly identical to those under California law. Similar rules to California's also govern "relation back" for compulsory counterclaims.

2. Cross-Claims

A claim by one defendant against a codefendant is called a cross-claim. FRCP 13(g). As under California law, cross-claims are never compulsory. The claims asserted must relate to the same transaction or occurrence, or the same property, that is the subject matter of the initial complaint.

3. Third-Party Complaints

A claim for indemnity by a defendant against a third party is called an impleader or third-party complaint. FRCP 14. As under California law, a third-party complaint is permissive.

E. Illustration

On July 4, 2023, Paley was swimming in Surprise Lake. Dixon accidentally ran into Paley with her jet ski, causing Paley to suffer a number of injuries. On July 2, 2025, Paley filed a complaint against Dixon in Tuolumne County Superior Court for damages related to his injuries. Two weeks later, Dixon answered Paley's complaint. Dixon simultaneously filed a cross-complaint for damages from the whiplash she suffered in the accident, alleging that Paley was negligently swimming in a boats-only part of the lake. The cross-complaint is compulsory, as it arises from the same occurrence as that alleged in the initial complaint. Although filed more than two years after the accident, Dixon's cross-complaint is not barred by the two-year statute of limitations for personal injuries in CCP § 335.1. As a compulsory cross-complaint, it relates back to the date of the filing of Paley's initial complaint. K.R.L. Partnership v. Superior Court, 120 Cal.App.4th 490, 15 Cal.Rptr.3d 517 (2004).

VI. ATTACKING THE PLEADINGS

Several types of responses are available to a defendant who objects to various aspects of the plaintiff's complaint. These devices may also be used to attack an answer or cross-complaint.

A. Responsive Pleading: Demurrer

While it has similarities to a motion, a demurrer is formally a responsive pleading. In its most common form, it is used to attack the allegations of the complaint on a number of alternative grounds. CCP §§ 422.10 & 430.10. A defendant may file a demurrer instead of, or at the same time as, filing the answer. CCP § 430.30(c). A plaintiff may also file a demurrer against a defendant's answer. CCP § 430.20. Before filing the demurrer, the demurring party must meet and confer with the party who filed the pleading to attempt to resolve the issues to be raised in the demurrer. CCP § 430.41(a).

1. Types of Demurrers

a. General Demurrer

A defendant may object on the ground that the "pleading does not state facts sufficient to constitute a cause of action." CCP § 430.10(e). This response, known as a general demurrer, may be addressed to the entire complaint or to any individual cause(s) of action within it. If the complaint states *any* legitimate cause of action, even if it is not the one intended by the plaintiff, the general demurrer addressed to the entire complaint must be overruled. A plaintiff may bring a demurrer on the ground that the defendant's answer fails to state facts sufficient to constitute a defense. CCP § 430.20(a). If a defendant objects to the complaint on the ground that the court lacks subject matter jurisdiction, that objection is usually considered to be a general demurrer rather than a special demurrer. CCP § 430.10(a).

b. Special Demurrer

In addition to the two general demurrer grounds stated above, a defendant may bring a special demurrer against the complaint on the following technical grounds:

- the person filing the complaint lacks the legal capacity to sue (see section I(B), above);
- there is another action pending between the same parties on the same cause of action;
- there is a defect or misjoinder of parties;
- the pleading is uncertain;
- in a contract action, it cannot be determined from the pleading whether the contract is written, oral, or implied by conduct; or
- certain required certificates were not filed.

CCP § 430.10(b)–(d) & (f)–(i). A plaintiff may file a special demurrer objecting to the answer on two grounds: (1) the answer is uncertain; or (2) it cannot be ascertained from the answer whether a contract pleaded in the answer is written or oral. CCP § 430.20(b)–(c).

2. Court's Consideration of Demurrer

The demurrer does not test the truth of the facts contained in the pleading. Rather, when a court considers a demurrer, it assumes the truth of any material allegations of fact that have been properly pleaded (but it does not accept as true conclusions of fact or law). John's Grill, Inc. v. Hartford Financial Services Group, Inc., 16 Cal.5th 1003, 323 Cal.Rptr.3d 875, 552 P.3d 1045 (2024). The court restricts its consideration to defects on the face of the complaint (and attachments that have been incorporated by reference), and to matters subject to judicial notice under Cal. Evid. Code §§ 450–460. A judge may sustain a demurrer either with or without leave to amend the complaint. The court ordinarily grants leave to amend if there is a reasonable probability that an amendment will cure the defect. A pleading can be amended a maximum of three times in response to a demurrer. CCP § 430.41(e)(1). If the court overrules the demurrer, the defendant must file an answer to the complaint.

3. *Compare Federal Procedure*

The grounds for demurrer have several counterparts in FRCP 12, but the different pleading standards existing in the federal and California courts create distinctions in the courts' consideration of these grounds. The federal equivalent of a general demurrer is a motion under FRCP 12(b)(6) for "failure to state a claim upon which relief can be granted." A party may also attack the court's subject matter jurisdiction (FRCP 12(b)(1)) and may object on the ground of "failure to join a party under Rule 19" (FRCP 12(b)(7)). In addition, a party may bring a motion for a more definite statement if the pleading "is so vague or ambiguous that the party cannot reasonably prepare a response." FRCP 12(e). This motion is similar to a special demurrer for uncertainty in California practice. There is no federal equivalent of the California special demurrer based on the inability to ascertain from the pleading whether a contract is oral or written. Alternatively, the grounds for objection in FRCP 12 may be asserted as defenses in a defendant's responsive pleading.

4. **Illustration**

The Primos are longtime Danger Demons season ticket holders and rabid fans. The Danger Demons have begun requiring a pat-down search of all ticketholders attending home games in their Yuba City stadium. The Primos objected to being forced to undergo the searches as a condition of retaining their season tickets and cheering on their beloved team. They filed suit against the Danger Demons in Sutter County Superior Court, alleging that the pat-downs violate their state constitutional right to privacy. The Danger Demons demurred to the complaint, contending that it did not state a cause of action because the Primos cannot show that they had a reasonable expectation of privacy. The superior court must base its ruling only on the contents of the complaint and must assume that all of the facts alleged in the Primos' complaint are true. The court may sustain the demurrer only if the complaint failed to state a cause of action under any possible legal theory. Further factual development was necessary before the Danger Demons could demonstrate that the allegations of the complaint failed to state a cause of action under any possible legal theory due to overriding concerns about safety. At the pleading stage,

> however, the complaint's privacy violation allegations were sufficient to survive demurrer. Sheehan v. San Francisco 49ers, Ltd., 45 Cal.4th 992, 89 Cal.Rptr.3d 594, 201 P.3d 472 (2009).

B. Motions to Attack Pleadings

1. General Procedural Requirements for Motions

A motion is an application to the court for an order. CCP § 1003. The rules governing pretrial motion practice are found primarily in the CCP, CRC, local court rules, and case law.

a. Papers

The moving party files and serves the following papers: (1) the motion (the actual request itself); (2) a "notice of motion," stating the time and place of the hearing and the grounds for the motion and the relief sought; (3) evidence in support of the requested order; (4) a memorandum of points and authorities; and (5) a proposed order. Before filing a demurrer or certain pleading and discovery motions, the moving party must first meet and confer with the opposing party in a reasonable and good faith effort to resolve the issues raised by the motion. Once the moving papers are served, the responding party may file a memorandum of points and authorities, evidence, and a proposed order in opposition to the motion. The moving party has the opportunity to file reply papers. Courts may enact local rules that permit or require electronic filing of documents. CCP § 1010.6; CRC 2.252.

b. Service of Moving Papers and Timing of Hearing

For most pretrial motions, the hearing date set forth in the notice of motion must be at least 16 court days after service by personal delivery of the moving papers, with longer notice periods if service is by mail, fax, or overnight delivery. CCP § 1005(b). Civil motion papers may also be served electronically. CCP § 1010.6. Some motions require lengthier notice periods (such as motions for summary judgment or for discretionary dismissal under the diligent prosecution statutes; see Chapter 5). The moving papers must be served on all parties who have appeared in the action, usually through the parties' respective attorneys of record.

c. **Tentative Ruling and Hearing**

In many superior courts, judges issue tentative rulings before the hearing on the motion. Depending on the tentative ruling, the parties may or may not decide to appear at the hearing for oral argument. If the parties appear at the hearing, the judge may enter a final ruling on the motion in open court or may take the matter "under submission" for determination at a later date. The judge's ruling is entered into the court minutes. The judge may also sign a formal written order, but it is not always required.

d. **Motions to Reconsider Prior Rulings or Renew Prior Motions**

If the trial court enters an interim or final order following a motion, a party may move the court to reconsider and perhaps modify or revoke the order. CCP § 1008(a). A party may also renew a motion previously brought before the court. CCP § 1008(b). If a party's application for reconsideration or renewal does not meet the strict requirements of section 1008, the court has no jurisdiction to consider it. CCP § 1008(e). The court, in its discretion, may impose sanctions for any violation of section 1008. CCP § 1008(d).

1) **Party's Motion for Reconsideration**

Any party affected by a trial court's ruling on a motion may request the court to reconsider the ruling and enter a different order. CCP § 1008(a). The statute contains several requirements:

- The party must seek reconsideration within ten days after service of notice of entry of the order.
- The motion for reconsideration must be made to the same judge or court that entered the order.
- The motion for reconsideration must be based on new or different facts, circumstances or law.

CCP § 1008(a).

2) **Party's Renewal of Previous Motion**

A party who previously made a motion and who is dissatisfied with the outcome may renew the motion with the court. CCP § 1008(b). Section 1008(b) applies broadly and governs virtually all renewed motions. See, e.g., Even Zohar Construction & Remodeling, Inc. v. Bellaire Townhouses, LLC, 61 Cal.4th 830, 189 Cal.Rptr.3d 824, 352 P.3d 391 (2015) (second application under CCP § 473(b) for relief from default judgment based on attorney fault must comply with section 1008). The moving party must show new or different facts, circumstances or law as a basis for the motion. The statute does not set out a time deadline for a renewal motion, and it does not require that the renewal motion be made to the same judge or court.

3) Reconsideration on Court's Own Motion

The strict requirements of CCP § 1008 apply only to party applications for reconsideration or renewal. The trial court possesses inherent authority to reconsider its prior rulings even in the absence of new or different facts, circumstances or law. A court may exercise its inherent authority on its own volition or at the suggestion of a party. Le Francois v. Goel, 35 Cal.4th 1094, 29 Cal.Rptr.3d 249, 112 P.3d 636 (2005).

4) *Compare Federal Procedure*

There is no exact counterpart of California's motion for reconsideration or renewal in the FRCP, but several federal rules address the district court's ability to revise or set aside orders. See Chapter 5(VIII).

5) Illustration

Pauline instituted dissolution of marriage proceedings against her husband, Drew, in Tehama County Superior Court. Under the couple's marital settlement agreement, Pauline was entitled to remain in the family home in Corning until the end of the school year in June. Pauline did not move out until August. At that point, Drew sought an order from the court that Pauline pay him a fair market rental for the period between June and August. The court granted the order. Pauline then moved the court to reconsider its order. In support of the motion, Pauline filed all of the same papers she had filed in response to Drew's original motion, including a declaration stating the text of an oral conversation she and Drew had in June in which Drew told Pauline that he would allow her to remain in the home until

> August. Pauline's application for reconsideration will be denied on the ground that it does not meet the strict requirements of CCP § 1008(a) because it did not include new or different facts, circumstances or law. The defective application may nevertheless prompt the court to exercise its inherent authority to reconsider its earlier order on its own motion and to change its ruling, even in the absence of new facts, circumstances or law. In re Marriage of Barthold, 158 Cal.App.4th 1301, 70 Cal.Rptr.3d 691 (2008).

2. Motion for Judgment on the Pleadings

a. Grounds for Motion

A motion for judgment on the pleadings has several similarities to a general demurrer. A defendant may bring this motion on only two alternative grounds: that the court lacks subject matter jurisdiction (CCP § 438(c)(1)(B)(i)); or that the complaint fails to state facts sufficient to constitute a cause of action (CCP § 438(c)(1)(B)(ii)). A plaintiff may move for judgment on the pleadings as to the defendant's affirmative defenses in the answer. CCP § 438(c)(1)(A). Material facts properly pleaded are deemed true, and the grounds for the motion must appear on the face of the pleading or be based on matters subject to judicial notice. CCP § 438(d). Like a demurrer, a motion for judgment on the pleadings may be granted with or without leave to amend. CCP § 438(h)(1). Unlike a demurrer, the court may grant judgment on the pleadings on its own motion. CCP § 438(b)(2).

b. Timing

A motion for judgment on the pleadings is sometimes referred to as a "delayed demurrer." A defendant may bring the motion after filing an answer and the time to file a demurrer has expired. CCP § 438(f)(2). The moving party must meet and confer with the opposing party before filing the motion papers, in an attempt to resolve the issues raised by the motion. CCP § 439.

c. *Compare Federal Procedure*

FRCP 12(c) provides for a motion for judgment on the pleadings "[a]fter the pleadings are closed—but early enough not to delay trial." The FRCP 12(c) motion is "functionally identical" to the FRCP 12(b)(6) motion to dismiss. U.S. ex rel. Cafasso v. General Dynamics C4 Systems, Inc., 637 F.3d 1047, 1054 n.4 (9th Cir.2011).

d. Illustration

Paloma sued Dove Co. in Mariposa County Superior Court for the wrongful death of her husband, Hernando. Paloma's complaint did not allege an employment relationship between Dove Co. and Hernando. An affirmative defense in Dove Co.'s answer, however, alleged that Hernando had been an employee, and that Paloma's remedy was exclusively through the workers' compensation system. Dove Co. then brought a motion for judgment on the pleadings on this ground. Although a motion for judgment on the pleadings is brought after the defendant has filed its answer, the motion cannot be based on matters raised via the answer. The court must view the complaint on its own to determine if its allegations state a cause of action. Thus, Paloma's failure to negate Dove Co.'s defense in her complaint is not a ground to grant the motion. Hughes v. Western MacArthur Co., 192 Cal.App.3d 951, 237 Cal.Rptr. 738 (1987).

3. Motion to Strike

A motion to strike may be used to attack a complaint on grounds not reachable through a demurrer or a motion for judgment on the pleadings.

a. Grounds for Motion

Within the time to file a responsive pleading, a party may move to "[s]trike out any irrelevant, false, or improper matter inserted in any pleading," or "[s]trike out all or any part of any pleading not drawn or filed in conformity with the laws of this state, a court rule, or an order of the court." CCP §§ 435(b)(1) & 436(a)–(b). The grounds for the motion to strike must appear on the face of the pleading or come from matters subject to judicial notice. CCP § 437. For example, a defendant might move to strike a demand for punitive damages in an ordinary contract action because punitive damages normally are not an available remedy for this type of claim. The moving party must meet and confer with the opposing party before filing the motion papers, in an attempt to resolve the issues raised by the motion. CCP § 435.5.

b. Compare: Demurrer

A motion to strike has several characteristics in common with a demurrer: (1) each is brought during the pleading stage; (2) each constitutes a general appearance if the defendant has not previously appeared; (3) each may be granted with or without leave to amend; and (4) the court's consideration of each is restricted to the face of the challenged pleading and to matters subject to judicial notice. While a demurrer resembles a motion, it is actually considered a pleading. CCP § 422.10. One important manifestation of this distinction is that the court may bring its own motion to strike (CCP § 436), whereas only a party may file a pleading, such as a demurrer.

c. Compare: Anti-SLAPP Motion to Strike

A defendant or cross-defendant may bring a special motion to strike, known as an anti-SLAPP motion. CCP § 425.16. See section VIII(C), below.

d. *Compare Federal Procedure*

A federal district court may strike from a pleading "an insufficient defense or any redundant, immaterial, impertinent, or scandalous matter." FRCP 12(f). Generally, a defendant must file a motion to strike within the time to respond to the complaint. The court may also strike matter from a pleading on its own motion.

e. Illustration

Larry is a lawyer representing Priya in her lawsuit against Darth. Larry drafted a complaint for Priya and filed it in Plumas County Superior Court. Larry neglected to sign the complaint, as required by CCP § 128.7(a). Larry discovered the omission, but he did not promptly file an amended complaint with a proper signature. Darth moved to strike the entire complaint because it was "not drawn or filed in conformity with the laws of this state" under CCP § 436(b). The court will likely grant the motion to strike with leave to amend. It would be an abuse of discretion to grant the motion without leave to amend because the defect is easily cured. Vaccaro v. Kaiman, 63 Cal.App.4th 761, 73 Cal.Rptr.2d 829 (1998).

VII. AMENDED PLEADINGS

Amendments to pleadings may occur at many points during a lawsuit, including during the pleading and discovery stages, after settlement negotiations, and during trial. Some amendments are permitted as a matter of right, and some require a court order. An amended complaint making material substantive changes supersedes the original pleading, unless the amended pleading is considered a "sham" because it suppresses or avoids an earlier unfavorable admission without explanation. Panterra GP, Inc. v. Superior Court, 74 Cal.App.5th 697, 289 Cal.Rptr.3d 743 (2022). An amended complaint must be served on all opposing parties, who must file new responsive pleadings.

A. Amendments as of Right

A party may amend a pleading once as a matter of right before an answer, demurrer or motion to strike is filed, or after a demurrer or motion to strike is filed and before it is heard. CCP § 472. The statute does not restrict the kinds of amendments a party may make as a matter of right.

1. *Compare Federal Procedure*

In federal practice, a plaintiff may amend the complaint "once as a matter of course" within 21 days of its service or 21 days after service of a required responsive pleading. FRCP 15(a)(1). Otherwise, a party must obtain leave of court (which is liberally granted) or the consent of the opposing party in order to amend. FRCP 15(a)(2).

2. Illustration

Portnoy was a shareholder and an employee of Drenka Corp. in Redlands. Portnoy sued Drenka Corp. and two of its officers, Roth and Zuckerman, in San Bernardino County Superior Court. Portnoy's complaint alleged Labor Code violations against Drenka Corp. and breach of fiduciary duty against the two corporate officers. In response to the complaint, Drenka Corp. filed an answer, and the officers filed a demurrer. Three days before the hearing of the officers' demurrer, Portnoy filed a first amended complaint without leave of court to address the issues raised by the demurrer. Portnoy's amended complaint is properly filed as of right under CCP § 472. Although Portnoy could no longer amend the complaint as of right as to Drenka Corp., since it had already filed its answer, he could amend without leave of court the breach of fiduciary duty cause of action because the officers' demurrer had not yet been heard. Drenka Corp.'s answer did not preclude Portnoy from amending the complaint as to Roth and Zuckerman. Barton v. Khan, 157 Cal.App.4th 1216, 69 Cal.Rptr.3d 238 (2007).

B. Amendments by Court Order

All other amendments not covered by CCP § 472 require leave of court. The court ordinarily liberally grants leave to amend.

1. After Demurrer or Motion to Strike

When a court sustains a demurrer or grants a motion to strike, it often grants leave to amend the subject pleading. The pleader normally has ten days to amend the pleading unless the court specifies a different time. CRC 3.1320(g).

2. Adding, Deleting or Correcting Parties

The court may grant leave to amend a pleading to add or remove parties, or to correct a mistaken name of a party. CCP § 473(a)(1). The addition of parties may run afoul of the statute of limitations unless the doctrine of "relation back" applies. (See section VII(C), below.)

3. Amendments Related to Doe Defendants

When a plaintiff is "genuinely ignorant" of a defendant's "name," the plaintiff may state that fact in the complaint and name the defendant as a fictitious "Doe." CCP § 474. The complaint must contain charging allegations against the Doe defendants. When the plaintiff discovers the defendant's true name, the complaint must be amended to substitute the true name for the Doe designation. The plaintiff may amend the complaint, even after the limitations period has expired, so long as the plaintiff was actually ignorant, at the time of filing the complaint, of the defendant's identity or of the facts giving rise to a cause of action against that defendant. The plaintiff has three years under the diligent prosecution statutes (see Chapter 5(III)(A)(1)) to amend the complaint and serve the substituted defendant. Fuller v. Tucker, 84 Cal.App.4th 1163, 101 Cal.Rptr.2d 776 (2000). If the amended complaint satisfies the requirements in section VII(C), below, it will relate back to the date of the filing of the original complaint.

a. *Compare Federal Procedure*

Doe defendants generally are not allowed in federal court pleadings. The district court will ignore fictitiously named defendants when a state court complaint is removed to federal court on the basis of diversity jurisdiction. 28 USC § 1441(b).

b. Illustration

Petunia's husband, Hiram, died of mesothelioma caused by his exposure to asbestos during his employment with Dredge Machinery in Lee Vining. Petunia filed a timely wrongful death action in Mono County Superior Court against Dredge Machinery and fictitious defendants designated as Does 1–10. When Petunia attempted to amend the complaint more than one year after filing the action to substitute Ducts & Drains, Inc. for Doe 1, Ducts & Drains filed a motion for summary judgment, arguing that that Petunia had not complied with CCP § 474 because she had not been genuinely ignorant of the identity of Ducts & Drains at the time she filed her action. In support of its motion, Ducts & Drains pointed to deposition testimony of a Dredge Machinery manager, who speculated that the Ducts & Drains products used by Dredge Machinery contained asbestos. The trial court granted summary judgment for Ducts & Drains on the ground that Petunia "knew or should have known" of the identity of Ducts & Drains at the time she filed her action. However, the correct standard is whether Petunia had actual knowledge of the identity of the defendant sued as a Doe. A plaintiff is not obligated to investigate facts she "should have known" prior to filing the complaint. Hahn v. New York Air Brake LLC, 77 Cal.App.5th 895, 293 Cal.Rptr.3d 119 (2022).

4. Other Court-Ordered Amendments

The court has broad discretion to order "an amendment to any pleading or proceeding in other particulars." CCP § 473(a)(1).

C. Statute of Limitations and Relation Back for Amended Pleadings

Amendments to pleadings to add new causes of action or new parties (named or Doe) may be subject to the bar of an applicable statute of limitations unless the doctrine of "relation back" applies. This doctrine allows the filing of an amended pleading to relate back to the date of the filing of the timely original complaint, thus making the amended pleading timely as well. An amended pleading must satisfy three requirements in order for the relation back doctrine to apply. It must:

- rest on the same general set of facts as the original pleading;

- seek recovery for the same injury or injuries as in the original pleading; and
- refer to the same accident and same offending instrumentality as in the original pleading.

Barrington v. A. H. Robins Co., 39 Cal.3d 146, 216 Cal.Rptr. 405, 702 P.2d 563 (1985). Relation back will not apply if the original pleading is devoid of factual allegations. Scholes v. Lambrith Trucking Co., 10 Cal.App.5th 590, 216 Cal.Rptr.3d 794 (2017), affirmed on other grounds, 8 Cal.5th 1094, 258 Cal.Rptr.3d 812, 458 P.3d 860 (2020).

1. *Compare Federal Procedure*

An amended pleading will relate back to the date of the filing of the original pleading if: (a) "the law that provides the applicable statute of limitations allows relation back" (FRCP 15(c)(1)(A)); or (b) "the amendment asserts a claim or defense that arose out of the conduct, transaction, or occurrence set out—or attempted to be set out—in the original pleading" (FRCP 15(c)(1)(B)). FRCP 15(c)(1)(A) appears to open the door to expanding Doe practice in federal court, at least for claims brought in diversity. While FRCP 15(c)(1)(C) provides a stricter relation back standard for a pleading that amends the "naming of the party against whom a claim is asserted," federal courts apply the more liberal standard of FRCP 15(c)(1)(A) when the claims are based on California substantive law. Provencio v. Vazquez, 258 F.R.D. 626 (E.D.Cal.2009).

2. **Illustration**

Patmore worked for Downton University in Gustine. Patmore's workload was consistently heavy, causing her to work overtime hours for which she was not paid. Downton University terminated her employment. Patmore filed a timely complaint against Downton University in Merced County Superior Court for overtime pay violations. After the statute of limitations had expired, Patmore filed an amended complaint seeking to add a cause of action for age discrimination. Even though the amended complaint names the same employer and addresses the same employment, the amended complaint will not relate back to the filing of the original complaint because the age discrimination claim does not arise out of the same general facts as the claim for overtime pay. Kim v. Regents of University of California, 80 Cal.App.4th 160, 95 Cal.Rptr.2d 10 (2000).

VIII. TRUTH IN PLEADING

A. Frivolous Pleadings

1. Sanctions Under CCP § 128.7

CCP § 128.7 imposes several requirements on parties and attorneys who present papers to a California court.

a. Signature

An attorney (or the party if not represented by an attorney) must sign every "pleading, petition, written notice of motion, or other similar paper." CCP § 128.7(a).

b. Certification

By signing, filing, submitting, or later advocating for any paper presented to the court, the attorney or unrepresented party certifies that:

- The paper is not being presented for any improper purpose, such as to harass or cause unnecessary delay;
- The claims, defenses, or other contentions in the paper are warranted by existing law or by a nonfrivolous argument for extending or modifying the law;
- The factual allegations have evidentiary support, or are likely to after a reasonable opportunity for discovery; and
- The denials of factual contentions are warranted by the evidence or are reasonably based on lack of information or belief.

CCP § 128.7(b). Sanctions are available, by motion of a party or the court, for violation of these requirements (except in discovery matters). CCP § 128.7(c) & (g). The party seeking sanctions must have exercised due diligence in bringing the motion. CCP § 128.7(c).

c. Sanctions

1) Purpose and Types of Sanctions

The purpose of section 128.7 sanctions is to "deter repetition of this conduct or comparable conduct by others similarly situated." CCP § 128.7(d). The court is authorized to issue both monetary and nonmonetary sanctions. Possible sanctions include payment of a penalty to the court, or a payment to the moving party of its reasonable attorney's fees and expenses incurred as a direct result of the violation of the statute. Id. A party who prevails on a sanctions motion under section 128.7 may also be entitled to reasonable expenses and attorney's fees for presenting or opposing the motion. CCP § 128.7(c)(1). A motion for sanctions brought for an improper purpose shall itself be the subject of a motion for sanctions. CCP § 128.7(h).

2) Safe Harbor Provision

The party seeking sanctions must serve the moving papers on the opposing party and allow the opponent 21 days to withdraw or correct the offending paper. If this "safe harbor" period expires without such withdrawal or correction, the moving party may proceed to file the motion with the court. CCP § 128.7(c)(1); and Primo Hospital Group, Inc. v. Haney, 37 Cal.App.5th 165, 249 Cal.Rptr.3d 601 (2019). The 21-day safe harbor period also applies to sanctions motions made by the court.

d. ***Compare Federal Procedure***

Because CCP § 128.7 was modeled on FRCP 11, California courts often rely on federal case law construing Rule 11 in applying that statute. Although the federal rule and the California statute are largely identical, some key distinctions exist:

- The California court assesses whether the moving party exercised due diligence in bringing a sanctions motion; FRCP 11 does not contain this requirement.
- The 21-day safe harbor provision in section 128.7 applies to motions by a party or by the court; under FRCP 11, the safe harbor period applies only to party motions.
- There is no provision in FRCP 11, as there is in section 128.7, authorizing sanctions for a motion for sanctions that was brought for an improper purpose.

e. Illustration

Paniz filed a complaint in Modoc County Superior Court against Demuth Catering Co., her employer, for demoting her from banquet manager to server. The complaint alleged that Paniz was demoted in retaliation for bringing the questionable food preparation practices of Demuth Catering to the attention of county health authorities. Paniz and Demuth Catering reached a settlement and filed a notice of the settlement with the court, which entered a dismissal with prejudice. Four months later, Paniz moved to vacate the settlement agreement and dismissal, contending that the confidentiality provision of the agreement prevented her from exposing Demuth Catering's alleged continued improper conduct. At the same time as filing its opposition to the motion to vacate, Demuth Catering served Paniz with a motion for sanctions pursuant to CCP § 128.7, on the ground that the motion to vacate the dismissal was frivolous. Nineteen days after the sanctions motion was served, the court denied Paniz's motion, ruling that there was no basis to vacate the dismissal. A week later, Demuth Catering filed its section 128.7 motion with the court. The court may not grant the sanctions motion because, under the statute's safe harbor provision, Paniz was required to have a full 21 days after service of the sanctions motion to correct or withdraw her motion to vacate before the section 128.7 motion was filed with the court. Because the court heard and ruled on the motion to vacate only 19 days after service of the sanctions motion, the section 128.7 safe harbor period had not yet expired. The burden was on Demuth Catering to ensure that the full safe harbor period was provided. It could have sought either a continuance of the motion to vacate or an order shortening the time to file its sanctions motion. Li v. Majestic Industry Hills, LLC, 177 Cal.App.4th 585, 99 Cal.Rptr.3d 334 (2009).

2. Sanctions Under CCP § 128.5

CCP § 128.5 permits the court to order a party or attorney to "pay the reasonable expenses, including attorney's fees, incurred by another party as a result of actions or tactics, made in bad faith, that are frivolous or solely intended to cause unnecessary delay." CCP § 128.5(a). While section 128.5 is not restricted to the presenting of papers, as is CCP § 128.7, section 128.5 contains several provisions that mirror the requirements of section 128.7. See, e.g., CCP §§ 128.5(f)(1)(B) (21-day safe harbor provision) & 128.5(g) (motion brought for improper purpose will itself be subject to motion for sanctions).

B. Vexatious Litigants

1. Designation as Vexatious Litigant and Security Requirement

A defendant (or respondent) may move the court to designate the plaintiff (or appellant) as a vexatious litigant. A vexatious litigant is a person who has:

- commenced or maintained in propria persona at least five lawsuits in the last seven years, and those suits have been resolved adversely to that person;
- repeatedly attempted to relitigate a matter that previously had been finally determined against that person;
- repeatedly filed unmeritorious motions, pleadings, or discovery requests, or has engaged in other frivolous or delaying tactics;
- previously been designated by a court as a vexatious litigant in a matter based on the same or similar facts or transaction; or
- commenced or maintained meritless litigation against someone protected by a restraining order issued against that person, causing harassment or intimidation.

CCP § 391(b). If the plaintiff is designated a vexatious litigant, and there is no reasonable probability that the plaintiff will prevail in the action, the defendant may move the court to require the plaintiff to furnish security in order to bring their lawsuit. CCP § 391.1(a). If the vexatious litigant fails to post the required security, the court will dismiss the action. CCP § 391.4.

2. Leave of Court to File Lawsuit

In addition to the above procedure, the presiding judge of the court may issue a prefiling order prohibiting a vexatious litigant from filing any new litigation in the state in propria persona without first obtaining leave of court. CCP § 391.7. The court subsequently may vacate the prefiling order and direct the removal of the person's name as a vexatious litigant if the facts have materially changed and the ends of justice would be served. CCP § 391.8.

3. *Compare Federal Procedure*

Although no federal equivalent of California's vexatious litigant statutes exists, the Ninth Circuit has allowed district courts to adopt local rules that permit judges to "proceed by reference to the Vexatious Litigants statute of the State of California." Ringgold-Lockhart v. County of Los Angeles, 761 F.3d 1057, 1061 n.1 (9th Cir.2014). Some federal courts have used their inherent power to issue narrowly tailored orders to limit the ability of a vexatious litigant to bring a lawsuit without leave of court. Sullivan v. Hyland, 647 F.Supp.2d 143 (D.Conn.2009). A district court might issue a writ pursuant to the All Writs Act, 28 USC § 1651(a), to address vexatious litigation.

4. Illustration

Over the course of a year, Puneet filed several actions in Yolo County Superior Court in pro per against Dam-It, a contractor located in Davis and specializing in the repair and prevention of flood damage. The court entered an order declaring Puneet to be a vexatious litigant. The court instituted a "prefiling order" prohibiting Puneet from filing any "new litigation" in pro per without approval of the superior court's presiding judge. CCP § 391.7(a). Six months later, Puneet's new attorney, Arnold, filed a lawsuit on Puneet's behalf against Donald, a former partner in a real estate investment. Puneet did not obtain court approval before filing the lawsuit against Donald. After several months, Arnold experienced an "irremediable breakdown in the attorney/client relationship" with Puneet. The court permitted Arnold to withdraw as counsel, but no new counsel was substituted. Donald immediately applied to the court to dismiss Puneet's action against him. Donald contended that Puneet's action had now become one filed in pro per, and Puneet had not obtained a prefiling order. Puneet, however, did not violate the prefiling order. He had filed his lawsuit against Donald through counsel, not in pro per. There was no prohibition against Puneet maintaining his action in pro per once it was on file. Instead, Donald could have sought an order requiring Puneet to furnish security before continuing to prosecute his action, on the ground that Puneet had no reasonable probability of prevailing. CCP § 391.1. If Puneet failed provide security as ordered, his action would then be subject to dismissal. Shalant v. Girardi, 51 Cal.4th 1164, 126 Cal.Rptr.3d 98, 253 P.3d 266 (2011).

C. Anti-SLAPP Motion to Strike

Spurred by "a disturbing increase in lawsuits brought primarily to chill the valid exercise of the constitutional rights of freedom of speech and petition," the California Legislature in 1992 authorized a special motion to strike lawsuits characterized as SLAPP (Strategic Litigation Against Public Participation) actions. CCP § 425.16(a). Anti-SLAPP motions are a mechanism to dispose of such lawsuits at the pleading stage, thereby avoiding the costs and delays of litigation. In order to encourage participation in matters of public importance, the anti-SLAPP statute is construed broadly. CCP § 425.16(a).

1. Features of Anti-SLAPP Motion

a. Respective Burdens of Parties

A defendant bringing an anti-SLAPP motion to strike has the initial burden to make a prima facie showing that the plaintiff's cause of action arises from protected activity: an act of the defendant in furtherance of the exercise of free speech or petition rights in connection with a public issue. Park v. Board of Trustees of California State University, 2 Cal.5th 1057, 217 Cal.Rptr.3d 130, 393 P.3d 905 (2017) (discussing nexus required between cause of action and protected activity). The defendant is not required to demonstrate that the plaintiff intended to chill his constitutional rights. Equilon Enterprises, LLC v. Consumer Cause, Inc., 29 Cal.4th 53, 124 Cal.Rptr.2d 507, 52 P.3d 685 (2002). Once the defendant makes the initial showing, the burden shifts to the plaintiff to establish a probability of prevailing on the merits of the claim. CCP § 425.16(b)(1). To carry this burden, the plaintiff must demonstrate that the complaint is legally sufficient and supported by enough admissible evidence to sustain a favorable judgment.

1) Defendant's Burden: Acts "In Furtherance"

An act of the defendant in furtherance of the right of petition or free speech must fall within one of four statutory categories:

- any statement or writing made before a legislative, executive, judicial or other official proceeding;
- any statement or writing made in connection with an issue under consideration or review by a legislative, executive, or judicial body, or

any other legally authorized official proceeding;

- any statement or writing made in a place open to the public or in a public forum, in connection with an issue of public interest; or
- any other conduct in furtherance of the exercise of the constitutional right of petition or free speech in connection with an issue of public interest.

CCP § 425.16(e)(1)–(4). Activity that is illegal as a matter of law does not constitute a protected exercise of First Amendment rights. Flatley v. Mauro, 39 Cal.4th 299, 46 Cal.Rptr.3d 606, 139 P.3d 2 (2006).

2) Defendant's Burden: Issue of Public Interest

The requirement that the defendant's speech or petition activity be connected to an issue of public interest is interpreted liberally. CCP § 425.16(a) & (b)(1). For purposes of CCP § 425.16(e)(4), " 'a matter of concern to the speaker and a relatively small, specific audience is not a matter of public interest,' and * * * '[a] person cannot turn otherwise private information into a matter of public interest simply by communicating it to a large number of people.' " Rand Resources, LLC v. City of Carson, 6 Cal.5th 610, 621, 243 Cal.Rptr.3d 1, 10, 433 P.3d 899 (2019). See also Geiser v. Kuhns, 13 Cal.5th 1238, 297 Cal.Rptr.3d 592, 515 P.3d. 623 (2022) (protest outside of plaintiff's home constituted speech in connection with issue of public interest).

3) Plaintiff's Burden: Probability of Prevailing

Once the defendant has satisfied its showing, the burden shifts to the plaintiff to establish a probability of prevailing on the merits. CCP § 425.16(b)(1). The plaintiff must meet its burden by providing competent admissible evidence that demonstrates that the cause of action has at least minimal merit (that is, the claim is legally sufficient and factually substantiated). The court accepts all evidence provided by the plaintiff as true for the purposes of the motion. If the plaintiff satisfies its burden, the anti-SLAPP motion will be denied.

4) Illustration

Proctor's Bakery is located in West Covina. Dirk Drama, a celebrity jeweler and mega social media influencer, ordered a cake from Proctor's Bakery for his son Josh's seventh birthday party, in a "mad scientist" theme. Dirk supplied Proctor's Bakery with a photo he had found on the internet to guide the design. When the cake arrived at the house the morning of the party, Dirk was shocked to find realistic-looking capsule pills made from frosting spilling out of a beaker decorating the top of the cake. Dirk took to social media to vent his rage, posting numerous diatribes on TikTok and Instagram (where he had a combined total of over 1.5 million followers) in which he threatened to put Proctor's Bakery out of business. Proctor's Bakery brought an action against Dirk in Los Angeles County Superior Court for libel and slander. Dirk filed an anti-SLAPP motion, contending that his social media posts were protected speech made in a public forum on an issue of public interest, under CCP § 425.16(e)(3). The court will deny Dirk's motion, finding that Dirk's statements were not made in connection with an issue of public interest. Dirk identified the issue of public interest as preventing children from confusing candy with pills. But "while 'candy confusion' might be an issue of public interest, [Dirk]'s statements did not discuss the danger of children confusing medications for candy. * * * [Dirk]'s statements did not seek public discussion of anything. They aimed to whip up a crowd for vengeful retribution." In addition, Dirk's status as a "celebrity" with a huge social media following does not turn a private dispute with Proctor's Bakery into a matter of public interest. At bottom, Dirk "is complaining about a cake order. He did not like the cake and he did not like the service. Those are not issues of public interest." Woodhill Ventures, LLC v. Yang, 68 Cal.App.5th 624, 632–633, 636, 283 Cal.Rptr.3d 507, 513, 516 (2021).

b. Timing

An anti-SLAPP motion generally must be filed within 60 days after service of the complaint or amended complaint. However, a court may in its discretion consider an anti-

SLAPP motion filed after this deadline. The court is required to hear the anti-SLAPP motion within 30 days of service of the motion unless the condition of the court's docket requires a later hearing. CCP § 425.16(f).

c. Discovery Stayed

Unless the court orders otherwise for good cause, the filing of an anti-SLAPP motion stays all discovery until the court rules on the motion. CCP § 425.16(g). The effect of this stay is to protect a defendant from the expense of discovery while the motion is pending.

d. Fees and Costs

A prevailing defendant on an anti-SLAPP motion is entitled to recover attorney's fees and costs. CCP § 425.16(c). The term "fees and costs" is ambiguous, but the legislative history indicates that the statute was intended to allow for the fees and costs associated with the motion and not with the entire litigation.

e. Appealability

An order granting or denying an anti-SLAPP motion under CCP § 425.16 is appealable. CCP §§ 425.16(i) & 904.1(a)(13). See Chapter 8(III)(A).

2. When Anti-SLAPP Motion Is Not Available

In response to what it found to be a "disturbing abuse" of the anti-SLAPP procedures, the California Legislature in 2003 exempted two categories of lawsuits from an anti-SLAPP motion:

a. Public Interest

Suits brought solely in the public interest or on behalf of the general public are not subject to an anti-SLAPP motion, as long as all of the following requirements are met:

- The plaintiff does not seek relief greater than or different from the relief sought for the general public;
- The lawsuit, if successful, would enforce an important right affecting the public interest and would confer a significant public benefit; and
- Private enforcement is necessary and places a disproportionate financial burden on the plaintiff.

CCP § 425.17(b); and Blanchard v. DIRECTV, Inc., 123 Cal.App.4th 903, 20 Cal.Rptr.3d 385 (2004).

b. Commercial Speech

Anti-SLAPP protections do not apply to causes of action arising from commercial speech when:

- The cause of action is against a person primarily engaged in the business of selling or leasing goods or services;
- The cause of action arises from a statement or conduct by that person consisting of representations of fact about that person's or a competitor's business, goods or services;
- The statement or conduct was made for the purpose of obtaining approval for, promoting, or securing sales or leases of, or commercial transactions in, the person's goods or services, or was made in the course of delivering the person's goods or services; and
- The intended audience for the statement or conduct is an actual potential customer or a person likely to influence an actual or potential customer, or the statement or conduct arose in connection with a regulatory approval process, proceeding or investigation.

CCP § 425.17(c); and JAMS, Inc. v. Superior Court, 1 Cal.App.5th 984, 205 Cal.Rptr.3d 307 (2016).

c. Illustration

In exploring ways to expand its clientele, Pretty Nails Salon, located in San Francisco, decided to advertise on the widely used review website Dealz. Pretty Nails was persuaded to deal with Dealz because the website employs an innovative review filter that, according to Dealz's representations, produces more reliable reviews by filtering out questionable and biased reviews, making the website more attractive to advertisers like Pretty Nails. After Pretty Nails signed on with Dealz, the salon received several reviews that it believed were inaccurate but which had not been filtered out. Pretty Nails sued Dealz in San Francisco County Superior Court for unfair competition and false advertising resulting from Dealz's representations regarding the quality of its review filter. Dealz responded by filing an anti-SLAPP motion to strike the complaint, alleging that the lawsuit interfered with its free speech rights in promoting the trustworthiness of its review filter and reviews. Dealz's motion will fail because it is subject to the commercial speech exception of CCP § 425.16(c). Dealz's "statements about its review filter—as opposed to the content of the reviews themselves—are commercial speech about the quality of its product (the reliability of its review filter) intended to reach third parties to induce them to engage in a commercial transaction (patronizing Dealz's website, which patronage induces businesses on Dealz to purchase advertising)." Moreover, Dealz's representations are statements of fact concerning the reliability of its review filters, not mere puffery or opinion. Thus, the anti-SLAPP statute did not apply to Dealz's commercial speech. Demetriades v. Yelp, Inc., 228 Cal.App.4th 294, 310, 175 Cal.Rptr.3d 131, 143 (2014).

3. SLAPPback Action

In 2005, the Legislature declared that a "SLAPPback" was distinguishable in character and origin from an ordinary malicious prosecution action. CCP § 425.18(a). A SLAPPback arises from a previous lawsuit dismissed pursuant to an anti-SLAPP motion. CCP § 425.18(b)(1). A defendant who previously prevailed on the anti-SLAPP motion (now the SLAPPback plaintiff) may bring a SLAPPback suit against the former plaintiff (now the SLAPPback defendant) to recover damages beyond the attorney's fees and costs awarded to the former prevailing defendant. CCP § 425.18(b)(1). The SLAPPback defendant may bring an anti-SLAPP motion against the SLAPPback suit, but many of the procedural protections for an anti-SLAPP movant are not available in the SLAPPback context. For example, the SLAPPback plaintiff may conduct discovery to oppose the anti-SLAPP motion. CCP § 425.18(c) & (e). See West v. Arent Fox LLP, 237 Cal.App.4th 1065, 188 Cal.Rptr.3d 729 (2015).

4. *Compare Federal Procedure*

Federal procedure does not authorize an anti-SLAPP motion. Several potential conflicts between federal procedure and the anti-SLAPP procedures exist. Makaeff v. Trump University, LLC, 715 F.3d 254, petition for rehearing denied, 736 F.3d 1180 (9th Cir.2013). For example, the burden on a plaintiff to establish a probability of prevailing on the merits at the pleading stage may run counter to FRCP 8(a)(2), which requires that the plaintiff merely provide a short and plain statement showing the pleader is entitled to relief. In addition, FRCP 56 allows a defendant to defeat meritless claims via summary judgment, but only later in the litigation (most notably after broad discovery has occurred). In contrast, an anti-SLAPP motion is filed much earlier in the litigation, and, once the motion is filed, discovery is stayed. Conflicts between California's anti-SLAPP provisions and federal procedures can lead to interesting *Erie* dilemmas in diversity actions. See Swierkiewicz v. Sorema N.A., 534 U.S. 506, 122 S.Ct. 992, 152 L.Ed.2d 1 (2002) (refusing to apply the discovery-limiting aspects of CCP § 425.16 because they directly collided with the discovery-allowing aspects of FRCP 56).

5. Illustration

During a contentious gubernatorial election, the incumbent, Governor Prescott, found himself battling against challenger Damon. In a former life, Prescott was a professional football player. Toward the end of his playing career, Prescott had admitted to using illegal, performance-enhancing drugs. During the campaign, Damon released a commercial that referred to Prescott as "an admitted drug user" and a "cheater." After losing the election, Prescott brought suit against Damon in Sacramento County Superior Court for defamation. Damon filed an anti-SLAPP motion, arguing that he was merely exercising his constitutionally protected right to free speech and that his comments addressed a matter of public concern—Prescott's qualifications to be Governor. When the burden shifted to Prescott, he could not show that Damon made the comments with the knowledge that they were false or with reckless disregard as to whether they were false. As such, he could not establish a probability that he would prevail on his defamation claim. The court will thus strike Prescott's complaint as a SLAPP. Conroy v. Spitzer, 70 Cal.App.4th 1446, 83 Cal.Rptr.2d 443 (1999).

IX. JOINDER

California applies liberal rules of joinder of causes of action and of parties.

A. Joinder of Causes of Action

Subject to the application of the doctrine of claim preclusion (see Chapter 9(II)(A)), a California plaintiff who brings a cause of action against one or more defendants is permitted to join any other causes of action she has against those defendants. CCP § 427.10(a). There is no requirement that the causes of action possess a common question of law or fact.

B. Permissive Joinder of Parties

1. Permissive Joinder of Defendants

The plaintiff may join several defendants in a single action if the action asserts against them: (a) a right to relief arising out of the same transaction, occurrence, or series of transactions or occurrences, *and* a question of law or fact common to all; or (b) an adverse claim, right or interest in the subject matter of the action. CCP § 379(a).

2. Permissive Joinder of Plaintiffs

CCP § 378(a) permits joinder of plaintiffs under the same liberal standard as that for permissive joinder of defendants.

3. *Compare Federal Procedure*

Permissive joinder of defendants and plaintiffs is liberally allowed under FRCP 20 under similar grounds as those found in the California statutes, as long as the requirements of subject matter jurisdiction are satisfied.

4. Illustration

Over one hundred borrowers residing in Williams sued Dishonest Mortgage Lenders in Colusa County Superior Court, alleging that Dishonest provided falsely inflated appraisals that exaggerated home prices and misrepresented or concealed the terms of its loans to plaintiffs in order to induce them to borrow. Dishonest filed a special demurrer on the ground of misjoinder of parties, contending that each plaintiff should have filed separate complaints because of the significant differences in their alleged injuries. The court will likely overrule the demurrer and allow all of the plaintiffs to be joined under CCP § 378(a). The potential liability of Dishonest to all borrowers is based on the same series of transactions and occurrences and the same alleged scheme. Permissive joinder of plaintiffs would promote judicial economy and access to evidence common to all claims. Petersen v. Bank of America Corp., 232 Cal.App.4th 238, 181 Cal.Rptr.3d 330 (2014).

C. Compulsory Joinder of Parties

1. Necessary Parties

A court must order joinder of a person who is subject to service of process (personal jurisdiction) and whose joinder will not deprive the court of subject matter jurisdiction, if that person's joinder satisfies at least one of the conditions set forth in CCP § 389(a):

- In his absence, complete relief cannot be accorded among those already parties; or
- He claims an interest in the subject matter of the action, and the disposition of the action in his absence may:
    - as a practical matter impair or impede his ability to protect his interest; or
    - subject existing parties to substantial risk of double, multiple or inconsistent obligations because of his claimed interest.

Doe v. Regents of University of California, 80 Cal.App.5th 282, 295 Cal.Rptr.3d 625 (2022).

2. Indispensable Parties

If joinder of a necessary party is not possible, the court must determine whether the action "in equity and good conscience" should proceed in the absence of the person, or whether it should be dismissed without prejudice because the person is considered "indispensable." CCP § 389(b). The inability to join an indispensable party does not render the court without jurisdiction (power) to proceed. Rather, the court decides in equity and good conscience *whether* it should proceed, considering such factors as the existence of prejudice to the absentee, and the adequacy of any judgment rendered in that person's absence.

3. *Compare Federal Procedure*

CCP § 389 is taken nearly verbatim from FRCP 19.

4. Illustration

Peach and her brothers, Biff and Buff, managed several family-owned companies in Porterville. A shareholders' election resulted in control of the companies resting in Declan Co., an entity connected to Biff and Buff. Peach filed an action against Declan Co. in Tulare County Superior Court, challenging the validity of the election on grounds of conflict of interest and breach of fiduciary duty. Declan Co. filed a motion for judgment on the pleadings, contending that Biff and Buff were necessary and indispensable parties to the action. The court will find that Biff and Buff must be joined as necessary and indispensable parties under CCP § 389(a) and (b). Peach's causes of action against Declan Co. were based on the brothers' self-dealing and breach of fiduciary duty. The brothers' absence from the lawsuit would impair their ability to protect their interests, and there would be a danger of inconsistent obligations as between Declan Co. and the brothers. Thus, Peach must name and serve Biff and Buff in the action, or risk dismissal if she fails to do so. Morrical v. Rogers, 220 Cal.App.4th 438, 163 Cal.Rptr.3d 156 (2013).

D. Special Joinder Devices

Several special procedures exist in California to join (or, in some cases, separate) parties and claims.

1. Consolidation and Bifurcation

a. Consolidation

When two or more actions are pending before a court, and the actions involve a common question of law or fact, the court may order a joint hearing of any or all issues in the actions, or it may consolidate the actions. CCP § 1048(a). If consolidation would create confusion, conflict or prejudice, the court may exercise its discretion to deny consolidation.

1) Complete Consolidation

Complete consolidation unites two or more lawsuits into a single action. The pleadings are combined into one set, and the allegations and affirmative defenses are treated in tandem. The court enters a single judgment. Because of the total merging of the actions, complete consolidation is ordered only when the parties in each action are identical and the causes of action could have been joined in a single lawsuit.

2) Partial Consolidation

An order of partial consolidation combines two actions in the same court for the purpose of trial. Partial consolidation promotes judicial economy and prevents duplication and inconsistency. Partial consolidation maintains the separate nature of each set of pleadings;

the court makes separate findings and judgments in each action.

3) Consolidation and Coordination of Actions in Different Courts

Noncomplex cases involving common questions that are pending in different courts may be ordered transferred to one court and consolidated with each other. CCP § 403. Complex cases pending in different courts may be coordinated under a more cumbersome procedure set forth in CCP § 404. Prescription Opioid Cases, 57 Cal.App.5th 1039, 272 Cal.Rptr.3d 99 (2020).

b. Bifurcation

A court may order separate trials of any causes of action or issues in a lawsuit if doing so would further convenience, avoid prejudice, or foster judicial economy. CCP § 1048(b). A common example is a court order of separate trials on the issues of liability and damages. An order of separate trials is often referred to as "bifurcation." The former label "severance" is still sometimes used.

c. *Compare Federal Procedure*

CCP § 1048 is largely modeled on FRCP 42.

d. Illustration

Pisces, Pesto, and Pram individually brought product liability suits alleging that cough syrup made by Drugsafe Co. in Willows was unsafe. In assessing whether the three actions should be consolidated, the Glenn County Superior Court found: (1) all plaintiffs had to use extensive expert testimony and scientific findings about the same product; (2) the jury would not be confused with only three plaintiffs; and (3) it was not likely that the jury would be prejudiced against Drugsafe just because there were three plaintiffs alleging the same side effects. On these facts, it was proper to consolidate the three cases. Todd-Stenberg v. Dalkon Shield Claimants Trust, 48 Cal.App.4th 976, 56 Cal.Rptr.2d 16 (1996).

2. Interpleader

a. Conflicting Claims

Interpleader permits a person or entity—known as the stakeholder—who is subject to multiple and inconsistent claims to the same property or funds to join all of the claimants in a single suit to resolve the controversy. CCP § 386(b). A defendant to an existing claim or claims may file an interpleader action as a cross-complaint, or may, before answering the complaint, apply to the court to deposit the property in question with the court. A party may also initiate an action in interpleader as a plaintiff when that party faces conflicting claims to the same property. Once the right to interplead has been granted and the deposit has been made, the stakeholder is discharged from liability to the claimants. CCP § 386(a) & (b).

1) **Stakeholder Interest**

Traditionally, interpleader actions could be brought only where the stakeholder explicitly disavowed any interest in the subject property. These actions were known as strict interpleader. It is not clear whether California continues to require that stakeholders disavow any interest in the interpleaded property. By permitting the stakeholder to deny liability "in part" to any of the claimants under CCP § 386(b), the stakeholder might impliedly be deemed to assert an interest in the property.

2) **Additional Claims Against Stakeholder**

In an interpleader action, the claimants to the subject property should raise only issues related to the interpleader action. Although claimants should not also raise independent claims against the stakeholder, the court may consider such claims. Claimants are not required to assert causes of action that would otherwise have to be pleaded in a compulsory cross-complaint.

b. ***Compare Federal Procedure***

Conceptually, federal interpleader practice under FRCP 22 and 28 USC § 1335 is similar to California practice. In contrast to the ambiguity in the California law, federal law is clear that interpleader is available even if the stakeholder is not completely disinterested. In federal court, a stakeholder may deny liability in whole or in part to any of the other claimants, and she may also claim a share of the subject property "in the nature of interpleader." FRCP 22; 28 USC § 1335. There is no limitation on additional claims against the stakeholder. Indeed, under FRCP 13, a claimant might be required to raise them.

c. Illustration

When Muriel was found dead outside her Placerville home, her death was investigated as a homicide. Her husband, Doron, became a prime suspect in her death. He stood to benefit from a sizable insurance policy taken out on Muriel's life. The carrier, Prime Insurance Co., refused to pay out any policy benefits while Doron was under investigation for Muriel's death. Prime Insurance, a disinterested stakeholder, filed a complaint in interpleader in El Dorado County Superior Court, alleging that it was uncertain whether it should pay the life insurance benefits to Doron or to Muriel's estate. Prime Insurance properly brought its interpleader action because, although only one liability existed, there were conflicting claims and a threat of double vexation. Prime Insurance appropriately relied on the court to determine to whom it was liable for the funds. Farmers New World Life Insurance Co. v. Rees, 219 Cal.App.4th 307, 161 Cal.Rptr.3d 678 (2013).

3. Intervention

a. Types of Intervention

Intervention allows a nonparty to an action to join as a party (either as a plaintiff or a defendant) if the nonparty has a sufficient interest in the subject matter of the litigation. There are two types of intervention: intervention of right and permissive intervention.

1) Intervention of Right

The court will order intervention if a nonparty establishes that:

- a statute entitles the nonparty to intervene in an action; or
- the nonparty satisfies all of the following criteria for intervention of right:
    - a showing of an interest in the subject matter of the action;
    - a showing that the disposition of the action may impede or impair the nonparty's ability to protect that interest; and
    - a timely application for intervention.

CCP § 387(b); and Carlsbad Police Officers Association v. City of Carlsbad, 49 Cal.App.5th 135, 262 Cal.Rptr.3d 646 (2020). If the requirements are met, the court must order intervention unless the nonparty's interest is already adequately represented by an existing party.

2) **Permissive Intervention**

a) **Requirements**

Intervention may be allowed in the court's discretion, upon timely application, where a nonparty has an "interest in the matter in litigation" or in the "success of either of the parties." CCP § 387(a). This provision has been interpreted to permit intervention when:

- the proper procedures have been followed;
- the nonparty has a direct and immediate interest in the action;
- the intervention will not enlarge the issues in the litigation; and
- the reasons for the intervention outweigh any opposition by the parties presently in the action.

City and County of San Francisco v. State, 128 Cal.App.4th 1030, 27 Cal.Rptr.3d 722 (2005).

b) **Direct and Immediate Interest**

The moving party's interest in the litigation must be direct and immediate. A consequential interest is not sufficient. It is not always easy to tell the difference. An interest is sufficiently direct where that party will benefit or suffer by the direct effect of the judgment, or where the judgment in itself adds to or diminishes that party's legal rights.

c) **Liberal Construction**

California follows a policy of liberal construction underlying the court's exercise of discretion for permissive intervention. Even if a party establishes the necessary interest for permissive intervention, however, the court may exercise its discretion to deny intervention where it would cause significant delay, reopen evidence, or enlarge the issues in the case.

b. Timeliness

The party seeking to intervene (both of right and permissively) must seek leave of court. The timeliness of the application for intervention depends on the circumstances of the case. The court will exercise its discretion to deny the motion to intervene where the moving party has not been diligent or there otherwise has been unreasonable delay.

c. *Compare Federal Procedure*

Federal intervention may be either mandatory (FRCP 24(a)) or permissive (FRCP 24(b)). While the federal and California provisions for intervention as of right are virtually identical, the standard for permissive intervention in FRCP 24(b) differs from that encompassed by CCP § 387(a). The federal court may permit a party to intervene when a federal statute grants a conditional right to intervene, or when a common question of law or fact exists between the main action and a claim or defense of the person seeking intervention. FRCP 24(b).

d. Illustration

Derrick Oil Corp. leased a parcel of land in Weaverville, with the intent of extracting any oil under the surface. Philo brought a quiet title action against Derrick Oil in Trinity County Superior Court, alleging that, under the terms of the deed to the parcel, he was entitled to extract any subsurface oil. Irma, who owns an adjacent parcel, feared that any oil extraction would cause subsidence in her parcel. Irma timely moved for permission to intervene in the action between Philo and Derrick Oil. Irma's motion will be denied, as the quiet title action between Philo and Derrick Oil would not have a direct and immediate effect on Irma's interest. Lindelli v. Town of San Anselmo, 139 Cal.App.4th 1499, 43 Cal.Rptr.3d 707 (2006).

4. Class Actions

a. Purpose of Class Actions

The class action procedure allows a person to bring a lawsuit on behalf of herself and others similarly situated. CCP § 382. Class actions are favored in California because they can provide effective relief to plaintiffs where the claim of any one individual plaintiff is too small to pursue individually. Because class actions involve the litigation of many claims at once, it is essential that a lead plaintiff fairly represent the class, that the class be well defined, and that adequate notice be given to class members. Although CCP § 382 authorizes class actions in California, it provides little instruction. As a result, FRCP 23 has long been used for guidance, as has Cal. Civ. Code § 1780 et seq. (Consumer Legal Remedies Act). Additionally, a substantial body of case law regarding class actions has developed in California.

1) Requirements

The essential requirements for a California class action are an ascertainable class and a community of interest among the members of the class. Sav-on Drug Stores, Inc. v. Superior Court, 34 Cal.4th 319, 17 Cal.Rptr.3d 906, 96 P.3d 194 (2004).

a) Ascertainable Class

Without a precisely framed class, capable of some objective definition, it becomes impossible for all potential plaintiffs to receive notice of the action. The class definition must allow identification of those who fit within the class and allow persons learning of the definition to determine whether or not they are members of the class.

b) Community of Interest

The community of interest requirement has three factors: (1) predominant common questions of law or fact; (2) class representatives whose claims are typical of the class members; and (3) class representatives who will adequately represent the class. Typicality does not require that a representative's claims be identical to those of the class members—only that the representative be similarly situated and similarly motivated. Adequacy requires that a representative vigorously seek all relief available to the class.

2) Number of Plaintiffs

The class members must be "numerous." CCP § 382. There is no requirement of a minimum number of plaintiffs. However, where a class is extremely small, the potential benefits of the class action procedure may give way to individual adjudication.

b. Grounds for Class Certification

California follows federal procedure in allowing for three general types of class actions: (1) those where plaintiffs might be prejudiced if their claims are handled separately; (2) those where declaratory or injunctive relief is appropriate; or (3) those where common questions predominate and a class action is more appropriate than any other method. FRCP 23(b). A class member may not opt out of the first two types of class actions, but she may opt out of the more general "common questions" class. In considering a motion for class certification, a court must analyze only whether the requirements of class certification have been met. Any inquiry into the merits of the underlying claims is improper. Linder v. Thrifty Oil Co., 23 Cal.4th 429, 97 Cal.Rptr.2d 179, 2 P.3d 27 (2000). An order denying class certification on all causes of action is immediately appealable. In re Baycol Cases I and II, 51 Cal.4th 751, 122 Cal.Rptr.3d 153, 248 P.3d 681 (2011).

c. Notice

Because the resolution of the class action will bind all class members and preclude any further action on the same claims, it is essential that class members be given adequate notice of the pendency of the action. However, in expansive classes involving small losses, California courts have recognized that "class actions should be permitted to proceed, where the economic realities involved in giving 'adequate' notice, compared to the small individual losses of class members, would effectively negate any class action." Cartt v. Superior Court, 50 Cal.App.3d 960, 971, 124 Cal.Rptr. 376, 384 (1975). CRC 3.766(f) authorizes notice via publication where personal notification is "unreasonably expensive" or where class members have an "insubstantial" stake in the action. The court has discretion to shift some or all of the burden of the cost of notice onto the defendant. "Opt-out" notice is generally acceptable, but the validity of "opt-in" notice is the subject of debate within the California courts. Los Angeles Gay and Lesbian Center v. Superior Court, 194 Cal.App.4th 288, 125 Cal.Rptr.3d 169 (2011).

d. Settlement

In determining whether a settlement is fair to the class members, the trial court considers a variety of factors on a case-by-case basis, including: "(1) the strength of plaintiffs' case, (2) the risk, expense, complexity and likely duration of further litigation, (3) the risk of maintaining class action status through trial, (4) the amount offered in settlement, (5) the extent of discovery completed and the stage of the proceedings, (6) the experience and views of counsel, and (7) the reaction of the class members to the proposed settlement." Munoz v. BCI Coca-Cola Bottling Co., 186 Cal.App.4th 399, 407–408, 112 Cal.Rptr.3d 324, 330–331 (2010). The most important task for the court is to balance the strength of the case for the plaintiffs on the merits against the amount offered in settlement.

e. *Compare Federal Procedure*

The federal and California class action practices follow many of the same general principles because California courts have long used FRCP 23 for guidance. However, there are some distinctions. A federal order denying class certification is subject to immediate appeal only at the discretion of the appellate court. FRCP 23(f). In federal practice, initially the plaintiff must bear the entire cost of providing notice to potential class members. In contrast to California's more lenient standard, federal procedure requires the best practicable notice possible under the circumstances, including individual notice to all members of the class who can be reasonably identified. FRCP 23(c)(2)(B).

f. Illustration

Peyton's home was located a short distance from Dorke Corp., a manufacturer of fertilizers located in Chowchilla. Peyton and several other residents living near the manufacturing plant filed suit in Madera County Superior Court against Dorke Corp. They alleged damages from the discharge of dangerous chemicals, which had contaminated the local drinking water. The plaintiffs sought class certification for a "medical monitoring class." The goal of the class action was to require Dorke Corp. to fund a court-supervised program for the medical monitoring of the class members. Although common issues existed among the potential class members, the individual

> issues actually predominated because of the presence of different levels of exposure and different monitoring needs among the class members. Therefore, class certification was not appropriate. Lockheed Martin Corp. v. Superior Court, 29 Cal.4th 1096, 131 Cal.Rptr.2d 1, 63 P.3d 913 (2003).

5. Representative Suits

a. Purpose

In representative suits, a person or entity is permitted to sue on behalf of the real parties in interest. Class actions are a form of representative suit. Representative actions are not always subject to the detailed procedural requirements for class actions; in particular, the representative is not always required to have an injury in fact that is typical of the represented group. For example, taxpayers, shareholders, homeowners' associations, and labor unions may bring certain types of representative suits. In class actions and other types of representative suits, those represented may be subject to claim and issue preclusion.

b. Unfair Competition Law (UCL)

One common category of representative suit is based on California's Unfair Competition Law, Cal. Bus. & Prof. Code § 17200 et seq. Relief in a representative suit under the UCL is limited to equitable remedies. The remedies may include injunctive relief and instances where losses of money or property can be restored through restitution to those who are direct victims of the defendant's unfair practices. Since the passage of Proposition 64 in 2004, representative suits brought under the UCL by persons who are not public officials must be certified as class actions under CCP § 382. The named plaintiff must show that he suffered injury in fact and lost money or property as a result of the unfair competition. In re Tobacco II Cases, 46 Cal.4th 298, 93 Cal.Rptr.3d 559, 207 P.3d 20 (2009).

c. Private Attorneys General Act of 2004 (PAGA)

PAGA permits an aggrieved employee to bring a representative action against the employer on behalf of herself and other similarly situated employees to recover civil penalties for Labor Code violations. Cal. Lab. Code § 2698 et seq. The action need not meet all of the requirements for a class action. The representative plaintiff is standing in the shoes of the State, which receives 75% of any recovery. The remaining 25% is distributed to the aggrieved employees. Estrada v. Royalty Carpet Mills, Inc., 15 Cal.5th 582, 317 Cal.Rptr.3d 219, 541 P.3d 466 (2024). See Chapter 5(I)(A)(2) for discussion of arbitration of PAGA claims.

d. Illustration

Dromio Corp. sold the tools it manufactured with a "Made in U.S.A." label. However, some components of the tools were of foreign origin. Pilch, shopping in Loyalton, purchased Dromio tools containing some foreign-made components. Pilch subsequently brought a representative suit in Sierra County Superior Court under California's Unfair Competition Law. The representative action for equitable relief was permissible because Pilch alleged that he and other consumers suffered an injury in fact from the incorrect label. Pilch alleged that the "Made in U.S.A." label was false, that he had relied on the label, and that he would not have purchased the tools otherwise. Pilch was not required to allege that the tools were defective because of the foreign-made parts. Kwikset Corp. v. Superior Court, 51 Cal.4th 310, 120 Cal.Rptr.3d 741, 246 P.3d 877 (2011).

SAMPLE EXAM QUESTIONS

OBJECTIVE QUESTIONS

The questions in this section are based on the following hypothetical:

Patrick had surgery at Cloverdale Public Hospital, a governmental entity. When he awoke from the surgery, he experienced numbness in his arm and hand. Patrick filed a medical malpractice action in Sonoma County Superior Court 11 months after his surgery, seeking damages for his personal injuries. In his verified complaint, Patrick named Cloverdale Public Hospital, Dr. Mel King (Patrick's surgeon), and a number of Doe defendants.

---

(1) True or False: Patrick may sue Cloverdale Public Hospital for his personal injuries as long as he filed his lawsuit within the relevant statute of limitations period.

(2) Patrick's complaint must include:

a. A short and plain statement of the claim showing that he is entitled to relief;

b. A statement of facts sufficient to constitute a cause of action in ordinary and concise language;

c. A demand for judgment specifying the amount of damages sought;

d. Both b and c.

(3) Cloverdale Public Hospital's answer to Patrick's complaint:

a. Must be verified because verified pleadings are required in personal injury actions;

b. Must be verified because verified answers are required of all defendants responding to a verified complaint;

c. Need not be verified because Cloverdale Public Hospital is a governmental defendant;

d. Need not be verified because verified answers are always optional under California law.

(4) True or False: In Patrick's personal injury action, Patrick is required to serve Dr. King with a statement of damages at the same time as serving the complaint.

(5) Which of the following would be an appropriate ground for a demurrer by Cloverdale Public Hospital to Patrick's complaint?

a. The allegations of the complaint show that Patrick has another action pending on the same causes of action against Cloverdale Public Hospital and Dr. King;

b. The prayer requests relief that is not supported by the allegations of the complaint;

c. Patrick improperly stated in the complaint the amount of damages he seeks;

d. None of the above.

(6) True or False: A demurrer filed by Cloverdale Public Hospital is timely if it is filed at the same time as the Hospital's answer.

(7) Which of the following is NOT an appropriate ground for Dr. King to file a motion to strike Patrick's complaint?

a. The complaint includes irrelevant matter;

b. The complaint does not state facts sufficient to constitute a cause of action;

c. The complaint contains false allegations;

d. The complaint includes allegations prohibited by a previous court order.

(8) True or False: Dr. King may not file a general denial to Patrick's complaint.

(9) The statute of limitations for a personal injury action like Patrick's:

a. Begins to run only from the date on which the wrongful act was done to Patrick (i.e., the date of the surgery);

b. Is actually a statute of repose;

c. May be tolled only for statutorily permitted reasons;

d. Might not begin to run until Patrick discovers or has reason to discover the harm.

(10) About 18 months after the complaint was filed, Patrick and his attorney learned during Dr. King's deposition that Patrick's injury was likely the result of the anesthesia. Patrick found out that Dr. Langdon was the anesthesiologist. Patrick's attorney promptly moved to amend the complaint to substitute Dr. Langdon's true name for one of the Doe defendants. Should the court permit the amendment?

a. Yes, because the amendment is part of the same transaction or occurrence as that pleaded in Patrick's complaint;

b. No, because the statute of limitations has expired as to Patrick's cause of action against Dr. Langdon;

c. Yes, because Patrick filed the amendment substituting Dr. Langdon for one of the Doe defendants as soon as he had actual knowledge that Dr. Langdon contributed to Patrick's injury;

d. No, because Patrick failed to investigate Dr. Langdon's involvement before Patrick filed his complaint.

(11) Patrick filed a motion to amend the complaint to add a cause of action for fraud against Dr. King. If the trial court denies Patrick's motion to amend the complaint, Patrick may:

a. Make an ex parte application to the court to reconsider its ruling;

b. Within ten days of the court's order denying the motion to amend, move the court to permit renewal of the motion to amend;

c. Refile all of the papers he presented to the court on the motion to amend and move the court to reconsider its denial of the motion;

d. Suggest to the court that it reconsider, on its own motion, the denial of the motion to amend.

(12) Which of the following complaints is most appropriately challenged by an anti-SLAPP motion to strike?

a. A college basketball player's libel suit against a blogger for a series of postings about the basketball player's alleged gambling addiction;

b. A class action filed by a group of homeowners concerned about noise and safety who seek an injunction against a group that protests the United States' dependence on oil by erecting human barricades across intersections in their neighborhood;

c. A suit for false advertising against the manufacturer of a "miracle cure" for baldness;

d. Patrick's complaint against Dr. King.

(13) Patrick wishes to bring a class action against Cloverdale Public Hospital on behalf of all patients who suffered injuries allegedly caused by poor sanitation practices. If Patrick seeks certification to proceed as a class action, he must show:

a. An ascertainable class;

b. That he can adequately represent the class and that his claims are typical of the entire class;

c. Common questions of law or fact that predominate;

d. All of the above.

The questions in this section are based on the following hypothetical:

Roman owns a piece of real property near San Juan Bautista to which he believed he had full and clear title. At one time the property was co-owned by three individuals: Lan, Gia and Noa. Roman bought the property from Lan, only afterward discovering that Gia and Noa were still owners. Roman sued Lan in San Benito County Superior Court for damages for failure to disclose, alleging that Lan knew of the existence of Gia and Noa's title when Lan sold the property to Roman.

---

(14) True or False: After Lan has answered the complaint, she may file a motion for judgment on the pleadings on any of the grounds available for a demurrer.

(15) True or False: Any amendments Roman may wish to make to his complaint require leave of court, which is granted liberally.

(16) Gia and Noa wish to intervene in the lawsuit between Roman and Lan. The court will order intervention:

a. Only if all parties in the action stipulate to Gia and Noa's intervention;

b. Even if Gia and Noa's intervention would substantially expand the issues in the lawsuit;

c. If Gia and Noa make a showing that their interests with respect to the property will be affected as a direct result of the judgment rendered in Roman's lawsuit;

d. As long as such a motion would be granted under the standards of FRCP 24(b).

(17) True or False: Lan may file a cross-complaint against Roman for damages arising out of a separate and unrelated business deal between them that went awry.

(18) Lan has filed an anti-SLAPP motion against Roman's complaint, which the court denied. Roman wants to bring a motion for sanctions under CCP § 128.7 on the ground that the motion was presented primarily to harass Roman and cause him unnecessary expense. The court:

a. Will deny the motion for sanctions because section 128.7 is not applicable to anti-SLAPP motions;

b. Is authorized to award Roman both deterrence sanctions as well as Roman's costs and attorney's fees if he is the prevailing party on the motion;

c. Will not require a 21-day safe harbor period because that requirement applies only when the court brings its own motion for sanctions;

d. Will impose sanctions if the filing of Lan's anti-SLAPP motion constitutes an action or tactic, made in bad faith, which is frivolous or solely intended to cause unnecessary delay.

Answers to Objective Questions

(1) **False.** Cal. Gov't Code § 945.4 states that a plaintiff may not file suit against a government entity until she has filed a claim with the relevant government agency. In addition, a notice of intention to sue a health care provider is required by CCP § 364.

(2) **b.** CCP § 425.10(a) requires that a complaint must contain: (1) a statement of the facts constituting the cause of action, in ordinary and concise language; and (2) a demand for judgment for the relief to which the pleader claims to be entitled. CCP § 425.10(b), however, provides that the amount of monetary damages shall not be pleaded in a personal injury action. Answer (a) sets out the federal standard in FRCP 8(a)(1).

(3) **c.** CCP § 446(a) does not require a governmental defendant to file a verified answer, even if the complaint is verified.

(4) **False.** Patrick is not required to serve a statement of damages simultaneously with his complaint. He must serve the statement upon request of Cloverdale Public Hospital or Dr. King. Additionally, the court may not enter a default judgment against either defendant unless Patrick has previously served the statement of damages. CCP § 425.11.

(5) **a.** This is a ground for a special demurrer. CCP § 430.10(c). Answers (b) and (c) are not grounds for a demurrer. They are more appropriately addressed via a motion to strike.

(6) **True.** CCP § 430.30(c) provides "a party objecting to a complaint or cross complaint may demur and answer at the same time."

(7) **b.** CCP § 436 states that a party may move the court to strike out "any irrelevant, false, or improper matters inserted in any pleading" or "all or any part of any pleading not drawn or filed in conformity with * * * an order of the court." Answer (b) states a ground for a general demurrer.

(8) **True.** Dr. King may not file a general denial under CCP § 431.30(b)(1) because Patrick's complaint is verified. Dr. King is required to file a verified answer containing specific denials.

(9) **d.** Under the general rule for defining the accrual of a cause of action, the statute of limitations starts to run when the wrongful act has been done or the liability arises. However, the discovery rule delays the accrual of the cause of action until the plaintiff discovers or has reason to discover the cause of action. Answer (b) is incorrect because a statute of repose provides that a defendant is liable only for certain periods of time, regardless of when the plaintiff actually sustained an injury. Answer (c) is incorrect because there are also equitable principles that may toll the running of the statute of limitations.

(10) **c.** Patrick must amend the complaint to substitute Dr. Langdon for one of the Doe designations once he is no longer genuinely ignorant of Dr. Langdon's identity or of the facts giving rise to a cause of action against Dr. Langdon. CCP § 474. For practical purposes, Patrick generally would have three years from the date he commenced his action to substitute Dr. Langdon and accomplish service of process. CCP § 583.210. Shorter deadlines would apply under Fast Track rules. (See Chapter 5(II)(B).)

(11) **d.** If Patrick applies to the court for reconsideration of its order or renewal of his motion, he must adhere to the jurisdictional requirements of CCP § 1008. However, Patrick is not precluded from suggesting to the court (e.g., in a case management conference) that the court might reconsider its ruling, and the court then may exercise its inherent power to grant reconsideration or renewal on its own motion.

(12) **a.** The basketball player's lawsuit appears to be a SLAPP because it arises from the blogger's posting in furtherance of his right to freedom of speech. Answer (b) arguably meets the requirements of a suit brought solely in the public interest or on behalf of the general public and therefore is exempt from an anti-SLAPP motion. CCP § 425.17(b). Answer (c) involves defendants who are engaged primarily in the business of selling goods and are likewise precluded from bringing an anti-SLAPP motion. CCP § 425.17(c). Answer (d) is incorrect because Patrick's lawsuit does not arise from any act of Dr. King in furtherance of Dr. King's free speech rights.

(13) **d.** All of these requirements must be satisfied for class certification. CCP § 382; Cal. Civ. Code § 1781.

(14) **False.** The only grounds for a motion for judgment on the pleadings that overlap with a demurrer are those based on lack of subject matter jurisdiction and on failure to state facts sufficient to constitute a cause of action or defense.

(15) **False.** Roman may amend his complaint without leave of court once before the answer or demurrer of a defendant is filed, or after the demurrer is filed and before it is heard. CCP § 472.

(16) **c.** The court will require a showing of a direct and immediate interest in the action such that the judgment will add to or diminish Gia's or Noa's rights. Answer (a) is incorrect because parties may not stipulate for intervention; a court order is required. Answer (b) is incorrect because intervention will be denied if it would substantially expand the issues in the lawsuit. Answer (d) is incorrect because the standard for permissive intervention under FRCP 24(b) is somewhat different than that under California law.

(17) **True.** Lan's permissive cross-complaint against Roman may allege any causes of action she has against Roman, even if they do not arise out of the same transaction or occurrence as those pleaded in Roman's complaint. CCP §§ 428.10(a) & 428.30.

(18) **b.** Sanctions under CCP § 128.7(d) are intended to deter repetition of the conduct by Lan or by others similarly situated. In addition, CCP § 128.7(c)(1) permits an award of costs and attorney's fees to the prevailing party incurred in making or opposing the sanctions motion. Answer (a) is incorrect because there is no express exemption of anti-SLAPP motions. Answer (c) is incorrect because the safe harbor period required under California law applies to motions brought either by the court or by a party. Answer (d) is incorrect because the grounds for an award of sanctions stated in answer (d) apply to CCP § 128.5, not to CCP § 128.7.

ESSAY QUESTIONS

A. Sally was riding in an Orange County transit bus to her doctor's appointment in Garden Grove, when suddenly a teenager approached her, punched her, knocked out two of her teeth, grabbed her purse, and jumped off the bus. Concerned passengers chased and caught the attacker. While criminal charges are currently pending against the attacker, Sally's attorney filed a civil lawsuit against the attacker and the County in Orange County Superior Court. In the cause of action against the attacker, Sally has described the facts of the incident, and she has sought damages on a number of intentional tort theories. In the cause of action against the County, the complaint pleads only that the County was negligent in failing to prevent the attack. Sally's complaint is demanding $10,000 for her medical and dental expenses, $25,000 for her pain and suffering, and $500,000 in punitive damages.

(1) Discuss the response(s) each of the defendants might file to Sally's complaint. Include a discussion of any timing issues that may be involved in the defendants' response(s).

(2) Assume that Orange County wishes to sue the bus manufacturer for indemnity because a mechanism on the bus that would have allowed the driver to alert the police failed to properly function. Via which procedural vehicle(s) may the County sue the bus manufacturer for indemnity?

B. Citizens Respecting Animals' Rights (CRAR) is a California nonprofit organization whose mission is to prevent cruelty toward animals throughout the state. As a pressure tactic, the group targets the employees of public and private organizations that conduct research and testing on animals. CRAR's members have directed their protest efforts toward thousands of employees of university laboratories, pharmaceutical manufacturers, and cosmetics companies.

Tony is a researcher at a cosmetic testing lab in Santa Maria. CRAR members have vandalized his house, yelled at his children as they waited for their school bus, and called Tony's house at all hours. CRAR members have gone to the homes of other lab employees, vandalized their property, set off alarms late at night, broken windows, spray-painted cars, left threatening telephone messages, and publicized the employees' private information on the internet.

Tony has filed a lawsuit against CRAR in Santa Barbara County Superior Court, seeking to enjoin the group from engaging in further harassing activity and seeking compensation for property damage and emotional distress the group has inflicted on Tony and his family. Tony's attorneys have suggested turning Tony's complaint into a class action.

(1) Discuss the potential for class certification and any barriers Tony might face.

(2) Identify and analyze the possible response(s) CRAR might file to Tony's lawsuit.

<u>Essay Answers</u>

<u>Essay A</u>

(1) <u>Defendants' Responses</u>

- Orange County's responses:
  - Failure to file a notice of claim:
    - When suing a governmental agency, Sally must first file a notice of the claim with the appropriate agency. Once the County has denied Sally's claim, she may proceed to file her complaint.
    - The County might attempt to file a demurrer to challenge the court's subject matter jurisdiction, Sally's lack of legal capacity to sue, or Sally's failure to state facts sufficient to constitute a cause of action. CCP § 430.10(a)–(b) & (e). But these grounds must be present on the face of the complaint or by matters subject to judicial notice. It is unlikely that Sally's failure to file a governmental claim meets this requirement.
    - The County might alternatively file a motion to strike the complaint because it was not filed in conformity with the laws of California which require Sally to file a governmental claim. CCP § 436(b). The court will be limited to considering the face of the complaint and matters subject to judicial notice.
    - If a demurrer and motion to strike are not proper ways to challenge the failure to file a prelawsuit governmental claim, the County may later bring a motion for summary judgment or summary adjudication. (See Chapter 5(VII)(A).)

- Failure to plead sufficient facts to constitute a cause of action:
  - The County may file a general demurrer on the ground that Sally has not met her burden under California's fact pleading requirement. CCP § 430.10(e). The complaint alleges negligence without any facts supporting the elements of the cause of action.
  - The County might alternatively file a motion for judgment on the pleadings on this ground after it has filed its answer. CCP § 438(c)(1)(B).
- Amount of damages:
  - The County may file a motion to strike the prayer of the complaint. No amount of damages may be stated in a personal injury unlimited civil case. CCP § 425.10(b).

- Attacker's responses:
  - The attacker probably has no ground to challenge the sufficiency of the complaint. The complaint appears to set out ultimate facts in support of the intentional tort causes of action.
  - There is no prelawsuit claim requirement Sally must satisfy as to the attacker (as she must when it comes to suing the County).
  - The attacker may bring a motion to strike the prayer of the complaint because it improperly states an amount of damages.

(2) Indemnity

- The County may file a permissive cross-complaint against the bus manufacturer under CCP § 428.10(b). The indemnity cause of action against the manufacturer arises out the same transaction or occurrence as the negligence cause of action in Sally's complaint.
- Alternatively, the County may bring a separate lawsuit against the manufacturer. The statute of limitations on an indemnity claim does not start to run until after a judgment against the County is entered.

Essay B

(1) Class Certification

- On a class certification motion, Tony must establish:
  - An ascertainable class in which common questions of law or fact predominate;

  - Numerosity;
  - Class representatives with claims typical of the class; and
  - Class representatives who can adequately represent the class.

- Ascertainable class, common questions of law or fact:
  - The CRAR campaign has resulted in damage to the property and disruption to the lives of many lab employees. Although common questions exist, the differences in the experiences and injuries of the employees may indicate that the common questions do not predominate.
  - Members of the class appear to be ascertainable.
- Numerosity:
  - It is not known how many potential class members there are, but it appears that the class would be sufficiently numerous to make the class action device appropriate.
- Class representatives with claims or defenses typical of the class:
  - Tony's claim is that CRAR's vandalism campaign resulted in property damage and harassment of his family.
  - Other members of the class have similar claims, although some might have had different experiences or degrees of injury.
- Class representatives who can adequately represent the class:
  - Tony's interests are likely congruent with other potential class members such that Tony will be motivated to vigorously litigate the issues.

(2) <u>CRAR's Responses</u>

- CRAR's principal response: anti-SLAPP motion to strike.
  - CRAR may contend that Tony's lawsuit has been brought to chill CRAR'S First Amendment right of freedom of speech, and that an anti-SLAPP motion is the appropriate response.
  - Two-step process:
    - CRAR first must show that Tony's causes of action arise out of CRAR's acts in furtherance of its free speech right in connection with a public issue.
    - The burden then shifts to Tony to establish a probability of prevailing on the merits.

- CRAR will not be able to satisfy its burden if the activity in question is illegal.
    - In this case, CRAR has committed harassment, trespassing, and vandalism while engaging in the protesting it claims is protected speech.
    - The court will likely deny the anti-SLAPP motion before the burden would be shifted to Tony.
- If defects in Tony's complaint appear on the face of the pleading, CRAR might file a general or special demurrer, a motion to strike, or a motion for judgment on the pleadings.

CHAPTER 4

DISCOVERY

I. DISCOVERY IN CALIFORNIA

A. Philosophy and Initial Disclosures

Discovery is the formal information-gathering portion of a lawsuit. The California discovery statutes are construed in favor of a liberal exchange of information. Discovery is intended to put the prospective evidence of the case out in the open, to narrow the issues, to promote settlement, and to prevent surprise at trial. Greyhound Corp. v. Superior Court, 56 Cal.2d 355, 15 Cal.Rptr. 90, 364 P.2d 266 (1961). The California discovery system is designed to be self-executing—implemented by the parties with minimal court intervention. In an action pending in state court, each party is entitled to discovery through properly propounded requests. Parties are not obligated to make any automatic disclosures, but in unlimited civil cases they may initiate mandatory disclosures similar to those required under the Federal Rules (see section I(B), immediately below). CCP § 2016.090.

B. *Compare Federal Procedure*

California's discovery statutes are generally more detailed than their federal rule counterparts. In contrast to California procedure, federal parties are obligated, independent of any request, to automatically disclose certain information at the outset of the action, including the identity of witnesses and copies of documents that may support the disclosing party's claims or defenses. FRCP 26(a)(1).

II. DISCOVERY SCOPE

A. Broad Scope

California's liberal philosophy of discovery is manifested in the expansive scope of discovery. A matter is discoverable as long as it is: (1) relevant to the subject matter of the action; (2) admissible, or reasonably calculated to lead to the discovery of admissible evidence;

and (3) not subject to a privilege or other protection from discovery. CCP § 2017.010.

B. Relevance and Admissibility

1. Relevance

Relevance to the subject matter of the action is a broad standard. A matter is relevant if it might aid a party in assessing the case, preparing it for trial, or facilitating a settlement. Stewart v. Colonial Western Agency, Inc., 87 Cal.App.4th 1006, 105 Cal.Rptr.2d 115 (2001). The concept of relevance is flexible, depending on the complexity of the issues in a case.

2. Reasonably Calculated to Lead to Discovery of Admissible Evidence

A matter need not be admissible in evidence to be discoverable, as long as its discovery might reasonably lead to the discovery of other evidence that would be admissible at trial. For example, a party may not object to discovery on the ground that the matter constitutes inadmissible hearsay if the hearsay might lead to admissible evidence.

3. *Compare Federal Procedure*

Federal law also imposes relevance limitations on the scope of discovery. FRCP 26(b)(1). The basic federal relevance standard, however, is stricter than that in California. Any nonprivileged matter is discoverable if it is relevant to "any party's claim or defense and proportional to the needs of the case, considering the importance of the issues at stake in the action, the amount in controversy, the parties' relative access to relevant information, the parties' resources, the importance of the discovery in resolving the issues, and whether the burden or expense or the proposed discovery outweighs its likely benefit." Id. In addition, "[i]nformation within this scope of discovery need not be admissible in evidence to be discoverable." Id.

4. Illustration

Posey filed suit in Santa Clara County Superior Court against 66 companies she believed were responsible for her exposure to asbestos and her subsequent illnesses. One of the defendant companies, Dusk Manufacturing, propounded an inspection demand to Posey. The demand included a request to inspect any documents Posey had submitted to any trusts administering asbestos-related claims for any of the other defendants in Posey's lawsuit. The documents are discoverable

> if they are relevant to the subject matter of the action and they are either admissible or reasonably calculated to lead to the discovery of admissible evidence (including admissions against interest). Rules of evidence that potentially exclude the admission of certain evidence at trial have no bearing on discoverability. Liberal policies underlie the discovery process, and substantial leeway is afforded to the party seeking discovery. Protective orders may be issued to narrow the breadth of discovery, if necessary. Volkswagen of America, Inc. v. Superior Court, 139 Cal.App.4th 1481, 43 Cal.Rptr.3d 723 (2006).

C. Privileges

1. Types of Privileges

California law recognizes a number of privileges that, if applicable, limit the scope of discovery. Some information and communications are subject to absolute privileges (e.g., attorney-client, physician-patient, clergy-penitent). Others (such as trade secrets and police personnel files) are subject to qualified privileges, requiring disclosure only if the interests of justice in permitting discovery outweigh the interests in preventing disclosure.

2. Privilege Procedure

A party may claim a privilege either by objecting to a discovery request on that ground (thereby forcing the proponent of the discovery to file a motion to compel further responses), or by filing a motion for a protective order. The court typically requires the party objecting on the ground of privilege to file a "privilege log" that sets out the basic information concerning items as to which the privilege applies and the ground for asserting the privilege.

3. Waiver

The holder of a privilege (e.g., client, patient, penitent, etc.) might waive the privilege by disclosing, or consenting to the disclosure of, a significant part of the communication. Waiver may also occur by failing to claim the privilege. An unintentional disclosure of privileged information by an attorney might constitute a waiver by the client, but California law is not definitive on this point.

4. *Compare Federal Procedure*

Federal law also limits the scope of discovery to matters that are not privileged. FRCP 26(b)(1). The Federal Rules of Evidence govern privilege issues in federal question cases, but in diversity cases, state law determines the availability and scope of a privilege. FRE 501. District courts evaluating claims of privilege often require the objecting party to provide a privilege log. FRCP 26(b)(5)(A).

5. Illustration

Penn, a former member of Deliverance Community Church in Buttonwillow, sued the Church in Kern County Superior Court for sexual abuse committed by a former youth minister when Penn was a minor. A year before the suit was filed, when the abuse allegations had come to light, the Church's head minister, Pastor Healy, had sent a letter to her congregation reaching out to members who might have been affected by the youth minister's abuse. Pastor Healy assured her congregants that all communications with her would be confidential. Pastor Healy received a dozen responses to her letter from members of the congregation (none of whom was a party to Penn's lawsuit). In the lawsuit, Penn served interrogatories and document demands on the Church, seeking identifying information about anyone with knowledge about the alleged sexual abuse committed by the youth minister. The Church responded with an objection based on the clergy-penitent privilege. Penn filed a motion to compel responses, arguing that the privilege did not apply because the letters to Pastor Healy were not confessional in nature and therefore were not penitential communications. The court will likely uphold the privilege. The communications were "penitential" because they were: (a) intended to be confidential; (b) actually made in confidence and not in the presence of any third persons; (c) made to a member of the clergy who, in the course of her practice, is accustomed to receiving such sensitive communications; and (d) made to a religious figure with a duty, under church tenets, to keep the communications confidential. Doe 2 v. Superior Court, 132 Cal.App.4th 1504, 34 Cal.Rptr.3d 458 (2005).

D. Work-Product Protection

An attorney's work product may be withheld from discovery in order to "[p]reserve the rights of attorneys to prepare cases for trial with that degree of privacy necessary to encourage them to prepare their cases thoroughly" and to "[p]revent attorneys from taking undue advantage of their adversary's industry and efforts." CCP § 2018.020. The attorney is the holder of work-product protection and thus may waive it.

1. Absolute Protection

Any writing that "reflects an attorney's impressions, conclusions, opinions, or legal research or theories is not discoverable under any circumstances." CCP § 2018.030(a). "Writing" is defined broadly to include such items as charts, graphs, photographs, recordings, pictures, videos, email and computer data. CCP § 2016.020(c); Cal. Evid. Code § 250.

2. Qualified Protection

Work product that is not absolutely protected may be subject to qualified protection. Qualified work product is not discoverable "unless the court determines that denial of discovery will unfairly prejudice the party seeking discovery * * * or will result in an injustice." CCP § 2018.030(b). Qualified protection is accorded only to derivative materials—those created or derived from an attorney's work on behalf of a client that reflect the attorney's strategy or interpretation. Examples of protected derivative materials include charts, reports, or compilations prepared by consultants. Examples of nonderivative materials that are not protected work product include witness statements that do not reflect counsel's evaluation, and documents identifying the location of physical evidence. Witness statements that are procured by an attorney are entitled to at least qualified protection. They receive absolute work-product protection if they are "inextricably intertwined" with the attorney's impressions. Coito v. Superior Court, 54 Cal.4th 480, 142 Cal.Rptr.3d 607, 278 P.3d 860 (2012).

3. *Compare Federal Procedure*

Federal work-product protection operates similarly to California's. Under the qualified work-product protection of FRCP 26(b)(3)(A), "a party may not discover documents and tangible things that are prepared in anticipation of litigation or for trial." One state/federal distinction is in the language regarding when qualified work product is subject to disclosure. Under the federal rule, disclosure is permitted if the party seeking discovery shows a "substantial need" for the information and cannot, without "undue hardship," find the "substantial equivalent" in another way. FRCP 26(b)(3)(A)(ii). California's statute requires a showing of undue prejudice or injustice. While California law offers absolute work-product protection for an attorney's mental impressions, conclusions, opinions and legal theories, federal protection for core work product is slightly more equivocal. Upjohn Co. v. United States, 449 U.S. 383, 101 S.Ct. 677, 66 L.Ed.2d 584 (1981); and Fireman's Fund Insurance Co. v. Superior Court, 196 Cal.App.4th 1263, 127 Cal.Rptr.3d 768 (2011). FRCP 26(b)(3)(B) provides only that the court "must protect against disclosure" of such material when the court has ordered that qualified work product be disclosed. A party or other person may request their own previous statement about the action or its subject matter, without need for the usual showing required for other work product. FRCP 26(b)(3)(C).

4. Illustration

Draxo Pharmaceuticals, headquartered in Paso Robles, makes and distributes Tranquility, a prescription antianxiety medication. Draxo sent a shipment of Tranquility to Pill Hill Drug Stores, Inc., a pharmacy chain with retail outlets all over Central California. Unfortunately, the bottles were mislabeled. Those customers who thought they were receiving Tranquility actually got WakeUp, a stimulant. Some of those customers suffered serious side effects from taking WakeUp, and word spread that Pill Hill was not committed to quality control. Pill Hill sued Draxo in San Luis Obispo County Superior Court for damages from lost business. During discovery, officers of Draxo met with the corporation's lawyers to discuss litigation strategy. At the meeting, one of Draxo's attorneys, Ace, took notes, which he later annotated with comments. Ace took the notes with him the next day to a deposition of one of Pill Hill's expert witnesses. When Ace entered the conference room, no one else had arrived, so he left his papers in the room and went to get a cup of coffee. When he returned, Pill Hill's counsel, Cap, was in the room, holding a copy of Ace's annotated notes. Cap claimed that while Ace was away, the court reporter had duplicated and given Cap a copy of the notes. Cap refused to return the copy of the notes to Ace. Ace moved to disqualify Cap and his firm from representing Pill Hill on the ground that Cap had acquired Ace's attorney work product without authorization. Because the notes contained Ace's strategic analysis, thought processes, and opinions about the lawsuit, they were subject to absolute work-product protection under CCP § 2018.030(a). Disqualification of Pill Hill's counsel was the appropriate remedy. Rico v. Mitsubishi Motors Corp., 42 Cal.4th 807, 68 Cal.Rptr.3d 758, 171 P.3d 1092 (2007).

E. Privacy

The California Constitution expressly provides an inalienable right of privacy. Cal. Const., art. I, § 1. Even if a matter is relevant, admissible and not privileged, it may still be shielded from discovery because its disclosure would violate the right to privacy.

1. Nature of Protection

Privacy protection is not absolute. When faced with a privacy objection, the court first evaluates whether the party claiming privacy protection:

- possesses a legitimate privacy interest;
- possesses a reasonable expectation of privacy under the particular circumstances; and
- has suffered a serious invasion of privacy.

Hill v. National Collegiate Athletic Association, 7 Cal.4th 1, 26 Cal.Rptr.2d 834, 865 P.2d 633 (1994). If these criteria are satisfied, the court then balances the need for the information to fairly resolve the suit against the privacy interest of the party opposing discovery. The party asserting the privacy interest has the burden to "establish its extent and the seriousness of the prospective invasion." The court must then weigh the interests of the party seeking the discovery. A showing of compelling need for the discovery is not always required. "Only obvious invasions of interests fundamental to personal autonomy must be supported by a compelling interest. * * * [W]henever lesser interests are at stake, the more nuanced framework * * * applies, with the strength of the countervailing interest sufficient to warrant disclosure of private information varying according to the strength of the privacy interest itself, the seriousness of the invasion, and the availability of alternatives and protective measures." Williams v. Superior Court, 3 Cal.5th 531, 557, 220 Cal.Rptr.3d 472, 494, 398 P.3d 69 (2017). Examples of information protected by privacy include personal financial records, membership in associations or groups, medical and personnel records, and sexual history.

2. *Compare Federal Procedure*

Although the U.S. Constitution does not contain an explicit privacy clause, as does the California Constitution, federal courts recognize a claim of privacy in the discovery context. The district court may balance the need for discovery against the need to protect a person from "annoyance, embarrassment, [or] oppression." FRCP 26(c)(1).

3. Illustration

Pilar married Dave in Weed, California. After they had been married about a year, a blood test revealed that Pilar was HIV positive. Pilar believed that Dave had infected her. Pilar sued Dave in Siskiyou County Superior Court for intentional and negligent infliction of emotional distress and for fraud. Pilar alleged that Dave knew he was HIV positive, but he did not tell Pilar, and he engaged in unprotected sex with her. In response, Dave alleged that he is HIV positive because Pilar infected him. Seeking to discover Dave's sexual history and the timing of his awareness of his HIV status, Pilar propounded interrogatories and a request for admissions on Dave. Dave objected on the ground that inquiry into his sexual history and behavior violated his right of privacy. Dave has a reduced expectation of privacy in this case because he has admitted that he is HIV positive and he has put his HIV status in controversy by alleging that Pilar infected him. Nevertheless, assuming Dave has established the three requirements for privacy protection, the court must balance Dave's right to privacy against Pilar's rights to ascertain the truth and to a fair trial. Pilar's requests, however, must be tailored to the time period between the earliest date on which Dave could have been infected until the date when Pilar and Dave ceased sexual relations. John B. v. Superior Court, 38 Cal.4th 1177, 45 Cal.Rptr.3d 316, 137 P.3d 153 (2006).

F. Other Limitations on Discovery

A court may issue a protective order to restrict discovery. (See section IV(C), below.)

III. DISCOVERY METHODS

A. Informal Discovery

During the pendency of a lawsuit, a party typically utilizes one of the statutorily approved methods of discovery. However, a party is not precluded from conducting its own lawful exploration of the facts using informal methods. For example, if the plaintiff was injured in a public location, she may visit that site to conduct an investigation or make observations. Pullin v. Superior Court, 81 Cal.App.4th 1161, 97 Cal.Rptr.2d 447 (2000). A party may also obtain information available through a public agency, over the internet, or through a cooperative third party, without the need for a formal discovery request.

B. Statutorily Authorized Discovery Methods

In unlimited civil cases, there are six distinct methods of discovery authorized under California's discovery laws: interrogatories, inspection demands, requests for admission, depositions, physical and mental examinations, and exchange of expert witness information. CCP § 2019.010. (See section III(C)(3), below, regarding more restricted discovery in limited civil cases.) In deciding which discovery devices to use in a given action, a party must consider such factors as cost, efficiency, timing, the respective benefits of written versus oral responses, and the value of spontaneous versus prepared responses.

1. Interrogatories

Interrogatories are written questions propounded by one party to another party. Interrogatories are a useful method to obtain basic background information about another party's claims, defenses, contentions or evidence.

a. Propounding Interrogatories

1) Form Interrogatories

The Judicial Council of California has made available a set of form interrogatories applicable to many types of civil lawsuits. CCP § 2033.710; Judicial Council Form DISC–001. A party may ask an unlimited number of form interrogatories of another party. CCP § 2030.030(a)(2).

2) Specially Drafted Interrogatories

A party may serve specially prepared (nonform) interrogatories that allow for questions more tailored to the litigation. These interrogatories typically seek detailed factual information as well as a party's contentions. A propounding party may ask up to a total of 35 specially drafted interrogatories of another party, unless the propounding party also serves a declaration attesting to the need for additional interrogatories. CCP §§ 2030.030–.050. In the absence of a declaration for additional discovery or a stipulation between the parties, specially drafted interrogatories in excess of 35 need not be answered. Specially drafted interrogatories are subject to a number of other restrictions—they may not include, for example, subparts, conjunctive or disjunctive questions, a preface, or instructions. Each interrogatory must be complete in and of itself, without reference to other interrogatories or outside matter. CCP § 2030.060.

b. Responding to Interrogatories

1) Types of Responses

Three types of responses to interrogatories are permitted:

- Answers: Answers must be complete and straightforward, based on information reasonably available to the responding party.
- Objections: Common objections include that a privilege or work-product protection exists, the numerical limit has been exceeded, or the interrogatories are burdensome or oppressive. Objections are waived by the failure to timely raise them, either in the response or by motion for protective order.
- Option to produce documents: If the interrogatories seek information contained in files or records, and the response requires compilation or summarization of information, the responding party may elect to allow the propounding party to inspect and copy records (if the burden of searching the records is substantially the same for both parties).

CCP §§ 2030.210–.220.

2) Timing and Verification of Response

The responding party must serve a response within 30 days of service of the interrogatories. CCP § 2030.260. An untimely response waives all objections to the interrogatories unless the court grants relief from the waiver. CCP § 2030.290. Interrogatory answers must be signed under oath by the responding party; objections must be signed by the attorney, but not under oath. CCP § 2030.250. An unverified response (where a verification is required) is treated as no response at all.

c. *Compare Federal Procedure*

Federal interrogatory practice is largely similar to California's. A key distinction is that a party in federal court may serve no more than a total of 25 interrogatories (including subparts) on another party unless the court orders or the parties stipulate otherwise. FRCP 33(a)(1). Although form interrogatories are not available in federal court, the automatic initial disclosures made after a federal action has been filed provide some of the information a party may obtain via California's form interrogatories. FRCP 26(a)(1).

d. Illustration

Plaintiff Peony took the deposition of defendant Delta in an action filed in Butte County Superior Court. The deposition yielded hundreds of pages of transcript. Following Delta's deposition, Delta propounded the following interrogatory to Peony: "Do you contend that any of the answers that Delta gave at her deposition are untrue? If so, identify the question asked and the answer given by stating the date of the deposition, the volume number, and the page and line number of the questions you contend that Delta answered untruthfully." Delta's interrogatory to Peony is not full and complete in and of itself, as required by CCP § 2030.060(d). A response to the interrogatory would require Peony to refer to and incorporate questions and answers from the hundreds of pages of Delta's deposition. Because the interrogatory essentially asks thousands of individual questions, it violates the "Rule of 35" of CCP § 2030.030(a)(1). If Delta had served a declaration for additional discovery (CCP § 2030.050) with the interrogatory, Peony's options would have been to answer the interrogatory without objection as to the number or form of individual questions, or to move for a protective order. Catanese v. Superior Court, 46 Cal.App.4th 1159, 54 Cal.Rptr.2d 280 (1996).

2. Inspection Demands

A party may make a written demand to inspect any document, tangible thing, or land of another party. Electronically stored information (ESI) is also discoverable (see section III(C)(1), below).

a. Propounding Demand

An inspection demand must contain a description of each item or a reasonably particular categorization of items, and a reasonable place and time for inspection (at least 30 days after service of the demand). CCP § 2031.030. There is no statutory limit to the number of inspection demands a party may serve on another party.

b. Responding to Demand

1) Types of Responses

The three types of permissible responses to an inspection demand are:

- Agreement to comply: The responding party agrees to produce the items requested that are in its possession, custody or control.
- Inability to comply: The responding party explains why, after a diligent search and reasonable inquiry, the items demanded cannot be produced.
- Objections: See Interrogatories, section III(B)(1)(b), above.

CCP §§ 2031.210–.240.

2) Timing and Verification of Response

The responding party must serve a written response within 30 days after service of the inspection demand. CCP § 2031.260. An untimely response waives all objections to the inspection demand unless the court grants relief from the waiver. CCP § 2031.300. A response containing an agreement to comply must be verified by the responding party. Any objections must be signed by the attorney for the responding party. CCP § 2031.250.

c. Obtaining Documents from Nonparty

Several statutes provide methods for obtaining documents from a nonparty. They include: CCP § 2020.010 et seq. (documents and business records from nonparty deponent); § 2034.010 et seq. (writings of expert); § 1985.3 (subpoena for personal records of consumer); and § 1985.6 (subpoena for employment records).

d. *Compare Federal Procedure*

FRCP 34 sets out a similar procedure for a request to produce documents or tangible things, or to enter onto land. However, a response to a Rule 34 request need not be verified by the responding party; it must only be signed by the attorney. Acceptable responses to a Rule 34 request are an agreement to allow inspection, an objection, or a statement that the responding party will produce copies of documents or electronically stored information instead of permitting inspection. There is no express option to state an inability to comply, as exists under the California statute. A party may obtain documents or electronically stored information from a nonparty via the subpoena procedure in FRCP 45.

e. Illustration

In her lawsuit in Inyo County Superior Court, plaintiff Pasha served a document demand on defendant Deco. Deco served a hybrid response, containing both specific responses to some requests and objections based on privilege to other requests. The response was served on time but was not verified by Deco. On her motion to compel further responses, Pasha argued that the lack of verification made the entire response untimely and thus resulted in a waiver of all objections. CCP § 2031.300(a). The court will reach a different conclusion. Objections set forth in a discovery response do not have to be verified by the party; they only need to be signed by the attorney. Only the fact-specific responses must be verified by a party. Deco's fact-specific responses were unverified, and thus untimely, and objections as to those requests were waived. However, the unverified objections signed by counsel were not waived. Pasha may move for an order to compel verified fact-specific responses, and she may seek sanctions for the untimely unverified response. Food 4 Less Supermarkets v. Superior Court, 40 Cal.App.4th 651, 46 Cal.Rptr.2d 925 (1995).

3. Requests for Admission

In contrast to the information-seeking nature of the written forms of discovery discussed above, requests for admission (RFA) allow the propounding party to obtain written responses from another party admitting or denying the truth of facts and other matters, as well as the genuineness of documents. CCP § 2033.010. Such admissions are binding against the responding party at trial and in any dispositive pretrial motions. CCP § 2033.410.

a. **Propounding Requests**

1) **Number and Format of RFA**

A party may use a Judicial Council form or may propound specially drafted RFA. CCP § 2033.710. In either case, the propounding party may request an unlimited number of RFA as to the genuineness of documents, but they are limited to 35 RFA for requests as to the truth of matters, unless a declaration for additional discovery is served with the RFA or the parties stipulate to an increased number. CCP §§ 2033.030–.050. Similar restrictions to those for interrogatories apply to RFA (e.g., no subparts, no conjunctive or disjunctive questions, etc.). CCP § 2033.060.

2) **Types of Requests**

In addition to RFA as to the genuineness of documents, a party may ask another party to admit or deny the truth of facts, opinions related to facts, and legal conclusions (i.e., the application of law to fact). CCP § 2033.010.

b. **Responding to Requests**

1) **Types of Responses**

A party may respond to RFA in three ways:

- Admission or denial: The responding party admits the portions of the RFA that are true and denies the remainder, based on readily available information.
- Inability to admit or deny: The responding party states that after a reasonable inquiry, she has insufficient information to admit or deny the RFA.
- Objections: See Interrogatories, section III(B)(1)(b), above.

CCP §§ 2033.220–.230.

2) **Timing and Verification of Response**

The response must be served within 30 days after service of the RFA. CCP § 2033.250. An untimely response waives all objections to the RFA. It also permits the propounding party to file a motion to deem the genuineness of documents and/or truth of matters contained in the RFA admitted (unless the responding party serves a proposed response that substantially complies with the statute before the hearing of the motion). CCP § 2033.280. A response containing admissions and denials must be verified under oath by the responding party. Objections are signed by the attorney. CCP § 2033.240.

c. **Amending or Withdrawing Admissions**

A responding party may move the court for an order permitting amendment or withdrawal of an admission (including a "deemed" admission). The court will grant the motion if the admission was a result of the responding party's mistake, inadvertence, or excusable neglect, and if no substantial prejudice will result to the propounding party. CCP § 2033.300.

d. ***Compare Federal Procedure***

FRCP 36 is largely similar to the California RFA statutes. One contrast is that there is no numerical limit on RFA for any purpose. Another important distinction is that in federal practice, a matter will automatically be deemed admitted if the responding party files an untimely response; no motion is required. FRCP 36(a)(3).

e. **Illustration**

Paolo placed his entire life savings into an investment vehicle managed by Doofus Financial, which is located in Oxnard. Doofus Financial promised spectacular financial returns, but in reality, risk was rampant and returns nonexistent. After Paolo lost all of his savings, he sued Doofus Financial in Ventura County Superior Court for fraud and related causes of action. Doofus Financial served Paolo with a set of requests for admission. Paolo requested a two-week extension to respond, to which Doofus Financial did not agree until the day after Paolo's responses should have been served. Paolo then served his responses to the RFA four days after they were due. Several days later, Doofus Financial filed a motion to deem its RFA admitted because of Paolo's tardy and purportedly inadequate responses. The court will rule against Doofus Financial because it has not filed an appropriate motion. If Paolo's responses were served before the hearing of the motion and were substantially compliant with the requirements of CCP § 2033.220, a motion to deem RFA

> admitted is not proper. If Doofus Financial believed Paolo's responses were deficient, it should have filed a motion to compel a further response under CCP § 2033.290. Assuming that the court grants that motion and orders further responses from Paolo, and assuming Paolo fails to comply with that order, Doofus Financial may then file a "deem admitted" motion based on Paolo's noncompliance with the court's order. St. Mary v. Superior Court, 223 Cal.App.4th 762, 167 Cal.Rptr.3d 517 (2014).

4. Depositions

Oral depositions permit a party to obtain the in-person pretrial testimony of an individual under oath. Oral depositions are the discovery device best suited to evaluating witness demeanor and to soliciting spontaneous responses. Depositions may also be taken on written questions.

a. Oral Depositions of Parties

1) Notice

A party initiates a deposition of another party by serving a notice on the deponent at least ten days before the date of the deposition. CCP § 2025.270. Service of a proper notice requires the deponent to appear and, if requested, to produce documents, unless the deponent serves timely objections or seeks a protective order. CCP § 2025.280. A notice to a corporation or other entity includes a description of the matters to be addressed at the deposition. The entity is then required to designate the officers, directors, or other persons most qualified to testify on those matters on behalf of the entity. CCP § 2025.230. A deposition notice may also be served directly on an officer, director, managing agent or employee of an entity. CCP § 2025.280.

2) Location of Deposition

The deposition of a natural person, including a party, must take place within 75 miles of the deponent's California residence. Alternatively, the deposing party may require the deponent to appear for a deposition in the county in which the action is pending at a place within 150 miles of the deponent's residence. CCP § 2025.250(a). A corporate party may be deposed within 75 miles of its designated principal California office, or at the same alternative location as discussed above regarding an individual deposition. CCP § 2025.250(b). The court may permit a deposition to take place at a more distant location. CCP § 2025.260. However, under CCP § 1989, a California court lacks the power to order a nonresident witness (party or nonparty) to come to the state for a deposition. Toyota Motor Corp. v. Superior Court, 197 Cal.App.4th 1107, 130 Cal.Rptr.3d 131 (2011).

3) Number of Depositions

Unless the court issues a protective order, a party may take an unlimited number of depositions in an unlimited civil action. Unless the court orders otherwise or a statutory exception applies, a deposition is limited to seven hours of total testimony. CCP § 2025.290. Only one deposition may be taken of a natural person unless the court orders successive depositions on a showing of good cause. CCP § 2025.610.

4) Conduct of Deposition

a) Scope of Examination

Deponents are required to answer questions based solely on their personal knowledge. They are not required to guess or to investigate or inquire of other sources. All parties have the right to attend a deposition and to cross-examine a deponent. The grounds for objection to questions are narrow, and some objections (such as those addressed to the form of the question and those based on privilege) are waived if not properly raised at the deposition. CCP § 2025.460.

b) Control of Questioning

If a deponent is subjected to abusive questioning, his counsel may object or may suspend the deposition and move for an order to limit or terminate questioning. CCP §§ 2025.460–.470. Court intervention also may be necessary if a deponent fails or refuses to answer questions or produce documents. CCP § 2025.480.

b. Oral Depositions of Nonparties

1) Subpoenas

A deposition of a nonparty witness is initiated by serving a subpoena. A deposition notice is not sufficient. The subpoena may require the following:

- oral testimony only;
- production of business records only; or
- both oral testimony and production of business records or other documents.

CCP § 2020.020. A witness may challenge the subpoena by serving written objections, a motion to quash or modify the subpoena, or a motion for protective order.

2) Personal Records of Consumer

Special rules apply to subpoenas for personal records of a consumer (e.g., bank, school, health) or employment records of an employee. See, e.g., CCP §§ 1985.3 & 1985.6.

c. Depositions on Written Questions

A party may take a deposition on written questions rather than orally. The deposition notice must attach the written direct examination questions. Other parties in the action may then serve cross-examination questions on the deponent (followed by redirect and recross questions). The party noticing the deposition may forward the direct examination questions to the deponent in advance of the deposition. However, the deponent may not preview the cross, redirect, or recross questions. The deponent may assert objections to questions or may seek a protective order. CCP § 2028.010 et seq.

d. Deposition Transcript

The deponent has the opportunity to review the deposition transcript and change any answers given at the deposition. She may then approve the transcript by signing it. Alternatively, she may refuse to approve it by not signing it. CCP § 2025.520. A party may use the deposition of another party or party-affiliated witness at trial for any purpose (i.e., as substantive evidence or for impeachment purposes). A nonparty deposition may be used to impeach that nonparty's testimony at trial. Any deposition may also be offered at trial if special circumstances exist, such as where a deponent is unavailable to testify at trial because of death or disability, or the deponent resides more than 150 miles from the place of the trial. CCP § 2025.620.

e. ***Compare Federal Procedure***

FRCP 30, 31, 32, and 45 govern depositions of parties and nonparties. Each side in a federal action is limited to ten depositions per side unless the court orders otherwise. FRCP 30(a)(2)(A)(i). In addition, in the absence of a court order, each deposition is limited to one day consisting of seven hours. FRCP 30(d)(1).

f. **Illustration**

Peggy sued her former employer, Draper Co., in Yuba County Superior Court for wrongful termination from her job in Olivehurst. Peggy's counsel took the deposition of Joan, a senior manager of Draper Co. Peggy's attorney asked Joan questions about Peggy's immediate supervisor, Cooper, and the quality of Cooper's working relationship with other female employees. Joan's lawyer instructed Joan not to answer on the ground that the information sought was irrelevant. The information was relevant to the subject matter of the action. Moreover, a relevance objection during the discovery phase is generally not a valid basis for instructing a deponent not to answer a question. A relevance objection is not waived even if it is not raised at the deposition. Stewart v. Colonial Western Agency, 87 Cal.App.4th 1006, 105 Cal.Rptr.2d 115 (2001).

5. **Physical and Mental Examinations**

Any party may take a physical or mental examination of a party or party affiliate whose physical or mental condition is "in controversy" in the action. CCP § 2032.020. A party's condition is in controversy if that party's pleadings allege physical or emotional injuries, or if discovery reveals that a party's physical or mental condition is relevant.

a. **Physical Examination of Plaintiff by Demand**

Assuming that the "in controversy" requirement is met, a defendant (or cross-defendant) is entitled to take one physical examination of the plaintiff (or cross-complainant) by serving a demand. No court order is required. CCP § 2032.220.

1) Limitations on Examination

The examination must be performed by a licensed physician or other licensed health care practitioner. CCP § 2032.020(b). It must not involve painful, protracted, or intrusive tests. The examination must take place within 75 miles of the examinee's residence. CCP § 2032.220(a).

2) Response to Demand

a) Timing of Response

A written response must be served within 20 days after service of the demand. CCP § 2032.230(b). An untimely response waives all objections to the demand. CCP § 2032.240.

b) Content of Response

The responding party may respond by:

- agreeing to comply in full;
- agreeing to comply upon specified conditions; or
- refusing to comply for reasons stated in the response.

CCP § 2032.230. There is no requirement that the response be verified.

b. Physical Examination by Court Order

Any additional physical examinations of a plaintiff beyond the one permitted on demand, and any physical examinations of a person other than the plaintiff, require leave of court based on a showing of good cause. CCP § 2032.310. The examination may not take place more than 75 miles from the examinee's residence, unless the court finds good cause and orders the moving party to make advance payment of reasonable travel expenses. CCP § 2032.320(e).

c. Mental Examination

A mental examination requires a court order. CCP § 2032.310. The moving party must show that the potential examinee's mental condition is in controversy and must establish good cause for the examination. A party might be able to avoid a mental examination by stipulating that: (1) no claim is being made for mental or emotional injuries beyond those usually associated with the physical injuries claimed; and (2) no expert testimony will be offered at trial to support a claim for damages for this usual mental or emotional distress. CCP § 2032.320.

d. Presence of Attorney

An examinee has the right to have an attorney (and a court reporter) present during any portion of a physical examination. CCP § 2032.510. During a mental examination, attorneys generally do not attend, as their presence might interfere with the rapport between the examiner and examinee. However, the court has discretion to permit the presence of the examinee's attorney. Vinson v. Superior Court, 43 Cal.3d 833, 239 Cal.Rptr. 292, 740 P.2d 404 (1987). In addition, the examinee has the right to audio record the mental examination in its entirety. CCP § 2032.530.

e. *Compare Federal Procedure*

FRCP 35 permits physical and mental examinations of parties whose condition is in controversy in the action. FRCP 35(a) requires leave of court for all examinations (physical and mental), a distinction from California's practice of allowing one physical examination of the plaintiff on demand if her physical condition is in controversy. An examinee in a federal action is not entitled to have an attorney present during any examination; a court may allow the attorney to be present only for good cause. FRCP 26(c)(1)(E).

f. Illustration

Pryce sued Doyle Motorcycles in Nevada County Superior Court, seeking damages for multiple injuries he sustained after a defective accelerator caused him to be thrown head first off his motorcycle while participating in a race near Truckee. In addition to alleging injuries to his neck, spine, ribs, and head, Pryce asserted that the crash also affected his cognitive and emotional functioning. Doyle Motorcycles served Pryce with a Demand for Independent Medical Examination, seeking "standard" and "routine" neurological (physical) and neuropsychological (mental) examinations. Pryce submitted to the physical examination, but he objected to the demand for the mental examination. Upon motion of Doyle Motorcycles, the trial court ordered Pryce to submit to a mental examination consisting of "standardized written psychological tests" to "test emotional and cognitive functioning." The order will not be upheld on appeal. A court's order for a mental exam must specify the diagnostic tests and procedures to be performed, as well as the scope and nature of the examination. CCP § 2032.320(d). The court's order did not comply with the statutory requirements because it did not describe the tests and procedures by name and with particularity. Its language was ambiguous and subject to multiple meanings among mental health professionals. Carpenter v. Superior Court, 141 Cal.App.4th 249, 45 Cal.Rptr.3d 821 (2006).

6. Expert Witness Discovery

Expert witness testimony is a common feature of civil trials. Pretrial exchange of expert witness information allows parties to conduct depositions in order to prepare to present or challenge expert testimony during trial. Parties may obtain discovery regarding those experts who have been retained to provide an expert opinion at trial. The opinions and work product of experts hired solely as consultants who will not testify at trial are not subject to discovery.

a. Exchange of Expert Witness Information

1) Procedure for Demand

Any party may serve on another party a written demand for exchange of expert witness lists. Service of the demand by one party obligates all others to make a simultaneous exchange. CCP § 2034.260(a). The demand must be in writing and must specify the date for the exchange of expert witness lists and any other materials included in the demand (such as expert witness declarations and discoverable writings of experts). CCP § 2034.230.

2) Timing of Demand and Exchange

Any party may make a demand on another party for disclosure of expert witnesses any time after the setting of the initial trial date. The deadline for the demand is ten days after the initial trial date has been set, or 70 days before the initial trial date, whichever is closer to the trial date. CCP § 2034.220. Any disclosed expert may be deposed before trial, so that all parties may better learn the nature of the expert's testimony. CCP § 2034.410. The simultaneous exchange of the expert witness information requested in the demand must take place 50 days before the initial date set for trial, or 20 days after service of the demand, whichever is closer to the trial date (unless the court orders a different date). CCP § 2034.230.

3) Contents of Demand

a) Information and Documents

A party may demand that the exchange include the name and address of any person whose expert witness testimony is expected to be offered at trial. The demand may also request the discoverable reports and other writings of an expert for whom an expert witness declaration must be served. CCP § 2034.210.

b) Expert Witness Declaration

If a designated expert is a party or an employee of a party, or the expert has been retained for the purpose of forming and stating an opinion at trial, the designation of that witness must include the submission of an expert witness declaration signed by the attorney for the party designating that expert. CCP § 2034.210(b). The declaration must include: (1) a statement of qualifications; (2) a statement of the general substance of the witness's expected testimony; and (3) a representation that the witness is sufficiently familiar with the pending action to submit to a deposition concerning his expected trial testimony. CCP § 2034.260.

b. Supplementing or Augmenting Expert Witness List

If an opponent's expert witness list states that the opponent intends to offer expert testimony at trial on a subject not addressed in other parties' lists, the other parties may supplement their lists with the names of witnesses whose expert opinion will be offered on those previously omitted subjects. CCP § 2034.280. A party may move the court to augment an expert witness list to add a subsequently retained expert, or to amend an expert witness declaration regarding the substance of the testimony a previously designated expert is expected to give. CCP § 2034.610.

c. Failure to Comply with Exchange Requirements

With some exceptions, the trial court will exclude the testimony of an expert witness if the party offering that testimony has unreasonably failed to list that witness as an expert, submit an expert witness declaration when one was required, produce requested discoverable writings of the expert, or make the expert available for deposition. CCP § 2034.300. In addition, if the substance of an expert's testimony is not disclosed in the expert witness declaration, and the expert broaches the previously undisclosed subject at trial, the testimony of that witness may be excluded. Bonds v. Roy, 20 Cal.4th 140, 83 Cal.Rptr.2d 289, 973 P.2d 66 (1999).

d. Conflict of Interest

A conflict of interest may arise when an expert has been consulted (but not retained for trial) by one party, is then dismissed, and is later hired by the opposing party to offer an opinion at trial. The expert may be disqualified if they actually possess confidential information obtained during the prior consultation. Potential access to confidential information is not sufficient to justify disqualification. Western Digital Corp. v. Superior Court, 60 Cal.App.4th 1471, 71 Cal.Rptr.2d 179 (1998).

e. *Compare Federal Procedure*

In contrast to California law, FRCP 26(a)(2) requires a party to automatically disclose, without formal demand, those expert witnesses who may testify at trial. The timing of the disclosure is ordinarily directed by the court. In the absence of court instruction or party stipulation, the federal rules require disclosure at least 90 days before trial. FRCP 26(a)(2)(D). Federal procedure also requires the equivalent of an expert witness declaration from a witness retained to provide expert testimony, in the form of a written report, signed by the witness, which must include: (1) a complete statement of all opinions and the basis for those opinions; (2) the data considered; (3) any exhibits that will be used to support the opinions; (4) the qualifications of the witness; (5) a list of any other cases in which the witness has testified over the last four years; and (6) the compensation to be paid to the witness. FRCP 26(a)(2)(B). A party may depose a "person who has been identified as an expert whose opinions may be presented at trial" but not those experts who are not expected to testify at trial. FRCP 26(b)(4)(A), (D).

f. Illustration

Patricia brought a medical malpractice action in Contra Costa County Superior Court against Dr. Dingleberry. The complaint alleged that Dr. Dingleberry negligently severed a nerve in Patricia's arm during a procedure performed at a hospital in Richmond. Both parties exchanged expert witness declarations. Dr. Dingleberry designated Dr. Einstein as an expert witness. Dr. Einstein's expert witness declaration stated that he would testify about the extent of Patricia's damages. On the last day of trial, Dr. Dingleberry's attorney sought to elicit testimony from Dr. Einstein about the applicable standard of care. Any such testimony should not be allowed because it would expand the general substance of the testimony noted in Dr. Einstein's declaration. Although Dr. Einstein's expert witness declaration could have been amended earlier to include the expanded testimony, it was too late at trial to seek an amendment. Bonds v. Roy, 20 Cal.4th 140, 83 Cal.Rptr.2d 289, 973 P.2d 66 (1999).

C. Additional Discovery Issues

1. Electronically Stored Information

The California Electronic Discovery Act, enacted in 2009, codified and streamlined the procedures for discovery of electronically stored information (ESI).

a. Form of Production

The propounding party may identify the form in which the ESI is to be produced. If no specific form of production is requested, the responding party may produce the ESI in any ordinarily maintained form. CCP § 2031.280. The responding party may object to the discovery or move for a protective order if the information is from a source that is not reasonably accessible because of undue burden or expense. CCP §§ 2031.060 & 2031.310. The court has discretion to order the propounding party to bear the expense of production or translation of compilations. CCP §§ 2031.060(e); 2031.280(e) & 2031.310(f). See also Toshiba America Electronic Components, Inc. v. Superior Court, 124 Cal.App.4th 762, 21 Cal.Rptr.3d 532 (2004). The same requirements apply to civil subpoenas for ESI. CCP § 1985.8; and Park v. Law Offices of Tracey Buck-Walsh, 73 Cal.App.5th 179, 288 Cal.Rptr.3d 202 (2021).

b. Sanctions

The ESI discovery statutes provide a safe harbor against the imposition of sanctions for failure to provide ESI that has been lost, damaged or destroyed due to the routine, good faith operation of an electronic information system. CCP §§ 1985.8(m)(1) & 2031.310(j).

c. Inadvertent Disclosure of Privileged or Protected ESI

A party who has inadvertently produced ESI that is subject to a privilege or work-product protection must notify the receiving party, who in turn must sequester the information. The receiving party must either return the ESI or must present it to the court for determination of the claim of privilege or protection. If the receiving party has already disclosed the information before notice from the propounding party, the receiving party must take reasonable steps to retrieve the ESI. CCP § 2031.285.

d. *Compare Federal Procedure*

The FRCP contain several provisions governing electronic discovery. For example, parties must include issues related to discovery of ESI in a discovery plan submitted to the court during a scheduling conference. FRCP 26(f)(3)(C). The court may issue sanctions when ESI has been lost because a party did not take reasonable steps to preserve it. FRCP 37(e). Parties are not required to provide electronic information not reasonably accessible to the responding party because of undue burden or expense, unless ordered otherwise by the court. FRCP 26(b)(2)(B). Although the cost of discovery is ordinarily borne by the responding party, the court may order costs to be shifted in whole or in part to the party propounding requests for electronic data that are not reasonably accessible. Zubulake v. UBS Warburg LLC, 217 F.R.D. 309 (S.D.N.Y. 2003).

e. Illustration

Pincer enrolled in the D'Arcy Culinary Academy's master chef program in Carmel-by-the-Sea. Pincer grew disillusioned with the program when he became aware of the school's low graduation rate and his dim employment prospects and expected earning capacity. He sued D'Arcy in Monterey County Superior Court for fraud, unfair competition, and related claims. Pincer had taken out substantial loans in order to attend D'Arcy. In the process of discovery, Pincer issued a business records subpoena to Frankie Max, an entity that services Pincer's student loans. Pincer sought ESI concerning his loan file. Frankie Max filed a motion to quash the subpoena on the grounds that it should be permitted to produce the information in hard copy form and should not be required to undergo the burden and expense of producing it in an electronic format. Under CCP § 1985.8, which governs discovery subpoenas seeking ESI, Pincer may specify the form in which the information should be produced and may require Frankie Max to translate any data compilations into a reasonably usable form. Pincer has acknowledged his obligation to pay the reasonable costs Frankie Max would incur in complying with the subpoena. Because the subpoena sought permissible discovery within the bounds of section 1985.8, Frankie Max has no substantial legal or factual basis for refusing to comply with it. Vasquez v. California School of Culinary Arts, Inc., 230 Cal.App.4th 35, 178 Cal.Rptr.3d 10 (2014).

2. Supplemental (Continuing) Discovery

a. No Obligation to Automatically Supplement

A California litigant is not required to automatically update any previous discovery responses that were true and correct when served. A party may propound a single supplemental interrogatory or inspection demand to obtain information acquired after the original responses were served. The supplemental interrogatory or inspection demand may be served twice before, and once after, the initial setting of the trial date. CCP §§ 2030.070 & 2031.050.

b. *Compare Federal Procedure*

In marked contrast to California procedure, a federal litigant has an affirmative duty to update all disclosures and discovery responses (interrogatories, document requests, or requests for admission) when the court so orders or when new information is acquired and is not known to the other party. FRCP 26(e).

c. Illustration

Parker received a cancer diagnosis. He sued his employer, Diechem Corp., in Placer County Superior Court, alleging

> that it knowingly exposed Parker to benzene and other dangerous chemicals in its factory in Roseville. Diechem propounded an interrogatory asking Parker to identify any persons who have knowledge of his work with Diechem. Parker responded that he did not know of anyone. Subsequently, Diechem brought a summary judgment motion against Parker. In response, Parker included with his opposition papers the declaration of Gord, whom Parker later recalled had worked with him at Diechem. Diechem objected to the declaration and sought to have it excluded on the ground that Parker should have supplemented his interrogatory answer when Gord's identity became known. However, under CCP §§ 2030.290 and 2030.300, Parker had no duty to supplement his interrogatory answer with the new information. As his initial responses were not willfully false, Parker was under no obligation to amend his answers in the absence of a supplemental interrogatory from Diechem. Therefore, Gord's declaration may be used in opposition to the summary judgment motion. Biles v. Exxon Mobil Corp., 124 Cal.App.4th 1315, 22 Cal.Rptr.3d 282 (2004).

3. Discovery in Limited Civil Cases

The use of some of the discovery tools discussed in section III(B), above, is curtailed in limited civil cases. Only one oral or written deposition is allowed, and each party is permitted to use a combined total of up to 35 interrogatories, requests for admission, and inspection demands against each adverse party. CCP §§ 94–95. However, a plaintiff in a limited civil case may obtain additional information by serving a case questionnaire on the defendant, requesting basic information such as identity of witnesses, relevant documents, and insurance coverage. If the plaintiff serves the defendant with a completed questionnaire along with the complaint, the defendant must serve a completed questionnaire with the answer. CCP § 93.

4. International Discovery

Document discovery and depositions in international litigation are subject to special procedures.

a. Discovery in Actions Pending in Another Nation or State

A party in a California action may take the deposition of another party or a nonparty in a foreign country. CCP § 2027.010. A deposition may be taken in California for an action pending in another country or state under the procedures set out in the Interstate and International Depositions and Discovery Act, CCP § 2029.100 et seq.

b. The Hague Evidence Convention on Taking Evidence Abroad in Civil or Commercial Matters

In addition to other means of obtaining discovery, a signatory to The Hague Evidence Convention in one country may send a Letter of Request to a signatory in another country requesting a deposition and/or documents of a witness in the second country.

c. *Compare Federal Procedure*

Federal courts may choose to utilize the discovery procedures under The Hague Evidence Convention. If the court does not require these procedures, the FRCP authorize discovery involving persons outside the United States. For example, FRCP 28(b) governs the taking of depositions in foreign countries under several scenarios, such as where there is an underlying treaty or convention or a letter of request.

IV. JUDICIAL OVERSIGHT OF DISCOVERY

A. Role of Court in Discovery

Although California discovery is intended to be self-executing, parties may need the assistance or intervention of the court. In some cases, a court order is required to undertake discovery. (See, e.g., mental examinations, section III(B)(5), above.) In others, discussed below, the court may be asked by a party to step into a discovery dispute and issue orders to compel compliance with the discovery statutes or to prevent or address misuse of the discovery process.

B. Orders Compelling Discovery

1. Compel Response to Discovery

If a party does not serve a timely written response to a discovery request, or serves a timely but unverified response, the propounding party may move the court for an order compelling a response. All objections to that discovery are deemed waived unless the responding party requests relief from the waiver by filing a response in substantial compliance with the statutory requirements. See, e.g., CCP §§ 2030.290 & 2031.300. An untimely response to RFAs allows the propounding party to file a motion to deem the requests admitted. See section III(B)(3), above.

2. Compel Further Response to Discovery

a. Procedure

If the responding party provides incomplete, evasive or otherwise improper written responses to discovery, or responds with unfounded objections, the propounding party may bring a motion to compel a further response. See, e.g., CCP §§ 2030.300 & 2031.310. For most motions, the moving party must file a separate statement, which places all of the disputed discovery requests, answers, objections, and basis for the moving party's position in one document. CRC 3.1345. The motion must be brought within 45 days of the challenged discovery response. See, e.g., CCP §§ 2030.300 & 2031.310(c). Generally, a motion to compel a further response will be granted if the moving party can show good cause for the discovery sought.

b. Meet and Confer

The parties to a motion to compel a further response must "meet and confer" about each matter in dispute before the moving party files the motion. The moving party must file a declaration showing that the parties made "a reasonable and good faith attempt at an informal resolution of each issue presented by the motion." CCP § 2016.040. There is no meet and confer requirement for motions to compel if the initial response is absent, untimely, or unverified.

3. Compel Compliance with Discovery Order

If a party fails to obey a court order compelling a further response to discovery, the court may impose sanctions for noncompliance. See, e.g., CCP §§ 2030.300(e); 2031.310(i) & 2033.290(e). See also section IV(D), below.

4. Compare Federal Procedure

Federal discovery motions are procedurally similar to those under California law. One distinction is that, unlike the California motions to compel further responses, which must be brought within the statutory time limit, federal motions must be brought only within a reasonable time, or as ordered by the court. FRCP 16(b)(3)(A) & 37(a).

5. Illustration

Piper sued Devin in Modoc County Superior Court over a dispute arising out of Piper's sale to Devin of a boat berthed at Goose Lake. Devin served Piper with a set of 23 special interrogatories. Piper objected to 20 of the interrogatories on the ground that they were "vague and ambiguous." In meeting and conferring regarding Piper's objections, Devin stated that the interrogatories were drafted in clear and unambiguous terms. Devin then filed a motion to compel further responses and to strike the objections, and for sanctions against Piper. The motion was accompanied by a "meet and confer" declaration. The court should grant the motion. All of Piper's objections were unreasonable, evasive, and lacking in legal merit. Piper's purpose was to delay and to obstruct the self-executing process of discovery. Piper must provide further responses to the interrogatories without objection. In addition, the court must impose a monetary sanction on Piper. Piper engaged in a misuse of the discovery process: (a) she interposed improper objections to valid discovery requests, forcing Devin to file his motion to compel further responses; and (b) she opposed Devin's motion without substantial justification. Clement v. Alegre, 177 Cal.App.4th 1277, 99 Cal.Rptr.3d 791 (2009).

C. Protective Orders

1. When Protective Order Available

The court may enter a protective order under several discovery statutes. One permissible ground is that the burden, expense, or intrusiveness of the discovery outweighs the likelihood that the discovery sought will lead to admissible evidence. CCP § 2017.020. Another is that the discovery sought is cumulative, duplicative, or unduly burdensome or expensive, or is obtainable from another source. CCP § 2019.030. In addition, many of the statutes authorizing the various methods of discovery contain specific provisions for protective orders to protect against annoyance, harassment or oppression. See, e.g., CCP § 2025.420 (depositions); § 2030.090 (interrogatories); § 2031.060 (inspection demands); and § 2033.080 (requests for admission). Before moving for a protective order, the moving party must meet and confer with the opposing party.

2. *Compare Federal Procedure*

FRCP 26(c)(1) authorizes a court to issue protective orders to protect "a party or person from annoyance, embarrassment, oppression, or undue burden or expense." The rule lists several forms of protective orders, which may be issued on a showing of good cause.

3. Illustration

Polluters, Inc., a chemical manufacturer, hired contractors to work with local businesses near Visalia to clean up dangerous residue generated by Polluters, Inc. and buried in landfill deposits years before. Elsa, an employee of Polluters, Inc., reported to a Polluters, Inc. manager that some of the contractors were being paid for services they were not actually providing. Polluters, Inc. filed suit in Tulare County Superior Court against these contractors for breach of contract and fraud. At his deposition, the Polluters, Inc. manager refused to disclose Elsa's identity. One of the defendant contractors moved to compel the manager to reveal Elsa's identity. In response, Elsa filed a sealed declaration stating that her life had been threatened because she had provided highly sensitive information about the contractors, and she sought a protective order. The court will prohibit disclosure of Elsa's identity. CCP § 2025.420(b)(9) permits a protective order requiring that "certain matters not be inquired into." The court must balance Elsa's interests against the contractors' need for the information. In the absence of a compelling reason for disclosure, the protective order will be issued because disclosure could jeopardize Elsa's safety. John Z. v. Superior Court, 1 Cal.App.4th 789, 2 Cal.Rptr.2d 556 (1991).

D. Sanctions

1. Availability of Sanctions

The court may sanction a party who misuses the discovery process. Misuse includes: failing to respond; providing evasive responses; raising unmeritorious objections; making or opposing (without substantial justification) a motion to compel discovery; failing to meet and confer to informally resolve a discovery dispute; and disobeying a court order to provide discovery. See CCP § 2023.010, and the individual statutes governing the different methods of discovery. Sanctions may be imposed on a party, its attorney, or both. Notice to all parties is required before any sanctions may be ordered.

2. Purpose of Sanctions

Discovery sanctions in California are not meant to punish. Their purpose is to compel disclosure and to compensate for enforcement of the discovery statutes. Discovery sanctions are not intended to create a reward or windfall, but rather to place the nonsanctioned party in the same position they otherwise would have occupied but for their opponent's misuse of the discovery process. City of Los Angeles v. Pricewaterhouse Coopers, LLP, 17 Cal.5th 46, 324 Cal.Rptr.3d 410, 553 P.3d 1194 (2024).

3. Types of Sanctions

CCP § 2023.030 sets out an escalating series of sanctions, which may be imposed for misuse of the discovery process:

- Monetary: Any misuse of the discovery process "shall" result in a monetary sanction unless the party subject to sanctions acted with "substantial justification" or monetary sanctions would be "unjust." Monetary sanctions are the most common form of discovery sanctions, typically covering the attorney's fees and costs incurred in compelling further responses.
- Issue: If a monetary sanction is ineffective, or a party has failed to comply with an order compelling further responses, the court may impose an issue sanction. This sanction designates certain facts as established.
- Evidence: If a party has engaged in severe misconduct, the court may order an evidence sanction, which precludes the sanctioned party from introducing certain matters into evidence.
- Contempt: The court may issue a contempt sanction in which the misuse of the discovery process is treated as a contempt of court.
- Terminating: Also known as the "doomsday" sanction, a terminating sanction may result from a party's egregious misconduct and can include striking all or part of the pleadings, staying further proceedings, dismissing the action, or rendering a default judgment.

4. *Compare Federal Procedure*

FRCP 37(b)–(f) sets out numerous federal sanctions available for many types of discovery misconduct. Federal discovery sanctions are largely the same as California's escalating set of sanctions. However, federal discovery sanctions can be more punitive in nature. Federal judges have greater leeway to impose discovery sanctions with the objective of deterring the misuse of discovery.

5. Illustration

After a long and complicated class action lawsuit in Glenn County Superior Court regarding defects in Duffy Computers' laptop covers, plaintiff Perren and defendant Duffy Computers reached a settlement. To the dismay of Duffy Computers' counsel, Perren's attorney, Amanda, requested attorney's fees of $25,000,000 for her work on the case. To determine whether documents existed to support such an "exorbitant" figure, Duffy Computers served a number of inspection demands, seeking Amanda's electronic billing records in their original unaltered format. Duffy Computers learned that before Amanda produced time and billing records in response to the demand, she had them converted to pdfs and then deleted the original electronic files. Duffy Computers filed a motion for monetary sanctions under CCP § 2023.010 for Amanda's misuse of the discovery process. To aid in its consideration of Duffy Computers' sanctions motion, the court ordered that Amanda allow an expert to conduct a forensic inspection of her computers, backup drives, and hard drives to determine whether any of the original data could be recovered. On the day before the inspection, Amanda refused to permit it to go forward. The court properly exercised its discretion in awarding $165,000 to Duffy Computers for its attorney's fees and costs resulting from Amanda's failure to comply with the court's forensic inspection order. Ellis v. Toshiba America Information Systems, Inc., 218 Cal.App.4th 853, 160 Cal.Rptr.3d 557 (2013), cert. denied, 572 U.S. 1138, 134 S.Ct. 2692, 189 L.Ed.2d 215 (2014).

E. Special Punitive Damages Discovery

1. Court Order for Financial Condition Discovery

To prevail on a claim for punitive damages, a plaintiff must establish, by clear and convincing evidence, "oppression, fraud, or malice." Cal. Civ. Code § 3294(a). Discovery of a defendant's financial condition is often necessary to make this showing. It aids in the determination of an amount of punitive damages sufficient to punish the defendant and deter future misconduct. Financial condition discovery is permitted only by court order under Cal. Civ. Code § 3295(c). The court will order such discovery only after it weighs the evidence presented by both parties and makes a determination that the plaintiff is "very likely * * * [to] prevail on his claim for punitive damages." Jabro v. Superior Court, 95 Cal.App.4th 754, 758, 115 Cal.Rptr.2d 843, 845 (2002).

2. ***Compare Federal Procedure***

In federal lawsuits seeking punitive damages, discovery of the financial condition of a defendant is normally permitted under the scope of discovery articulated in FRCP 26(b)(1). There is no special order or showing required, although the defendant may seek a protective order under FRCP 26(c)(1).

3. **Illustration**

Pax was an investor in a limited partnership that owned two movie theaters in Clovis. Pax filed suit in Fresno County Superior Court against the general partner, Derry, for mismanagement of funds. Pax included a claim for punitive damages in his complaint. Pax served a document request on Derry seeking detailed financial information about Derry and the partnership. When Derry refused to provide it, Pax moved to compel production. Derry opposed the motion on the ground that the information was protected under Cal. Civ. Code § 3295. Section 3295 significantly limits a plaintiff's access to financial information for the purpose of a punitive damages claim. However, if the financial discovery is fundamentally related to the cause of action, and the plaintiff is likely to prevail on the merits, financial condition discovery will be permitted. Pax's claims against Derry arise out of Derry's alleged misappropriation of funds, and his financial records are key to Pax's proof. Rawnsley v. Superior Court, 183 Cal.App.3d 86, 227 Cal.Rptr. 806 (1986).

F. Completion of Discovery

1. Discovery Cutoff

Discovery must be completed on or before 30 days before the initial trial date set in an action. Motions regarding discovery must be heard on or before 15 days before the initial trial date. CCP § 2024.020(a). A continuance or postponement of the trial date does not extend the time for completing discovery unless the court makes an order reopening discovery. CCP § 2024.020(b). In cases involving discovery following a mistrial, an order granting a new trial, or a remand for a retrial following a reversal on appeal, discovery is reopened and a new completion date is set based on the initial date of the new trial. Fairmont Insurance Co. v. Superior Court, 22 Cal.4th 245, 92 Cal.Rptr.2d 70, 991 P.2d 156 (2000).

2. *Compare Federal Procedure*

The district court sets the time for the completion of discovery as part of its scheduling order under FRCP 16(b)(3)(A). The rule does not define "completion of discovery," but district court local rules or the court's case management order may provide more specific guidance. On a showing of good cause, a party may seek an order from the court to extend the discovery cutoff date. FRCP 16(b)(4).

3. Illustration

Petula sued Duke in Santa Cruz County Superior Court for damages resulting from a fire that Duke allegedly set on Petula's property in Watsonville. Petula served Duke with a document demand. Duke assured Petula that he would serve a timely response, but he did not do so. Duke cancelled his deposition twice, and, when he finally appeared, he did not bring the requested documents. He promised to send them, but he never did. One day before the cutoff date for bringing discovery motions, Petula filed a motion to compel production of the documents and for sanctions. The motion would be heard after the cutoff date. Duke objected to the motion on the ground that it was untimely. The court will grant the motion. Duke gave Petula several false assurances that he would produce the requested documents. He is thus equitably estopped from relying on the discovery motion cutoff date. Sears, Roebuck & Co. v. National Union Fire Insurance Co., 131 Cal.App.4th 1342, 32 Cal.Rptr.3d 717 (2005).

SAMPLE EXAM QUESTIONS

OBJECTIVE QUESTIONS

The questions in this section are based on the following hypothetical:

While strolling at an indoor shopping mall in Ione, Adam slipped on the floor, fell, and broke his ankle. He realized that someone had spilled a drink in the spot where he had slipped. After consulting with an attorney, Adam filed suit in Amador County Superior Court against the shopping mall's owner, Super Shop, Inc.

---

(1) Adam's attorney hired an expert who went to the mall during ordinary business hours and conducted some experiments on the slipperiness of the floor. Super Shop's attorney contends that the experiments do not constitute permissible discovery. Is the discovery proper or improper?

a. The discovery is improper because the attorney was required to serve a statutorily authorized discovery request on Super Shop;

b. The discovery is improper unless the expert obtained the permission of Super Shop before he arrived at the mall to conduct his experiment;

c. The discovery is proper as long as the expert who conducted the experiment does not testify at the trial;

d. The discovery is proper because parties are permitted to conduct lawful, informal discovery without the necessity of a discovery request.

(2) True or False: Adam's attorney made notes on pages containing the transcript of interviews that the attorney directed be conducted with witnesses to Adam's fall. The notes reflected the attorney's thoughts about the credibility of each witness's perceptions. The notes are discoverable by Super Shop if the court determines that denial of discovery will unfairly prejudice Super Shop in the preparation of its defense.

(3) Adam wishes to take the depositions of Super Shop, and of a witness (not a party to the lawsuit) who observed Adam's fall. Which of the following is true about these depositions?

a. Each deposition that Adam wishes to take may not be lengthier than eight hours;

b. Adam may notice the deposition of Super Shop, but he must serve a deposition subpoena on the person who witnessed the fall;

c. Adam may use the deposition transcripts of both deponents at trial for impeachment purposes only;

d. All objections to questions Adam's attorney asks at the two depositions are waived at trial unless raised on the record at the deposition.

(4) True or False: If the trial court orders a new trial in Adam's action, no further discovery will be permitted because discovery must have been completed at least 30 days before the date initially set for trial.

(5) Super Shop has served Adam with a set of 40 inspection demands for documents. Adam served a timely response, signed by Adam's attorney, containing only objections to all of the document demands. Super Shop responded by immediately filing a motion to compel further responses to the inspection demands, and for sanctions. What result?

a. The motion to compel should be denied because Super Shop's motion does not show that Super Shop met and conferred with Adam to attempt to resolve the discovery dispute before filing the motion;

b. The motion to compel should be granted because Adam did not verify the response;

c. Even if the motion to compel is granted, the motion for sanctions should be denied because sanctions are proper only if Adam fails to comply with the order compelling further responses;

d. The motion to compel should be denied because Super Shop propounded a number of inspection demands in excess of the statutory limit and did not include a declaration for additional discovery.

(6) True or False: If Adam seeks discovery of electronically stored information from Super Shop, the court may exercise its discretion to shift to Adam the cost of providing the discovery.

(7) True or False: As in federal practice, Adam may propound no more than 35 requests for admission on Super Shop.

(8) If Adam fails to respond to Super Shop's interrogatories in a timely manner:

a. Adam waives any objections to the interrogatories;

b. Adam waives any right to exercise the option to produce writings;

c. Adam is subject to an evidence sanction unless he can show good cause for the failure to respond on time;

d. Both a and b.

(9) True or False: In California, it is not a valid objection to Super Shop's interrogatories for Adam to respond that the matter to be discovered is not admissible evidence.

(10) After Adam has responded to Super Shop's interrogatories, Super Shop may later obtain supplemental/updated information from Adam in which way?

a. Adam is obligated to update the information in his original responses without a formal request from Super Shop;

b. Super Shop may propound a supplemental interrogatory to Adam as of right twice before the setting of the initial trial date, and once after the trial date is set;

c. Super Shop may propound a supplemental interrogatory to Adam only if the court grants leave to do so on a showing of good cause;

d. The discovery statutes do not give Super Shop the right to request that Adam update his original responses, and they do not obligate Adam to automatically update his responses.

(11) True or False: Any witness who will provide expert testimony for Adam at trial must submit an expert witness declaration to Super Shop.

(12) Super Shop wishes to obtain an initial physical examination of Adam. Super Shop:

a. Must obtain an order from the court after establishing good cause for the examination;

b. Must ensure that only a licensed physician conducts the examination;

c. May demand that Adam submit to the examination without leave of court provided the examination is not painful, protracted or intrusive and occurs within 75 miles of Adam's home;

d. Must agree to let a medical professional of Adam's choosing participate in conducting the examination.

(13) Assume that Super Shop contends that Adam's mental condition is in controversy in the action. Adam has moved for a protective order to prevent Super Shop from inquiring into his mental condition in any deposition, based on Adam's right to privacy. The privacy objection:

a. Will require the court, as a threshold matter, to balance Adam's privacy interest against Super Shop's interest in disclosure;

b. Will not be upheld for a minimal invasion of privacy, even if Adam has a legitimate privacy interest and a reasonable expectation of privacy;

c. Will not be upheld because privacy is not a proper ground to limit discovery in California;

d. Serves as an absolute protection against disclosure.

(14) True or False: The court may permit Adam's attorney to be present during any mental examination conducted on Adam.

Answers to Objective Questions

(1) **d.** Parties are permitted to conduct lawful informal discovery. The mall is open to the public, and the expert was not required to seek permission or make a formal discovery request before conducting his investigation.

(2) **False.** The notes of Adam's attorney are subject to absolute work-product protection, while the witness statements themselves would be subject to at least qualified work-product protection. Coito v. Superior Court, 54 Cal.4th 480, 142 Cal.Rptr.3d 607, 278 P.3d 860 (2012). The court would examine the prejudice to Super Shop only for materials subject to qualified protection. CCP § 2018.030.

(3) **b.** A deposition notice is used for a deposition of a party (corporate or individual), but a subpoena is issued to compel a nonparty to attend a deposition.

(4) **False.** The general discovery cutoff rule is 30 days before the initial trial date. CCP § 2024.020. However, the court may set a new cutoff date if a new trial is ordered. CCP § 2024.050(a).

(5) **a.** A motion to compel a further response to an inspection demand must be accompanied by a "meet and confer" declaration. CCP §§ 2031.310(b)(2) & 2016.040. Answer (b) is incorrect because Adam need not verify a response containing only objections; it is sufficient that the response is signed by the attorney. Answer (c) is incorrect because monetary sanctions are mandatory under CCP § 2031.310(h) if Super Shop's motion is granted, unless the court finds that Adam acted with substantial justification in opposing the motion or if the imposition of a sanction is unjust. Answer (d) is incorrect because there is no statutory limit on the number of inspection demands that may be served.

(6) **True.** Although the expense of providing electronic discovery is usually borne by the responding party, the court has discretion to shift the cost to the propounding party. CCP §§ 2031.060(e); 2031.280(e) & 1985.8(f).

(7) **False.** There is no numerical limit for requests for admission in the federal system. California permits 35 requests for admission concerning the truth of matters, but an unlimited number of requests concerning the genuineness of documents. CCP § 2033.030(a).

(8) **d.** Both (a) and (b) are correct. An untimely response waives all objections to the interrogatories (including privilege and work-product protection) and the right to produce writings as permitted under CCP § 2030.230. See CCP § 2030.290. Answer (c) is incorrect because the court would not impose this escalated type of sanction for an initial failure to serve a timely response to the interrogatories.

(9) **True.** A matter need not be admissible evidence in order to be discoverable. It is sufficient that the discovery request be reasonably calculated to lead to the discovery of admissible evidence. CCP § 2017.010.

(10) **b.** Adam must update his interrogatory responses only if Super Shop serves one or more proper and timely supplemental interrogatories on him. CCP § 2030.070.

(11) **False.** An expert witness declaration is required only for a designated expert who is a party or an employee of a party, or who has been retained by a party for the purpose of expressing an expert opinion. CCP §§ 2034.210(b) & 2034.260. Adam's treating physician, for example, would not require an expert witness declaration because, although he might provide an expert opinion at trial, he was retained to treat Adam's injuries and not to be an expert witness.

(12) **c.** Because Adam is seeking recovery for personal injuries, Super Shop may demand one physical examination of him by a licensed health care practitioner or physician without leave of court as long as the two requirements noted in answer (c) are met. CCP § 2032.220.

(13) **b.** Adam must have experienced a serious invasion of his privacy. Answer (a) is incorrect because the court performs this balancing only after it determines that the initial three prongs are satisfied. Answer (c) is incorrect because the California Constitution, art. I, sec. 1, enshrines a right to privacy. Answer (d) is incorrect because a privacy objection does not automatically provide absolute protection.

(14) **True.** While infrequently exercised, the court has discretion to permit Adam's attorney to attend the mental examination. Even if the court does not permit the attorney's attendance, Adam still has the right to audio record the examination. CCP § 2032.530.

ESSAY QUESTION

Wynn hired XYZ Construction, Inc. (XYZ) to remodel his roomy but run-down cabin in Big Bear Lake, a city in San Bernardino County. Wynn, who lived 275 miles away in Lemoore (Kings County), did not supervise the construction on a day-to-day basis. He did, however, go to Big Bear Lake every other weekend to check on XYZ's progress. During one of his trips, Wynn began to suspect XYZ of shoddy construction.

Six months later, XYZ completed the construction job. Shortly after moving his belongings into the cabin, Wynn discovered that his suspicions were correct—XYZ had significantly cut corners during the construction. Wynn consulted Lucia, a construction defect lawyer he knew from Lemoore, who recommended that Wynn sue XYZ. Wynn filed a negligence and breach of contract lawsuit (unlimited civil case) against XYZ in San Bernardino County Superior Court.

Lucia has utilized a variety of discovery tools on behalf of Wynn to obtain information from XYZ. First, she sent a set of 22 form interrogatories and 31 special interrogatories (several of which had subparts and compound questions) to XYZ. Second, she propounded 15 inspection demands for production of documents, including several documents Lucia believed were in the possession of XYZ's attorneys regarding their investigation of the Big Bear Lake job site. Finally, Lucia noticed 21 depositions, including the depositions of XYZ and numerous independent subcontractors. In the notice to XYZ, Lucia specifically requested that the owner/CEO of XYZ and XYZ's supervisor of the Big Bear Lake construction job appear for depositions on behalf of the company.

Lucia heard "through the grapevine" that after the construction was completed, the supervisor had sustained a serious back injury, was in the middle of an ugly divorce, and had started taking medication for depression. As a result, Lucia served a demand for physical and mental examinations of the XYZ supervisor. Lucia requested that the examinations take place in Lemoore where suitable examiners are available, even though the supervisor lives in Big Bear Lake.

XYZ has failed to respond to any of the interrogatories, document demands, deposition notices, and examination demands.

Lucia has hired two construction defect experts to testify at trial about the construction plans, the feasibility of those plans, and the ways in which XYZ failed to comply with the plans.

You are an associate in Lucia's office. Lucia has asked to you to analyze the following issues:

(1) What objections might XYZ raise in response to the discovery requests Lucia made on behalf of Wynn?

(2) How may XYZ be compelled to respond to Wynn's discovery requests, and what is the possibility of obtaining sanctions against XYZ for its failure to respond?

(3) What is Lucia's obligation to provide information to XYZ about the expert witnesses hired on behalf of Wynn?

<u>Essay Answer</u>

(1) <u>XYZ's Objections</u>

- Interrogatories:
    - 31 special interrogatories: may violate limit of 35 because subparts and compound questions count as additional interrogatories. If there are more than 35, XYZ is required to answer only the first 35.
    - If the special interrogatories number more than 35, Wynn should have served a Declaration for Additional Discovery with the interrogatories.

  - Wynn may serve an unlimited number of form interrogatories.
- Inspection demands for documents:
  - There is no limit to the number of document demands Wynn may serve, so the 15 demands are not objectionable for that reason. If the requests are unduly burdensome or expensive, XYZ may move for a protective order.
  - Documents in the possession of XYZ's attorneys regarding their investigation may be protected by the work-product doctrine or the attorney-client privilege.
- Depositions:
  - XYZ might object to the notice of the deposition of XYZ. Wynn must identify the topics of the deposition of XYZ, and the company would then designate the person(s) most knowledgeable to testify on the areas described in the notice. Wynn may also directly notice the depositions of XYZ's officers and managers. Since the independent contractors are not parties to the lawsuit and are not employees of XYZ, Lucia must subpoena their deposition attendance; a deposition notice is not the proper method.
  - There is no limit on the number of depositions Wynn may take (as compared to the limit of ten under the FRCP), unless XYZ files a motion for protective order to limit the number.
- Physical and mental examinations:
  - Wynn may not demand examinations of the supervisor. The governing statute provides that a defendant is entitled to one physical examination of a plaintiff whose physical condition is "in controversy" in the action. Here, Wynn (the plaintiff) is not entitled to demand a physical examination of an employee of the defendant. Also, the supervisor has not put his physical condition in controversy, so the court will not likely grant such a request.
  - The court will not order a mental examination of the supervisor because his mental condition is not in controversy. Moreover, the supervisor's objection based on privacy would likely prevail.
  - If the examinations are ordered, they must take place within 75 miles of the supervisor's residence, or the court must find good cause for the travel and order Wynn to pay the supervisor in advance for reasonable travel expenses. CCP § 2032.320(c).

(2) Motion to Compel Response and for Sanctions

- There is no meet and confer requirement for a motion to compel a response to discovery. (A motion to compel a further response requires the moving party to submit a meet and confer declaration with the motion.)
- An untimely response to Wynn's discovery requests waives any objections XYZ has to the discovery, unless the court relieves XYZ of its waiver.
- The court must award monetary sanctions against the party who unsuccessfully made or opposed the motion to compel, unless that party acted with substantial justification or the sanction is otherwise unjust.

(3) Expert Witness Discovery

- Wynn has no obligation to provide information about Wynn's expert witnesses unless XYZ or Wynn demands that all parties simultaneously exchange expert trial witness information.
    - If an exchange demand is made, all parties must provide the names and addresses of their respective testifying experts.
    - For each expert who is a party or employee of a party or who has been retained for the purpose of expressing an expert opinion at trial, the designation of that witness must include an expert witness declaration with:
        - a brief narrative of the expert's qualifications and general substance of the expected testimony;
        - a representation that the expert will testify at trial; and
        - a representation that the expert is sufficiently familiar with the action that he will be able to give a meaningful deposition.
    - A demand for mutual production of reports and writings of the expert may be included for any expert for whom an expert witness declaration is required.

CHAPTER 5

DISPOSITION WITHOUT TRIAL

I. ALTERNATIVE DISPUTE RESOLUTION

"Alternative dispute resolution" refers to "a process, other than formal litigation, in which a neutral person or persons resolve a dispute or assist parties in resolving their dispute." CRC 3.800. Either through agreement or by order of court, parties may utilize dispute resolution devices that bypass or minimally involve the court system. Principal examples of these devices (discussed below) include contractual arbitration, judicial arbitration, and mediation.

A. Contractual Arbitration

1. Arbitration Policy

a. California Arbitration Act

The California Legislature has enacted a detailed statutory scheme to implement a system of private dispute resolution by way of contractual arbitration. CCP §§ 1280–1296. The statutes reflect a state policy in favor of contractual arbitration because it is perceived as a prompt and relatively cost-effective dispute-resolution tool. At the same time, the California Supreme Court has traditionally placed limitations on the unfettered enforcement of arbitration agreements in several contexts (e.g., violations of statutory rights, unconscionability, class action waivers; see below).

b. Federal Arbitration Act

The Federal Arbitration Act (FAA) governs written arbitration agreements involving interstate or international commerce. 9 USC § 1 et seq. Like the California arbitration statutes, the FAA manifests a strong federal policy favoring contractual arbitration. The FAA accomplishes this policy goal through an equal treatment principle: "A court may invalidate an arbitration agreement based on 'generally applicable contract defenses' like fraud or unconscionability, but not on legal rules that 'apply only to arbitration or that derive their meaning from the fact that an agreement to arbitrate is at issue.' " Viking River Cruises, Inc. v. Moriana, 596 U.S. 639, 650, 142 S.Ct. 1906, 1917, 213 L.Ed.2d 179 (2022).

c. Federal Preemption

To accomplish this policy goal, the FAA "preempts any state rule discriminating on its face against arbitration—for example, a 'law prohibit[ing] outright the arbitration of a particular type of claim.' And not only that: The Act also displaces any rule that covertly accomplishes the same objective by disfavoring contracts that (oh so coincidentally) have the defining features of arbitration agreements." Kindred Nursing Centers L.P. v. Clark, 581 U.S. 246, 251, 137 S.Ct. 1421, 1426, 197 L.Ed.2d 806 (2017).

2. Arbitration Agreements

a. Arbitrability and Enforceability

A written agreement to arbitrate a current or future dispute is valid and enforceable unless a ground exists for revocation of the agreement. CCP § 1281. The parties' agreement defines the scope of private arbitration and the powers of the arbitrator. If a question arises as to the arbitrability of an issue, the court, not the arbitrator, decides it (unless the arbitration agreement clearly delegates that authority to the arbitrator).

1) Grounds for Revocation

Grounds for revocation of the arbitration agreement include lack of agreement, fraud in the inducement of the arbitration clause, illegality, and unconscionability.

2) Unconscionability

A court may refuse to enforce an arbitration agreement it finds to be unconscionable. Cal. Civ. Code § 1670.5. Unconscionability may be *procedural* (focusing on whether the contract was obtained through oppression, surprise, or the like), or *substantive* (focusing on whether the terms of the agreement are overly harsh or one-sided). The unconscionability defense requires both forms to be present. Depending on the degree of unconscionability, the court may void the entire contract or sever the unconscionable portions. Ramirez v. Charter Communications, Inc., 16 Cal.5th 478, 322

Cal.Rptr.3d 825, 551 P.3d 520 (2024). In cases where the FAA applies and preempts state law, the availability of the unconscionability ground has been the subject of judicial scrutiny in light of the strong federal policy favoring the enforceability of arbitration agreements. See OTO, L.L.C. v. Kho, 8 Cal.5th 111, 251 Cal.Rptr.3d 714, 447 P.3d 680 (2019), cert. denied, 590 U.S. 978, 141 S.Ct. 85, 207 L.Ed.2d 170 (2020).

3) Illustration

Emmett experienced severe psychotic episodes as a young adult, prompting his admission to Diagnostic Treatment Center (DTC), a residential facility in Red Bluff. A day after his admission, Emmett was found hanged in his room. His mother, Phyllis, brought an action for wrongful death in Tehama County Superior Court arising from Emmett's suicide, alleging that Emmett had been left unsupervised, and he had not received necessary medication in a timely manner. Emmett had signed an arbitration agreement upon his admission to the facility. In opposition to DTC's motion to compel arbitration of Phyllis' claims, Phyllis contended that the arbitration agreement was both procedurally and substantively unconscionable. First, given the unequal bargaining positions of the parties and Emmett's impaired mental state at the time he was presented with the agreement, Emmett had no meaningful opportunity to negotiate the arbitration clause, resulting in procedural unconscionability. Second, the arbitration agreement was substantively unconscionable because it contained one-sided, "punitive" provisions that gave DTC more favorable terms than those given to Emmett. For example, the agreement imposed a damages cap, and it required Emmett to unilaterally release DTC from almost "any conceivable claim." The court will likely agree with Phyllis on both grounds. Nelson v. Dual Diagnosis Treatment Center, Inc., 77 Cal.App.5th 643, 663, 292 Cal.Rptr.3d 740, 756 (2022).

b. Classwide Arbitration

Arbitration on a classwide basis requires the parties' unambiguous consent. Epic Systems Corp. v. Lewis, 584 U.S. 497, 138 S.Ct. 1612, 200 L.Ed.2d 889 (2018). California courts had traditionally invalidated class action waivers in arbitration agreements. Gentry v. Superior Court, 42 Cal.4th 443, 64 Cal.Rptr.3d 773, 165 P.3d 556 (2007), cert. denied, 552 U.S. 1296, 128 S.Ct. 1743, 170 L.Ed.2d 541 (2008); and Discover Bank v. Superior Court, 36 Cal.4th 148, 30 Cal.Rptr.3d 76, 113 P.3d 1100 (2005). In light of the U.S. Supreme Court's decisions in AT&T Mobility LLC v. Concepcion, 563 U.S. 333, 131 S.Ct. 1740, 179 L.Ed.2d 742 (2011), and Morgan v. Sundance, Inc., 596 U.S. 411, 142 S.Ct. 1708, 212 L.Ed.2d 753 (2022), the California Supreme Court now considers most class action waivers to be enforceable. Quach v. California Commerce Club, Inc., 16 Cal.5th 562, 323 Cal.Rptr.3d 126, 551 P.3d 1123 (2024); and Iskanian v. CLS Transportation Los Angeles, LLC, 59 Cal.4th 348, 173 Cal.Rptr.3d 289, 327 P.3d 129 (2014).

c. Representative Actions

When it comes to representative actions, such as those pursuing relief for California Labor Code violations under the Private Attorneys General Act of 2004 (PAGA), the U.S. Supreme Court has held that an employee's individual claims may be compelled to arbitration (thus preempting *Iskanian* on this point). Viking River Cruises, Inc. v. Moriana, 596 U.S. 639, 142 S.Ct. 1906, 231 L.Ed.2d 179 (2022). While nonindividual claims theoretically may be litigated in court by a representative, the U.S. Supreme Court suggested in *Viking River Cruises* that a representative whose individual claims have been ordered to arbitration is no longer considered an aggrieved employee and thus has no statutory standing to pursue a representative action in court. However, the California Supreme Court subsequently disagreed with that interpretation of state law, holding that *Viking River Cruises* misconstrued PAGA. "[W]here a plaintiff has filed a PAGA action comprised of individual and non-individual claims, an order compelling arbitration of individual claims does not strip the plaintiff of standing to litigate non-individual claims in court." Adolph v. Uber Technologies, Inc., 14 Cal.5th 1104, 1123, 310 Cal.Rptr.3d 668, 680, 532 P.3d 682 (2023).

d. Arbitration of Statutory Rights

Statutory rights (such as those under the California Fair Employment and Housing Act) may be subject to arbitration if the arbitration agreement and process meets certain requirements: (1) the agreement must provide for neutral arbitrators; (2) the agreement may not limit the type of relief available or the scope or amount of any remedies; (3) the parties must be afforded an adequate opportunity for discovery; (4) the agreement must provide for a written award that, under the appropriate circumstances, may be subject to judicial review; and (5) when an employer requires its employees to submit to arbitration, the agreement must not require the employee to pay costs and arbitration fees beyond what the party would have to pay in a court proceeding. Armendariz v. Foundation Health Psychcare Services, Inc., 24 Cal.4th 83, 99 Cal.Rptr.2d 745, 6 P.3d 669 (2000). See also Ramirez v. Charter Communications, Inc., 16 Cal.5th 478, 322 Cal.Rptr.3d 825, 551 P.3d 520 (2024) (applying *Armendariz*).

3. Obtaining Arbitration

a. Demand for Arbitration

A party to the agreement typically sets the arbitration in motion by making a demand on the other party for arbitration. If there is no question as to the arbitrability of the dispute or the enforceability of the agreement, the arbitration proceeds without court intervention.

b. Court Involvement

1) Petition to Compel Arbitration

If a party has made an arbitration demand and the demand is refused—but no lawsuit has yet been initiated—the demanding party may invoke court assistance by filing a petition to compel arbitration. The court will examine the parties' arbitration agreement and decide whether the issues in dispute are arbitrable. If so, the court will order the parties to arbitrate unless it finds that the demanding party has waived the right to arbitration or that the agreement is unenforceable. CCP § 1281.2.

2) Motion to Compel Arbitration and to Stay Proceedings

If a party to an arbitration agreement has already filed suit instead of pursuing arbitration, the party who wishes to proceed with arbitration may file a motion to compel arbitration. The court conducts the same inquiry as it does on a petition to compel arbitration.

CCP § 1281.2. In addition, the moving party may request a stay of the court proceedings. CCP § 1281.4.

3) Waiver of Right to Compel Arbitration

The court may find that a party has waived the right to compel or demand arbitration if that party has performed acts inconsistent with the right to arbitration. Such acts may include active participation in litigation, unreasonable delay in seeking arbitration, or bad faith conduct. Because California law favors arbitration, a strong showing of waiver must be made; however, demonstrating prejudice is not required. Quach v. California Commerce Club, Inc., 16 Cal.5th 562, 323 Cal.Rptr.3d 126, 551 P.3d 1123 (2024) (following Morgan v. Sundance, Inc., 596 U.S. 411, 142 S.Ct. 1708, 212 L.Ed.2d 753 (2022)).

c. Illustration

Precious and Darling were partners in a tax preparation company located in South Lake Tahoe. After Darling left the partnership, Precious filed a lawsuit in El Dorado County Superior Court, alleging that Darling took all of the client files and most of the office furniture when starting a competing tax preparation company in Grizzly Flats. After filing the complaint in court, Precious moved for a preliminary injunction, opposed Darling's demurrer to the complaint, propounded many discovery requests, demanded a jury trial at a case management conference, and posted jury fees. About six months after the litigation commenced, Darling filed a cross-complaint against Precious, alleging damages resulting from the dissolution of the partnership. In response to Darling's cross-complaint, Precious filed a motion to compel arbitration of the entire dispute, based upon an arbitration clause contained in the original partnership agreement. The court will probably conclude that Precious waived the contractual right to arbitrate. The court must find by clear and convincing evidence that Precious had constructive or actual knowledge of the right to arbitrate and, by implication, intentionally abandoned that right through the conduct of initiating and litigating the action. A reasonable fact finder would likely conclude that Precious had abandoned the right to enforce the arbitration clause. The court does not need to find that Darling suffered prejudice before ruling that Precious waived the right.

> Hofer v. Boladian, 111 Cal.App.5th 1, 332 Cal.Rptr.3d 506 (2025).

4. Arbitration Proceedings

Arbitration agreements often specify that the arbitration proceedings will be conducted according to the rules of a particular alternative dispute resolution organization such as the AAA (American Arbitration Association) or JAMS (Judicial Arbitration and Mediation Services).

a. Selection of Neutral Arbitrator

1) Obligation of Impartiality

Arbitrators are required to act with impartiality. They have a continuing duty to disclose potential biases. CCP § 1281.9. A party may seek to disqualify the arbitrator by bringing a timely motion.

2) Parties' Agreement

The parties' agreement may specify the method by which the arbitrator (or arbitrators) will be selected. If the agreement calls for a single arbitrator, each party must agree on the selection. If the arbitration agreement calls for a panel of three arbitrators, sometimes each side selects one arbitrator, and those arbitrators agree on the selection of the third arbitrator. Often the parties agree in advance to be bound by the arbitrator-selection rules of a particular ADR organization.

3) Compare: Private Judges

a) Temporary Judges

Parties to an existing lawsuit may agree to use the services of a temporary judge to hear their dispute. Temporary judges are subject to the disclosure obligations and conduct requirements in CRC 2.831 et seq. and the California Code of Judicial Ethics (Canon 6). Temporary judges are compensated by the parties. See Jolie v. Superior Court, 66 Cal.App.5th 1025, 281 Cal.Rptr.3d 610 (2021).

b) Referees

Alternatively, the court may appoint a referee. References may be voluntary (subject to the parties' consent) or involuntary (resulting from the motion of a party or the court). Referees may adjudicate an entire matter and render a binding decision (general reference), or they may issue an advisory decision subject to court approval (special reference). In the absence of economic hardship, the parties generally pay a pro rata share of the referee's fee. CCP §§ 638–639; CRC 3.900 et seq.; Code of Judicial Ethics (Canon 6). See Yu v. Superior Court, 56 Cal.App.5th 636, 270 Cal.Rptr.3d 606 (2020).

b. Discovery and Evidence

The right to discovery in contractual arbitration proceedings is restricted by statute. CCP §§ 1283.05 & 1283.1. The arbitrator is not required to follow the rules of evidence and procedure. CCP § 1282.2(d).

5. Arbitration Award

a. Requirements for Award

At the conclusion of the arbitration, the arbitrator renders a written, signed award that includes the arbitrator's determination of the issues presented. CCP § 1283.4. The arbitrator serves a signed copy of the award on all of the parties. CCP § 1283.6.

b. Confirmation of Award

A party to arbitration may petition the court to confirm the arbitration award. Upon confirmation, the court enters judgment on the award, which may be enforced like any other court judgment. CCP § 1287.4.

c. Judicial Review of Award

One of the hallmarks of contractual arbitration is that the award is considered final and binding. It is subject to judicial review on only very narrow statutory grounds authorizing vacation or correction of the award.

1) **Vacating Arbitration Award**

A court must vacate an arbitration award if it determines that:

- The award was obtained by corruption or fraud;
- There was corruption of any of the arbitrators;
- The rights of a party were substantially prejudiced by misconduct of a neutral arbitrator;
- The arbitrator exceeded her powers and the award cannot be corrected without affecting the merits of the decision;
- The arbitrator substantially prejudiced a party by refusal to postpone a hearing on sufficient cause, refusal to hear material evidence, or other conduct contrary to the arbitration statutes; or
- The arbitrator failed to disclose disqualifying information or failed to disqualify herself upon receipt of a timely demand.

CCP § 1286.2.

2) **Correcting or Modifying Arbitration Award**

A court must modify or correct an arbitration award if it determines that:

- The arbitration award evidences a miscalculation of figures or a mistaken description of a person or thing;
- The arbitrator exceeded her powers but the award may be corrected without affecting the merits of the decision; or
- The award was imperfect in a matter of form not affecting the merits of the controversy.

CCP § 1286.6.

3) **Judicial Review of Arbitrator Error**

Generally, an arbitration award may not be reviewed for errors of law or fact, even if those errors appear on the face of the award and cause substantial injustice. Moncharsh v. Heily & Blase, 3 Cal.4th 1, 10

Cal.Rptr.2d 183, 832 P.2d 899 (1992). Parties to contractual arbitration assume the risk of arbitrator error in exchange for a speedy and less expensive resolution of their dispute. The California Supreme Court has mitigated the harshness of this position by permitting judicial review of arbitrator error when the parties have included in their agreement a clear, unambiguous, and express provision stating that the arbitrator will be deemed to have exceeded his powers if he commits error. Cable Connection, Inc. v. DIRECTV, Inc., 44 Cal.4th 1334, 82 Cal.Rptr.3d 229, 190 P.3d 586 (2008).

d. Appeal

A party may appeal from: (1) an order dismissing or denying a petition to compel arbitration; (2) an order dismissing a petition to confirm, correct or vacate and award; (3) an order vacating an award; (4) a judgment entered on the award; or (5) a special order after final judgment. CCP § 1294. In an appeal from a judgment following confirmation of the award, review is limited to the grounds set forth in CCP § 1286.2 for vacating the award. The appellate court does not review the merits of the dispute or the arbitrator's reasoning.

e. *Compare Federal Procedure*

The grounds for vacating, modifying, or correcting a federal arbitration award are similar to those permitted under California law. See 9 USC §§ 10–11. The statutes do not allow for judicial review of the arbitrator's error of law, and they do not permit parties to agree to expanded judicial review beyond the grounds listed in the statute. Hall Street Associates, L.L.C. v. Mattel, Inc., 552 U.S. 576, 128 S.Ct. 1396, 170 L.Ed.2d 254 (2008). Some courts, however, have set aside arbitration awards for arbitrator error on the nonstatutory basis of the arbitrator's "manifest disregard of the law." See, e.g., Biller v. Toyota Motor Corp., 668 F.3d 655 (9th Cir.2012). The grounds for a federal appeal of an arbitration ruling are narrow. 9 USC § 16.

f. Illustration

Purchasers retained Ditz Realty to serve as their real estate agents in buying a home in Arbuckle. They entered into a real estate purchase contract that called for arbitration of any disputes arising out of the agreement.

> The clause required the arbitrator to "render an award in accordance with California substantive law." After Purchasers paid for the home and moved in, they discovered extensive termite, earthquake, and moisture damage, which made the house uninhabitable. Purchasers and Ditz Realty arbitrated Purchasers' damages claims, which resulted in an award for Purchasers. Ditz Realty brought a motion in the Colusa County Superior Court to vacate the award. The motion contended that the arbitrator committed several errors of law, and that the language of the parties' arbitration agreement called for an expanded scope of review that would permit the court to determine whether the arbitrator committed error. Parties to an arbitration agreement are free to include in their agreement an express and unambiguous statement that the arbitrator does not have the power to commit legal errors, and that such errors are subject to judicial review. A claim of such legal error would then be a ground to vacate the award. But the agreement between Ditz Realty and Purchasers did not contain such a clear and explicit statement. By merely agreeing to the application of California substantive law, the parties did not evince an agreement to subject the award to judicial review for errors of law. Gravillis v. Coldwell Banker Residential Brokerage Co., 182 Cal.App.4th 503, 106 Cal.Rptr.3d 70 (2010).

B. Judicial Arbitration

1. Characteristics of Judicial Arbitration

Judicial arbitration is a dispute-resolution process conducted under the auspices of and managed by the superior court to attempt to resolve smaller civil actions without trial. CCP § 1141.10 et seq.; CRC 3.811 et seq. The term "judicial arbitration" is somewhat of a misnomer, since it is not true binding arbitration to which the parties have agreed, and it is not conducted by a sitting judge.

2. Obtaining Judicial Arbitration

a. Actions Subject to Judicial Arbitration

Any superior court with at least 18 judges may mandate judicial arbitration for unlimited civil cases in which the amount in controversy is $50,000 or less for each plaintiff. Limited civil cases may also be ordered into judicial arbitration if a court's local rule so provides. CCP § 1141.11.

In addition, parties may stipulate to judicial arbitration, or the plaintiff may elect to participate in judicial arbitration and agree that any award will not exceed $50,000. CCP § 1141.12.

b. Cases Exempt from Judicial Arbitration

Actions exempt from the requirement of judicial arbitration include class actions, family law matters, probate cases, small claims appeals, unlawful detainer proceedings, and those actions involving a nonfrivolous or substantial request for equitable relief. CRC 3.811; CCP § 1141.13.

3. Arbitration Proceedings

a. Selection of Arbitrator

The parties to judicial arbitration may stipulate to the selection of an arbitrator. In the absence of a stipulation or a local rule governing the selection of arbitrators, the court provides names of potential arbitrators to the parties and appoints an arbitrator who has not been rejected by the parties. CRC 3.815. The arbitrator is typically an attorney or retired judge.

b. Conduct of Arbitration

Unlike contractual arbitration, parties to judicial arbitration possess full discovery rights. CRC 3.822. With certain limited exceptions, judicial arbitration is conducted according to the rules of evidence and procedure. CRC 3.823.

c. Arbitration Award and Judgment

The arbitrator must render a written and signed award determining the issues presented. Within ten days after the conclusion of arbitration, the arbitrator must file the award with the court clerk and provide proof of service upon all parties. CRC 3.825. The clerk enters the award as a judgment if no party has requested a new trial (trial de novo) within 60 days after the arbitrator has filed the award. CRC 3.827. The judgment has the same effect as any court judgment, except that it may not be appealed. CCP § 1141.23. The judgment may be vacated by the trial court only on limited grounds, including those provided in CCP § 1286.2 (a)(1)–(3) for vacation of contractual arbitration awards (see section I(A)(5)(c), above), or on a ground provided in CCP § 473 for vacation of judgments and orders. CRC 3.828.

4. Trial De Novo

a. Request for Trial De Novo

Within 60 days after the arbitrator has filed the award with the clerk, a party may request a trial de novo as to both law and facts. CRC 3.826(a); CCP § 1141.20(b). The case must proceed to trial under the court's case management order. CRC 3.826(b). Neither the parties nor the court may refer to the arbitration at the trial de novo. CRC 3.826(c); CCP § 1141.25. Discovery is not allowed after an arbitration award and before the trial de novo except by stipulation of the parties or by court permission on a showing of good cause. CCP § 1141.24.

b. Outcome of Trial De Novo

If the judgment entered following the trial de novo is less favorable than the arbitration award for the party who requested the trial, the court must order that party to pay certain costs and fees, unless the order would create substantial economic hardship. CCP § 1141.21(a).

5. *Compare Federal Procedure*

Each district court must authorize the use of at least one type of alternative dispute resolution process. 28 USC § 651. The district court may make a referral to court-annexed arbitration only where the parties consent. Court-annexed arbitration is prohibited when the action is based on a constitutional or civil rights violation, or when the amount in controversy exceeds $150,000. 28 USC § 654(a).

6. Illustration

Padma filed a breach of contract complaint against Daphne in Madera County Superior Court. After numerous pretrial proceedings and a settlement conference, Padma and Daphne stipulated to submit the case to "binding" arbitration. The stipulation referred to the Judicial Arbitration Act and included a waiver of the right to a trial de novo. The court will employ the ordinary rules of contract interpretation to determine whether the parties have agreed to contractual or judicial arbitration. Despite the agreement to pursue "binding arbitration," the parties appeared to have intended to seek judicial arbitration with an advance waiver of the trial de novo right (a right that arises only in the judicial arbitration context). Porreco v. Red Top RV Center, 216 Cal.App.3d 113,

264 Cal.Rptr. 609 (1989). See also Rivera v. Shivers, 54 Cal.App.5th 82, 268 Cal.Rptr.3d 392 (2020) (citing *Porreco*).

C. International Arbitration

California has enacted the California International Arbitration and Conciliation Act (CCP § 1297.11 et seq.) to encourage and facilitate dispute resolution within the state involving foreign parties. The Act applies to commercial arbitrations in which any one of the following conditions is present:

- The parties' places of business are in countries other than where the arbitration agreement was executed;
- The dispute has close connections with a third country, or a substantial portion of the parties' agreement is supposed to be performed in that third country;
- The agreement expressly states that the subject matter of the arbitration agreement relates to commercial interests in more than one country; or
- The subject matter of the arbitration agreement is otherwise connected to commercial interests in more than one country.

CCP § 1297.13. See also Chapter 7(II)(A)(4) on recognition and enforcement of foreign arbitration awards.

D. Mediation

Mediation is "a process in which a neutral person or persons facilitate communication between the disputants to assist them in reaching a mutually acceptable agreement." CCP § 1775.1(a). The California Legislature has recognized the importance of mediation for the timely, informal, and cost-efficient resolution of disputes. CCP § 1775.

1. Mediation Programs

a. Court-Annexed Mediation

California has enacted the Civil Action Mediation Act. CCP §§ 1775 et seq. Currently, only the Los Angeles County Superior Court is statutorily required to participate in this program, but the superior courts of other counties may elect to participate as well (and several have). CCP § 1775.2.

1) Actions Submitted to Mediation

The court determines the amenability of a matter to mediation on a case-by-case basis, not categorically.

CRC 3.891(b). The court may order cases into mediation on largely the same basis as those ordered into judicial arbitration, including those in which the amount in controversy does not exceed $50,000 for each plaintiff. CCP § 1775.5. In addition, parties may stipulate to submit their matter to mediation, regardless of the amount in controversy. CRC 3.891(a)(2). Unlike judicial arbitration, however, an action may be submitted to mediation even if it requests equitable relief. Cases referred to judicial arbitration may not also be ordered submitted to mediation. CCP § 1775.4.

2) Selection and Role of Mediator

The mediator is selected from a panel maintained by the court, unless the parties stipulate to the selection of a mediator. CCP § 1775.6. The mediator does not have decisionmaking power; the role is to facilitate the process by which the parties reach their own voluntary agreement. Jeld-Wen, Inc. v. Superior Court, 146 Cal.App.4th 536, 53 Cal.Rptr.3d 115 (2007); CRC 3.853.

3) Conclusion of Mediation

The mediation must be completed within 60 days of the reference to mediation, unless the court extends the deadline for good cause. CRC 3.896(c). The mediator must file with the court a Statement of Nonagreement if no settlement has been reached. CCP § 1775.9. In order to preserve confidentiality, no other information may be included in the statement. If no agreement has been reached, the case is returned to the trial calendar.

b. Voluntary Mediation

Some courts that have not elected to establish a court-annexed mediation program have adopted voluntary mediation programs. Courts cannot require participation, and there are no sanctions for failing to participate. Berkeley Cement, Inc. v. Regents of University of California, 30 Cal.App.5th 1133, 242 Cal.Rptr.3d 252 (2019).

c. "Binding" Mediation

Parties may agree to "binding mediation," a seeming contradiction in terms. "In binding mediation, the mediator conducts a mediation and, if a settlement is not reached, the mediator decides the matter by reaching a fair settlement figure." Bowers v. Raymond J. Lucia Companies, 206 Cal.App.4th 724, 734, 142 Cal.Rptr.3d 64, 71 (2012).

2. Confidentiality of Mediation Proceedings

a. Written or Oral Communications

Unless an express statutory exception exists, parties and mediators are prohibited from disclosing any written or oral communications made during mediation. Such communications are not discoverable or admissible. Cal. Evid. Code § 1119. The confidentiality continues after the mediation ends. Id. § 1126. Under certain limited conditions, however, a written or oral settlement agreement reached during mediation may be disclosed. Id. §§ 1123–1124.

b. Reports or Findings

A mediator may not submit to the court any reports or findings related to the conduct of the mediation, unless the parties agree otherwise. Cal. Evid. Code § 1121; and Cassel v. Superior Court, 51 Cal.4th 113, 119 Cal.Rptr.3d 437, 244 P.3d 1080 (2011). However, a party may advise the court about bad faith conduct by other parties during the mediation. Foxgate Homeowners' Association, Inc. v. Bramalea California, Inc., 26 Cal.4th 1, 108 Cal.Rptr.2d 642, 25 P.3d 1117 (2001).

3. *Compare Federal Procedure*

The district court may utilize "special procedures to assist in resolving the dispute when authorized by statute or local rule." FRCP 16(c)(2)(I). All district courts, by local rule, must require civil litigants to consider using at least one alternative dispute resolution process (including mediation) during the litigation. 28 USC § 652(a). While there is no federal mediation privilege, courts are required to adopt local rules to provide for appropriate confidentiality of ADR proceedings. 28 USC § 652(d).

4. Illustration

Paki was injured in an airplane crash in Vallejo. He filed a personal injury lawsuit in Solano County Superior Court against Dusty Air Co. In an attempt to resolve the dispute, the parties held a mediation session. When the case did not settle, a second mediation session was scheduled, and each side submitted mediation briefs to the mediator. Dusty Air's attorney stated in his brief that Paki's attorney had communicated a settlement demand for $1 million, an amount far lower than Paki's earlier demand. On the day before the second mediation, an email exchange occurred between counsel for Paki and Dusty Air discussing the discrepancy in the settlement demands and the authority of Paki's counsel to lower the demand. The emails referred to and quoted from the mediation brief. The second mediation session settled the case, but Paki brought a malpractice action against his attorneys based on the less favorable settlement Paki received. The contents of the mediation briefs and emails are protected by confidentiality and may not be used as evidence in the malpractice action. Wimsatt v. Superior Court, 152 Cal.App.4th 137, 61 Cal.Rptr.3d 200 (2007).

II. CASE MANAGEMENT

A. Court's Obligation

Superior court judges are responsible for "active management and supervision of the pace of litigation from the date of filing to disposition." CRC 3.713(c); see also Cal. Gov't Code § 68607. Unless a case is exempt, the court must hold an initial case management conference within 180 days after the filing of a civil complaint to review the case and make initial determinations about alternative dispute resolution or trial setting. CRC 3.721; 3.722. In addition to the initial conference, the court may set additional case management conferences, either on its own motion or pursuant to a request by a party. CRC 3.723. The court must render a case management order setting forth a schedule for future events in the litigation and addressing other issues of case management. CRC 3.728.

B. Case Disposition ("Fast Track")

The Legislature, in enacting the Trial Court Delay Reduction Act (TCDRA, frequently referred to as "Fast Track"), authorized the Judicial Council to adopt statewide rules of court, and the superior courts to adopt local rules, to achieve the goal of expeditious disposition of superior court actions.

1. Case Disposition Time Goals

a. Unlimited and Limited Civil Cases

The TCDRA applies to all general civil cases, except those exempted or excluded from the Act. (See next paragraph.)

Under the case disposition rules applicable to Fast Track, the court should attempt to dispose of 75 percent of unlimited civil cases within 12 months, 85 percent within 18 months, and 100 percent within 24 months. For limited civil cases, the disposition goals are 90 percent within 12 months, 98 percent within 18 months, and 100 percent within 24 months. CRC 3.714(b).

b. Exempt Cases

Uninsured motorist cases, cases included in a petition for coordination, and collections cases are exempt from the Fast Track case disposition rules. CRC 3.712(b)–(d). In addition, the court may exempt cases from the disposition time goals if it determines that they involve exceptional circumstances, in which case the court should attempt to dispose of the action within three years. CRC 3.714(c). Juvenile, probate, and domestic relations cases shall not be assigned to a delay reduction program. Cal. Gov't Code § 68608(a).

c. Factors in Determining Disposition Goal

The court must consider each case on its own merits in setting case disposition goals. CRC 3.714. The court evaluates several factors in determining the appropriate disposition time goal, including: the number of parties, causes of action, and cross-complaints; the complexity of the issues; the nature and extent of discovery; and the estimated length of trial. CRC 3.715.

2. Pretrial Time Goals

With exceptions, the TCDRA requires service of the complaint within 60 days of filing, and service of a responsive pleading within 30 days of service of the complaint. The parties may also stipulate to one continuance within 30 days of service of the responsive pleadings. A superior court may generally impose its own time periods for other litigation activities, such as service of a cross-complaint, but the court cannot impose shorter time periods for these specific events than are permitted under statute. Cal. Gov't Code § 68616.

3. Sanctions

The TCDRA gives judges the broad power to "impose sanctions authorized by law" in order to achieve the purpose of the statutes. Cal. Gov't Code § 68608(b). Permissible sanctions may range from monetary sanctions to termination of the litigation. A judge may dismiss a plaintiff's action or strike a defendant's pleading only if less severe sanctions would not be effective. Id. However, the judge may not dismiss or strike a party's pleadings when counsel, and not the party, was responsible for failing to comply with Fast Track rules. CCP § 575.2(b); and Garcia v. McCutchen, 16 Cal.4th 469, 66 Cal.Rptr.2d 319, 940 P.2d 906 (1997).

4. *Compare Federal Procedure*

FRCP 1 states aspirationally that the rules "should be construed * * * to secure the just, speedy, and inexpensive determination of every action and proceeding." The FRCP do not require judges to dispose of a certain percentage of cases within a given time period. However, the rules do provide time frames for certain litigation events. For example, service of summons and complaint must be completed within 90 days of filing, and the defendant ordinarily must serve the response to the complaint within 21 days of service of summons and complaint. See FRCP 4(m) & 12(a)(1)(A). Moreover, the district court must promptly issue a scheduling order based on service upon or appearance of the defendant. FRCP 16(b)(2).

5. Illustration

Restaurant owner Pierre filed suit in Stanislaus County Superior Court against his landlord, Della Corp., for failure to comply with the terms of his lease for his restaurant, Magnifique, located in Modesto. Pierre's attorney, Arlo, attempted to serve the complaint on the president of Della Corp. six times over the course of 70 days, but he was unsuccessful. Local Fast Track rules required plaintiffs to complete service within 60 days of the filing of the complaint. The court issued an order to show cause for the failure to timely serve Della Corp. Arlo did not appear at the order to show cause hearing, and the judge dismissed Pierre's case in its entirety. The dismissal is inappropriate for two reasons: (a) the judge did not consider whether less severe sanctions might be effective; and (b) Pierre's lawsuit cannot be terminated as a sanction for Arlo's failure to comply with the Fast Track rules. Service of process is ordinarily within the power of counsel, not of the client. Therefore, monetary sanctions should be imposed only on Arlo for failure to timely serve the complaint. Tliche v. Van Quathem, 66 Cal.App.4th 1054, 78 Cal.Rptr.2d 458 (1998).

III. DISMISSALS

A. Involuntary Dismissal Under Diligent Prosecution Statutes

For cases not part of the TCDRA, the superior court is authorized to involuntarily dismiss a plaintiff's action under what are known as "diligent prosecution" statutes. CCP § 583.110 et seq. These statutes obligate plaintiffs (and cross-complainants) to diligently manage their lawsuits and move them forward. CCP § 583.130. Involuntary dismissal may occur if the plaintiff fails to complete service of process or to bring the action to trial within the applicable deadlines. The court may dismiss on motion of a party or on its own motion. Involuntary dismissals are without prejudice and may be either mandatory or discretionary.

1. Failure to Serve Complaint

a. Mandatory Dismissal

In non-Fast Track actions, the plaintiff must serve the defendants (both named and Doe) with the summons and complaint within three years after commencement of the action. CCP § 583.210(a). In addition, the plaintiff has 60 days beyond the time the summons and complaint must be served upon a defendant to file proof of service with the court. CCP § 583.210(b). If the plaintiff fails to meet these deadlines, dismissal is mandatory. CCP § 583.250(b).

1) Tolling

Dismissal of the plaintiff's action for failing to timely serve process may be delayed if a statutory tolling provision applies. The time during which any of the following statutory excuses lasts is excluded from the calculation of the three-year deadline:

- The defendant was not amenable to the process of the court;
- The prosecution of the action or proceedings in the action was stayed and the stay affected service;
- The validity of service was the subject of litigation by the parties; or
- Service, for any other reason, was impossible, impracticable, or futile due to causes beyond the plaintiff's control.

CCP § 583.240. The plaintiff has the burden to show that a valid excuse exists and that the plaintiff exercised reasonable diligence in attempting to serve process.

2) **Other Extensions**

In addition to the above tolling provisions, the three-year deadline may be extended by the parties via written stipulation or oral agreement in open court. CCP §§ 583.220 & 583.230.

b. **Discretionary Dismissal**

The court has discretion to involuntarily dismiss an action that has not been served within two years from the filing of the complaint. CCP § 583.420(a)(1). In exercising its discretion, the court must consider the factors found in CRC 3.1342(e), including: the nature and complexity of the case; the extent of any settlement negotiations; the plaintiff's diligence in attempting to achieve service of process; and the nature of any delays attributable to the parties. A court considering a discretionary dismissal motion often focuses on whether the plaintiff has a reasonable excuse for the delay, and whether the defendant has been prejudiced. Putnam v. Clague, 3 Cal.App.4th 542, 5 Cal.Rptr.2d 25 (1992). The court may toll the two-year period on any of the grounds applicable under the provisions for tolling the three-year mandatory dismissal deadline for failure to serve process, discussed in section III(A)(1)(a), above. See CCP § 583.240.

2. **Failure to Bring Case to Trial**

a. **Mandatory Dismissal**

The court must involuntarily dismiss a plaintiff's action if it has not been "brought to trial" within five years of its filing. CCP §§ 583.310 & 583.360.

1) **"Brought to Trial"**

"Trial," in the context of the diligent prosecution statutes, commences when the jury panel is sworn (jury trial) or when the first witness is sworn (court trial). Pretrial proceedings that result in a final disposition of an action may constitute "trial" for this purpose (such as an order granting summary judgment or an order sustaining a demurrer without leave to amend).

2) **Tolling**

In calculating the five-year period in which the action must be brought to trial, the court will not include in the calculation the time during which any of the following occurred:

- The jurisdiction of the court to try the action was suspended;
- Prosecution or trial of the action was stayed or enjoined; or
- Bringing the action to trial, for any other reason, was impossible, impracticable, or futile.

CCP § 583.340. The plaintiff has the burden to show the existence of one of the statutory excuses and to establish reasonable diligence at all stages of the litigation in attempting to bring the case to trial. Bruns v. E-Commerce Exchange, Inc., 51 Cal.4th 717, 122 Cal.Rptr.3d 331, 248 P.3d 1185 (2011). If, after a period of tolling, fewer than six months remain in which to bring the action to trial, the action may not be dismissed as long as trial commences within six months after the conclusion of the period of tolling. CCP § 583.350.

3) **Other Extensions**

The five-year deadline may be extended by written stipulation or oral agreement in open court. CCP § 583.330.

b. **Discretionary Dismissal**

The court has discretion to dismiss an action that has not been brought to trial within two years of its filing. CCP § 583.420(a)(2)(B); CRC 3.1340. The court must apply the factors found in CRC 3.1342(e) in exercising its discretion to dismiss. The same tolling provisions as apply in the mandatory dismissal context also apply to discretionary dismissals for failure to bring the case to trial. CCP §§ 583.420(b) & 583.340. See section III(A)(2)(a), above.

3. **Diligent Prosecution Statutes and TCDRA**

A case that is subject to the Trial Court Delay Reduction Act ("Fast Track"; see section II(B), above), may be involuntarily dismissed under different (usually much shorter) time limits than those imposed by the diligent prosecution statutes. For example, under Cal. Gov't Code § 68616 and the local rules of many superior courts, a court may involuntarily dismiss an action if the plaintiff has failed to serve process on the defendant within 60 days of the filing of the complaint. The diligent prosecution statutes do not limit the court's power to dismiss an action under another applicable statute or court rule or under the court's inherent authority. CCP § 583.150.

4. *Compare Federal Procedure*

A defendant may move the court for an involuntary dismissal of an action under FRCP 41(b) if the plaintiff has failed to prosecute, to comply with the Federal Rules, or to comply with an order of the court. The district court also possesses inherent power to dismiss on its own motion. With limited exceptions, such an involuntary dismissal is with prejudice. Rule 41(b), unlike the California diligent prosecution statutes, does not state the types of conduct that constitute a failure to prosecute, and does not include specific time limits and tolling provisions. Federal courts are reluctant to impose a drastic measure such as dismissal unless the conduct of the plaintiff has demonstrated willful or repeated delay or noncompliance, and prejudice to defendant.

5. Illustration

Pedro filed a qui tam action in Trinity County Superior Court on behalf of the State of California against Dorian Medical Corp. for insurance fraud. The applicable statutes required that this type of action be filed under seal to give the relevant governmental agencies an opportunity to investigate the allegations and determine whether they will intervene in the action. During the 912-day period during which the action was under seal, Pedro was unable to serve the complaint on Dorian Medical or take other litigation steps. Once the governmental agencies determined they would not intervene, the court lifted the seal and prosecution of the action proceeded. When five years had elapsed from the date of Pedro's filing of the action, Dorian Medical moved for mandatory dismissal for failure to bring the matter to trial within five years. Pedro will successfully argue that the 912-day period during which the action was maintained under seal tolled the five-year statute because the action was "enjoined or stayed" under CCP § 583.340(b), thus preventing Pedro from prosecuting the lawsuit. State ex rel. Sills v. Gharib-Danesh, 88 Cal.App.5th 824, 304 Cal.Rptr.3d 865 (2023).

B. Other Involuntary Dismissals

Additional statutory bases for involuntary dismissal include the following scenarios:

- The court sustains a demurrer or grants a motion to strike as to the entire complaint without leave to amend (CCP § 581(f));
- The plaintiff fails to timely amend the complaint when leave to amend has been granted (CCP § 581(f));
- The court orders a terminating sanction for misuse of the discovery process or for a party's violation of Fast Track rules (CCP § 2023.030(d); Cal. Gov't Code § 68608(b)); or
- The plaintiff or the defendant fails to appear for trial (CCP § 581(b)).

C. Voluntary Dismissals

A plaintiff may voluntarily dismiss her action, or may request the court to dismiss the action, at any time before "the actual commencement of trial." CCP § 581(b)(1) & (c). This dismissal may be either with or without prejudice.

1. Commencement of Trial

The actual commencement of trial precludes a plaintiff from dismissing her action without prejudice. Under CCP § 581(a)(6), "trial" commences at any of the following points:

- the beginning of opening statement or argument;
- if there is no opening statement, the time of the administration of an oath or affirmation to the first witness; or
- the introduction of any evidence.

Courts have expanded the definition of "trial" to include various dispositive pretrial proceedings in which the court makes a final determination of an issue of law or fact. Franklin Capital Corp. v. Wilson, 148 Cal.App.4th 187, 55 Cal.Rptr.3d 424 (2007). Examples include: the filing of a motion for terminating sanctions in a discovery dispute; a tentative ruling sustaining a demurrer without leave to amend; and an order sustaining a demurrer with leave to amend where the time for amendment has expired.

2. With or Without Prejudice

Dismissal with prejudice precludes a plaintiff from bringing a new action based on the same causes of action as in the dismissed action. Dismissal without prejudice permits the plaintiff to bring a new lawsuit on the same causes of action, assuming those causes of action are not barred by the applicable statute(s) of limitations. Once trial has actually commenced, a voluntary dismissal may be entered only with prejudice, unless the court orders otherwise for good cause or the affected parties consent to a dismissal without prejudice. CCP § 581(c).

3. *Compare Federal Procedure*

In contrast to the unlimited number of voluntary pretrial dismissals without prejudice permitted under the California statute, FRCP 41(a)(1) permits a plaintiff to voluntarily dismiss the action only once without leave of court. Moreover, if the plaintiff has already voluntarily dismissed a previous action on the same claim, the voluntary dismissal is with prejudice. FRCP 41(a)(1)(B). The right of voluntary dismissal without leave of court is available only if the defendant has not answered or filed a summary judgment motion, or if all parties who have appeared in the action stipulate to the dismissal. In all other circumstances, the plaintiff must obtain court permission to voluntarily dismiss their case. FRCP 41(a)(2). The California Supreme Court will be addressing the preclusive effect of FRCP 41(a)(1)(B)'s two-dismissal rule on claims filed in California courts. Doe v. Marysville Joint Unified School District, 98 Cal.App.5th 95, 316 Cal.Rptr.3d 382 (2023) (second voluntary dismissal of federal cases had claim-preclusive effect on state court action), rev. granted, 319 Cal.Rptr.3d 885, 545 P.3d 883 (2024).

4. Illustration

Pluck, a talented 18-year-old musical theatre performer, attended Dancer Academy, a private performing arts high school in Ross. Pluck was frequently taunted and bullied by other students on campus, to the point where she wanted to drop out of school. Pluck filed suit against Dancer Academy in Marin County Superior Court for intentional infliction of emotional distress and negligent supervision. Dancer Academy filed a motion for summary judgment. One day before Pluck's opposition to the summary judgment motion was due, she moved to dismiss her action without prejudice. Pluck may voluntarily dismiss her case without prejudice any time prior to the actual commencement of trial. Pluck moved to dismiss before several key litigation events had occurred: the deadline for filing opposition to the summary judgment motion; the date of the hearing on the motion; and the court's tentative ruling.

> As the case was dismissed before a stage where a final ruling on the summary judgment motion was a "mere formality," Pluck's voluntary dismissal was timely. Zapanta v. Universal Care, Inc., 107 Cal.App.4th 1167, 1173, 132 Cal.Rptr.2d 842, 846 (2003).

IV. DEFAULT AND DEFAULT JUDGMENT

A. Entry of Default

Entry of default and entry of default judgment are two distinct procedures. If a defendant fails to file a timely answer, demurrer, or other statutorily permitted response to the complaint, the plaintiff may seek the entry of the defendant's default. CCP § 585. The plaintiff must request the court clerk to enter the defendant's default—it is not automatic. After the clerk enters the default, the defendant has no right to appear or participate in the proceedings or to receive notices (except notice that its default has been entered). The court no longer has jurisdiction over the defendant, except to consider a motion to set aside the default.

B. Entry of Default Judgment

Upon the entry of default, the plaintiff may seek a default judgment against the defendant. CCP § 585.

1. Entry of Default Judgment by Clerk

In limited circumstances—actions arising from a contract or a judgment for a fixed amount of damages, where service of process was achieved other than by publication—the court clerk may enter a default judgment. CCP § 585(a).

2. Entry of Default Judgment by Court

In all other cases, the court must enter the default judgment after the plaintiff provides the court with evidence to "prove up" her right to relief. CCP § 585(b).

a. Prove-Up Hearing

The court must conduct a "prove-up hearing" at which the plaintiff appears either in person or through submission of affidavits. The defendant has no right to receive notice of, or to appear at, the prove-up hearing—even to contest the amount of damages.

b. Amount of Recovery

1) If No Answer

"[I]f there is no answer," the amount awarded to the plaintiff on a default judgment must not exceed the amount pleaded in the prayer of the complaint (or the body of the complaint if the prayer is defective). CCP § 580(a). In personal injury or wrongful death cases, in which the amount of damages must not be stated in the complaint (see Chapter 3(III)(B)), the amount awarded to the plaintiff on a default judgment must not exceed that set out in the plaintiff's statement of damages under CCP § 425.11. Punitive damages (the amount of which also must not be stated in the complaint) may not exceed the amount demanded in the plaintiff's statement of punitive damages under CCP § 425.115. The plaintiff must have served the defendant with the statement of damages and/or punitive damages (when applicable) before the court will enter default judgment. Due process considerations require that the defendant must have adequate notice of the specific relief that the plaintiff seeks against him. A penalty default (resulting, for example, from striking the defendant's answer as a sanction) is treated as though no answer had been filed in the action. Greenup v. Rodman, 42 Cal.3d 822, 231 Cal.Rptr. 220, 726 P.2d 1295 (1986).

2) In All Other Cases

"[I]n any other [unlimited civil] case, the court may grant the plaintiff any relief consistent with the case made by the complaint and embraced within the issue." CCP § 580(a). In limited civil cases, the types of relief that may be granted are statutorily restricted. CCP § 580(b).

C. Setting Aside Default and Default Judgment

1. Discretionary or Mandatory Relief from Default and/or Default Judgment

The defendant may move the court to vacate the entry of default and/or default judgment under CCP § 473(b). The statute contains both discretionary and mandatory relief provisions, as well as time limits for filing the motion. See section VIII(A), below.

2. Vacating Default and Default Judgment Based on Lack of Actual Notice

If service of process did not result in actual notice to the defendant in time to respond to the complaint, the defendant may move to set aside any resulting default and/or default judgment. CCP § 473.5. The defendant must seek relief within a reasonable time, in no case later than two years after entry of default judgment or 180 days after service of written notice that a default or default judgment has been entered (whichever is earlier). The court has discretion to set aside the default and/or default judgment so long as the defendant's lack of actual notice was not caused by his avoidance of service or by inexcusable neglect.

D. *Compare Federal Procedure*

FRCP 55(b) permits entry of a default judgment by either the clerk or the court. In contrast to California procedure, a defendant who has made a previous appearance in federal proceedings has a right to be notified of a prove-up hearing and to appear to contest the plaintiff's showing. FRCP 55(b)(2). A federal court may set aside an entry of default on a showing of good cause. A final default judgment may be vacated as provided in FRCP 60(b). FRCP 55(c).

E. Illustration

Palti and Decker became involved in a romantic relationship in Rancho Mirage while Decker was still married. As the relationship progressed, Decker promised Palti that he would pay all of Palti's living expenses for the rest of Decker's life, among other representations. When the relationship soured and Decker ceased paying, Palti filed an action in Riverside County Superior Court, seeking an accounting of all property Decker had purchased and income he had earned during the relationship. The prayer of Palti's complaint did not contain a specific dollar figure for monetary damages; it demanded recovery "in a sum to be proven at trial." Decker did not respond to the complaint, and the clerk of the court entered his default. At the prove-up hearing, Palti presented detailed evidence from a forensic accountant of the amount of his damages. The trial court entered default judgment and granted some, but not all, of the monetary relief Palti had sought. Decker, who was not present at the hearing, thereafter filed a motion to set aside the default and default judgment because the complaint did not state a specific amount of damages, in violation of CCP § 580(a). In reconciling section 580(a) with the characteristics of an accounting, the court will require a plaintiff

> to plead an *estimated* amount of damages, even if he is not able to state a precise sum in the prayer. Due process requires that the complaint must put a defaulting defendant on notice of the maximum amount of a potential judgment against him. Palti is not relieved of the obligation to provide that notice to Decker, even in an accounting action where he does not yet know the specific amount of his damages. Sass v. Cohen, 10 Cal.5th 861, 272 Cal.Rptr.3d 836, 477 P.3d 557 (2020).

V. SETTLEMENT

The vast majority of California civil lawsuits settle before trial. California has a strong policy in favor of settlement, which furthers judicial efficiency by disposing of cases prior to trial. The court may, either on a party's or its own motion, set a mandatory settlement conference. CRC 3.1380. However, parties have no obligation to settle.

A. Settlement Agreement

1. Dismissal of Action

When the parties agree on the terms of a settlement of the entire case, the plaintiff must file a request for dismissal with the court within 45 days of the settlement. CRC 3.1385(b). Dismissal of all causes of action against a defendant or cross-defendant terminates that party's involvement in the lawsuit, and the court ceases to have jurisdiction over that party.

2. Entry of Judgment and Enforcement of Agreement

When the parties have stipulated to a settlement, they may move the court to enter judgment pursuant to the terms of the settlement. CCP § 664.6(a). The stipulation may be made either in a writing signed by the parties or their attorneys outside the court, or orally before the court. CCP § 664.6(b). The court may not modify or add to the terms of the settlement. Leeman v. Adams Extract & Spice, LLC, 236 Cal.App.4th 1367, 187 Cal.Rptr.3d 220 (2015). The court does not automatically oversee the enforcement of a settlement agreement. The parties to the settlement may request in writing, prior to dismissal, that the court retain jurisdiction to enforce the terms of the settlement until performed. CCP § 664.6(a). Enforcement of the agreement may alternatively be sought by filing a separate action in equity.

B. Terms of Settlement

1. Settlement Allocation

Where there are multiple defendants, and one defendant settles with the plaintiff, the other defendants are entitled to have any amount of economic (compensatory) damages they owe in a subsequent judgment offset by the amount the settling defendant paid. CCP § 877(a). However, no defendant is entitled to any offset for the noneconomic (pain and suffering) damages paid by the settling defendant, because liability for noneconomic damages is several and can never be shared. Espinoza v. Machonga, 9 Cal.App.4th 268, 11 Cal.Rptr.2d 498 (1992). Each defendant may be held liable for noneconomic damages only in proportion to its percentage of overall fault. Cal. Civ. Code § 1431.2; and Weidenfeller v. Star and Garter, 1 Cal.App.4th 1, 2 Cal.Rptr.2d 14 (1991).

2. Good Faith Settlement

a. Good Faith Settlement Determination

Where there are multiple defendants and one of the defendants settles with the plaintiff, any party to the action is entitled to a hearing to determine whether the settlement was entered in good faith. CCP § 877.6. Otherwise, the possibility exists of one defendant settling for an extremely low amount, leaving the remaining defendants exposed to disproportionate liability. If the court determines that a settlement reached with one joint defendant was not made in good faith, the settlement amount is credited against any damages awarded the plaintiff. However, the nonsettling defendants are entitled to contribution from the settling defendant in the amount in excess of the nonsettling defendants' equitable shares of liability. In contrast, if the settlement was made in good faith, there is no right of contribution from the settling defendant. Leung v. Verdugo Hills Hospital, 55 Cal.4th 291, 145 Cal.Rptr.3d 553, 282 P.3d 1250 (2012).

b. Factors

For a court to deem a settlement to be in good faith, it must be reasonably within the range of the share for which the settling defendant could have been liable. Tech-Bilt, Inc. v. Woodward-Clyde & Associates, 38 Cal.3d 488, 213 Cal.Rptr. 256, 698 P.2d 159 (1985). Determining whether a settlement was entered in good faith requires a rough approximation based on the facts known at the time of the settlement and includes consideration of such factors as: the solvency and insurance limits of the settling defendant; any appearance of fraud or collusion in the settlement; and the recognition that a party typically pays less in settlement than at trial.

3. *Compare Federal Procedure*

While settlement is encouraged in federal practice, the FRCP provide only general authority to the trial judge to facilitate settlement, leaving the particulars to local rules or specific statutes. See FRCP 16(a)(5) & (c)(2)(I). Federal practice does not involve inquiring into the good faith of the settlement by one of multiple defendants. Instead, if the settling defendant settles for an amount that turns out to be less than its proportionate liability as determined at trial, the remaining defendants are entitled to a dollar-for-dollar setoff credit from the settling defendant. McDermott, Inc. v. AmClyde, 511 U.S. 202, 114 S.Ct. 1461, 128 L.Ed.2d 148 (1994).

4. Illustration

After undergoing many tests, Pello received a diagnosis of cancer. He believed the cancer resulted from his lifelong voracious consumption of ultra-processed snack foods containing chemical additives and preservatives, which some scientists have identified as suspected carcinogens. Pello sued 46 different snack food manufacturers for his injuries in San Mateo County Superior Court. Before trial, Pello settled with 45 of the manufacturers for a total of $1,500,000, and he released them from all claims arising from his alleged carcinogen exposure. At trial, the jury found the one remaining defendant, Dalton Industries, liable for Pello's injuries. The jury found Pello's economic damages to be $1,000,000 and his noneconomic damages for pain and suffering to be $3,500,000. The jury apportioned 2% of the fault for Pello's injuries to Dalton Industries. To determine how much Dalton Industries owed Pello, the trial court first divided Pello's economic damages ($1,000,000) by his total damages ($4,500,000) to determine what percentage of his total damages were economic damages (22%). The trial court then multiplied the total pretrial settlement amount ($1,500,000) by 22% to determine what amount of the pretrial settlement was for economic damages ($333,333). Because economic damages are joint and several, Dalton Industries, as the sole remaining defendant, was liable for $666,667 in economic damages ($1,000,000 as assigned by the jury, minus the $333,333 already paid in settlement). Because noneconomic damages are several (and thus not shared), Dalton Industries was liable for $70,000 in noneconomic damages ($3,500,000 as assigned by the jury, multiplied by 2% fault assigned to Dalton Industries). Pello may not recover the remainder of his noneconomic damages. Jones v. John Crane, Inc., 132 Cal.App.4th 990, 35 Cal.Rptr.3d 144 (2005).

VI. OFFER OF JUDGMENT

A. Statutory Basis

California's offer of judgment procedure, as set forth in CCP § 998, reflects the state's policy of encouraging settlements. Section 998 contains a statutory exception to the general rule under CCP § 1032(b) that a prevailing party is entitled to recover costs of suit as a matter of right. Under CCP § 998, a party, even if not the prevailing party as defined by section 1032(b), may recover their costs and possibly expert witness fees if: (1) they submit a timely written section 998 offer to another party; (2) the offer is not accepted; and (3) the party who failed to accept the offer does not obtain a more favorable judgment at trial or more favorable award in contractual arbitration.

B. Offer

1. Form and Timing

As late as ten days before trial, any party may serve on any other party a written section 998 offer of judgment. CCP § 998(b). The offer must state the terms and conditions of the proposed judgment and must contain a provision allowing the offeree to accept the offer by signing a statement of acceptance. CCP § 998(b).

2. Revocation

The offeror may revoke an offer any time prior to acceptance. T.M. Cobb Co. v. Superior Court, 36 Cal.3d 273, 204 Cal.Rptr. 143, 682 P.2d 338 (1984). A simple letter by the offeror sent prior to notification of the offeree's acceptance is sufficient. Death of the offeror or offeree, or a subsequent offer by the offeror, will serve as a revocation of any standing section 998 offer.

3. Token Offer Limitation

CCP § 998 contains an implied requirement that the offer be in good faith. A token or nominal offer does not meet this requirement. For an offer to meet the good faith requirement, it must "carry with it some reasonable prospect of acceptance. * * * [A] party having no expectation that his offer will be accepted will not be allowed to benefit from a no-risk offer made for the sole purpose of later recovering large expert witness fees." Adams v. Ford Motor Co., 199 Cal.App.4th 1475, 1483, 132 Cal.Rptr.3d 424, 430–431 (2011). Even a very modest offer can fulfill the good faith requirement if a defendant reasonably believes there is no liability. When a rejected offer turns out to be more favorable than the judgment received, that outcome is prima facie evidence that the offer was made in good faith and was reasonable.

C. Response to Offer

1. Acceptance

The acceptance must be communicated to the offeror before the time for acceptance expires. For an acceptance to be effective, it must be in writing, signed by the accepting party's counsel (or by the accepting party if she does not have representation), and filed with the court. Upon its filing, the judge or clerk must enter judgment in accordance with the offer. CCP § 998(b)(1). The acceptance must be unconditional. Siri v. Sutter Home Winery, Inc., 82 Cal.App.5th 685, 298 Cal.Rptr.3d 576 (2022).

2. Offer Not Accepted

If the offer is not accepted within 30 days after it was made, or before trial or arbitration, whichever comes first, the offer is deemed withdrawn. It cannot be presented at trial as evidence. CCP § 998(b)(2). Rejection of a section 998 offer must be unequivocal. Madrigal v. Hyundai Motor America, 17 Cal.5th 592, 331 Cal.Rptr.3d 15, 565 P.3d 714 (2025). Mere criticism, requests for a better offer, or making a counteroffer do not serve as rejections for section 998 purposes.

D. Effect of Failing to Accept Section 998 Offer

1. Plaintiff's Failure to Accept Defendant's Offer

If the defendant submits a section 998 offer to the plaintiff, the offer is not accepted, and the plaintiff fails to obtain a more favorable trial judgment or arbitration award, the plaintiff may not recover her postoffer costs and must pay the defendant's postoffer costs. Furthermore, the court may, in its discretion, award postoffer expert witness fees and costs to the defendant. CCP § 998(c)(1). The defendant's costs are deducted from the plaintiff's award, and if the defendant's costs exceed the plaintiff's award, judgment for the defendant will be entered in the net amount. CCP § 998(e).

2. Defendant's Failure to Accept Plaintiff's Offer

If the plaintiff submits a section 998 offer to the defendant, the offer is not accepted, and the defendant fails to obtain a more favorable trial judgment or arbitration award, the defendant must pay the plaintiff's costs of suit. In addition, the court may, in its discretion, order the defendant to pay the plaintiff's postoffer expert witness fees. CCP § 998(d).

E. *Compare Federal Procedure*

In contrast to California practice authorizing any party to make a section 998 offer, FRCP 68(a) permits only the defendant to make an offer of judgment. The federal rule does not apply to judgments in favor of defendants. For a defendant to recover costs under Rule 68, the plaintiff must obtain a judgment less favorable than the offer. Delta Air Lines, Inc. v. August, 450 U.S. 346, 101 S.Ct. 1146, 67 L.Ed.2d 287 (1981). The postoffer costs awarded under FRCP 68(d) are those authorized by the relevant underlying substantive statute. If that statute defines costs as including attorney's fees, those fees are awardable under FRCP 68. Marek v. Chesny, 473 U.S. 1, 105 S.Ct. 3012, 87 L.Ed.2d 1 (1985). Finally, 28 USC § 1821(b) sets a maximum attendance fee of $40 per day per witness (lay or expert) unless there is specific statutory or contractual authorization that would allow for a greater amount.

F. Illustration

Distracted Construction Co. was the general contractor hired to build a new library at a law school in Irvine. Distracted Construction entered into a subcontract with Pricey Builders to perform framing work. When that work ended up costing more than anticipated, Pricey Builders sued Distracted Construction in Orange County Superior Court for $400,000, alleging that Distracted Construction's poor management caused Pricey Builders to incur cost overruns for which it should be compensated. In an effort to settle the case, Distracted Construction presented a written section 998 offer in the amount of $100,000, which Pricey Builders summarily rejected. Distracted Construction then prepared for trial in earnest, retaining experts to serve as consultants and trial witnesses. At trial, the jury rendered a verdict for Pricey Builders for $80,000. Since this outcome was less favorable than the amount of Distracted Construction's section 998 offer, the court ordered Pricey Builders to pay Distracted Construction's postoffer costs of suit, which amounted to $90,000. In addition, the court exercised its discretion to award Distracted Construction $40,000 toward the costs of the services of its expert witnesses. Despite the fact that Pricey Builders was the "prevailing party," it ended up owing Distracted Construction a net award of $50,000. Scott Co. v. Blount, Inc., 20 Cal.4th 1103, 86 Cal.Rptr.2d 614, 979 P.2d 974 (1999).

VII. SUMMARY JUDGMENT AND SUMMARY ADJUDICATION

A. Summary Judgment

A party may move for summary judgment against an adverse party one time on the ground that the entire action has no merit or that there is no defense to the action. CCP § 437c(a)(1) & (4). A trial court may grant a motion for summary judgment if the parties' papers show that "there is no triable issue as to any material fact and that the moving party is entitled to a judgment as a matter of law." CCP § 437c(c). If granted, summary judgment disposes of all causes of action in a complaint or all defenses in an answer, leaving nothing for further adjudication. California's summary judgment law conforms "largely but not completely" to the federal procedures. Aguilar v. Atlantic Richfield Co., 25 Cal.4th 826, 849, 107 Cal.Rptr.2d 841, 860, 24 P.3d 493 (2001).

1. Papers Filed on Motion

a. Moving Party

The moving party must support the motion with evidence in the form of "affidavits, declarations, admissions, answers to interrogatories, depositions, and matters of which judicial notice shall or may be taken." CCP § 437c(b)(1). Additionally, the moving party must file a "separate statement," which sets out the material facts contended to be undisputed and references to the evidence that supports those material facts. CCP § 437c(b)(1); CRC 3.1350(d) & (h). A notice of the motion and a memorandum of points and authorities are also required. CRC 3.1350(c).

b. **Opposing Party**

In addition to presenting evidence and a memorandum of points and authorities in opposition to the motion, the opposing party must file a separate statement stating whether each of the moving party's facts is disputed or undisputed and noting supporting evidence for each allegedly disputed fact. The opponent may also present additional material facts in dispute. CCP § 437c(b)(3); CRC 3.1350(e)–(f).

c. **Evidentiary Objections**

A party may make objections to the evidence presented in the other party's papers. Evidentiary objections must be made no later than the time of the hearing or they are deemed waived. CCP § 437c(b)(5). A timely objection is not waived by the trial court's failure to expressly rule on it; the objection is preserved for appeal. CCP § 437c(q); and Reid v. Google, Inc., 50 Cal.4th 512, 113 Cal.Rptr.3d 327, 235 P.3d 988 (2010). In the absence of objections that the trial court sustains, the court is deemed to have considered all evidence presented by the parties and all inferences reasonably deducible from the evidence. CCP § 437c(c).

2. **Parties' Respective Burdens**

a. **Moving Party's Burdens**

1) **Burdens of Persuasion, Production and Proof**

At all stages of the summary judgment process, the moving party bears the burden of persuasion that there is no triable issue of material fact. The moving party also initially possesses the burden of production of evidence to establish a prima facie showing that there are no material facts in dispute. See CCP § 437c(p). The standard of proof that would apply at trial is relevant in a summary judgment motion. If the plaintiff is the moving party, she must produce evidence establishing the underlying facts by a preponderance of evidence or clear and convincing evidence, depending on the appropriate trial standard of proof. If the defendant is the moving party, he must present evidence that would permit the trier of fact to *not* find any underlying material fact according to the relevant standard of proof at trial. *Aguilar*, 25 Cal.4th at 851, 107 Cal.Rptr.2d at 862, 24 P.3d 493.

2) Satisfying Moving Party's Burden of Production

To meet its burden of production, the moving party must present evidence, not merely argument. A moving defendant must show that one or more elements of the plaintiff's cause of action cannot be established, or that there is a complete defense to the cause of action. CCP § 437c(p)(2). The moving defendant may: (a) affirmatively negate an element of the plaintiff's cause of action; (b) demonstrate that the process of discovery has yielded no evidence to support an element of a cause of action; or (c) show that a complete defense to the cause of action exists. A moving plaintiff may show that there is no defense to a cause of action by providing evidence to support each element of the cause of action. CCP § 437c(p)(1). The moving plaintiff need not affirmatively disprove defenses.

b. Opposing Party's Burden of Production

If the moving party satisfies the burden of production by establishing a prima facie case showing no material facts in dispute, the burden of production shifts to the opposing party to present evidence that at least one triable issue of material fact exists. CCP § 437c(p). The opposing party may seek a continuance of the hearing date in order to conduct necessary discovery to oppose the motion. The request must show why such discovery could not have been completed earlier. CCP § 437c(h).

3. Timing of Notice and Hearing

Summary judgment motions are subject to the lengthiest notice period of any California motion. The moving party must serve the papers on all other parties at least 81 days prior to the date of the hearing. The notice period may be longer if the papers are served by a method other than personal delivery. CCP § 437c(a). The motion may be served electronically, which extends the notice period by two days. CCP § 1010.6(a)(3); and Cole v. Superior Court, 87 Cal.App.5th 84, 303 Cal.Rptr.3d 296 (2022). The opposing party must file and serve any opposition to the motion at least 20 days before the hearing. CCP § 437c(b)(2). The moving party must file any reply papers at least 11 days before the hearing. CCP § 437c(b)(4). The motion must be heard at least 30 days before the scheduled trial date. CCP § 437c(a)(3). See Robinson v. Woods, 168 Cal.App.4th 1258, 86 Cal.Rptr.3d 241 (2008).

4. Entry of Judgment and Appellate Review

In granting or denying summary judgment, the trial court must render a detailed order setting out the reasons for its ruling and referring specifically to the supporting and opposing evidence on the motion. CCP § 437c(g). The Court of Appeal may review the entry of summary judgment as a final appealable judgment. It may also review the entry of any other nonfinal order related to the motion upon petition for extraordinary writ. CCP § 437c(m)(1). (See Chapter 8(III)(B)(1), regarding extraordinary writs.)

5. *Compare Federal Procedure*

FRCP 56, governing summary judgment, is far less detailed than its California statutory equivalent. In a series of cases, the U.S. Supreme Court liberalized the federal summary judgment standards, encouraging courts to utilize such motions to dispose of cases. See, e.g., Celotex Corp. v. Catrett, 477 U.S. 317, 106 S.Ct. 2548, 91 L.Ed.2d 265 (1986). California's summary judgment law and procedures are largely identical to those under the federal rule and cases. Some notable differences are as follows: (a) FRCP 56(c) allows a party to move for summary judgment without presenting any supporting affidavits, but the moving party must cite to particular parts of materials in the record or show that the materials do not establish that a genuine dispute exists. In California, the moving defendant may not merely rely on argument, but must present evidence. (b) FRCP 56 does not require a separate statement, as does the California statute and rule of court. (c) The federal notice period for summary judgment motions is much shorter than in California: 14 days under FRCP 6(c)(1) (or longer by local rule). (d) FRCP 56(b) permits a party to file a motion for summary judgment at any time until 30 days after the close of all discovery. No provision in the rule governs how early the motion may be filed, in contrast to the California statute.

6. Illustration

Perth bought a real estate parcel from Dunne Properties. The land was part of a development in Sonora in which high-end vacation homes would be constructed among the hills and valleys. When landslides damaged their parcel, Perth filed an action against Dunne Properties and its principals in Tuolumne County Superior Court for fraud and negligence due to poor soil testing and remediation. Dunne Properties filed a summary judgment motion based on several defenses it raised in its answer. The moving papers included a 50-page separate statement of undisputed material facts. Perth's opposition papers included a 155-page separate statement that did not comply in numerous respects with the requirements of CRC 3.1350, which governs content and format. Specifically, the opposition separate statement "improperly cit[ed] to numerous undisputed material facts for specific arguments in the opposition, which undisputed material facts were then supported by multiple paragraphs of multiple declarations, at times by every paragraph of nearly every declaration on file." This opposition statement would have required the court and the defendants to sift through many thousands of pages of materials to determine the factual basis for Perth's contentions. The judge issued an order requiring Perth to comply with CRC 3.1350 and gave them several opportunities to remedy the defective separate statement. They failed to do so. The judge has discretion under CCP § 437c(b)(3) to grant Dunne Properties' summary judgment motion based on Perth's noncompliant separate statement. Rush v. White Corp., 13 Cal.App.5th 1086, 1088, 221 Cal.Rptr.3d 240, 241 (2017).

B. Summary Adjudication

1. Grounds for Motion

A motion for summary adjudication may be filed as a separate motion or as an alternative to a motion for summary judgment. CCP § 437c(f)(2). The motion for summary adjudication is resolved "in all procedural respects" in the same manner as a summary judgment motion. Id. Summary adjudication motions may be brought only on the following limited grounds:

- A cause of action has no merit or there is no defense to a cause of action;
- An affirmative defense to a cause of action has no merit;
- A claim for punitive damages under Cal. Civ. Code § 3294 has no merit; or
- A defendant did or did not owe a duty to the plaintiff.

CCP § 437c(f)(1). Motions for summary adjudication may be filed more than once in an action. CCP § 437c(a)(4).

2. Effect of Granting of Motion

If the trial court grants summary adjudication on one or more of the above matters, the prevailing party no longer needs to present evidence on that matter at trial. The motion must completely dispose of the matter to which it is addressed.

3. ***Compare Federal Procedure***

"Partial summary judgment" under FRCP 56(a) is the counterpart of California's summary adjudication. Unlike the California statute, FRCP 56(a) does not limit the specific issues on which a party is authorized to move for partial summary judgment.

4. **Illustration**

Phyre filed suit in Lake County Superior Court against her former attorney Daryl for legal malpractice. Daryl had represented Phyre in a lawsuit she filed against her previous business partners. In the subsequent malpractice complaint, Phyre sought two items of compensatory damages based on Daryl's alleged negligence: recovery of the unreasonably high settlement amount Daryl negotiated for her to pay to her former partners; and "lost opportunities" that she did not pursue based on Daryl's faulty legal advice. Daryl subsequently filed a motion for summary adjudication to dispose of the claim for lost opportunity damages. Summary adjudication is not appropriate, and the court should deny the motion. Summary adjudication of a claim for damages is permitted only on the issue of punitive damages, not compensatory damages. CCP § 437c(f)(1). Moreover, adjudication of Phyre's lost opportunity damages claim would not completely dispose of the cause of action for legal malpractice. DeCastro West Chodorow & Burns, Inc. v. Superior Court, 47 Cal.App.4th 410, 54 Cal.Rptr.2d 792 (1996).

VIII. RELIEF FROM ORDERS AND JUDGMENTS

A trial court may relieve a party from an order or judgment under limited circumstances.

A. Discretionary Versus Mandatory Relief

1. Discretionary Relief: Party Fault

Under CCP § 473(b), a party or its legal representative may move the court to set aside or vacate a judgment, dismissal, order, or other proceeding (e.g., entry of default) "taken against him or her through his or her mistake, inadvertence, surprise, or excusable neglect." Attorney fault is imputed to the client. Relief under this segment of section 473(b) is discretionary. The motion must be brought "within a reasonable time, in no case exceeding six months" after the judgment or proceeding was taken. CCP § 473(b). Hence, an application for relief may be well within the six-month time limit but still be deemed untimely if the court determines that it was not diligently filed. Benjamin v. Dalmo Manufacturing Co., 31 Cal.2d 523, 190 P.2d 593 (1948). The motion must be accompanied by a copy of the answer or other pleading the moving party intends to file if the motion is granted.

2. Mandatory Relief: Attorney Fault

If a party's motion is accompanied by an affidavit from an attorney attesting to the attorney's mistake, inadvertence, surprise, or neglect (excusable or not), the court *must* set aside any resulting default judgment or judgment of dismissal entered against the party. CCP § 473(b). The rationale behind this provision is "to alleviate the hardship on parties who lose their day in court due solely to an inexcusable failure to act on the part of their attorneys." Zamora v. Clayborn Contracting Group, Inc., 28 Cal.4th 249, 257, 121 Cal.Rptr.2d 187, 193, 47 P.3d 1056 (2002). If the motion is made within six months of the entry of judgment, and the attorney's affidavit demonstrates that the judgment was actually caused by his conduct, relief from the judgment is mandatory. The court will require the attorney to pay reasonable legal fees and costs to the opposing counsel or parties. CCP § 473(b).

B. Void Judgments and Orders

CCP § 473(d) permits the court to set aside any void judgment or order upon a noticed motion by a party. In addition, the court has inherent power to set aside a judgment void on its face. A judgment or order is void if the court had no power or jurisdiction to enter the judgment or grant the relief.

C. Stipulated Vacation of Judgment

A trial court may vacate a judgment in order to "amend and control its process and orders so as to make them conform to law and justice." CCP § 128(a)(8). An appellate court, however, may not reverse or vacate a judgment based on stipulation of the parties unless: (1) "There is no reasonable possibility that the interests of nonparties or the public will be adversely affected by the reversal"; and (2) "The reasons of the parties for requesting reversal outweigh the erosion of public trust that may result from the nullification of a judgment and the risk that the availability of stipulated reversal will reduce the incentive for pretrial settlement." Id. The statutory language creates a presumption against stipulated reversals. Hardisty v. Hinton & Alfert, 124 Cal.App.4th 999, 21 Cal.Rptr.3d 835 (2004).

D. *Compare Federal Procedure*

FRCP 60 is similar to CCP § 473(b). In federal court, a party may be relieved from a final judgment, order, or proceeding on account of the following:

- mistake, inadvertence, surprise or excusable neglect;
- newly discovered evidence;
- fraud, misrepresentation or misconduct by the opposing party;
- void judgment;
- the judgment has been satisfied, released or discharged, the judgment is based on an earlier judgment that has been reversed or vacated, or applying the judgment prospectively is no longer equitable; or
- any other reason that justifies relief.

FRCP 60(b). In contrast to the California statute, FRCP 60 does not compel mandatory relief from judgment in the event an attorney attests to his fault. All motions under FRCP 60(b) must be made within a reasonable time, and motions made on the first three grounds listed in FRCP 60(b) may be made no more than one year after the entry of the judgment or order or the date of the proceeding. FRCP 60(c)(1); and Coney Island Auto Parts Unlimited, Inc. v. Burton, 607 U.S. ___, 146 S.Ct. 579, ___ L.Ed.2d ___ (2026). FRCP 60(d)(1) also acknowledges that the rule does not limit the district court's power to "entertain an independent action to relieve a party from a judgment, order, or proceeding." FRCP 54(b) authorizes the district court to revise a nonfinal order at any time before final judgment is entered.

E. Illustration

Avery was an overworked first-year associate at the nepotistic law firm of Smith, Smith, Smith, Smith & Smith, LLP, in Carpinteria. Avery was assigned to prepare a CCP § 998 offer on behalf of the firm's client, Paprika, who was suing Death Wish Cigarette, Gun, Alcohol and Explosives Emporium in Santa Barbara County Superior Court. The section 998 offer was supposed to propose settlement in favor of Paprika for $2,000,000. However, Avery inadvertently proposed settlement *against* Paprika for $2,000,000. Death Wish jumped at the offer, and the trial court entered judgment accordingly. Paprika fired the Smith firm and sought immediate discretionary relief from the judgment under CCP § 473(b). The trial court will likely exercise its discretion to grant the motion because the judgment was entered due to Avery's mistake and excusable neglect (which are imputed to his client Paprika), and the motion was timely filed. However, unless Avery filed an affidavit attesting to his neglect, the court was not *required* to set aside the judgment. Zamora v. Clayborn Contracting Group, Inc., 28 Cal.4th 249, 121 Cal.Rptr.2d 187, 47 P.3d 1056 (2002).

CHAPTER 5

SAMPLE EXAM QUESTIONS

OBJECTIVE QUESTIONS

The questions in this section are based on the following hypothetical:

Mia was fired from her job in Portola as a technician in the bottling department of Swill Beverage Co. (known for its ubiquitous advertising slogan, "Swill is Swell!"). Mia sued Swill in Plumas County Superior Court for wrongful termination based on sex discrimination, under California's Fair Employment and Housing Act (FEHA). She seeks compensatory damages of $40,000.

---

(1) Mia's lawsuit is placed within the court's "Fast Track" system, pursuant to the Trial Court Delay Reduction Act. This system is:

a. Applicable only in unlimited civil cases;

b. Inapplicable in domestic relations, juvenile, probate and wrongful termination cases;

c. Intended to ensure that all nonexempt civil cases are disposed of within two years after filing;

d. Intended to weed out unmeritorious cases during the early stages of a lawsuit.

(2) True or False: Assume that Mia's attorney failed to appear for three case management conferences after receiving notice and being ordered by the court to attend. Despite the attorney's misconduct, the trial court may not dismiss Mia's action as a sanction.

(3) Mia wishes to voluntarily dismiss her lawsuit. The dismissal:

a. May be filed without seeking leave of court after the court's tentative ruling granting Swill's motion for summary judgment;

b. May be entered upon oral or written request to the court at any time before commencement of the trial;

c. Is always without prejudice;

d. Both b and c.

(4) Assume that Mia's action is governed by California's diligent prosecution statutes. Those statutes:

a. Provide that the judge has discretion to dismiss the case if Mia has not brought it to trial within two years of the filing of the complaint;

b. Provide that the judge must dismiss the case if Mia has not brought it to trial within five years of the filing of the complaint;

c. Set out absolute time limits that are not subject to expansion or tolling;

d. Both a and b.

(5) Assume that Swill has not filed a response to the complaint and the court has entered its default. Before obtaining a default judgment against Swill, Mia must:

a. Give Swill notice of the court's prove-up hearing;

b. Re-serve Swill with the complaint;

c. Serve Swill with a statement of damages noting the amount of compensatory damages sought;

d. None of the above.

(6) Assume that the court enters a default judgment against Swill. Swill wishes to submit a motion for relief from the judgment, accompanied by an affidavit provided by its attorney stating that the default judgment occurred because the attorney neglected to calendar the deadline for filing Swill's answer. The motion:

a. Must be filed within a reasonable time after the entry of judgment, but in no case later than six months after entry of judgment;

b. Will be granted in the court's discretion as long as it is timely and the attorney's neglect was excusable;

c. Must be granted as long as it is timely, even if the attorney's negligence was inexcusable;

d. Must be accompanied by the answer to the complaint that Swill proposes to file.

(7) True or False: Summary adjudication is an appropriate motion for Swill to bring against Mia if Swill contends that Mia owed Swill a duty as an employee to use her best efforts to complete her work tasks.

(8) If Swill brings a motion for summary judgment against Mia, Swill must:

a. Serve the notice of motion and supporting papers on Mia at least 81 days before the hearing;

b. Have its motion heard at least 20 days before the scheduled trial date;

c. Satisfy its burden of persuasion before the burden shifts to Mia to show a triable issue of material fact;

d. Serve a separate statement of disputed material facts and the evidence supporting those facts.

(9) Mia wishes to make a CCP § 998 offer of judgment to Swill. Which of the following is NOT true about a section 998 offer of judgment?

a. Mia's section 998 offer must be submitted in writing;

b. Mia may expressly revoke her section 998 offer at any time prior to Swill's acceptance;

c. Mia may not make a section 998 offer because only defendants may make such offers;

d. If Mia's section 998 offer is not accepted before trial or within 30 days of the offer, whichever is earliest, it is deemed withdrawn.

(10) True or False: Assume that Mia's employment agreement requires her to arbitrate any dispute she might have with Swill. The court will not enforce the arbitration agreement between Mia and Swill because statutory FEHA claims must be adjudicated only by a court, not in arbitration.

(11) True or False: If the dispute between Mia and Swill is arbitrated, Mia may request the superior court to vacate the resulting arbitration award if the face of the award contains a material error that causes substantial injustice to Mia.

(12) True or False: Any dispute regarding whether Mia's claims against Swill are arbitrable under the arbitration agreement will be determined by the arbitrator, unless the agreement requires that determination to be made by the court.

(13) True or False: If the court submits Mia's action to judicial arbitration, the court may not also require that Mia and Swill participate in court-annexed mediation.

Answers to Objective Questions

(1) **c.** California's "Fast Track" case management system sets the goal that 100% of nonexempt limited and unlimited civil cases should be resolved within two years of filing. CRC 3.714(b). Answer (a) is incorrect because Fast Track applies to both unlimited and limited civil cases. Answer (b) is incorrect because, while juvenile, probate, and domestic relations cases are statutorily excluded from Fast Track requirements, wrongful termination cases are not. Cal. Gov't Code § 68608(a). Answer (d) is incorrect because no evaluation of the merit of the action is undertaken as part of the Fast Track procedures.

(2) **True.** If the failure to comply with the court orders to appear at the conferences is the fault of Mia's attorney and not of Mia, the court may not dismiss Mia's case as a sanction. CCP § 575.2(b). Additionally, the court may order dismissal only if it appears that less severe sanctions would not be effective. Cal. Gov't Code § 68608(b).

(3) **b.** Voluntary dismissals may be entered at any time prior to commencement of trial upon written or oral request to the court. CCP § 581(b)(1).

(4) **d.** Both (a) and (b) are correct. Subject to statutory tolling provisions, if Mia fails to bring her case to trial two years after the action was filed, the court has discretion to dismiss it. CCP § 583.420(a)(2)(B); CRC 3.1340. The court must dismiss the action if it is not brought to trial within five years. CCP §§ 583.310 & 583.360. Answer (c) is incorrect because the diligent prosecution statutes allow for expansion or tolling of the deadlines under specific circumstances.

(5) **d.** None of these requirements applies to Mia's action. Answer (c) is incorrect because Mia is not required to serve a statement of damages on Swill under CCP § 425.11; her action is not one for personal injury or wrongful death.

(6) **c.** If a timely motion to set aside the judgment is accompanied by a declaration attesting that the judgment was the result of the attorney's fault (including inexcusable neglect), the court must grant the motion. CCP § 473(b). Answers (a), (b), and (d) refer to requirements for discretionary relief.

(7) **False.** Summary adjudication may be used to adjudicate whether Swill (the defendant) owes Mia (the plaintiff) a duty, but not to adjudicate whether Mia owes Swill a duty. CCP § 437c(f)(1).

(8) **a.** Swill must file its motion at least 81 days before date of the hearing. CCP § 437c(a)(2). Answer (b) is incorrect because the motion must be heard at least 30 days before the scheduled trial date. Answer (c) is incorrect because the burden of persuasion always remains with the moving party; it is the burden of production that may shift to Mia. Answer (d) is incorrect because Swill must submit with its motion a separate statement of *undisputed* material facts. CCP § 437c(b)(1).

(9) **c.** Either party may make a written section 998 offer in California. CCP § 998(b). In contrast, FRCP 68 permits only a defendant to make an offer of judgment. Answers (a), (b), and (d) accurately describe California's section 998 procedures.

(10) **False.** FEHA and other statutory claims may be subject to contractual arbitration as long as: (a) the agreement provides for neutral arbitrators; (b) the agreement does not limit the type of relief available or the scope or amount of any remedies; (c) Mia and Swill are afforded adequate opportunity for discovery; (d) the agreement provides for a written award that, under the appropriate circumstances, may be subject to judicial review; and (e) in requiring Mia and other employees to submit to arbitration, the agreement does not require Mia to pay costs and arbitration fees beyond what she would have to pay in a court proceeding. Ramirez v. Charter Communications, Inc., 16 Cal.5th 478, 322 Cal.Rptr.3d 825, 551 P.3d 520 (2024); and Armendariz v. Foundation

Health Psychcare Services, Inc., 24 Cal.4th 83, 99 Cal.Rptr.2d 745, 6 P.3d 669 (2000).

(11) **False.** The arbitration award may be vacated on very limited grounds, including that the arbitrator exceeded his powers. CCP § 1286.2. Normally, error by the arbitrator is not one of those grounds, even if the error is material and substantially prejudices Mia. Judicial review on the ground of arbitrator error may be obtained only if the arbitration clause contained an express and unambiguous statement that the arbitrator will be deemed to have exceeded his powers if he committed an error of law or fact.

(12) **False.** The question of arbitrability will be resolved by the court, unless the arbitration agreement clearly designates that the arbitrator will decide.

(13) **True.** The court may not order cases that it has referred to judicial arbitration into mediation. CCP § 1775.4.

ESSAY QUESTION

Jerry was employed as a mechanical engineer for 30 years. During that time, he worked for several employers on numerous job sites, including eight years on naval vessels in San Diego. Shortly after his retirement, Jerry discovered he had mesothelioma, a type of cancer caused by exposure to asbestos fibers. Jerry filed a product liability action in San Diego County Superior Court against Largely Avoidable Contamination, Inc. (LAC), a manufacturer and supplier of asbestos to the U.S. Navy during the time Jerry was working on naval ships. Jerry is seeking $500,000 in general damages, $250,000 in special damages, including medical costs, and an additional $1,000,000 in punitive damages.

LAC immediately noticed Jerry's deposition. During the deposition, Jerry admitted that while he had heard of LAC, he did not know whether LAC had manufactured the asbestos he was exposed to on the naval vessels, and he could not remember ever receiving any shipments of LAC products.

Immediately following Jerry's deposition, LAC sent Jerry an email offering to settle the case for $10,000 pursuant to CCP § 998. The offer was kept open for 30 days. Further, LAC immediately filed and served a summary judgment motion based on Jerry's testimony at the deposition.

Please analyze the following issues:

(1) Has LAC made a proper section 998 offer of judgment? Assuming that the offer is proper, what is required of Jerry to accept the section 998 offer?

(2) What are the consequences to Jerry if he rejects or fails to respond to the section 998 offer of judgment and then recovers nothing at trial?

(3) What is the likelihood that the court will grant LAC's summary judgment motion?

Answer to Essay Question

(1) Section 998 Offer of Judgment

- Requirements for offer: must be in writing; must specify that the offer is made pursuant to CCP § 998; and must be made at least ten days before the start of trial. It must contain the offer itself and the terms of the judgment, and it must include a provision that allows Jerry to indicate his acceptance by signing a statement of acceptance. CCP § 998(b).
  - Here, LAC has made a written offer expressly under section 998. An email constitutes a writing. The statute does not require a signed offer.
  - It is not known from the facts whether the offer includes a provision regarding Jerry's acceptance of the offer.
  - The offer appears to be timely.
  - Is the offer token or nominal? Given the doubt about whether LAC manufactured the asbestos in question, LAC's offer probably reflects its good faith belief in its lack of liability because Jerry may not be able to prove causation.
- Acceptance of offer:
  - Jerry must make an unequivocal acceptance of the offer in writing, signed by his attorney. The acceptance must be filed with the court and must be communicated to LAC before the time for acceptance expires.

(2) Failure to Accept Section 998 Offer

- If Jerry does not respond to the offer within 30 days, the offer is deemed withdrawn. If Jerry intends to reject the offer, he must do so in an unequivocal writing within 30 days.
  - If Jerry rejects or does not respond to the offer, and he then fails to obtain a more favorable judgment at the trial, Jerry may not recover his postoffer costs, and he must pay LAC's costs from the time of the offer. The court also has discretion to award expert witness fees and costs to LAC. CCP § 998(c)(1).
  - LAC's costs are deducted from Jerry's judgment. If LAC's costs exceed Jerry's judgment, the court will enter judgment for LAC in the net amount. CCP § 998(e).

- More favorable judgment at trial: Jerry must actually obtain more than the amount of the section 998 offer. Here, Jerry would have to recover more than $10,000.
- The postoffer costs Jerry might be required to pay include:
    - Filing costs
    - Service of process costs
    - Cost of making motions
    - Cost of deposition transcripts
    - Fees for appearances and travel of lay witnesses
- Expert witness fees:
    - CCP § 998(c)(1) makes an award of expert witness fees to LAC discretionary.

(3) <u>Summary Judgment Motion</u>

- Standard: LAC must show that the action has no merit by establishing that there is no triable issue of material fact and that LAC is entitled to judgment as a matter of law.
    - Burden: LAC has the burden of persuasion throughout the process. LAC also has the initial burden of production to make a prima facie showing that the sole cause of action for product liability has no merit.
        - A cause of action has no merit when one or more elements cannot be established. Here, LAC will likely focus on the element of causation.
        - LAC may meet its burden of production by showing that despite an adequate opportunity for discovery, Jerry's discovery responses are factually devoid. Alternatively, LAC may affirmatively negate the causation element with evidence of its own.
        - LAC's motion must be supported by evidence and must include a separate statement of undisputed material facts.
        - If LAC satisfies its burden of production, the burden shifts to Jerry to produce evidence establishing a triable issue of material fact. Jerry must submit a separate statement in response to LAC's separate statement.
- Application:
    - Jerry admitted during his deposition that he does not know whether LAC manufactured the asbestos to which he was

exposed. Moreover, Jerry had many jobs where he could have been exposed to asbestos.

- LAC will likely offer Jerry's factually devoid deposition testimony as evidence that there is no triable issue with regard to the element of causation. The burden of production will then shift to Jerry to provide evidence to show LAC's products actually caused his injuries.
- Unless Jerry can provide such evidence, LAC will likely prevail on summary judgment.

CHAPTER 6

TRIAL

I. SETTING TRIAL DATE

A. Trial Setting Conference

The court must conduct an initial case management conference within 180 days of the filing of the complaint. CRC 3.721 & 3.722. The case may be set for trial at the initial conference, but it is more likely that trial setting will occur at a later conference scheduled at the court's discretion. CRC 3.723. In setting a case for trial, the court must consider a variety of factors listed in CRC 3.729, including the number of parties in the action, the complexity of the issues, and the amount of discovery yet to be conducted.

B. Trial Setting Preference

Some parties are entitled to preference in trial setting, such as those over the age of 70, those with a terminal illness, and those under the age of 14 claiming wrongful death or personal injury damages. CCP § 36.

II. OBTAINING A JURY TRIAL

A. Right to Trial by Jury

The right to a jury trial is one of the fundamental rights afforded to litigants in a court action. As guaranteed by the California Constitution, "[t]rial by jury is an inviolate right and shall be secured to all." Cal. Const., art. I, § 16. The jury trial right is also provided by statute. See CCP § 631(a) ("The right to a trial by jury * * * shall be preserved to the parties inviolate."). The Seventh Amendment of the United States Constitution is not applicable to the states and thus does not govern the right to a jury trial in civil actions in state court.

1. When Right Attaches: Historical Approach

In deciding whether the right to a jury trial attaches under the California Constitution, California courts have adhered to a historical approach, assessing whether a jury right existed at common law in 1850, the year in which the jury trial provision was first included in the California Constitution. Thus, if an action would have been subject to a right to a jury trial at common law (including English common law) in 1850, then there is a constitutional right to a jury trial for that action today in California's courts. Nationwide Biweekly Administration, Inc. v. Superior Court, 9 Cal.5th 279, 261 Cal.Rptr.3d 713, 462 P.3d 461 (2020). In recognition of the fact that the law has evolved and new causes of action have come into being since 1850, the right to a jury has been "extended to cases of like nature as may afterwards arise." Franchise Tax Board v. Superior Court, 51 Cal.4th 1006, 125 Cal.Rptr.3d 158, 252 P.3d 450 (2011).

a. Law Versus Equity

Generally, a litigant is entitled to a jury in civil actions at law but not in actions in equity. "The form of relief sought in the complaint is a reliable indicator whether the action is legal or equitable." Valley Crest Landscape Development, Inc. v. Mission Pools of Escondido, Inc., 238 Cal.App.4th 468, 491, 189 Cal.Rptr.3d 259, 278 (2015) (express indemnity claim seeking monetary damages was considered legal issue, entitling cross-defendant to jury trial). Actions that are statutorily deemed *legal*, and thus within the domain of the jury, include those for:

- recovery of specific, real, or personal property;
- money due under a contract;
- damages for breach of contract;
- damages for fraud;
- damages for negligence;
- damages for injury to real or personal property; and
- damages for violation of a statute.

CCP § 592.

Matters that are considered *equitable*, and thus subject to trial by the court, include:

- requests for injunctive relief;
- specific performance of a contract;
- petitions to compel arbitration;
- rescission of a contract;
- damages or relief under the doctrine of promissory estoppel;

- paternity actions; and
- defenses such as claim or issue preclusion and equitable estoppel.

1) "Gist of the Action"

In many actions, there is a mix of legal and equitable issues and causes of action. If these issues are intertwined to such a degree that they cannot reasonably be separated, the court will employ the "gist of the action" test in its historical analysis. When the action deals mainly with ordinary common law rights that would have been tried to a jury in 1850, it is an action at law and a jury right generally exists. Conversely, if the action depends primarily on the application of equitable doctrines, no jury right attaches. *Nationwide Biweekly Administration*, 9 Cal.5th at 318, 261 Cal.Rptr.3d at 738–739, 462 P.3d 461.

2) "Equity First" Rule

If the issues are severable, the court can hold separate nonjury and jury phases. California ordinarily follows the "equity first" rule—equitable causes of action are tried first by the court, followed by legal causes of action tried by the jury. But this rule is not rigid. A court has discretion to decide whether to try the equitable or legal issues first. Cal. Evid. Code § 320; and Darbun Enterprises, Inc. v. San Fernando Community Hospital, 238 Cal.App.4th 399, 191 Cal.Rptr.3d 340 (2015). This choice can impact the case in at least two ways: (a) the decision rendered in the first phase may render the second phase moot; and (b) findings of fact made during the first phase are binding on the trier of fact during the second phase.

3) Equitable "Clean-Up" Doctrine

California observes the equitable clean-up doctrine, which precludes the right to a jury trial in actions in which the legal issues are "incidental" to the equitable issues. Benach v. County of Los Angeles, 149 Cal.App.4th 836, 57 Cal.Rptr.3d 363 (2007).

b. *Compare Federal Procedure*

One of the most salient differences between the California and the federal systems is the derivation of the right to a jury trial. The Seventh Amendment to the U.S.

Constitution provides: "In Suits at common law, where the value in controversy shall exceed twenty dollars, the right of trial by jury shall be preserved * * *." However, since this amendment has not been applied to the states, the California right to a jury in civil trials derives from the state Constitution only. There is no need to follow U.S. Supreme Court precedent interpreting the Seventh Amendment. Although the U.S. Supreme Court revised the historical test starting in the late 1950s, and expanded the right to trial by jury, the California Supreme Court has adhered to its own long-standing historical test. When an action in federal court involves both equitable and legal issues, the jury will almost always hear the legal issues first. As a result of the expansion of the jury right, the federal system has also rejected the equitable clean-up doctrine; no legal issues are considered "incidental." While there are many differences between the federal and California jury trial rights, there is one important similarity: the U.S. Congress and the California Legislature each have the power to create the right to a jury trial by statute for additional causes of action, such as those in equity or in special proceedings.

c. Illustration

While driving on the Golden Gate Bridge, careless driver Daisy was talking on her cell phone and trying to add low calorie sweetener to her half-caff, no foam, double shot, extra hot, ultra-super grande, vanilla-hazelnut latte with extra whipped cream and chocolate shavings. Immersed in her multitude of tasks, she forgot to keep an eye on the road and she ran into the back of Paddy's car. Both Paddy and Daisy were uninjured, but Paddy's car sustained $3000 in damage, which was not covered by his auto insurance. Paddy sued Daisy in the small claims division of the Marin County Superior Court to recover the cost of repairs. Judgment was entered for Paddy. In response to Daisy's small claims appeal (i.e., trial de novo request) in the superior court, Paddy demanded a jury trial, even though the small claims statutes do not provide for one. The court must deny his demand. While damages for negligence are considered legal in nature, and thus triable by jury, a jury trial was typically not available under English common law for small monetary claims such as Paddy's at the time of the ratification of the California Constitution. Because cases involving small sums of money were usually adjudicated by juryless tribunals in

> 1850, Paddy has no constitutional right to a jury in either the small claims division or in the trial de novo in superior court. Crouchman v. Superior Court, 45 Cal.3d 1167, 248 Cal.Rptr. 626, 755 P.2d 1075 (1988).

2. Securing a Jury

a. Jury Demand

A party must make a timely and proper demand for a trial by jury. A demand is considered timely if it is made at the time the cause is first set for trial, or within five days after notice of setting if the trial date is set without notice or stipulation. CCP § 631(f)(4). This demand requires only that the party announce, either in writing or orally, that a jury is wanted. Once this demand has been properly made, it applies to the original trial and any subsequent retrials that may occur. In addition to making a timely demand, a party must post jury fees in advance of the trial. CCP § 631(b)–(c). Starting on the second day of trial, and every day thereafter, the party must provide another deposit equal to that day's jury fees. CCP § 631(e).

b. Waiver of Jury Trial Right

The California Constitution provides that a party may waive the right to a jury. Cal. Const., art. I, § 16. Waiver may occur in several ways, including: failing to appear at trial; filing written consent to a bench trial with the court clerk; orally consenting to waiver in open court; failing to make a timely demand for a jury; and failing to deposit jury fees on time. CCP § 631(f). The means of waiver can be created only by the Legislature. Grafton Partners L.P. v. Superior Court, 36 Cal.4th 944, 32 Cal.Rptr.3d 5, 116 P.3d 479 (2005) (predispute waiver of right to jury in a court trial is not enforceable). In contrast, a party may waive the right to a jury by agreeing to a valid contract clause providing for binding arbitration in place of a trial in court if a dispute arises. Armendariz v. Foundation Health Psychcare Services, Inc., 24 Cal.4th 83, 99 Cal.Rptr.2d 745, 6 P.3d 669 (2000). A party may also waive the right to a jury by entering into a contract with a valid forum selection clause providing for litigation in a jurisdiction that does not afford civil litigants the same right to trial by jury as litigants in California courts enjoy. EpicentRx, Inc. v. Superior Court, 18 Cal.5th 58, 334 Cal.Rptr.3d 702, 572 P.3d 1 (2025).

c. Relief from Waiver

Even if a party waives the right to a jury, deliberately or inadvertently, the court may grant relief from this waiver. CCP § 631(g). Though left to the discretion of the court, California has a policy favoring relief from waiver of the jury right. In general, such a motion will be granted unless it would create substantial hardship to the opposing party. Boal v. Price Waterhouse & Co., 165 Cal.App.3d 806, 212 Cal.Rptr. 42 (1985).

d. Expedited Jury Trial

California permits parties to a pending lawsuit to choose to conduct an expedited jury trial. CCP § 630.01 et seq.; CRC 3.1545 et seq. The expedited process imposes strict limits on length of trial (three hours per side), number of jurors (eight or fewer), and number of peremptory challenges (three per side). It also restricts the ability to bring motions for directed verdict, JNOV and new trial. The verdict is binding and not subject to appeal except upon very narrow grounds. To use the expedited jury trial process, the parties must agree to a "high/low" figure for damages, where the plaintiff is ensured of a minimum recovery and the defendant knows its maximum potential liability. The jury is not made aware of the high/low calculation.

e. *Compare Federal Procedure*

FRCP 38(b) requires a party to serve a timely written demand for a jury trial or else the right is waived. A party may waive the right to a jury by stipulation of the parties (FRCP 39(a)(1)), or the parties may withdraw a jury demand by consent (FRCP 38(d)). The court may reinstate a jury trial after a waiver (FRCP 39(b)), but federal courts are less generous than California courts in restoring a jury trial after an inadvertent waiver. There is no specific federal counterpart in the FRCP to California's expedited jury trial procedure. However, federal judges may conduct a summary jury trial if authorized by local rule. FRCP 16(c)(2)(I).

f. Illustration

Preston sued Darlene for breach of contract damages in Alpine County Superior Court. Preston demanded a jury trial. Before trial was to begin, Preston was required to submit various trial documents to Darlene and to the

> court, pursuant to a local court rule. When Preston failed to comply, the court deemed his jury trial demand waived and set the matter for a bench trial. The court lacked authority to take this action. CCP § 631(f) provides the exclusive grounds for waiver or forfeiture of the right to jury trial. "Failure to prepare trial documents in accordance with local rules does not fall within any of the means of waiver specified in section 631." A waiver that does not fit into one of the statutory grounds is unenforceable. Amato v. Downs, 78 Cal.App.5th 435, 445, 293 Cal.Rptr.3d 682, 689 (2022).

B. Stages of Jury Selection

1. Jury Pool

Each year, the jury commissioner of every county superior court must compile a master list of names from which the court may summon potential jurors for jury duty. CCP § 198(b). Prospective jurors for the master list may be chosen from any sources that will provide a "representative cross section of the population of the area served by the court." CCP § 197(a). At a minimum, a representative cross section can be derived by selecting names of potential jurors from voter registration lists, Department of Motor Vehicles lists, and lists of resident state tax filers. CCP § 197(b)(2). The master list is then narrowed down to eliminate persons not qualified for jury service. CCP § 198(c). Those disqualified from jury service include noncitizens, minors, incarcerated persons, and conservatees. CCP § 203(a). Those persons on the qualified juror list are eligible to be summoned at random to appear for jury service.

2. Jury Venire

When prospective jurors are summoned from the jury pool to the court for possible jury service, they may request postponement of jury service or may seek to be excused from service based on "undue hardship." CCP § 204(b). Acceptable hardship excuses include lack of reasonably available transportation, extreme financial burden, and risk of mental or physical harm. CRC 2.1008(d). The summoned jurors who remain for potential selection after the court grants postponements and hardship excuses constitute the jury venire.

3. Jury Panel

When a particular superior court department or courtroom has a need for jurors, a group of prospective jurors is randomly assigned from the venire and sent to the courtroom to undergo voir dire. CCP § 194(q). (Voir dire is discussed in section II(D)(1), below.) Before voir dire commences, the entire panel is sworn. It is from the jury panel that the actual jurors who will hear the case will be selected.

4. Petit Jury

Those members of the jury panel who are not excused during voir dire become the members of the petit jury before whom the action is tried. The petit jury may also include alternate jurors.

C. Composition of Jury Venire

1. Representative Cross Section of Community

The California Supreme Court has interpreted the constitutional right to a jury trial under article 1, section 16, to mean that a party is entitled to a jury drawn from a representative cross section of the community. Williams v. Superior Court, 49 Cal.3d 736, 263 Cal.Rptr. 503, 781 P.2d 537 (1989). This requirement is also statutory. CCP § 204(a). At each stage of the jury selection process, persons from distinctive or cognizable groups within the community may not be systematically excluded. People v. Anderson, 25 Cal.4th 543, 106 Cal.Rptr.2d 575, 22 P.3d 347 (2001). California courts apply the standards developed in criminal cases under the Sixth Amendment to civil cases, too, because the entire jury trial right is guaranteed in that one provision of the state Constitution. California law is sometimes more strict than federal law, but it cannot be less strict.

2. Test for Violation of Representative Cross Section Requirement

To establish a prima facie showing that the representative cross section requirement has been violated, a party must satisfy a three-pronged test:

- The excluded group is a distinctive or cognizable group in the community;
- The representation of this group in the jury venire is not "fair and reasonable" when compared to the number of such persons in the community; and
- The underrepresentation is due to systematic exclusion of that group in the process of jury selection.

Duren v. Missouri, 439 U.S. 357, 99 S.Ct. 664, 58 L.Ed.2d 579 (1979). If the objecting party establishes a prima facie case under this test, the burden shifts to the opposing party to provide a more precise statistical showing that no significant disparity exists, or a compelling justification for the procedure that has resulted in the disparity. People v. Burgener, 29 Cal.4th 833, 129 Cal.Rptr.2d 747, 62 P.3d 1 (2003).

a. **Prong 1: Cognizable or Distinctive Group**

In the context of challenging the jury venire, a group is considered cognizable or distinctive if: (1) the members of the group "share a common perspective arising from their life experience in the group"; and (2) "no other members of the community are capable of adequately representing the perspective of the group." People v. Garcia, 77 Cal.App.4th 1269, 1276–1279, 92 Cal.Rptr.2d 339, 343–345 (2000). In general, groups based on race, gender and religion have been considered cognizable. California also recognizes groups based on sexual orientation as distinctive. Id. In contrast, characteristics such as age and socioeconomic status are insufficient to establish a cognizable group when a party challenges the venire. (Compare the more expansive categories of cognizable groups for the purpose of exercising peremptory challenges during voir dire; see section II(D)(2)(b), below.)

b. **Prong 2: Fair and Reasonable Representation**

1) **Tests for Measuring Disparity**

California courts currently use two tests for measuring underrepresentation. The "absolute disparity" test calculates the difference between the group's percentage in the jury-eligible population and the group's percentage in the jury venire. For example, if African Americans comprise 5 percent of the eligible population but only 3 percent of the jury venire, the absolute disparity would be 2 percent (5% – 3% = 2%). The "comparative disparity" test calculates the percentage by which the number in the jury venire is below the number in the jury-eligible population. This figure is calculated by taking the absolute disparity and dividing it by the jury-eligible population. Returning to the above example, the comparative disparity would be 40 percent (2% ÷ 5% = 40%).

2) **Problems with Disparity Tests**

The courts have failed to establish a clear threshold for when a disparity becomes impermissible. The California Supreme Court has ruled that absolute disparities between 2.7 percent and 4.3 percent and comparative disparities between 23.5 percent and 37.4 percent are allowable. People v. Ramos, 15 Cal.4th 1133, 64 Cal.Rptr.2d 892, 938 P.2d 950 (1997). Both the absolute and comparative disparity tests have been criticized for statistically distorting the underrepresentation of the excluded group.

3) **Definition of Community**

For the purpose of the fair and reasonable representation requirement, the term "community" refers to the judicial district in which the case is tried. "Community" does not necessarily refer to the entire county in which the court sits or the location of the incident that gave rise to the suit. Williams v. Superior Court, 49 Cal.3d 736, 263 Cal.Rptr. 503, 781 P.2d 537 (1989). For example, each of the 12 judicial districts within the Los Angeles County Superior Court is considered a "community" for purposes of this test.

c. **Prong 3: Systematic Exclusion**

Statistical proof of a disparity in prong 2 does not, in itself, satisfy the objecting party's burden of proof. To establish a violation of the representative cross section requirement, the objecting party must also prove that the disparity is the product of an improper feature of the jury selection process. The party may show that the criteria for selection are not random or neutral. If the criteria are neutral, the challenging party may attempt to establish that they are applied in a constitutionally impermissible way that accounts for the disparity. People v. Burgener, 29 Cal.4th 833, 129 Cal.Rptr.2d 747, 62 P.3d 1 (2003).

3. ***Compare Federal Procedure***

A federal jury must be "selected at random from a fair cross section of the community in the district or division wherein the court convenes." 28 USC § 1861. A potential juror cannot be excluded because of race, color, religion, sex, national origin, or economic status. 28 USC § 1862. Compare CCP §§ 231.5 & 231.7. One notable difference between California and federal law is the definition of "community." Under federal law, each district court may decide to adopt either a district-wide or a division-wide jury pool. 28 USC §§ 1861 & 1863. California's four U.S. district courts encompass far larger communities than the county-based ones that state superior courts draw upon.

4. Illustration

After several months of living next to his new neighbors, the Daffodils, in Mammoth Lakes, retiree Pug Pugnacious filed a nuisance suit against them in Mono County Superior Court. In the complaint, Pugnacious alleged that the Daffodils would often play music after 6 p.m. and could be heard talking in their backyard as late as 7:45 p.m. When the suit reached the jury selection stage, Pugnacious was appalled to find an absence of senior citizens in the jury venire. He moved to quash the venire on the ground that the venire did not constitute a representative cross section of the community. Pugnacious provided statistical evidence that senior citizens make up five percent of Mono County, but only four percent of the jury venire. The court will deny the motion to quash on three independently sufficient grounds. First, distinctions based on age do not establish a cognizable group when claiming that a jury venire is not composed of a representative cross section of the community. Second, the absolute disparity of one percent and comparative disparity of 20 percent are well within the acceptable range. Third, Pugnacious failed to provide proof that this disparity was a product of an impermissible feature of the jury selection process that resulted in systematic exclusion of senior citizens. Thus, Pugnacious cannot establish a violation of the fair cross section requirement. People v. Burgener, 29 Cal.4th 833, 129 Cal.Rptr.2d 747, 62 P.3d 1 (2003).

D. Composition of Petit Jury

1. Voir Dire

a. Purpose of Voir Dire

The petit jury is selected via the process known as voir dire. In Anglo-Norman (a dialect of Old French), the term "voir dire" translates as "to speak the truth." In modern French, it is translated as "to see and to say." Voir dire consists of a series of questions from the judge and counsel to the prospective jurors on the jury panel. Voir dire serves two main purposes: (1) it helps assure that the jury is fair and impartial; and (2) it aids counsel in the intelligent exercise of challenges. CCP § 222.5.

b. Conduct of Voir Dire

Before any party questions the prospective jurors, the judge usually conducts an examination after discussion with the attorneys. This inquiry largely consists of questions regarding the person's ability to serve as an impartial juror. Once the judge completes this examination, the parties have the opportunity to question the prospective jurors. The judge may exercise her discretion to set reasonable limits. CCP § 222.5; CRC 3.1540.

2. Challenges to Prospective Jurors

Challenges to prospective jurors during the voir dire phase fall into two categories: challenges for cause; and peremptory challenges. Challenges for cause are exercised first, followed by peremptory challenges. CCP § 226(c).

a. Challenges for Cause

1) Number

There is no limit to the number of challenges for cause. These challenges can be lodged either in writing or orally. CCP § 226(b).

2) Grounds

There is no limit as to the number of grounds that can be raised against a given prospective juror. There are three distinct grounds on which an attorney may exercise a challenge for cause, in the following order:

a) Challenge for General Disqualification

A prospective juror may be challenged for general disqualification if the prospective juror: (1) lacks the qualifications required by law to be a competent juror; or (2) has a disability or incapacity that renders the juror unable to perform the duties of a juror without prejudice to the challenging party. CCP § 228.

b) Challenge for Implied Bias

In some situations, the law presumes that a juror is biased and thus not fit to serve as a juror. Such circumstances include the following:

- The prospective juror is related by blood or marriage to any party, to an officer of a corporate party, or to any witness or victim in the case within the fourth degree;
- The relationship between the prospective juror and a party is of a kind listed in CCP § 229(b) (such as landlord-

tenant, employer-employee, principal-agent, or debtor-creditor);

- The prospective juror has served as a witness or juror in a trial with the same parties or involving the same offense or cause of action;
- The prospective juror has an interest in the litigation;
- The prospective juror has an unqualified belief or opinion based on knowledge of material facts; or
- The prospective juror has enmity against, or bias toward, either party.

CCP § 229.

c) Challenge for Actual Bias

A prospective juror may be challenged for actual bias when they have shown "a state of mind * * * in reference to the case, or to any of the parties, which will prevent the juror from acting with entire impartiality, and without prejudice to the substantial rights of any party." CCP § 225(b)(1)(C).

b. Peremptory Challenges

Peremptory challenges permit a party to remove prospective jurors for any reason that does not violate constitutional or statutory limitations. These challenges are often exercised to remove jurors thought to be unsympathetic or overly opinionated.

1) Number

Unlike the unlimited quantity of challenges for cause, each party gets a limited number of peremptory challenges. In most situations, each party may exercise up to six peremptory challenges. If there are more than two parties, the court will divide the parties into two or more sides and allow each side eight peremptory challenges. If there are more than two sides, the court will grant additional peremptory challenges as "the interests of justice may require." CCP § 231(c). The exercise of peremptory challenges alternates between the sides until all challenges have been used or until both sides consecutively choose not to exercise a challenge. CCP § 231(d).

2) Constitutional Limitations

While peremptory challenges may be exercised without giving a reason, they cannot be used to deliberately and systematically exclude cognizable groups from the jury. This sort of exclusion violates both the Equal Protection Clause of the Fourteenth Amendment of the United States Constitution, and the California Constitution's representative cross section requirement.

a) Test Under Equal Protection Clause of Federal Constitution

The test for a violation of the Equal Protection Clause often arises in the context of a *Batson* challenge. Batson v. Kentucky, 476 U.S. 79, 106 S.Ct. 1712, 90 L.Ed.2d 69 (1986). The objecting party has the initial burden to establish a prima facie case of discrimination by showing that the circumstances surrounding the challenge raise an inference of discrimination. Johnson v. California, 545 U.S. 162, 125 S.Ct. 2410, 162 L.Ed.2d 129 (2005). If the objecting party is successful, the burden shifts to the opponent to provide a neutral explanation for the challenge. The objecting party then has the opportunity to show that the explanation for the challenge is a pretext and that there was purposeful discrimination. Id. The court decides whether the objecting party has proven purposeful discrimination. If the appellate court finds a *Batson* violation or finds that the trial court applied an incorrect standard, it orders limited remand of the case to the trial court rather than automatic reversal of the trial court judgment. People v. Johnson, 38 Cal.4th 1096, 45 Cal.Rptr.3d 1, 136 P.3d 804 (2006). Race and gender discrimination dominate the case law in this area.

b) Test Under California Constitution

Under California law, peremptory challenges are presumed to be properly exercised. To overcome this presumption, the objecting party must: (1) create as complete a record of the circumstances surrounding the challenge as possible; (2) establish that the challenged prospective jurors were part of a cognizable group; and (3) establish a reasonable inference that the excluded jurors were challenged because they were members of the cognizable group. If the objecting party is successful is making this showing, the burden shifts to the opposing party to establish that the challenges were not the product of group bias alone. People v. Wheeler, 22 Cal.3d 258, 148 Cal.Rptr. 890, 583 P.2d 748 (1978). In contrast to a federal *Batson* challenge—where the court typically orders a limited remand—a successful *Wheeler* challenge on California constitutional grounds results in automatic reversal of the trial court judgment. People v. Johnson, 38 Cal.4th 1096, 1105, 45 Cal.Rptr.3d 1, 7, 136 P.3d 804 (2006) (Werdegar, J., concurring).

3) Statutory Limitations

In all cases to be tried by a jury in state court, "[a] party shall not use a peremptory challenge to remove a prospective juror on the basis of an assumption that the prospective juror is biased merely because of a characteristic listed or defined in [Cal. Gov't Code § 11135]." CCP § 231.5. Those characteristics include "sex, race, color, religion, ancestry, national origin, ethnic group identification, age, mental disability, physical disability, medical condition, genetic information, marital status, or sexual orientation." Cal. Gov't Code § 11135(a).

The Legislature has statutorily modified the *Wheeler/Batson* procedure for many types of cases. CCP § 231.7. Starting with criminal cases in 2021, and extended in 2026 to specified civil cases, especially civil rights actions (see CCP § 231.7(k)), the statute makes it harder for attorneys in the applicable cases to defend peremptory strikes on neutral grounds. In the cases that fall under CCP § 231.7, the trial courts will not screen challenges to peremptory strikes, as is done in those civil cases to which *Wheeler/Batson* still applies under CCP § 231.5. In CCP § 231.7 cases, attorneys who use peremptory challenges can be asked their reasons, and the proffered reasons are tested against an objective standard, rather than against a subjective standard. CCP § 231.7(d)(1). The Legislature has deemed that the objectively reasonable person "is aware that unconscious bias, in addition to purposeful discrimination, have resulted in the unfair exclusion of potential jurors in the State of California." CCP § 231.7(d)(2)(A). The statute also lists 13 ostensibly neutral reasons that are presumed to be invalid unless the party exercising the challenge can, by clear and convincing evidence, overcome the presumption by showing that the proffered reason bears on the prospective juror's ability to be fair and impartial in the particular case. CCP § 231.7(e).

3. Jury Size

Historically, the petit jury has been composed of 12 jurors. However, California law permits smaller juries in civil cases. "[T]he Legislature may provide that the jury shall consist of eight persons or a lesser number agreed on by the parties in open court." Cal. Const., art. I, § 16. See also CCP § 220.

4. *Compare Federal Procedure*

Federal voir dire, in contrast to California's procedure, is largely conducted by the judge. FRCP 47. Though federal judges may allow the attorneys to ask questions of prospective jurors, this practice is more prevalent in state court. Another notable difference is that parties in federal civil cases have only three peremptory challenges. 28 USC § 1870. The U.S. Supreme Court has found race, gender, and ethnic origin to be improper bases for peremptory challenges. The Ninth Circuit also recognizes sexual orientation as an impermissible ground for peremptory challenges. SmithKline Beecham Corp. v. Abbott Laboratories, 740 F.3d 471 (9th Cir.2014). Finally, FRCP 48 sets the number of jurors at between six and 12. Six jurors is the bare minimum for federal constitutional purposes. Colgrove v. Battin, 413 U.S. 149, 93 S.Ct. 2448, 37 L.Ed.2d 522 (1973).

5. Illustration

Ponce, owner of an apartment building in Fort Bragg, brought an unlawful detainer action in Mendocino County Superior Court against Dimitri, a tenant in the building. Dimitri had refused to pay rent over a six-month period because he believed that the landlord-tenant system was fundamentally disadvantageous to tenants and concentrated power in the hands of a few wealthy landowners. During voir dire, Dimitri tried to procure a sympathetic jury by using his peremptory challenges to remove prospective jurors perceived to be

> affluent. Dimitri's attorney exercised peremptory challenges against three company CEOs, two law firm partners, and one state lottery winner. Ponce objected that this tactic violated the California Constitution's representative cross section requirement. Dimitri's counsel admitted that he was trying to excuse wealthy jurors but contended that doing so was permissible under California law. The court should agree. While there was a reasonable inference that prospective jurors were being challenged because of their membership in a specific group, distinctions based on wealth are not cognizable like distinctions based on race, gender, religion, or sexual orientation. Economic groups do not share a common perspective arising out of their life experience, and other members of the community are capable of adequately representing their perspective on the jury. Accordingly, Ponce's objection will be overruled. (If, however, the issue in the case were based on one of the specified categories of civil cases (such as discrimination in housing) listed in CCP § 231.7(k)(2), Dmitri's counsel would have a much more difficult time defending the strategy of excluding wealthy jurors.) People v. Garcia, 77 Cal.App.4th 1269, 92 Cal.Rptr.2d 339 (2000).

III. CHALLENGES TO TRIAL JUDGE

Once an action is assigned to a superior court trial department, the trial judge may be disqualified, either through a challenge for cause or a peremptory challenge. These challenges may also be used to disqualify a superior court judicial officer other than the trial judge, such as a law and motion judge, settlement judge, commissioner, or referee. The disqualification statutes do not apply to appellate judges.

A. Challenges for Cause

1. Grounds for Disqualification

Disqualification is required for cause if a statutory ground exists under CCP § 170.1. These include circumstances where the judge:

- has personal knowledge of disputed evidentiary facts;
- has a physical impairment that would render her unable to properly conduct the proceeding;
- has a financial interest in the subject matter of or a party to the proceeding; or

- believes there is a substantial doubt as to her capacity to be impartial.

In addition, disqualification is mandatory under an objective standard if a "person aware of the facts might reasonably entertain a doubt that the judge would be able to be impartial." CCP § 170.1(a)(6)(A)(iii); and North American Title Co. v. Superior Court, 17 Cal.5th 155, 326 Cal.Rptr.3d 582, 557 P.3d 1180 (2024).

2. Procedure

The judge herself initially determines whether grounds for disqualification exist. As soon as the judge is aware of any ground for disqualification for cause, she must cease participation in the proceedings (except for exercising a very limited power to act pending assignment to a new judge), unless the parties and attorneys waive the disqualification. CCP § 170.3. If a judge ought to disqualify herself but refuses or fails to do so, a party may file with the court clerk a statement of the grounds for disqualification.

B. Peremptory Challenges

A party or attorney may challenge a trial judge on the ground that the judge is prejudiced against the party or attorney, without providing any further reasons for the challenge. CCP § 170.6. Each side may exercise this peremptory challenge once as a matter of right. A formal written motion is not required—the challenge may be made orally with no prior notice. As long as the challenge is timely and properly brought, the trial judge must promptly recuse herself. If she fails to do so, any subsequent orders or judgments are void as being in excess of jurisdiction. Prescription Opioid Cases, 57 Cal.App.5th 1039, 272 Cal.Rptr.3d 99 (2020).

C. *Compare Federal Procedure*

A district court judge must disqualify himself for cause "in any proceeding in which his impartiality might reasonably be questioned," as well as under several grounds similar to those listed in the corresponding California statute. 28 USC § 455. In addition, a party may file an affidavit setting forth specific facts and reasons that the assigned judge has a personal bias or prejudice against him or in favor of an opposing party. 28 USC § 144. There is no federal equivalent of California's judicial peremptory challenge.

D. Illustration

Judge Julie issued numerous rulings concerning marital dissolution and child custody matters in contentious proceedings between Fred and Wilma in Humboldt County Superior Court. Wilma and her attorney began to notice that Judge Julie consistently ruled to Wilma's disadvantage in motions and requests. For example, Judge Julie: (1) refused several times to review Wilma's attorney's time sheets on her request for attorney's fees; (2) threatened to reduce Wilma's spousal support by 50% if she pursued an appeal of the judge's attorney's fees rulings; and (3) continued to rely on the opinion of a questionable therapist regarding child custody and visitation issues and gave the therapist virtually unfettered control over Wilma's contact with her children. Wilma made a motion under CCP § 170.1(a)(6)(A)(iii) to disqualify Judge Julie for cause on the ground that her conduct and remarks raised a reasonable doubt as to whether she could be an impartial judge. Although the mere fact that Judge Julie has repeatedly ruled against Wilma does not automatically establish bias, Judge Julie's pattern of behavior creates an objective doubt that she will be able to be impartial. In such a case, fairness would be best served by assigning the entire matter to another judge. In re Marriage of Tharp, 188 Cal.App.4th 1295, 116 Cal.Rptr.3d 375 (2010).

IV. CONDUCT OF JURY TRIAL

A. Order of Proceedings

A jury trial follows a statutorily determined order unless the trial judge rules otherwise. CCP § 607. The trial generally proceeds as follows:

- The plaintiff makes her opening statement;
- The defendant makes his opening statement after the plaintiff's statement, or waits until after the plaintiff has presented her evidence;
- The plaintiff presents her evidence;
- The defendant makes his opening statement if he has not already done so;
- The defendant presents his evidence;
- The parties offer rebuttal evidence;

- The plaintiff presents her closing argument;
- The defendant presents his closing argument;
- The court instructs the jury;
- The jury deliberates; and
- The jury renders a verdict.

B. Opening Statements and Closing Arguments

1. Opening Statements

The opening statement is an opportunity for both parties to set out the nature of the action and the facts that will be presented to the jury during the trial proceedings. It is considered a key component of the trial because it often influences the jurors' perception of the case. Argument is not permitted during the opening statement.

2. Closing Arguments

Closing argument is counsel's final opportunity to communicate with the jurors and attempt to shape their interpretation of the evidence before the jury begins its deliberations. The court may admonish the jury and/or strike counsel's remarks if the argument contains irrelevant or inflammatory matter, or if it appeals to the jurors' prejudices or emotionalism. For example, reciting the Golden Rule to the jury constitutes improper argument. Janice H. v. 696 North Robertson, LLC, 1 Cal.App.5th 586, 205 Cal.Rptr.3d 103 (2016).

C. Commenting on the Evidence

1. Power to Comment

Judges have the power to "make any comment on the evidence and the testimony and credibility of any witness as in [their] opinion is necessary for the proper determination of the cause." Cal. Const., art. VI, § 10.

a. What Judges May Say

Judges have great leeway in commenting on evidence while charging the jury. Orient Handel v. United States Fidelity and Guaranty Co., 192 Cal.App.3d 684, 237 Cal.Rptr. 667 (1987). If a judge's statement is "accurate, temperate, and 'scrupulously fair,' " and it does not state an opinion "on the ultimate issue," then the comment will be permissible. People v. Melton, 44 Cal.3d 713, 735, 244 Cal.Rptr. 867, 878, 750 P.2d 741 (1988).

b. Limits on Judge's Power to Comment

While the judge's power is rather sweeping, it is not unlimited. In commenting, the judge may not, for example, withdraw material evidence from the jury's consideration, distort the record, or usurp the jury's ultimate fact-finding authority. See Haluck v. Ricoh Electronics, Inc., 151 Cal.App.4th 994, 1007, 60 Cal.Rptr.3d 542, 551 (2007) (judge's improper comments in front of jury "mocked plaintiffs and their testimony and impugned their credibility").

2. *Compare Federal Procedure*

The Federal Rules are silent on the power of federal trial judges to comment on evidence. The general tenor of federal case law is that federal judges, like their California counterparts, have the power to comment on the evidence (though they often choose not to exercise it). The U.S. Supreme Court has referred to the ability to comment on the evidence as one of the "essential prerogatives of the trial judge." Quercia v. United States, 289 U.S. 466, 469, 53 S.Ct. 698, 699, 77 L.Ed. 1321 (1933). Generally, comments are unacceptable if they are prejudicial or affect the jury's ability to pass upon the evidence in a fair and dispassionate way.

3. Illustration

Presley won a pickleball match at the ultra-exclusive Newport Beach country club, Diamond Hills. At the end of the match, Presley approached the net to shake his opponent's hand. In an effort to further display his athletic prowess, Presley attempted to jump over the net, only to catch his foot, fall forward, and break both of his wrists. Presley brought a negligence suit in Orange County Superior Court against Diamond Hills, claiming that the net was too high and that this "defect" was the cause of his injuries. At the end of the trial and after the jury instructions had been read, a clearly exasperated trial judge launched into the following monologue before the jury began its deliberations:

> Ladies and gentlemen of the jury, I will be honest with you. I was not supposed to be here this week. I was supposed to be on vacation. I had a tee time at Pebble Beach! Do you know how hard those are to get? But instead, I am stuck here, just like you, dealing with some knucklehead who injured himself being a show-off. Here's the deal. There is no evidence that there was a defect, let

> alone one that caused Mr. Presley's injuries. The verdict you render should be for the defendant, and if it is not, I will order a directed verdict for it.
>
> The jury returned a verdict for Diamond Hills. Presley made a timely motion for a new trial, but the court denied it. On appeal, Presley argued that the judge's statements were beyond the scope of permissible comment on the evidence. The appellate court will likely agree with Presley's position, noting that the trial judge made two main mistakes: (a) his comments were addressed not only to the evidence, but also to the ultimate question of liability; and (b) he expressly directed a verdict with his comments. As such, Presley would be entitled to a new trial. Lewis v. Bill Robertson & Sons, Inc., 162 Cal.App.3d 650, 208 Cal.Rptr. 699 (1984).

D. Instructions on the Law

During a jury trial, the court has the responsibility of instructing (or "charging") the jury on relevant matters of law. CCP § 607a. Ultimately, courts strive to craft instructions that are correct and neutral statements of law that are easily understandable by the jurors. See CRC 2.1050; 1 CACI Preface.

1. Sources of Proper Jury Instructions

a. Form Instructions

Form instructions are the source of the majority of jury instructions. Because they are predrafted, they are easy to use and generally accepted as accurate. While form instructions are commonly used, in rare circumstances they can be successfully challenged as inaccurate, irrelevant, or otherwise flawed. Mitchell v. Gonzales, 54 Cal.3d 1041, 1 Cal.Rptr.2d 913, 819 P.2d 872 (1991).

1) CACI Instructions

The Judicial Council of California approved the use of the California Civil Jury Instructions (known as CACI) in 2003. CACI constitute the official civil jury instructions in California. CRC 2.1050(a). The use of these instructions is strongly encouraged (CRC 2.1050(e)) and even mandatory in some counties. See, e.g., Fresno County Superior Court Rule 4.1.9 (CACI "shall be used wherever applicable"); and Madera County Superior Court Rule 2.3.1 ("In all jury trials it is the policy of the Court to use the instructions contained in * * * CACI, * * * as appropriate."). CACI include introductory, evidentiary, and concluding instructions as well as a variety of substantive instructions. CACI have supplanted other form instructions as the official instructions in California courts because they provide legally accurate instructions that are written at a high school level of comprehension.

2) BAJI Instructions

The widely used predecessors to CACI were the California Jury Instructions, Civil (commonly referred to as the "Book of Approved Jury Instructions" or "BAJI"). Much like CACI, BAJI contain introductory, evidentiary, concluding, and substantive instructions. While CACI have superseded BAJI as the approved instructions, courts still occasionally use BAJI. See Baumgardner v. Yusuf, 144 Cal.App.4th 1381, 51 Cal.Rptr.3d 277 (2006) (trial court's refusal to use BAJI instruction instead of CACI version was prejudicial because CACI instruction did not provide complete recital of relevant law).

b. Other Sources of Instructions

Instructions may be derived from relevant statutory language or appellate opinions. Other sources of jury instructions include form books, practice guides, legal treatises, restatements of law, and legal and common dictionaries.

2. Submission of Proposed Jury Instructions

a. Timing of Submissions

Prior to the swearing of the first witness, the parties are expected to submit proposed jury instructions "covering the law as disclosed by the pleadings." CCP § 607a. Prior to closing arguments, additional proposed instructions may be submitted regarding questions of law developed by the evidence during the trial that were not disclosed by the pleadings. After closing arguments, the court may give instructions on issues raised during the arguments but not addressed by previous instructions that were given or rejected. If a proposed instruction is submitted late, the court has the discretion to refuse to use it.

b. Court's Responsibilities After Submission

Once counsel have submitted proposed jury instructions, the court must decide whether each proposed instruction should be accepted, rejected, or modified, determine whether any additional instructions should be given, and apprise counsel of the instructions the court intends to give. CCP § 607a. The court may refuse to issue a party's proposed jury instruction if it is incomplete, erroneous, or a misstatement of the law. Swanson v. Marley-Wylain Co., 65 Cal.App.5th 1007, 80 Cal.Rptr.3d 496 (2021).

3. Charging the Jury

a. Timing of Instructions

Traditionally, the court charges the jury directly before or just after closing arguments. The court retains the power to instruct the jury at other times, such as at the commencement of the trial. CCP § 607. In some instances, rereading or giving additional instructions may be necessary after deliberations have begun.

b. Juror Comprehension of Instructions

Usually, instructions are presented both orally and in writing. In most cases, judges will read the instructions to the jurors first and then allow them to take a complete copy of the instructions into the jury room during deliberations. If the jurors "desire to be informed of any point of law arising in the cause," they may be brought into court and provided with the information they request "in the presence of, or after notice to, the parties or counsel." CCP § 614. California has instituted additional rules intended to increase juror comprehension of jury instructions, including requiring that jurors be permitted to take written notes during trial and instructions, and allowing trial judges to preinstruct juries immediately after being sworn. CRC 2.1031–2.1035.

4. Deliberations

After the court submits the case to the jury and the jury retires to begin its deliberations, the jurors must be kept together under the supervision of a court officer until they reach a verdict or the court discharges them. The officer must ensure that no improper communications are made to the jury during their deliberations, which must take place in secret. CCP § 613. The only items ordinarily permitted in the jury room are papers that were entered into evidence, exhibits that the court may deem proper, jury instructions, and notes taken by individual jurors. CCP §§ 612 & 612.5. Jurors may request the officer to bring them back into court for testimony to be reread or jury instructions to be clarified. Counsel for all parties must be notified and present in court when the court provides the jury with additional information. CCP § 614.

5. *Compare Federal Procedure*

Unlike California practice, which requires instructions to be proposed early in the trial process, federal parties usually submit instructions "[a]t the close of evidence or at any earlier reasonable time that the court orders." FRCP 51(a). Another difference between the two systems is the use of form instructions. While California has an "approved" set of official form instructions (CACI), the federal system does not. Unofficial form instructions (Federal Jury Practice and Instructions) exist, but use of these instructions is less prevalent than the use of CACI in California.

6. Illustration

Paris was riding her e-bike in Daly City with her Chihuahua, Tinkerbell, in the front cargo box. A dump truck owned and driven by Ditch made an illegal turn and collided with Paris. The impact caused serious injuries to Paris. Tinkerbell was unharmed. At the time of the accident, Ditch had a contract with Daly City to haul and deliver asphalt to various road repair projects. Paris sued Ditch and Daly City for her personal injuries in San Mateo County Superior Court. Following the presentation of evidence at the trial, the court informed the jury that it had to determine whether Ditch was an employee of Daly City or an independent contractor. If Ditch were found to be an employee, Daly City would be vicariously liable for his negligent conduct. The instruction given to the jury stated that Ditch must be deemed an employee if Daly City had the right to control how Ditch performed his work. Based on this instruction, the jury concluded that Ditch was an employee. The court's instruction, however, was an incorrect statement of the law because right of control is one factor—but not the only factor—in determining whether Ditch is an employee or independent contractor. Instead, the jury should have been instructed to apply a multifactor test. It was reasonably probable that the erroneous instruction prejudicially affected the jury's determination that Ditch was an employee of Daly City, especially given the substantial evidence Daly City presented at trial from which the jury could have concluded that Ditch met the criteria of an independent contractor. Bowman v. Wyatt, 186 Cal.App.4th 286, 111 Cal.Rptr.3d 787 (2010).

E. Verdicts

1. Nonunanimous Verdicts

Unanimity is not required of a civil jury verdict in California. A valid verdict may be reached by three-fourths of the jurors. Cal. Const., art. I, § 16; CCP § 618.

2. General, Special and Hybrid Verdicts

a. General Verdicts

A general verdict finds in favor of either the plaintiff or the defendant. CCP § 624. The jury does not specify the reasons for its decision. This is the most commonly used form of verdict in civil cases.

b. Special Verdicts

1) When Used

A special verdict sets out the jury's factual findings on all of the issues presented at trial. The judge then applies the appropriate law to those findings to reach a judgment in the case. CCP § 624. The use of special verdicts is normally within the discretion of the trial judge. Their use is not required except in a handful of situations, such as where the jury renders a verdict for punitive damages. CCP § 625.

2) Agreement on Each Finding Not Required

Under the three-fourths rule, any nine jurors in a jury of 12 may render a valid verdict on each question within the special verdict form. It is not required that the same nine jurors agree on each component of the special verdict. Resch v. Volkswagen of America, Inc., 36 Cal.3d 676, 205 Cal.Rptr. 827, 685 P.2d 1178 (1984).

c. Hybrid Verdicts

In some cases, the jury may render a "hybrid" verdict, which is a general verdict accompanied by responses to specific questions that disclose the basis for the jury's decision. CCP § 625.

3. *Compare Federal Procedure*

A federal jury may render a general verdict, special verdict, or general verdict accompanied by answers to interrogatories. FRCP 49. A federal civil jury verdict must be unanimous unless the parties stipulate otherwise. FRCP 48(b).

4. Illustration

After eating lunch at Delicious, a restaurant near the Santa Cruz Beach Boardwalk, Pascal tripped and fell while walking down a ramp leading from the restaurant to the parking lot, sustaining severe injuries. The ramp is owned and maintained by Delicious. Pascal sued Delicious in Santa Cruz County Superior Court for premises liability. At trial, the jury was instructed to render a special verdict on Delicious' liability. The jury's special verdict found that Delicious' negligence and the dangerous condition of the ramp were causes of Pascal's injuries. In response to Question #5 on the special verdict form, however, the jury found that the dangerous condition of the ramp did *not* create a reasonably foreseeable risk of the type of injury Pascal suffered. Finding these responses to be inconsistent, the trial court sent the jury back for further deliberations. When the jury returned, Question #5 was answered "yes." The judge did not err in requesting the jury to conduct further deliberations. The court did not guide the jury toward a particular outcome. It merely pointed out the unclear set of responses and "provided the jury with an opportunity to render a verdict in accordance with its deliberations." Mizel v. City of Santa Monica, 93 Cal.App.4th 1059, 1073, 113 Cal.Rptr.2d 649, 659 (2001).

F. Impeachment of Verdict

1. Jury Misconduct

Cal. Evid. Code § 1150 provides the basis for the impeachment of a jury verdict: "Upon an inquiry as to the validity of a verdict, any otherwise admissible evidence may be received as to statements made, or conduct, conditions, or events occurring, either within or without the jury room, of such a character as is likely to have influenced the verdict improperly." The statute requires objective evidence of misconduct. Evidence of a juror's subjective "mental processes" is not admissible. Examples of impeachable jury misconduct are:

- refusal to follow the court's jury instructions;
- reliance on outside evidence;
- juror inattentiveness and distraction at trial; or
- performance of experiments.

2. *Compare Federal Procedure*

To impeach a federal verdict, a juror may testify regarding whether (1) "extraneous prejudicial information was improperly brought to the jury's attention"; (2) "an outside influence was improperly brought to bear upon any juror"; or (3) "a mistake was made in entering the verdict on the verdict form." FRE 606(b). Evidence of a juror's mental processes or emotions during the deliberations is not permitted.

3. Illustration

Percy sued Dragster Motor Co. in San Luis Obispo County Superior Court for injuries he sustained when the self-driving system in his Dragster 5000 XS sports car failed, and Percy collided with a utility pole in the town of Avila Beach. At the conclusion of the trial, the jury rendered a verdict for Percy. Dragster Motor Co. challenged the verdict on the grounds of juror misconduct. Dragster obtained a declaration from one juror stating that another juror appeared to be sleeping during trial, and two other jurors were surreptitiously sending text messages to each other during the presentation of evidence. A court may discharge a juror upon good cause if the juror is unable to perform their duties, which must be established as a "demonstrable reality" in the record. The court abuses its discretion if it does not conduct an adequate inquiry into allegations of a juror's misconduct before ordering discharge. "In most instances, the court will interview all of the jurors before deciding whether a juror is unable or unwilling to deliberate. At a minimum, it must interview more than the complaining jurors." Shanks v. Department of Transportation, 9 Cal.App.5th 543, 553, 215 Cal.Rptr.3d 359, 367 (2017).

V. JUDICIAL CONTROL OVER JURY VERDICT

California law provides several devices that permit a judge to take a case away from the jury at various stages of the trial, both before and after the jury has rendered a verdict.

A. Nonsuit

1. Nature of Device

Nonsuit allows the trial court to partially or fully resolve the case at an early stage of a trial. The defendant may challenge the legal sufficiency of the plaintiff's causes of action without losing the right to present a defense. CCP § 581c(a). Only a defendant may bring a motion for nonsuit.

a. Timing

The defendant may move for nonsuit at one of two times: (1) at the completion of a plaintiff's opening statement; or (2) after the plaintiff has presented her evidence. CCP § 581c(a).

b. Standard for Granting Nonsuit

A defendant's motion for nonsuit will be granted if the plaintiff's opening statement or presentation of evidence is insufficient to support a prima facie showing of each element of the plaintiff's causes of action.

1) After Plaintiff's Opening Statement

A motion for nonsuit will be granted following a plaintiff's opening statement if, after the plaintiff has summarized all the facts that she expects to prove at trial, the court finds that those facts would be legally insufficient to establish one or more of the essential elements of the plaintiff's case. Nonsuit after a plaintiff's opening statement, however, is highly disfavored and will not be granted unless it is clear that the plaintiff will be unable to make out a prima facie case. The court normally grants the plaintiff a chance to amend the opening statement. Panico v. Truck Insurance Exchange, 90 Cal.App.4th 1294, 109 Cal.Rptr.2d 638 (2001).

2) After Plaintiff's Presentation of Evidence

Alternatively, nonsuit may be granted at the close of the plaintiffs' evidence. A trial court may not grant a defendant's motion for nonsuit if the evidence viewed most favorably to the plaintiff would support a jury verdict in favor of the plaintiff. The court does not weigh the evidence on a nonsuit motion. The court must disregard any conflicting evidence and draw all legitimate inferences from the evidence in the plaintiff's favor. Bjoin v. J-M Manufacturing Co., 113 Cal.App.5th 884, 336 Cal.Rptr.3d 475 (2025).

2. Complete and Partial Nonsuit

If complete nonsuit is not appropriate, the court may grant nonsuit as to certain causes of action brought by a plaintiff, certain defendants, certain plaintiffs, or one of several cases that have been consolidated for trial. CCP § 581c(b).

3. *Compare Federal Procedure*

Federal procedure does not have a precise equivalent of California's nonsuit. The motion for judgment as a matter of law under FRCP 50(a) is the federal counterpart to California's directed verdict motion; it can serve a function similar to a motion for nonsuit. (See section V(B), below.)

4. Illustration

After repeatedly watching his favorite heist film, "Glittering Gems," Ronnie Robber decided to burglarize Princess Jewels, a jewelry store around the corner from his home in Culver City. During his burglary attempt, Robber damaged several glass display cases, broke the locks on several secure jewelry drawers, and drilled holes into the store's safe. Before he could flee with any glittering gems, the police arrived. Robber was arrested and convicted, but he lacked the funds necessary to pay restitution to Princess Jewels for the damage he had caused. Princess Jewels brought a civil action against Dreck Motion Pictures, the producer of the movie "Glittering Gems," for the damage. At the commencement of the trial in Los Angeles County Superior Court, the attorney for Princess Jewels gave his opening statement. He failed to mention that he would present evidence at trial tending to show that in distributing "Glittering Gems," Dreck recklessly or deliberately encouraged people to commit burglary, an essential element of Princess Jewels' claim. At the close of Princess Jewels' opening statement, Dreck moved for nonsuit. Although nonsuit following opening statement is disfavored, the court will grant the nonsuit motion if the opening statement showed that Princess Jewels cannot make out a prima facie case against the studio on all elements of its cause of action. Olivia N. v. National Broadcasting Co., 126 Cal.App.3d 488, 178 Cal.Rptr. 888 (1981), cert. denied, 458 U.S. 1108, 102 S.Ct. 3487, 73 L.Ed.2d 1369 (1982).

B. Directed Verdict

1. Nature of Device

A directed verdict motion permits the moving party (either the plaintiff or the defendant) to test the legal sufficiency of the opponent's causes of action or defenses. CCP § 630(a).

a. Timing

An important difference between a motion for directed verdict and a motion for nonsuit is the timing. Any party may move for a directed verdict only after all parties have presented their evidence. CCP § 630(a).

b. Standard for Granting Directed Verdict

The standard for granting a directed verdict is the same as that for a nonsuit motion. If a party brings a motion for directed verdict at the close of all of the evidence, that motion is properly granted if, "disregarding conflicting evidence, and indulging every legitimate inference which may be drawn from the evidence in favor of the party against whom the verdict is directed * * * there is no evidence of sufficient substantiality to support a verdict in favor of such party." Newing v. Cheatham, 15 Cal.3d 351, 358–359, 124 Cal.Rptr. 193, 198, 540 P.2d 33 (1975). As in a nonsuit motion, the trial court in a directed verdict motion does not weigh the evidence.

2. Partial Directed Verdict

The court is empowered to grant a partial directed verdict when appropriate. CCP § 630(b). The court may direct a verdict on some of many claims or defenses, as to one of many coparties, or on the issue of liability (leaving the issue of amount of compensatory and/or punitive damages up to the jury).

3. *Compare Federal Procedure*

Judgment as a matter of law is the federal counterpart to California's directed verdict. A judgment as a matter of law is properly granted "[i]f a party has been fully heard on an issue during a jury trial and the court finds that a reasonable jury would not have a legally sufficient evidentiary basis to find for the party on that issue." FRCP 50(a). A motion for judgment as a matter of law may be made at any time before the case is submitted to the jury, including after the opening statement. FRCP 50(a)(2).

4. Illustration

Police Officer Peter sued the Desert Hot Springs Police Department in Riverside County Superior Court for wrongful discharge. Peter alleged that his employment was improperly terminated during his probationary period because of a perceived severe hearing disability. After Peter's presentation

> of evidence, the Department brought a directed verdict motion, arguing that in presenting his case at trial, Peter had failed to make a prima facie showing that he was initially qualified to be hired for his position. The court should grant the motion because the evidence presented by Peter is insufficient to permit the jury to render a verdict in his favor. Peter cannot establish that he satisfied the qualifications for the position for which he applied because he did not successfully complete the hearing examination. Quinn v. City of Los Angeles, 84 Cal.App.4th 472, 100 Cal.Rptr.2d 914 (2000).

C. Judgment Notwithstanding the Verdict

1. Nature of Device

A motion for judgment notwithstanding the verdict (JNOV) allows a trial court to resolve an issue in favor of the moving party after the jury has returned a verdict to the contrary. The motion is similar to the common law motion for judgment *non obstante veredicto.* As such, judgment notwithstanding the verdict is typically referred to by the acronym JNOV. Similar to the motions for nonsuit and directed verdict, a motion for JNOV challenges the legal sufficiency of the opposing side's evidence. A JNOV motion may be brought by either party (provided the jury has returned a verdict against that party) or, occasionally, by the court on its own motion. CCP § 629.

a. Timing

A JNOV motion is made after the jury has rendered its verdict. The moving party must make the motion within the time to serve and file a notice of intent to move for new trial. CCP §§ 629 & 659. (See section V(D)(1), below.) A trial court is without jurisdiction to consider an untimely JNOV motion. When the trial court makes a motion for JNOV sua sponte, the law is unclear whether the court must adhere to the time limits applicable to party motions. Compare Espinoza v. Rossini, 247 Cal.App.2d 40, 55 Cal.Rptr. 205 (1966) (stating that the strict time limits for a JNOV motion apply to litigants and courts alike) with Sturgeon v. Leavitt, 94 Cal.App.3d 957, 156 Cal.Rptr. 687 (1979) (disregarding the time limits for a JNOV motion that the trial court initiated).

b. Standard for Granting Motion for JNOV

The court is authorized to grant a motion for JNOV whenever a motion for directed verdict would have been granted had it previously been brought. CCP § 629. In other words, JNOV should be granted when the evidence is insufficient to support a verdict in favor of the nonmoving party. Kephart v. Genuity, Inc., 136 Cal.App.4th 280, 38 Cal.Rptr.3d 845 (2006). Essentially, the standards for granting a nonsuit, directed verdict, and JNOV are the same. A trial judge may grant a JNOV even if a previous directed verdict motion was denied. A party is not required to have brought a directed verdict motion before moving for JNOV.

2. Partial JNOV

There is no clear statutory authority for the granting of a partial JNOV. At least one court has reasoned that JNOV motions should be treated the same as nonsuits and directed verdicts, both of which may be partially granted. Beavers v. Allstate Insurance Co., 225 Cal.App.3d 310, 274 Cal.Rptr. 766 (1990).

3. Motions for JNOV and New Trial

JNOV motions and motions for new trial are frequently filed simultaneously and in the alternative. CCP § 629. The court then has the option of granting one motion and denying the other. Foxcroft Productions, Inc. v. Universal City Studios LLC, 76 Cal.App.5th 1119, 292 Cal.Rptr.3d 310 (2022). See section V(D), below.

4. Compare Federal Procedure

In the federal system, what used to be called JNOV is now referred to as a "renewed motion for judgment as a matter of law." FRCP 50(b). The standard is identical to the one for a preverdict motion for judgment as a matter of law (directed verdict): whether "the evidence, construed in the light most favorable to the nonmoving party, permits only one reasonable conclusion, and that conclusion is contrary to that of the jury." White v. Ford Motor Co., 312 F.3d 998, 1010 (9th Cir.2002). In order to bring a renewed motion for judgment after the jury has rendered a verdict, a federal court litigant must first have made a motion for judgment as a matter of law (i.e., directed verdict motion) after the opposing side has been fully heard on an issue. FRCP 50(b). The rationale for this extra step is that the Seventh Amendment states that "no fact tried by a jury shall be otherwise re-examined by any Court of the United States." A "renewed" motion for judgment as a matter of law is allowed because the motion is not viewed as a "reexamination." Rather, "the court is considered to have submitted the action to the jury subject to the court's later deciding the legal questions raised" by the previously submitted motion for judgment. FRCP 50(b); see also Weisgram v. Marley Co., 528 U.S. 440, 120 S.Ct. 1011, 145 L.Ed.2d 958 (2000). California, not being bound by the Seventh Amendment, does not require this formality.

5. Illustration

Play Toys, Inc. sued Darn Fun Co. in Ventura County Superior Court for allegedly copying a product idea. Both companies, within a month of each other, had put on the market a stuffed animal that "giggles" when bounced. The jury heard evidence that about a year before the launch of the product, an employee at Play Toys had shown a prototype to a manager at Darn Fun. There was also contradictory evidence presented that Darn Fun actually got the idea for the toy from other sources. The jury returned a verdict in favor of Play Toys. Darn Fun immediately moved for JNOV. The court will deny the JNOV motion because, viewed favorably toward Play Toys—the opponent of the motion—substantial evidence existed to support the jury's verdict in favor of Play Toys. Wolf v. Walt Disney Pictures and Television, 162 Cal.App.4th 1107, 76 Cal.Rptr.3d 585 (2008).

D. Motion for New Trial

1. Nature of Motion

Often coupled with a motion for JNOV, a motion for new trial asks the court to reexamine one or more issues after a trial has taken place and a verdict has been rendered. A party, however, also may bring a motion for new trial where an issue of fact or law has been decided without a trial judgment, such as summary judgment, directed verdict, nonsuit, judgment on the pleadings, or an excessive or inadequate default judgment. The trial court shall grant a new trial motion when it is "of the opinion that the error complained of has resulted in a miscarriage of justice." Cal. Const., art. VI, § 13.

a. Grounds for New Trial Motion

The court has no inherent power to order a new trial on its own motion. A party's motion for new trial must be based on one of the grounds enumerated in CCP § 657:

- Irregularity in the proceedings of the court, jury or adverse counsel (§ 657(1)). Example: erroneous exclusion of evidence, if the court's ruling prejudiced the moving party's right to a fair trial.

- Misconduct of the jury (§ 657(2)). Example: improper communications during jury deliberations.
- Accident or surprise during trial, which ordinary prudence could not have guarded against despite the diligence of the moving party (§ 657(3)). Example: the adverse party calls an expert witness who was not previously disclosed. This ground does not include a simple mistake or negligence of counsel; the accident or surprise must have a prejudicial effect on the moving party.
- Newly discovered material evidence, which the moving party could not have discovered and produced at trial, despite reasonable diligence (§ 657(4)). Example: willful suppression of material evidence during discovery and trial.
- Excessive or inadequate damages (§ 657(5)). Example: the jury applied an incorrect standard in calculating damages. This statutory ground typically results in a limited new trial on the issue of damages only.
- Insufficient evidence to justify the verdict (§ 657(6)). Example: the court reweighs the evidence and assesses the credibility of witnesses to determine if the weight is against the verdict. This ground is the most common basis for a new trial motion.
- The verdict or other decision is against law (§ 657(6)). Example: the jury has rendered a verdict contrary to the jury instructions.
- An error in law during the trial (§ 657(7)). Example: the court has given an erroneous jury instruction. The error must have been prejudicial, and the moving party must have objected to the error during the trial.

b. Judge's Consideration of New Trial Motion

1) Reweighing the Evidence

In contrast to motions for nonsuit, directed verdict, and JNOV, certain grounds for a new trial permit the judge to reweigh the evidence. This ability is most often exercised when the motion is based on the ground that the evidence was insufficient to justify the verdict (CCP § 657(6)) or that damages awarded were excessive or inadequate (CCP § 657(5)). Because of this power to reweigh the evidence, the judge is sometimes characterized as a "thirteenth juror." In this role, the judge is entitled to disbelieve witnesses and draw reasonable inferences counter to those of the jury. Fountain Valley Chateau Blanc Homeowner's Association v. Department of Veterans Affairs, 67 Cal.App.4th 743, 79 Cal.Rptr.2d 248 (1998).

2) Written Specifications for Court's Ruling

The court is obligated to provide specific written reasons for its ruling granting or denying the new trial motion. The requirement of written reasons forces the court to deliberate when exercising its broad discretion. In addition, written reasons make the appeal more meaningful by focusing the reviewing court's attention on the part of the record that served as the basis for the trial court's order. If the trial court grants the motion but fails to provide specific reasons for its order, the burden of persuasion on appeal is on the respondent (the party seeking to uphold the order). Oakland Raiders v. National Football League, 41 Cal.4th 624, 61 Cal.Rptr.3d 634, 161 P.3d 151 (2007).

3) Conditional New Trial: Additur and Remittitur

An order for a new trial may be made conditional on the plaintiff's agreement to instead accept what the court deems to be a fair and reasonable lower amount of damages (remittitur), or the defendant's agreement to pay a higher amount of damages (additur). CCP § 662.5.

c. Timing

Litigants seeking a new trial must file a notice of intention to move for a new trial: (1) before the entry of judgment; (2) within 15 days of the clerk's mailing of the notice of entry of judgment, or 15 days after service on the moving party by another party of written notice of entry of judgment, or 180 days after entry of judgment, whichever is earliest; or (3) within 15 days after another party has moved for a new trial. CCP § 659(a). These deadlines are jurisdictional. They cannot be extended by stipulation of the parties or order of the court. In re Marriage of Beilock, 81 Cal.App.3d 713, 146 Cal.Rptr. 675 (1978). Under CCP § 660, the court has 75 days within which it must render an order granting a new trial. Thereafter, the court has no jurisdiction to grant the motion, and it is deemed denied by operation of law.

2. *Compare Federal Procedure*

The federal version of a motion for new trial under FRCP 59 is similar to a motion for new trial under the California system. Federal trial judges are given broad discretion when ruling on such a motion. A new trial may be granted "for any reason for which a new trial has heretofore been granted in an action at law in federal court." FRCP 59(a)(1)(A). One major distinction between California and federal new trial motions is that the Seventh Amendment has been interpreted to not permit additur (although remittitur is allowed). The timing requirement for bringing a new trial motion is less complicated in federal court. The motion must be filed no later than 28 days after the entry of judgment. FRCP 59(b).

3. **Illustration**

Pearl sued canine clothing manufacturer Doggie Enterprises, maker of Round of A-Paws, whose marketing slogan was "Round of A-Paws: Where your puppy's clothing will always get a standing ovation." Pearl hired attorney Adele Addled to represent her in this action in Calaveras County Superior Court. Pearl claimed that a bejeweled, argyle doggie sweater-vest produced by the defendant caused her teacup Yorkie to break out in a rash and lose clumps of its hair during a doggie fashion show in Copperopolis. During the jury trial, Addled did a very poor job of representing Pearl. To make matters worse, during jury deliberations Pearl found out that Addled was not licensed to practice law in California. Once the jury returned an adverse verdict, Pearl made a timely motion for a new trial on the ground that her attorney's incompetence and lack of licensure constituted "irregularity in the proceedings." CCP § 657(1). The court will grant the new trial motion because Addled's actions constituted fraud on the court and denied Pearl a fair trial. Russell v. Dopp, 36 Cal.App.4th 765, 42 Cal.Rptr.2d 768 (1995).

VI. COURT TRIAL

A. Judge as Trier of Fact

If there is no request for a jury trial, or a jury is not appropriate, the judge serves as the trier of fact. In that role, the judge evaluates conflicts in the evidence and assesses the credibility of witnesses. In many respects, a court (or bench) trial proceeds in the same order as a jury trial. CCP § 607.

B. Motion for Judgment

1. Procedure

After a party's presentation of evidence, the other party may move for judgment. CCP § 631.8(a). The judge is not limited to considering only the legal sufficiency of the nonmoving party's evidence, as she would be in a motion for nonsuit, directed verdict, or JNOV in a jury trial. The judge may weigh the evidence and decide issues of credibility. If the judge grants the motion and enters judgment, she must issue a statement of decision. If the court denies the motion, the moving party may proceed with its presentation of evidence.

2. *Compare Federal Procedure*

The district court in a nonjury case may enter judgment on partial findings. "If a party has been fully heard on an issue during a nonjury trial and the court finds against the party on that issue, the court may enter judgment against the party on a claim or defense that, under the controlling law, can be maintained or defeated only with a favorable finding on that issue." FRCP 52(c). The district court is free to weigh the evidence, but it must support the judgment with findings of fact and conclusions of law, as provided in FRCP 52(a). The court may decline to render judgment until the close of all evidence.

3. Illustration

Prichard had worked for DryRiver Corp., a wireless internet provider located in Dunsmuir, for three years as manager of network operations. Prichard alleged in a complaint filed in Siskiyou County Superior Court that he had been misclassified as an exempt employee, depriving him of overtime pay and rest breaks. The trial court commenced a bench trial. After Prichard completed his presentation of evidence, DryRiver filed a motion for judgment on the ground that substantial evidence showed that Prichard had been properly classified as an administratively exempt employee. Substantial evidence

> presented by Prichard supported the findings that he regularly exercised discretion and independent judgment on issues of significance, his duties involved high-level decisionmaking, and he otherwise contributed to the management of the business operations. After weighing the evidence as the trier of fact, the trial court will likely grant the motion and enter judgment for DryRiver. Combs v. Skyriver Communications, Inc., 159 Cal.App.4th 1242, 72 Cal.Rptr.3d 171 (2008).

C. Statement of Decision

1. Tentative Decision

In a court trial lasting longer than one day, the court must render a tentative decision, orally or in writing. The tentative decision is not the judgment itself and is not binding on the court or parties. The court may ultimately render a different judgment. CRC 3.1590(b).

2. Timing and Contents of Statement of Decision

The trial court is not required to issue a statement of decision unless requested by a party within ten days of the court's announcement of its tentative decision. CCP § 632. The court is not required to prepare findings of fact and conclusions of law. The statement of decision sets forth the court's explanation of the legal and factual basis for the court's decision on each major disputed issue. Any objections to the statement of decision must be presented to the court in a timely fashion. CCP § 634.

3. Doctrine of Implied Findings

In the absence of a party's request for a statement of decision, the doctrine of implied findings requires an appellate court to presume that the trial court made all of the findings of fact necessary to support the judgment. A party may avoid the application of this doctrine by requesting a statement of decision and bringing any omissions or ambiguities to the attention of the trial court. Fladeboe v. American Isuzu Motors Inc., 150 Cal.App.4th 42, 58 Cal.Rptr.3d 225 (2007).

4. *Compare Federal Procedure*

FRCP 52(a)(1) requires the judge in a court trial to make findings of fact and conclusions of law, without need of a request from a party. The court then enters judgment under FRCP 58.

5. Illustration

Plum sued Deegan in Inyo County Superior Court for specific performance of a contract for acquisition of real estate located in Bishop. The judge tried the case without a jury and entered judgment for Plum. Deegan made an oral request for a written statement of decision from the judge. The judge stated that she had provided the parties with the statement of decision in the form of oral discussion between the parties and the court during post-trial proceedings, and in the court reporter's transcript from those proceedings. These items will not suffice. Upon the request of a party, the trial court must prepare a single document constituting a written statement of decision. Failure to do so results in reversible error. Whittington v. McKinney, 234 Cal.App.3d 123, 285 Cal.Rptr. 586 (1991).

SAMPLE EXAM QUESTIONS

OBJECTIVE QUESTIONS

The questions in this section are based on the following hypothetical:

Quinn sued Dump Co. in San Joaquin County Superior Court arising from the emission of allegedly toxic fumes from Dump Co.'s manufacturing plant located near Quinn's residence in Manteca. Quinn's suit seeks damages for his respiratory and other bodily injuries, as well as a permanent injunction requiring Dump Co. to reduce or eliminate the toxicity of its emissions. Quinn has requested a jury trial.

---

(1) True or False: In cases like Quinn's, involving both legal and equitable forms of relief, California follows the federal practice in which Quinn's claim for damages must be tried first before a jury, and the claim for injunctive relief will be tried later before the judge.

(2) Unless Quinn and Dump Co. agree to fewer jurors, the jury must have at least ___ jurors on it:

a. 6;

b. 8;

c. 10;

d. 12.

(3) True or False: Quinn and Dump Co. are entitled to three peremptory juror challenges each.

(4) Which of the following is a permissible reason for Dump Co. to use one of its peremptory challenges to remove a prospective juror:

a. The person's race;

b. The person's gender;

c. The person's sexual orientation;

d. None of the above.

(5) True or False: Dump Co.'s peremptory challenge of the trial judge may be made orally with no advance notice.

(6) True or False: Quinn's attorney may submit proposed jury instructions at any time prior to the delivery of closing arguments.

(7) If Dump Co. wishes to move for a nonsuit based on Quinn's opening statement, Dump Co.:

a. Must wait until after Quinn and Dump Co. both have presented their respective evidence;

b. Must wait until after the jury has returned a verdict;

c. May move at the conclusion of Quinn's opening statement on the ground that the facts Quinn summarized in his opening statement are legally insufficient to support a jury finding in Quinn's favor;

d. None of the above.

(8) True or False: Quinn does not have to move for a directed verdict in order to preserve the right to move for a judgment notwithstanding the verdict (JNOV).

(9) The trial judge may grant a motion for a new trial for Dump Co. on which of the following grounds:

a. Dump Co.'s discovery of new material evidence, as long as the evidence could not reasonably have been discovered before trial;

b. Misconduct by a juror;

c. Excessive amount of damages awarded to Quinn by the jury;

d. All of the above.

(10) True or False: If Quinn's suit is tried by the court instead of by a jury, the judge is required to issue a statement of decision after rendering her tentative decision, even if neither Quinn nor Dump Co. requests the statement.

(11) True or False: If Quinn waived his right to a jury trial by failing to deposit advance jury fees, the court has discretion to relieve Quinn of his waiver.

(12) True or False: If Quinn establishes an absolute disparity of 12% between the percentage of Latino jurors in the jury venire as compared to the percentage of Latino individuals in San Joaquin County, that showing is sufficient for Quinn to establish a systematic exclusion of Latino jurors.

(13) True or False: A jury verdict in favor of Dump Co. need not be unanimous.

(14) True or False: Quinn and Dump Co. may execute a stipulation to conduct an expedited jury trial prior to Quinn's filing an action in court.

Answers to Objective Questions

(1) **False.** California has rejected the federal practice of trying legal claims to a jury before trying equitable claims to the court. California generally follows the "equity first" doctrine, whereby equitable claims are first tried before the judge, and then legal claims are tried before the jury. However, the court has discretion to have the jury decide the legal claims first.

(2) **b.** Article I, section 16 of the California Constitution permits the Legislature to provide that civil juries must contain at least eight people,

unless both parties consent to fewer jurors. CCP § 220 allows the parties to agree to 12 or fewer jurors.

(3) **False.** In California, each side in an action involving two parties is entitled to six peremptory challenges. CCP § 231(c). In federal court, and in California expedited jury trials, each side gets three.

(4) **d.** Answers (a)–(c) are improper bases for peremptory challenges under California statute. CCP § 231.5 prohibits using a peremptory challenge to remove a juror on the "assumption" that the juror is biased because of a characteristic listed in Cal. Gov't Code § 11135(a). The characteristics listed in section 11135(a) include race, gender and sexual orientation (among several others). In addition, in criminal and certain categories of civil trials, there is an even more stringent review if a party is alleged to be trying to use a peremptory challenge to remove a juror because of the juror's "race, ethnicity, gender, gender identity, sexual orientation, national origin, or religious affiliation, or the perceived membership of the prospective juror in any of those groups." CCP § 231.7.

(5) **True.** Under CCP § 170.6(a)(2), a party may exercise one peremptory challenge of a judge, either orally or in writing, without any advance notice.

(6) **False.** Each party must submit proposed jury instructions to the trial judge in writing before the first witness is sworn. Quinn may submit additional proposed instructions before closing arguments begin if the evidence introduced additional issues that were not adequately addressed by the earlier submission of proposed instructions. CCP § 607a.

(7) **c.** CCP § 581c(a) permits a defendant to move for a nonsuit after the completion of the plaintiff's opening statement. The court must determine whether the facts that Quinn's attorney presented in the opening statement are legally insufficient. (Alternatively, Dump Co. could wait until after Quinn presents his evidence and make its motion based on the insufficiency of that evidence.)

(8) **True.** Unlike federal practice, California law does not require a party to move for directed verdict before filing a motion for JNOV.

(9) **d.** All of the grounds listed are among those set out in CCP § 657.

(10) **False.** The trial court is not required to issue a statement of decision unless Quinn or Dump Co. requests one within ten days of the court's announcement of its tentative decision. CCP § 632.

(11) **True.** Failure to deposit advance jury fees waives the right to a jury trial. CCP § 631(d)(5). The court, however, has discretion "upon just terms" to relieve Quinn of his waiver. CCP § 631(e).

(12) **False.** Absolute disparity is an example of one of the tests applied by the courts to satisfy the second prong of the *Duren* analysis (whether the representation of Latinos in the jury venire was not "fair and reasonable"

when compared to the number of Latinos in the community). Even assuming that a 12 percent absolute disparity is sufficient to meet prong two, Quinn must still satisfy prong three: the disparity must be due to a systematic exclusion of Latinos from the jury venire.

(13) **True.** California does not require unanimous verdicts in civil cases. Three-fourths of the jurors may render a verdict.

(14) **False.** Only parties to an already-filed action may agree to submit to an expedited jury trial. CCP § 630.03(c).

<u>ESSAY QUESTIONS</u>

A. Shira, a certified golf pro, filed suit in Sacramento County Superior Court against her former employer, Regal-Links, for wrongful termination and breach of contract. Shira is seeking damages and back pay, as well as an injunction ordering Regal-Links to give back Shira's job at its golf course in Isleton. The litigation is well into the discovery process, and Regal-Links' summary judgment hearing is scheduled in three weeks. Although the case is set for trial in three months, neither party has requested a jury trial.

(1) You are the chief legal counsel for Regal-Links. You suspect that Shira will want her case tried before a jury and that she will make that request if Regal-Links' summary judgment motion is denied and the case progresses to trial. You believe that it is more advantageous to Regal-Links to have the case tried before the judge. What arguments might you make to limit Shira's access to a jury trial, should she request one?

(2) Assume that Shira's case has been set for a jury trial. The jury panel is undergoing the process of voir dire. Counsel for Regal-Links has exercised peremptory challenges to remove all people from the jury who are or appear to be under the age of 30. Discuss whether these challenges are proper under California law.

B. Kate was injured in a one-car accident while driving near Redding. She was not hospitalized and did not lose any work as a result of the accident. The initial police report stated that the accident was a result of rainy weather and slippery roads. Despite the findings in the accident report, Kate's lawyer, Liora, filed suit in Shasta County Superior Court against Auto Group, the car's manufacturer, alleging that malfunctioning brakes and various design defects in the car caused or contributed to the accident.

During the opening statement, Liora described Kate's theory that the accident was, in fact, caused by the car's defects, and Liora noted in summary form some of the supporting evidence. After Liora presented her opening statement, Auto Group's attorney, April, moved for a nonsuit, which the judge denied. Liora then proceeded with the presentation of Kate's case. Liora, however, did not offer any expert testimony or other evidence that might establish by a preponderance of evidence that a design defect caused or contributed to Kate's accident. April moved for a directed verdict on behalf of Auto Group, which the judge denied.

After jury deliberations, the jury returned a verdict in favor of Kate, awarding her $3,000,000 in damages. Promptly following the jury verdict, April filed two motions on behalf of Auto Group: one for judgment notwithstanding the verdict (JNOV), and alternatively one for new trial based on excessive damages. The judge denied the JNOV motion. The judge granted the motion for new trial unless Kate accepted a judgment with the damages reduced to $500,000.

Discuss whether the judge's ruling on each of the four motions (nonsuit, directed verdict, JNOV and new trial) was correct.

Answers to Essay Questions

Essay A

(1) Right to Jury Trial

- Shira's entitlement to jury trial:
    - Shira's right does not come from the U.S. Constitution's Seventh Amendment, but rather from California Constitution, art. I, § 16. The right attaches to those causes of action for which a jury trial would have been available under the common law in existence in 1850. California statutes also provide for the right to jury trial for particular causes of action. See, e.g., CCP § 592.
    - Shira has brought both a legal cause of action and an equitable cause of action. Parties generally are entitled to a jury on legal claims, but not on equitable claims. In California, equitable claims are generally tried first, then legal claims (but the court has discretion to reverse the order).
    - The request for an injunction stemming from the wrongful termination allegation will likely be tried first before the judge. Then the jury will try the legal issues, including entitlement to back pay. The jury will be bound by the judge's findings.
    - If Shira's damages and injunctive claims are so intertwined that they cannot be easily separated, the court will determine the "gist of the action." If the court decides that the gist is legal, the jury will try all claims. If the gist is equitable, the court will try all claims.
    - If the legal issues are considered incidental to the equitable issues, the equitable clean-up doctrine would apply and would preclude a jury trial.

- Waiver of right to jury trial:
  - A party must request jury trial in a timely manner—usually in the complaint or answer, but at least at or shortly after the time the case is set for trial. CCP § 631(d)(4). The requesting party also must place a deposit for the cost of the first day (and after each day of trial must place an additional deposit). CCP § 631(b)–(c).
  - Waiver can include: failing to timely demand jury trial; written or oral consent; or failure to deposit jury fees. CCP § 631(d).
  - The court has discretion to relieve a party of a jury trial waiver on just terms. CCP § 631(e).
  - Shira's case has been set for trial, the discovery process has been ongoing, and a summary judgment motion is on the law and motion calendar. Shira has not demanded a jury trial at any stage. Shira appears to have waived her right to a jury trial. But the court may relieve her of the waiver in its discretion.

(2) Regal-Links' Peremptory Challenges

- CCP § 231.5 prohibits the removal of a juror on the assumption that they are biased because they possess one or more of the characteristics listed in Cal. Gov't Code § 11135(a). Age is included in this list, so Regal-Links' pattern of challenges of young prospective jurors can be tested under the *Wheeler/Batson* process. If Shira had alleged in the complaint that discrimination (based on, for example, race or sexual orientation) was a reason for her termination, the more stringent procedures of CCP § 231.7 could potentially apply to test Regal-Links' peremptory challenges. But age is not included in the list of characteristics in section 231.7(a), so CCP § 231.5 will govern the analysis.
- Under the case law interpreting article VI, section 16 of the California Constitution, the jury must be drawn from a representative cross section of the community. To determine whether removing people under 30 is a *constitutionally* impermissible ground for the exercise of peremptory challenges, the court must determine whether this age group constitutes a distinctive or cognizable group in the community.
- The cognizable group test focuses on whether:
  - The members of the group share a common perspective arising from their life experience in the group; and

- No other members of the community can adequately represent the perspective of the group.
    - People under 30 cannot be said to share a common perspective. Young people come from a variety of backgrounds and experiences. Although there may be some common characteristics that younger age groups possess, there is a great deal of variation. Some people under 30 may experience discrimination based on their age, but the group as a whole does not generally have a history of persecution on account of age.
    - Members of other age groups may be able to represent the perspective of people under 30 on the jury.
- Based on this test, the peremptory challenges are likely to be constitutionally permissible because people under 30 do not constitute a cognizable or distinctive group in the community. Nevertheless, based on the applicable California statute, CCP § 231.5, a peremptory challenge on the basis of age should not be allowed.

Essay B

- Nonsuit:
    - Standard: nonsuit is granted if the plaintiff's opening statement has failed to present a prima facie case of each element of the plaintiff's causes of action. The motion may be granted only if it is certain that the facts stated would be insufficient to support a jury verdict in the plaintiff's favor.
        - Only a defendant may move for nonsuit, either after the plaintiff's opening statement or after the plaintiff's presentation of evidence. CCP § 581c(a).
    - Defendant Auto Group timely moved for nonsuit after Liora's opening statement on behalf of Kate.
        - During opening statement, Liora told the jury about some of the evidence she planned to present on the theory that design defects in the car caused the accident.
        - The court properly denied the nonsuit.
        - A nonsuit motion is rarely granted based on the opening statement. Even if nonsuit were appropriate, the court would likely give Liora an opportunity to amend the opening statement rather than grant nonsuit at this stage. Auto Group might also have waited to bring a nonsuit motion until after Liora presented Kate's evidence.

- Directed verdict:
  - Standard: a directed verdict will be granted if, disregarding conflicting evidence and viewing the evidence in the light most favorable to the nonmoving party, the evidence is legally insufficient to support a verdict in favor of the nonmoving party.
    - The standard is same as that for nonsuit, but a directed verdict motion may be made by either the plaintiff or defendant after both sides have presented their evidence. CCP § 630(a).
  - Auto Group moved for a directed verdict at the conclusion of Kate's evidence. The motion is premature under California law, but would be timely under FRCP 50.
  - If the directed verdict motion had been timely, the court probably should have granted it. Liora failed to introduce any evidence suggesting that a design defect caused by Auto Group was the cause of the accident.
- JNOV:
  - Standard: JNOV should be granted when the nonmoving party's evidence is insufficient to support a verdict in its favor, and no reasonable jury could have returned the verdict that was rendered.
    - Either party may move for JNOV after the jury's verdict. CCP § 629. The timing is the same as that for a motion for new trial. CCP §§ 629; 659.
    - The standard is the same as that for nonsuit and directed verdict, but the JNOV motion is made after the jury's verdict.
    - JNOV motions are often combined with motions for new trial.
  - Kate's evidence was insufficient to prove that a design defect caused the accident. Even if the judge denied the directed verdict motion, the JNOV motion should have been granted.
- New trial:
  - Standard: the court may grant a new trial on one or more of the statutory grounds in CCP § 657. The trial court proceedings must have resulted in a "miscarriage of justice." Cal. Const., art. VI, § 13.
    - A new trial may be granted on the ground of excessive damages. CCP § 657(5). The court may make its new

trial order conditional on Kate's acceptance of a lower amount of damages (remittitur), as long as the reduced amount is fair and reasonable. CCP § 662.5.

    - The timing requirements for bringing a motion for new trial are jurisdictional. CCP § 659.

- The court may order a conditional new trial if it concludes that the jury awarded Kate excessive damages for the harm she proved had occurred. If Kate refuses the reduced award, the court will grant Auto Group's motion for a new trial.

CHAPTER 7

SECURING AND ENFORCING JUDGMENTS

I. PROVISIONAL REMEDIES FOR SECURING JUDGMENTS

Provisional remedies are pretrial procedures that help assure that a defendant will be able to satisfy a judgment if the plaintiff prevails.

A. Attachment for Security

Attachment for security is a statutory tool allowing a plaintiff to secure a defendant's (or potential judgment debtor's) property prior to the resolution of litigation. Attachment serves as security against any potential damages the plaintiff might be awarded at the conclusion of litigation and ensures that the plaintiff will actually recover those damages. See CCP § 482.010 et seq.

1. Claims Subject to Attachment

Attachment applies only to a claim for money based on a contract of a fixed or readily ascertainable amount of $500 or more. CCP § 483.010(a). The claim may be unsecured or secured by personal (not real) property. CCP § 483.010(b). In an action against an individual defendant, an attachment may be issued only on a claim arising out of the defendant's conduct of a trade, business, or profession. CCP § 483.010(c).

2. Right to Attach Order

The court must enter a right to attach order authorizing a writ of attachment. The right to attach order is ordinarily issued after notice and hearing, but in cases of great or irreparable injury to the plaintiff, the court may issue an ex parte order. CCP §§ 484.010; 484.040 & 485.220. See also Western Steel and Ship Repair, Inc. v. RMI, Inc., 176 Cal.App.3d 1108, 222 Cal.Rptr. 556 (1986).

3. Property Subject to Attachment

Any property of a corporation or other business entity may be attached. CCP § 487.010(a). As to an individual defendant, only nonexempt property (such as real property, accounts receivable or equipment) may be attached. CCP § 487.010(c). All other property of an individual is exempt. CCP § 487.020.

4. *Compare Federal Procedure*

FRCP 64(a) authorizes federal courts to follow the attachment laws of the state in which the court is located in order to seize and secure property to satisfy a judgment. The U.S. Supreme Court has emphasized the importance of providing a defendant with advance notice and an opportunity to be heard as means of protecting the defendant's due process rights. United States v. James Daniel Good Real Property, 510 U.S. 43, 114 S.Ct. 492, 126 L.Ed.2d 490 (1993).

5. Illustration

Ophelia Owner entered a commercial lease agreement with Tessa Tenant for office space in Woodland. Ophelia filed suit against Tessa in Yolo County Superior Court for breach of the lease based on Tessa's failure to make timely payments under the lease. Ophelia applied for a right to attach order for $60,000 to cover the amount of money Tessa still owed under the lease. Tessa filed opposition to the request for attachment. Ophelia's reply papers set out several new legal arguments. The court issued the right to attach order without a hearing. The court does not have discretion to issue the order without a hearing. CCP § 484.040. Tessa must be given a chance to respond to the new arguments set forth in Ophelia's reply papers. Hobbs v. Weiss, 73 Cal.App.4th 76, 86 Cal.Rptr.2d 146 (1999).

B. Preliminary Injunctions and Temporary Restraining Orders

1. Preliminary Injunctions

A preliminary injunction allows a court to preserve the status quo pending the final determination of an underlying action at trial. See generally CCP §§ 526 & 527.

a. Requirements for Preliminary Injunction

Notice and an opportunity to be heard are absolute requirements for the issuance of a preliminary injunction. In addition, injunctive relief involves consideration of two core matters by the court:

- the inadequacy of any existing remedies at law, including whether the moving party will suffer irreparable harm before the case can been fully adjudicated; and
- the likelihood that the moving party (usually the plaintiff) will succeed on the merits of the underlying action.

After analysis of the above factors, the court balances the harm likely to be suffered by the moving party if the injunction is denied versus the harm likely to be suffered by the nonmoving party if the injunction is granted. People v. Uber Technologies, Inc., 56 Cal.App.5th 266, 270 Cal.Rptr.3d 290 (2020).

1) Inadequacy of Existing Remedies at Law and Irreparable Harm

The moving party must show that money damages will provide inadequate redress for any pending harm. Pacific Decision Sciences Corp. v. Superior Court, 121 Cal.App.4th 1100, 18 Cal.Rptr.3d 104 (2004). If money damages can provide sufficient redress, the movant will not suffer irreparable harm and cannot obtain injunctive relief. Irreparable harm is presumed where constitutional rights or real property rights are involved.

2) Reasonable Probability of Success

The moving party has the burden to demonstrate facts sufficient to show a "reasonable probability" of success on the merits. Fleishman v. Superior Court, 102 Cal.App.4th 350, 125 Cal.Rptr.2d 383 (2002). The court must make credibility assessments and weigh the evidence, even though a full factual record does not yet exist. If it clearly appears that the moving party cannot succeed on the underlying action, the injunction will be denied.

3) Sliding Scale

Some courts employ a "sliding scale" approach in analyzing the core factors. Under this analysis, a party who makes a stronger showing of likelihood to prevail on the merits may make a lesser showing of harm that would result if the injunction is not granted. People v. Uber Technologies, Inc., 56 Cal.App.5th 266, 270 Cal.Rptr.3d 290 (2020).

4) Balancing Respective Harms

The court must weigh the respective harms to the parties. "If the denial of an injunction would result in great harm to the plaintiff, and the defendants would suffer little harm if it were granted, then it is an abuse of discretion to fail to grant the preliminary injunction." Robbins v. Superior Court, 38 Cal.3d 199, 205, 211 Cal.Rptr. 398, 401, 695 P.2d 695 (1985). Because of the inherently equitable nature of injunctive relief, the outcome of an application for an injunction often turns on the relative harm to each party.

b. Types of Preliminary Injunctions

1) Mandatory and Prohibitory Injunctions

Mandatory injunctions command a party to perform (or to continue to perform) a particular action. Prohibitory injunctions, which are more common, command a party to cease or refrain from a particular action. Whether an injunction is mandatory or prohibitory depends not on its label but on its effect. Because mandatory injunctions compel a party to act, they may be stayed pending appeal of the injunction. Prohibitory injunctions may not be stayed on appeal.

2) Statutory Injunctions

Various statutory claims give rise to injunctive relief. Among these are: claims of harassment (CCP § 527.6); fraudulent transfer (Cal. Civ. Code § 3439.07); restraint of trade (Cal. Bus. & Prof. Code § 16753); and misappropriation of trade secrets (Cal. Civ. Code § 3426 et seq.). The moving party seeking a statutory injunction must show a likelihood of success on the merits and that it will suffer greater harm if the injunction is denied than the nonmoving party will suffer if the injunction is granted. The inadequacy of legal remedies is effectively already established by the applicable statutory provisions.

c. Security

The moving party is required to post a bond—also called an "undertaking"—if the court grants its request for a preliminary injunction. CCP § 529(a). This security is designed to cover any damages that the nonmoving party incurs if the injunction turns out to have been incorrectly issued. The injunction is not effective until the undertaking is posted. Certain parties are exempt from the bond requirement, including indigent parties, parties in a marital dissolution dispute, and governmental entities. CCP § 529(b).

2. Temporary Restraining Orders

A temporary restraining order (TRO) requires the same showing by the moving party as needed for a preliminary injunction: inadequate remedies at law and irreparable harm; a reasonable probability of success on the merits; and a balancing of comparative harms. TROs, however, are short in duration (typically 10–15 days), although they can be extended upon notice to the opposing party. TROs are normally issued pending a hearing on a preliminary injunction. TROs, unlike preliminary injunctions, can be issued ex parte on a showing that: (a) the moving party will suffer great harm before the matter can be heard with notice to the nonmoving party; and (b) the moving party attempted to give the opposing party notice. CCP § 527(c); and Ross v. Figueroa, 139 Cal.App.4th 856, 43 Cal.Rptr.3d 289 (2006). A bond is not mandatory for a TRO to issue.

3. *Compare Federal Procedure*

A federal preliminary injunction may issue only after notice to the opposing party, whereas a TRO may be granted without notice under limited circumstances. FRCP 65 (a)–(b)(1). The test for granting preliminary injunctive relief under FRCP 65 is similar to California's. "A plaintiff seeking a preliminary injunction must establish that he is likely to succeed on the merits, that he is likely to suffer irreparable harm in the absence of preliminary relief, that the balance of equities tips in his favor, and that an injunction is in the public interest." Winter v. Natural Resources Defense Council, 555 U.S. 7, 20, 129 S.Ct. 365, 375, 172 L.Ed.2d 249 (2008). *Winter* questioned the "sliding scale" approach used by some California state courts, where a weaker showing of harm may be offset by a stronger showing of likelihood of prevailing on the merits. As an additional threshold matter, before a preliminary injunction may issue in federal court, the plaintiff must make a showing that subject matter jurisdiction exists. FRCP 65(c) requires the posting of an undertaking to obtain a TRO or preliminary injunction, in an amount the court deems proper.

4. Illustration

Prince Entertainment, Inc. is in the business of providing live adult entertainment at restaurants it runs in San Diego County. As the COVID-19 pandemic gained momentum, the State of California and the County of San Diego issued restrictions on restaurants, which had the effect of curtailing Prince's adult entertainment business. Prince Entertainment sued the state and county in San Diego County Superior Court, seeking a preliminary injunction to prevent the enforcement of the public health restrictions. The injunction will not be issued. First, Prince Entertainment cannot demonstrate it is likely to prevail on the merits. The public health restrictions placed on restaurants do not violate Prince Entertainment's First Amendment rights because the restrictions are unrelated to suppression of expression. Second, a request to enjoin public agencies (state and county) from performing their duties requires Prince Properties to make a "significant showing" of irreparable harm, which it has failed to do. Third, the requested injunction is unreasonably vague. It would prohibit enforcement of all but "essential" restrictions, but it does not specify what those essential protocols are. It thus failed to provide reasonable notice of the conduct it seeks to restrict. Midway Venture LLC v. County of San Diego, 60 Cal.App.5th 58, 65, 274 Cal.Rptr.3d 383, 392 (2021).

II. ENFORCEMENT OF JUDGMENTS AND ORDERS

Once the plaintiff has obtained a judgment against the defendant, several statutory tools are available to the plaintiff to enforce and collect on the judgment.

A. Execution

1. California Money Judgments

Money judgments are not self-executing. Judgment creditors must follow detailed procedural steps set forth by state law to collect on money judgments. Judgments are enforceable for a period of ten years following the date of entry. CCP § 683.020. A judgment creditor may renew a judgment for additional ten-year periods by filing a renewal application before the current ten-year period has expired. CCP §§ 683.120 & 683.180. See also Backlund v. Stone, 115 Cal.App.5th 580, 338 Cal.Rptr.3d 251 (2025). The judgment creditor often records the judgment in the counties where the judgment debtor owns property in order to create a lien.

a. Writ of Execution

The judgment creditor may apply to the court clerk to issue a writ of execution to enforce a money judgment. CCP § 699.510. Once the judgment creditor obtains a writ of execution, the creditor then compels the levying officer (typically the sheriff) to enforce the judgment. Id. A levy creates an execution lien that is satisfied by selling or taking possession of the judgment debtor's property (real or personal). CCP §§ 697.710 & 701.510. The judgment debtor must be served with notice of the levy. CCP § 700.010. The notice identifies the property subject to the levy and informs the judgment debtor of its rights and duties under the levy. CCP § 699.540.

b. Property Exempt from Writ of Execution

All of the judgment debtor's property (personal and real) is subject to levy under a writ of execution unless the property is exempt. CCP §§ 695.010(a) & 699.710. Examples of exempt property include: the combination of equity in and proceeds from motor vehicles, in the amount of $8625 (CCP § 704.010); reasonably necessary household furnishings (CCP § 704.020); reasonably necessary and actually used "tools of the trade" up to $10,950 (CCP § 704.060(a)); and jewelry, heirlooms, and works of art up to $10,950 (CCP § 704.040). See Cal. Form EJ–156 (Apr. 1, 2025) (current dollar amounts of exemptions). A judgment debtor may claim a "homestead" exemption on his principal dwelling, ranging from $300,000 to $600,000, adjusted for inflation. CCP §§ 704.710–.780. Exemptions not claimed in a timely manner are waived, subjecting the property to enforcement of the judgment. CCP § 703.030(a). A judgment debtor's wages may be levied (garnished) to satisfy a judgment, but a percentage will be shielded from garnishment. CCP § 706.050.

c. Sale of Levied Property

The levying officer must sell all property levied upon in order to satisfy a money judgment. CCP § 701.510. The levying officer must first serve notice of the intended sale on the judgment debtor, either personally or by mail. CCP § 701.530. The proceeds of the sale must be distributed in order of priority until the money is exhausted. Certain creditors, such as tax authorities or mechanic's lien holders, may be entitled to higher priority to the proceeds.

2. Enforcement of Sister State Money Judgments

The enforcement in California of money judgments rendered in other states is accomplished via the expedited procedures of the Sister State Money-Judgments Act. CCP § 1710.10 et seq.; and Kahn v. Berman, 198 Cal.App.3d 1499, 244 Cal.Rptr. 575 (1988). The judgment creditor files an application for entry of the judgment in the superior court in the county where the judgment debtor resides, or in any county if the judgment debtor is not a resident of California. CCP §§ 1710.15 & 1710.20. The court clerk enters the judgment pursuant to the same procedures as California money judgments. CCP § 1710.25. The judgment creditor then serves the notice of entry of the judgment on the judgment debtor. CCP § 1710.30. The sister state judgment has the same effect as a judgment originally entered in California. CCP § 1710.35; and Casey v. Hill, 79 Cal.App.5th 937, 294 Cal.Rptr.3d 298 (2022).

3. Enforcement of Foreign Money Judgments

Under California's Uniform Foreign-Country Money Judgments Recognition Act (CCP § 1713 et seq.), a judgment creditor cannot enforce a money judgment from a foreign country in the expedited manner permitted for enforcement of sister state judgments. A foreign judgment may be enforced only by filing an original action and providing proper service of process. CCP § 1718; and Renoir v. Redstar Corp., 123 Cal.App.4th 1145, 20 Cal.Rptr.3d 603 (2004).

4. Enforcement of Arbitration Awards

Contractual arbitration awards rendered in California or in another state may be enforced even if they are not reduced to a court judgment. A foreign arbitration award is enforceable pursuant to treaty. Dial 800 v. Fesbinder, 118 Cal.App.4th 32, 12 Cal.Rptr.3d 711 (2004). See, e.g., New York Convention on the Recognition and Enforcement of Foreign Arbitral Awards, which is incorporated into the Federal Arbitration Act. See also Chapter 5(I)(C) for discussion of California's international arbitration statutes.

5. *Compare Federal Procedure*

Federal law provides that "[e]very judgment rendered by a district court within a State shall be a lien on the property located in such State * * * under the same conditions as a judgment of a court of general jurisdiction in such State, and shall cease to be a lien in the same manner and time." 28 USC § 1962. Thus, with some exceptions, federal courts sitting in California will follow the state's enforcement of judgments law as long as the judgment debtor resides within the state. See also FRCP 64(a) (federal courts may apply state enforcement of judgments law) & 69(a)(1) (state law governs the enforcement of a judgment in federal courts unless a federal statute applies). State court judgments are accorded full faith and credit in the federal courts. 28 USC § 1738.

6. Illustration

Pippa won a money judgment against Dubya, a Greeley Hill antiques dealer, in Mariposa County Superior Court. Pippa properly followed all procedures for enforcing the judgment via a writ of execution. Dubya claimed that three items of personal property were exempt from execution: a sewing machine; a pressing iron; and a surveyor's kit. Dubya contended that these items fell within the "tools of the trade" exemption of CCP § 704.060(a) because they constituted an integral part of Dubya's business and served as tools to attract consigners. Dubya's exemption request will be denied because those items constitute inventory of his business, not tools of his trade. Examples of the types of items held exempt under section 704.060(a) are computers to operate an online business, a safe for a jewelry business, and a truck used by a traveling repair person. Kono v. Meeker, 196 Cal.App.4th 81, 126 Cal.Rptr.3d 208 (2011).

B. Receivers

1. Appointment of Receiver

Receivers serve as officers of the court to collect money to satisfy a judgment or to manage property during pending litigation when there is a chance the property might be transferred or reduced in value before the conclusion of the action. The court may appoint a receiver after a judgment has been rendered if the judgment creditor establishes that a receivership is a "reasonable method to obtain the fair and orderly satisfaction of the judgment." CCP § 708.620. Alternatively, the court may appoint a receiver during the litigation. CCP § 564. The receiver serves as a fiduciary of both parties and must exercise great care when managing the given property. If a receiver breaches her fiduciary duty, she may be held personally liable. City and County of San Francisco v. Daley, 16 Cal.App.4th 734, 20 Cal.Rptr.2d 256 (1993).

2. *Compare Federal Procedure*

Federal courts may also appoint receivers. FRCP 66. The appointment of a receiver is regarded as an extraordinary remedy.

3. Illustration

Pimple sued Dimple in Sonoma County Superior Court for breach of a lease agreement. Pimple obtained a judgment for $38,000. Pimple placed a lien on Dimple's bank account, but it had a balance of only $2000. Dimple operates a popular and successful esthetics spa in Healdsburg, where Pimple had obtained facials in the past. Although Pimple suspected that Dimple had ownership interests in several rental properties throughout the county, Dimple stated that her interests in those properties were subject to a trust agreement whereby Dimple's mother-in-law received the rental income. Given the difficulty Pimple experienced in tracking down Dimple's properties and confirming the nature of her interests, the court will likely grant Pimple's request that it appoint a receiver to oversee the collection of the remaining $36,000 of the judgment out of the income generated from Dimple's esthetics spa. Medipro Medical Staffing LLC v. Certified Nursing Registry, Inc., 60 Cal.App.5th 622, 274 Cal.Rptr.3d 797 (2021).

C. Contempt of Court

A court order entered against a party may be enforced by contempt proceedings in the event the order is disobeyed. A party may behave in other ways that constitute contempt of court, such as unlawfully interfering with the court's process or proceedings, disorderly conduct toward a judge during a proceeding, or unlawfully detaining a witness or party going to court. CCP § 1209. Contempt may be either direct (in the presence of the court) or indirect (outside the presence of the court). CCP § 1211. In addition to statutory contempt measures, a court has inherent power to punish a party for conduct that interferes with the orderly proceedings of the court. CCP § 128(a)(3).

1. Elements of Contempt

To find contempt, the following elements must be established:

- entry of a valid order;
- actual knowledge of the order;
- ability to comply with the order; and

- willful failure to comply with the order.

In re Ivey, 85 Cal.App.4th 793, 102 Cal.Rptr.2d 447 (2000).

2. Types of Contempt

a. Civil Contempt

A party commits civil contempt by disobeying a court order benefiting another party. Typically, civil contempt proceedings are coercive in nature—the contempt order is intended to persuade the disobedient party to comply with the court order by imposing a fine (up to $1000), jail time (up to five days), or both. CCP § 1218(a). See Kim v. R Consulting & Sales, Inc., 67 Cal.App.5th 263, 281 Cal.Rptr.3d 918 (2021) (discussing quasi-criminal nature of civil contempt).

b. Criminal Contempt

Criminal contempt occurs when a party willfully disobeys a court order or is disrespectful toward the court or a judge. The purposes of punishing the contemptuous party in this context are to preserve the integrity of the court and to protect the administration of justice. Willful disobedience of a court order may constitute a misdemeanor under Cal. Penal Code § 166(a)(4).

3. Contempt Proceedings

a. Protections

Several constitutional protections are available to the contemnor because of the quasi-criminal nature of civil contempt proceedings. Such protections include a presumption of innocence, right to cross-examine adverse witnesses, and assistance of counsel. A right to a jury trial exists only if the fixed sentence to be imposed exceeds six months of incarceration.

b. Due Process

Whether a contempt order violates a contemnor's due process rights depends on the punishment. If the court's punishment is conditioned on compliance with the original order—e.g. the party shall be incarcerated until she complies—the order is not criminal in nature. The proceeding need only comply with *civil* due process requirements, such as providing notice to the party and affording an opportunity to be heard. However, if the court's punishment is not conditioned on compliance, but rather is entirely punitive (e.g., the party must pay a $15,000 fine for disrespect to the court), the contempt is considered criminal, and the alleged contemnor is entitled to *criminal* due process protections. Hicks v. Feiock, 485 U.S. 624, 108 S.Ct. 1423, 99 L.Ed.2d 721 (1988).

4. *Compare Federal Procedure*

Federal contempt proceedings are similar to California's and are subject to the same due process limitations. Notably, however, federal contempt sanctions usually are not subject to the strict fine and jail time limitations imposed by statute in California. Some federal courts have ordered multimillion-dollar fines as well as lengthy terms of imprisonment. See American Airlines, Inc. v. Allied Pilots Association, 228 F.3d 574 (5th Cir.2000) (affirming contempt fine of $45.5 million). But see United Mine Workers v. Bagwell, 512 U.S. 821, 114 S.Ct. 2552, 129 L.Ed.2d 642 (1994) (contempt fine exceeding $50 million considered criminal in nature and can be imposed only through jury trial).

5. Illustration

Archie is an attorney practicing in Hollister in San Benito County. Archie represented a client on a matter that was pending before the California Court of Appeal for the Sixth Appellate District. Archie filed a petition for rehearing containing "nine pages of text that more closely resembled a rant than a petition." For example, Archie lashed out with "jeremiads about 'society going down the tubes' and courts whose decisions are based not on a reading of the law but on their general corruption and openness to political influence." The Court of Appeal held Archie in direct contempt under CCP § 1209(a) for impugning the integrity of the trial and appellate court in the petition. It fined him $2,000 and ordered the judgment of contempt to be forwarded to the State Bar of California. In re Mahoney, 65 Cal.App.5th 376, 378–380, 280 Cal.Rptr.3d 2, 3–4 (2021), cert. denied, 595 U.S. ___, 142 S.Ct. 1117, 212 L.Ed.2d 12 (2022).

III. COSTS AND ATTORNEY'S FEES

A. Costs

1. Right to Costs

The right to recover costs of suit is created by statute. Historically, the "American Rule" has required that costs, like attorney's fees, be borne by each party. Today, however, the governing statutes have effectively reversed the historical presumption. The main costs statute, CCP § 1032(b), states that, except as otherwise expressly provided by statute, the "prevailing party" is entitled to costs as a matter of right. Examples of statutory exceptions include CCP § 998 (offer of judgment; see Chapter 5(VI)), and Cal. Gov't Code § 12965 (FEHA).

2. Prevailing Party

a. Statutory Definitions

The prevailing party, who is entitled to recovery of costs as a matter of right, is statutorily defined as:

- the party with a net monetary recovery;
- a defendant in whose favor a dismissal is entered;
- a defendant where neither the plaintiff nor the defendant obtains any relief; or
- a defendant as against those plaintiffs who do not recover any relief against that defendant.

CCP § 1032(a)(4).

b. Court's Discretion

If a party's recovery is nonmonetary or otherwise does not fit into one of the statutory definitions, the court must designate the prevailing party. Under these circumstances, the court then exercises its discretion to allow costs or not. If it does allow costs, it may apportion them between the parties. CCP § 1032(a)(4); and Lincoln v. Schurgin, 39 Cal.App.4th 100, 45 Cal.Rptr.2d 874 (1995).

3. Recovery of Costs

a. Allowable Costs

Costs must be "allowable," as defined by CCP § 1033.5. Allowable costs include: filing, motion and jury fees; juror expenses; deposition fees; regular witness fees; and court reporter fees. CCP § 1033.5(a). Expert witness fees are not allowable costs, unless the experts were ordered by the court to appear. CCP § 1033.5(a)(8) & (b)(1). Cost items that are not allowable unless expressly authorized by law include investigation expenses in preparing for trial and transcripts of court proceedings not ordered by the court. CCP § 1033.5(b). Costs for other items not specifically addressed by statute may be allowed in the discretion of the court. CCP § 1033.5(c)(4).

b. Other Requirements

Any expenses, including those expressly allowed by law, must:

- be actually incurred;
- be reasonably necessary to the conduct of the litigation (rather than merely convenient or beneficial to its preparation); and
- not exceed a reasonable amount.

CCP § 1033.5(c).

4. Attorney's Fees as Costs

Attorney's fees are considered an allowable cost when authorized by contract, statute or law. CCP § 1033.5(a)(10). Statutes providing for "costs and attorney's fees" are uniformly interpreted to allow the recovery of attorney's fees as a component of the costs if permitted under CCP § 1033.5(a)(10)(B). CCP § 1033.5(c)(5).

5. *Compare Federal Procedure*

Under FRCP 54(d)(1), a federal district court "should" award costs to the prevailing party. Unlike California, the district court does not award costs as a matter of right to the prevailing party. The federal court retains substantial discretion. The applicable federal statute, 28 USC § 1920, lists limited categories of allowable costs. The entitlement to an award of attorney's fees as costs is less clear under federal law than under California law. An example of the confusion is the provision in FRCP 68 for shifting costs based on an offer of judgment. The cost award varies depending upon the definition of "costs" in the underlying federal statute involved in the suit. Marek v. Chesny, 473 U.S. 1, 105 S.Ct. 3012, 87 L.Ed.2d 1 (1985).

6. Illustration

Polly was fired from her job in Chilcoot. She sued her employer, Dolly's Diner, for wrongful termination in Plumas County Superior Court. The case went to trial, and the jury found for Dolly's Diner. Pursuant to CCP § 1032, Dolly's Diner, as the prevailing party, sought recovery of the costs of preparing photocopies of exhibits, exhibit binders, and closing argument demonstratives. Dolly's Diner did not actually use those items at trial. Polly opposed these costs. Dolly's Diner may recover the cost of preparing these materials only if they were "reasonably helpful to aid the trier of fact." CCP

> § 1033.5(a)(13). Since they were not presented to the trier of fact, the cost of their preparation is not allowable. However, the court has discretion to allow those costs under CCP § 1033.5(c)(4). Even though the materials were not used at trial, the costs will be recoverable if they were reasonably necessary to the conduct of litigation and were reasonable in amount. Segal v. ASICS Corp., 12 Cal.5th 651, 288 Cal.Rptr.3d 742, 502 P.3d 389 (2022).

B. Attorney's Fees

1. Right to Recover Attorney's Fees

California follows the "American Rule," under which each side bears its own attorney's fees unless a law or the parties' agreement provides otherwise. CCP § 1021. However, California recognizes important exceptions based on fee-shifting statutes, contractual fee provisions, and equitable doctrines. CCP § 1033.5(a)(10).

a. Statutory Fee Shifting

Several California statutes provide for the shifting of the entitlement to recover attorney's fees.

1) Private Attorney General

California's "private attorney general" statute encourages parties to bring lawsuits to vindicate the public interest. It awards attorney's fees to the successful party in an action that resulted in the "enforcement of an important right affecting the public interest," as long as:

- a significant benefit has been conferred on the general public or a large class of people (beyond the litigating party);
- "the necessity and financial burden of private enforcement" make a fee award appropriate; and
- the fee is not paid out of the recovery.

CCP § 1021.5; and Let Them Choose v. San Diego Unified School District, 103 Cal.App.5th 953, 323 Cal.Rptr.3d 521 (2024). A plaintiff is typically considered the successful party if she served as a "catalyst motivating defendants to provide the primary relief sought" or "activat[ed] defendants to modify their behavior." Graham v. Daimler-Chrysler Corp., 34

Cal.4th 553, 567, 21 Cal.Rptr.3d 331, 341, 101 P.3d 140 (2004). The plaintiff need not have obtained all of the relief sought in the lawsuit.

2) Other Fee-Shifting Statutes

Some fee-shifting statutes provide that the losing party must pay the prevailing party's attorney's fees. Other provisions are "one way," awarding fees to a prevailing plaintiff, but not to a prevailing defendant. Compare, e.g., Cal. Lab. Code § 218.5 (two-way fee-shifting statute for actions to recover unpaid wages, fringe benefits, or health and welfare or pension fund contributions) with Cal. Lab. Code § 1194 (one-way fee-shifting statute for actions to recover unpaid minimum wage or overtime compensation).

b. Contractual Fee Shifting

Parties to a contract are free to provide for the shifting of attorney's fees by agreement. CCP § 1021. One-way fee provisions in a contract—awarding fees to one specified party or the other in an action on the contract—are interpreted by California courts as two-way provisions in which the prevailing party is entitled to recover fees. Cal. Civ. Code § 1717(a).

1) Prevailing Party on the Contract

The fee-shifting provision of Cal. Civ. Code § 1717 permits an award of fees to the "party prevailing on the contract." The prevailing party is defined as "the party who recovered a greater relief in the action on the contract." Cal. Civ. Code § 1717(b)(1). The court has discretion to determine that there is no party prevailing on the contract. In addition, there is no prevailing party if the action has been dismissed voluntarily or pursuant to settlement. Cal. Civ. Code § 1717(b).

2) Prevailing Party on Noncontract Claims

A prevailing party's entitlement to recovery of attorney's fees under Cal. Civ. Code § 1717 for noncontract (e.g., tort) claims that are conjoined with contract claims must be determined under the terms of the contract's attorney's fee provision. Eden Township Healthcare District v. Eden Medical Center, 220 Cal.App.4th 418, 162 Cal.Rptr.3d 932 (2013).

c. Equitable Fee Shifting

California recognizes a few equitable exceptions to the American Rule. One significant exception is the "common fund." Where a party brings an action to preserve a common fund of money, often in a class action, that party is entitled to attorney's fees paid out of the fund. The California Supreme Court created another exception in Brandt v. Superior Court, 37 Cal.3d 813, 210 Cal.Rptr. 211, 693 P.2d 796 (1985), where the court held attorney's fees to be a compensable form of damages when an insurer refused in bad faith to pay policy benefits. California courts retain the authority to recognize new equitable exceptions. Serrano v. Priest, 20 Cal.3d 25, 141 Cal.Rptr. 315, 569 P.2d 1303 (1977).

2. Calculating Attorney's Fees

Whether entitlement to fees is based on statute, contract or equitable principles, California generally determines the appropriate amount of attorney's fees by multiplying the reasonable hourly rate for comparable work in the legal community by the reasonable (not actual) number of hours expended, arriving at a figure known as the "lodestar." The trial court has wide discretion in determining the actual fee, and it may adjust the lodestar higher for novel and difficult questions, particular skill in litigation, the extent to which the case precluded the attorneys from working on other matters, and the "contingent nature of the fee award." Ketchum v. Moses, 24 Cal.4th 1122, 1132, 104 Cal.Rptr.2d 377, 384, 17 P.3d 735 (2001). The lodestar method of calculating attorney's fees is contrasted with the "cost plus" method, in which the actual number of hours expended is multiplied by the attorney's actual hourly rate.

3. *Compare Federal Procedure*

The U.S. Supreme Court has held that the American Rule is a " 'bedrock principle' " from which the Court does "not deviate * * * 'absent explicit statutory authority.' " Baker Botts L.L.P. v. ASARCO LLC, 576 U.S. 121, 126, 135 S.Ct. 2158, 2164, 192 L.Ed.2d 208 (2015). There are many federal fee-shifting provisions tied to specific statutes. Most prevailing party statutes are interpreted to provide for attorney's fees for a prevailing plaintiff, but not for a defendant unless the plaintiff's action was frivolous, unreasonable, or without foundation. Christiansburg Garment Co. v. EEOC, 434 U.S. 412, 98 S.Ct. 694, 54 L.Ed.2d 648 (1978). In contrast to California's private attorney general statute—CCP § 1021.5—there is no federal omnibus private attorney general statute. The party must prevail on a cause of action based on a statute that specifically allows the award of fees. Moreover, federal law does not recognize the "catalyst" theory in determining whether the plaintiff was the prevailing party under a statute. Rather, the plaintiff must have obtained a judgment on the merits or a court-sanctioned consent decree. Lackey v. Stinnie, 604 U.S. 192, 145 S.Ct. 659, 221 L.Ed.2d 63 (2025). In calculating the amount of attorney's fees to be awarded, enhancements to the basic lodestar figure are largely disapproved in federal court. Perdue v. Kenny A. ex rel. Winn, 559 U.S. 542, 130 S.Ct. 1662, 176 L.Ed.2d 494 (2010).

4. Illustration

Put It Elsewhere! (PIE) was formed by a group of concerned homeowners who wanted to keep the City of Dublin from building a four-story housing development for senior citizens in their neighborhood. The Dublin city council held a hearing and granted approval for the development. PIE brought suit in Alameda County Superior Court against the City of Dublin, alleging due process violations because Dublin did not give PIE a fair hearing, and attacking the project on various environmental and zoning grounds. The court agreed that PIE did not receive a fair hearing and ordered Dublin to hold a rehearing. The court reserved the other issues. After the rehearing, Dublin again approved the project. PIE returned to court to challenge the project on the environmental and zoning grounds, but it was unsuccessful. PIE then sought to recover its attorney's fees under CCP § 1021.5, California's private attorney general statute. The requirements of section 1021.5 have been satisfied. Although PIE was unsuccessful in preventing the project from going forward, it accomplished other worthy outcomes. The lawsuit resulted in additional public input, increased citywide accountability, and improvements to the hearing process. Bowman v. City of Berkeley, 131 Cal.App.4th 173, 31 Cal.Rptr.3d 447 (2005).

SAMPLE EXAM QUESTIONS

OBJECTIVE QUESTIONS

The questions in this section are based on the following hypothetical:

Lenny Landlord owned several houses in Brawley. Two of these houses had been vacant for some time, and they became sites of drug use and dealing by nonresidents of the neighborhood. Ned Neighbor brought a lawsuit in Imperial County Superior Court against Landlord for maintaining a nuisance. Neighbor sought damages as well as a preliminary and a permanent injunction mandating that Landlord abate the nuisance and provide adequate maintenance and supervision of his properties.

---

(1) True or False: Neighbor may seek prejudgment attachment of Landlord's property to ensure that Landlord will be able to satisfy any possible judgment in Neighbor's favor.

(2) In deciding whether to grant Neighbor's application for a preliminary injunction, which of the following must the court consider?

a. Neighbor's likelihood of success on the merits;

b. Whether there is an inadequate remedy at law, so that Neighbor will suffer irreparable harm before the case can be fully heard;

c. The harm that Neighbor will suffer if the injunction is denied, balanced against the harm that Landlord will suffer if the injunction is granted;

d. All of the above.

(3) True or False: Due process requires that Landlord must receive notice before the court issues a preliminary injunction against him.

(4) True or False: If Neighbor is designated the prevailing party after trial, he may recover only those allowable costs specifically enumerated by statute.

(5) In the *Neighbor v. Landlord* litigation, who will be designated a prevailing party entitled to an award of costs as of right?

a. Landlord, if Neighbor voluntarily dismissed him from the action;

b. Neighbor, if he won a permanent injunction against Landlord;

c. Neither Neighbor nor Landlord, because an award of costs as of right is permitted only when the litigation arises from a contract which entitles the prevailing party to recover costs under the contract;

d. Neither Neighbor nor Landlord, because the litigation did not arise from a statutory claim for which an award of costs to the prevailing party is statutorily required.

(6) The court is considering whether Landlord has committed contempt of court. Which of the following most accurately describes the difference between the concepts of civil and criminal contempt?

a. Civil contempt is a violation of an order issued in civil proceedings, while criminal contempt is a violation of an order issued in criminal proceedings;

b. Civil contempt can occur when one party fails to comply with a court order benefiting another party, while criminal contempt can remedy an act of disrespect or disobedience against the court;

c. In civil contempt proceedings, the court may impose only fines, while in criminal contempt proceedings it may order only incarceration;

d. None of the above.

(7) True or False: Neighbor may request the court to appoint a receiver either during the pendency of the lawsuit or after he wins a judgment.

(8) True or False: The court may not issue a temporary restraining order against Landlord unless Neighbor posts an undertaking.

(9) True or False: Neighbor could potentially recover attorney's fees under the private attorney general statute even if he did not obtain all of the relief he was seeking.

(10) If Neighbor wins a judgment for damages against Landlord and then seeks to enforce the judgment:

a. Landlord's own place of dwelling is automatically exempt from execution of the judgment;

b. The procedures governing enforcement of Neighbor's California money judgment are identical to those governing enforcement of foreign money judgments;

c. Neighbor must serve Landlord with a notice that his property is subject to a levy;

d. Neighbor's judgment will expire after ten years and may not be renewed.

<u>Answers to Objective Questions</u>

(1) **False.** CCP § 483.010 provides that prejudgment attachments may issue only in contract actions from which a claim for money arises. Neighbor's lawsuit is a tort action.

(2) **d.** The court will order injunctive relief only if all of these requirements are satisfied.

(3) **True.** The court may grant a preliminary injunction only after Landlord has been notified and given an opportunity to respond. In contrast, a temporary restraining order may be issued without notice.

(4) **False.** Items of costs that are not specifically included in the listing of allowable costs of CCP § 1033.5(a) may nevertheless be allowed in the court's discretion. CCP § 1033.5(c)(4).

(5) **a.** CCP § 1032(a)(4) sets out the definitions of a prevailing party who may recover costs as a matter of right. One of those definitions is "a defendant in whose favor a dismissal is entered." Answer (b) is incorrect because Neighbor is a plaintiff who has won nonmonetary relief. This outcome does not fit any of the four categories of section 1032(a), which would have resulted in an award of costs as a matter of right. Therefore, Neighbor is governed by the second sentence of that section, where the court decides who is the prevailing party, and a cost award is discretionary. Answers (c) and (d) are incorrect because an award of costs is not dependent on whether the litigation arose from contract or statute.

(6) **b.** Civil contempt orders are intended to force a party to comply with an adverse order that benefits another party. Criminal contempt orders punish disobedience or disrespect directed at the court. The court may order a fine and/or incarceration in both civil and criminal contempt.

(7) **True.** The court may appoint a receiver either during the litigation (CCP § 564) or after judgment (CCP § 708.620).

(8) **False.** Unlike preliminary injunctions, where an undertaking is typically required, the plaintiff need not post a bond when the court grants a temporary restraining order, unless the court orders otherwise.

(9) **True.** If Neighbor obtained limited relief, he may recover a lower amount of attorney's fees. In addition, if Neighbor acted as a catalyst that motivated Landlord to change his behavior, Neighbor will be considered the prevailing party entitled to attorney's fees.

(10) **c.** Notice to the judgment debtor of the levy is required. CCP § 700.010. Answer (a) is incorrect because the homestead exemption is not automatic; it must be claimed. In addition, the exemption might not protect the entire market value of the home. Answer (b) is incorrect because the enforcement of foreign money judgments involves the filing of an original action and the service of process. Answer (d) is incorrect because a judgment expires ten years after its entry, but it may be renewed for additional ten-year periods. CCP §§ 683.120 & 683.180.

ESSAY QUESTION

Brothers Mike and Kyle grew up in Atascadero. Mike and Kyle inherited from their parents a substantial estate consisting of a large home, a guesthouse, and a vineyard on a six-acre plot of land. The title to the estate is in the names of both Mike and Kyle. Kyle, a somewhat underhanded businessperson, sold the estate without Mike's consent to

DOG Properties, a strip mall developer who planned to demolish the home, guesthouse, and vineyard, and build a shopping center. Mike sued both Kyle and DOG Properties in San Luis Obispo County Superior Court for damages and for recovery of the family estate (to which Mike has great sentimental attachment).

DOG Properties is eager to begin development. Mike has requested a temporary restraining order and preliminary injunction to prevent DOG Properties from demolishing the buildings and vineyard pending adjudication of the propriety of the transfer of the estate to DOG Properties.

(1) Should the court grant the temporary restraining order? Should the court grant the preliminary injunction? Discuss the analysis the court must undertake for each form of relief.

(2) Assume Mike ultimately prevails in the lawsuit and obtains a judgment for damages from DOG Properties and Kyle for wrongful transfer. Discuss what steps Mike might take to enforce the judgment.

(3) Assume that before trial, Mike decides to voluntarily dismiss his lawsuit against Kyle, and the court enters a judgment of dismissal as to Kyle. Mike's action against DOG Properties proceeds through trial, where Mike obtains a judgment for damages. Discuss the entitlement of Kyle and Mike to recover their respective costs and attorney's fees.

Answer to Essay Question

(1) Temporary Restraining Order and Preliminary Injunction

- Temporary Restraining Order:
  - TRO will be issued if irreparable injury will occur before a preliminary injunction hearing can be held.
    - The court will issue a TRO for a period of 15 days if no notice is provided to DOG Properties.
  - Mike must show:
    - Irreparable injury will occur without the issuance of the TRO;
    - No adequate remedy at law;
    - Reasonable probability that Mike will prevail on his cause of action against DOG Properties; and
    - The harm to Mike if the TRO is denied outweighs the harm to DOG Properties and Kyle if the TRO is issued.
  - Mike may obtain the TRO ex parte if he would suffer irreparable harm if the matter had to wait to be heard on notice to DOG Properties and Kyle.

- Although a bond is usually not required for a TRO, the court has discretion to require an undertaking from Mike.
- Application:
  - Irreparable injury: Mike likely has a successful argument for irreparable injury. DOG Properties seems eager to begin demolition. Mike also has great sentimental attachment to the estate, so if DOG Properties demolishes the buildings and the vineyard on the estate, it is likely irreplaceable to Mike.
  - No adequate remedy: If not stopped quickly, DOG Properties will likely demolish the buildings and vineyard on the estate before Mike can have the matter tried, and damages will be inadequate to compensate for the loss.
  - Probability of prevailing: Mike will probably be able to make a prima facie showing of the elements of his cause of action against DOG Properties and Kyle. Mike is a rightful owner of his parents' estate and did not consent to its sale. Further, the facts indicate that DOG Properties and Kyle were acting in bad faith.
  - Balance of harms: Mike's harm would be the destruction of the buildings and the vineyard, whereas the harm to DOG Properties would be monetary in the sense that its construction project would be delayed. Therefore, Mike's harm probably outweighs the harm to DOG Properties.
  - Notice: Mike will probably argue that providing notice of the TRO might provoke DOG Properties to hurriedly demolish the buildings and vineyard and thus could cause more damage.
  - Undertaking: The court might require Mike to post a bond before it will issue the TRO. However, that is within the judge's discretion to decide.

- Preliminary Injunction:
  - The court will apply the elements listed above for a TRO.
  - The court will not issue a preliminary injunction in the absence of notice to DOG Properties and Kyle.
  - Mike will be required to provide an undertaking before the preliminary injunction will issue.

(2) Enforcement

- Alternatives:
  - Writ of Execution: Mike may apply for a writ of execution to enforce the money judgment. Assets belonging to DOG Properties and Kyle may then be sold by the levying officer to satisfy the judgment. DOG Properties and Kyle may attempt to claim various exemptions.
  - Appointment of a receiver: Mike could request the appointment of a receiver to collect money from businesses operated by DOG Properties or Kyle. However, this is an extraordinary remedy, and likely is a last resort.

(3) Costs and Attorney's Fees

- Kyle's Costs and Fees:
  - Kyle is entitled to recover his costs as a prevailing party because he is a defendant in whose favor a dismissal was entered. CCP § 1032(a)(4).
  - Kyle is not entitled to recover his attorney's fees under any statute, contract or law. CCP § 1033.5(a)(10). Mike's lawsuit was not an action on a contract, so there is no fee-shifting available under Cal. Civ. Code § 1717. Even if section 1717 applied to Mike's action, Kyle would still not be entitled to his attorney's fees because a party who is voluntarily dismissed from the action is not considered a prevailing party.
- Mike's Costs and Fees:
  - Mike is entitled to recover his costs as a prevailing party because he received a net monetary recovery against DOG Properties. CCP § 1032(a)(4).
  - Mike is not entitled to recover his attorney's fees under any statute, contract or law. CCP § 1033.5(a)(10). The American Rule applies, requiring Mike to bear his own attorney's fees.

CHAPTER 8

APPELLATE REVIEW

I. RIGHT OF APPEAL

The California Constitution sets out the jurisdiction (power) of the appellate courts. See Cal. Const., art. VI, §§ 11, 12. But it is statutory law that largely determines the types of judgments and orders from which a party may appeal. CCP § 904.1. In addition, judicially created doctrines and exceptions (see section III(A)(2), below) have expanded the availability of appeal beyond what is provided by statute. A right of appeal may not be conferred by stipulation, consent, estoppel or waiver. In appropriate cases, a party may seek review via a petition for extraordinary writ instead of by appeal (see section III(B)(1), below). The California Court System chart in Chapter 1(A)(3) summarizes the appellate and original jurisdiction of the three levels of state courts.

A. Review by Superior Court Appellate Division

1. Limited Civil Cases

A party in a limited civil case has a right to appeal from a judgment, but only to the appellate division of the superior court. CCP §§ 77(e) & 904.2. See also Dedication and Everlasting Love to Animals v. City of El Monte, 85 Cal.App.5th 113, 301 Cal.Rptr.3d 141 (2022). The Court of Appeal may hear an appeal of a limited civil case judgment only if the superior court certifies the appeal, or if the Court of Appeal determines, on its own motion, that transferring the case to the Court of Appeal is appropriate. CCP § 911.

2. Small Claims Cases

A defendant (but not a plaintiff) may "appeal" a small claims judgment to the superior court. The superior court proceedings are not actually an appeal. Instead, the superior court conducts a trial de novo. The judgment of the superior court is not appealable. CCP § 116.780. Postjudgment orders rendered by the superior court to enforce the judgment are reviewable by that court's appellate division. General Electric Capital Auto Financial Services, Inc. v. Appellate Division of Superior Court, 88 Cal.App.4th 136, 105 Cal.Rptr.2d 552 (2001).

B. Review by Court of Appeal

1. Superior Court Rulings in Unlimited Civil Cases

Appealable judgments and orders rendered by the superior court in unlimited civil cases generally may be appealed to the Court of Appeal. See CCP § 904.1. The Court of Appeal also hears petitions for extraordinary writs.

2. Administrative Rulings

The Court of Appeal has jurisdiction over appeals and writ proceedings from decisions of the Workers' Compensation Appeals Board, Agricultural Labor Relations Board, and Public Employment Relations Board.

C. Review by California Supreme Court

1. Civil Cases

California Supreme Court review of civil decisions of the Court of Appeal is discretionary. Grounds for review include securing uniformity of decisions or settling important questions of law. CRC 8.500(b)(1). The process of appeal to the Supreme Court is initiated by the filing of a petition for review within ten days after the decision of the Court of Appeal becomes final. CRC 8.500(a) & (e). The California Supreme Court grants review in only two to five percent of the civil matters in which a petition is filed.

2. Criminal Cases

The California Supreme Court has discretion to review decisions of the courts of appeal in criminal matters. However, all criminal judgments imposing the death penalty are automatically appealed directly from the superior courts to the Supreme Court.

3. Administrative Rulings

The California Supreme Court has original jurisdiction over review of certain decisions of the Public Utilities Commission, recommendations of the State Bar in attorney admission and disciplinary proceedings, and recommendations from the Commission on Judicial Performance on disciplinary proceedings regarding judges.

II. NATURE OF REVIEW BY COURT OF APPEAL

The purpose of review by the Court of Appeal is to correct prejudicial error committed by the trial court. (See section VI, below.) The Court of Appeal does not retry the trial court action. It bases its review on the trial court record, applying the appropriate standard of review (see section V, below).

A. Presumption of Correctness

The trial court's judgment or order is generally presumed to be correct. The appellant must demonstrate prejudicial (reversible) error. Jameson v. Desta, 5 Cal.5th 594, 234 Cal.Rptr.3d 831, 420 P.3d 746 (2018). Ambiguities in the trial court record are resolved in favor of affirming the trial court order or judgment. The trial court's decision will be affirmed as long as it was correct, even if the court's reasoning was incorrect.

B. Trial Court Record and Appellant's Burden

It is the appellant's burden to demonstrate prejudicial error through an adequate trial court record. The central role played by the record in the appellate process compels trial attorneys to be mindful of creating an adequate record in which grounds for appeal have been preserved. The record should reflect that the appellant interposed timely and proper objections during the trial court proceedings in order to prevent waiver of those objections on appeal. Generally, the appellant is not permitted to raise matters before the Court of Appeal that were not included and preserved in the trial court record.

C. Statement of Decision

In a nonjury (court) trial, a party may request the trial court to issue a statement of decision explaining the legal and factual bases for its decision as to each controverted issue. CCP §§ 632 & 634. (See Chapter 6(VI)(C).) The Court of Appeal may use the statement of decision in its review of the trial court judgment to determine if the decision is both factually and legally supported. If the appellant failed to request a statement of decision, the Court of Appeal will imply findings in support of the judgment. Atkinson v. Department of Motor Vehicles, 102 Cal.App.5th 997, 322 Cal.Rptr.3d 198 (2024).

D. Appellate Court Dispositions

An appellate court "may affirm, reverse, or modify" the trial court judgment or order, and may "direct the proper judgment or order to be entered, or direct a new trial or further proceedings to be had." CCP § 43. Reversal may be accompanied by directions to the trial court to proceed in a particular manner.

III. APPEALABILITY

A threshold issue for an appellate court is whether the judgment or order before it is appealable. This can be a challenging inquiry, one with serious consequences. "[T]he existence of an appealable judgment is a jurisdictional prerequisite to an appeal. A reviewing court must raise the issue on its own initiative whenever a doubt exists as to whether the trial court has entered a final judgment or other [appealable] order or judgment." Thompson v. Ioane, 11 Cal.App.5th 1180, 1189, 218 Cal.Rptr.3d 501, 508 (2017). The appellate court reviews only those orders and judgments specified in the notice of appeal, which is liberally construed. If a party fails to file a timely notice of appeal from an appealable judgment or order, the chance to obtain appellate review is forfeited. In re Baycol Cases I and II, 51 Cal.4th 751, 761 n.8, 122 Cal.Rptr.3d 153, 160 n.8, 248 P.3d 681 (2011) (describing California's " 'one shot' rule"). If an appeal is taken from a nonappealable judgment or order, the appellate court must dismiss the appeal, unless it exercises its discretion to treat the infirm appeal as a petition for an extraordinary writ. See also section III(B), below.

A. Appealable Judgments and Orders

1. One Final Judgment Rule

a. Appeal from Judgment

CCP § 904.1(a)(1) codifies the one final judgment rule, permitting an appeal from "a judgment" in the action. A judgment is defined as "the final determination of the rights of the parties in an action or proceeding." CCP § 577. Normally, only one final judgment is rendered by the trial court, from which the appellant files a notice of appeal. The appellate court seeks to avoid piecemeal appeals of nonfinal trial court orders or judgments.

b. Finality

An order or judgment is considered final "when it terminates the litigation between the parties on the merits of the case and leaves nothing to be done but to enforce by execution what has been determined." Dana Point Safe Harbor Collective v. Superior Court, 51 Cal.4th 1, 5, 118 Cal.Rptr.3d 571, 577, 243 P.3d 575 (2010). Labeling a judgment or order as final is not determinative. The appellate court considers the actual content and effect of the disposition.

c. *Compare Federal Procedure*

Federal appellate courts review "final decisions" of the district courts. 28 USC § 1291. Similar to the California standard, a final decision is one that " 'ends the litigation on the merits and leaves nothing for the court to do but execute the judgment.' " Ray Haluch Gravel Co. v. Central

Pension Fund, 571 U.S. 177, 183, 134 S.Ct. 773, 779, 187 L.Ed.2d 669 (2014). A federal judgment must be set forth in a separate document. FRCP 58.

d. Illustration

Ally, Bally and Cally were partners in the ownership and management of an apartment building in Rocklin. Ally accused Bally and Cally of violating the partnership agreement by failing to maintain accurate records and properly account for rental income. Ally brought suit in Placer County Superior Court to dissolve the partnership and sell the assets. The trial court entered judgment for dissolution of the partnership and sale of the apartment building. The judgment did not specify the ownership interests of each partner, did not completely provide for the allocation of sale proceeds, and did not state how partnership costs and expenses would be allocated among the partners. Bally and Cally filed a notice of appeal from the judgment. The appeal will be dismissed because it was not taken from a final judgment. The judgment did not resolve several key matters, requiring the trial court to conduct additional proceedings. Because piecemeal appeals are disfavored, Bally and Cally must wait to appeal until after the trial court enters a single, complete and final resolution of the issues. Kinoshita v. Horio, 186 Cal.App.3d 959, 231 Cal.Rptr. 241 (1986).

2. Judicially Created Exceptions to One Final Judgment Rule

a. Actions Involving Multiple Parties or Causes of Action

1) Judgment Final as to Party

In actions involving multiple plaintiffs or defendants, a judgment is considered final as to a party if it leaves no issue for further determination for that particular plaintiff or defendant, even if further proceedings are pending against other parties. Hydrotech Systems, Ltd. v. Oasis Waterpark, 52 Cal.3d 988, 277 Cal.Rptr. 517, 803 P.2d 370 (1991).

2) Compare: Multiple Causes of Action

In actions involving multiple causes of action, there is no appealable judgment until all causes of action are finally determined. If some causes of action are ordered to be tried separately and reach final determination, but additional causes of action remain for disposition, an appeal from a judgment adjudicating the separately tried causes of action is premature. Morehart v. County of Santa Barbara, 7 Cal.4th 725, 29 Cal.Rptr.2d 804, 872 P.2d 143 (1994). Moreover, if the additional causes of action are voluntarily dismissed without prejudice, with a waiver of the statute of limitations, the judgment on the adjudicated causes of action is not final and appealable. Kurwa v. Kislinger, 57 Cal.4th 1097, 162 Cal.Rptr.3d 516, 309 P.3d 838 (2012).

3) *Compare Federal Procedure*

Under FRCP 54(b), a district court may enter a judgment as to fewer than all parties *and* claims, as long as the court expressly determines that there is no just reason for delay and directs the entry of a partial final judgment. If the court does not make this express determination and direction, any judgment as to fewer than all parties or claims is not considered a final judgment and is thus not appealable.

4) Illustration

A Deeliver Co.'s driver hit Polka's car with his truck in Downieville while making deliveries under a contract with Fedecks. Polka sued both Deeliver Co. and Fedecks for damages in Sierra County Superior Court. The trial court entered summary judgment for Fedecks and dismissed it from the lawsuit. Polka's lawsuit against Deeliver Co. continued. Two months later, the trial court entered summary judgment for Deeliver Co. One month after that, Polka filed a notice of appeal from the two summary judgments entered for Fedecks and Deeliver Co., respectively. The appeal from the judgment for Fedecks was untimely. The trial court rendered a final appealable judgment as to Fedecks separately from the judgment for Deeliver Co., and Polka should not have waited until the second judgment to seek appeal as to both defendants. The judgment for Fedecks was final as to that party because it left no further issues to be resolved and was not dependent on the court's ruling as to Deeliver Co. Therefore, the untimely appeal from the judgment for Fedecks should be dismissed.

> Millsap v. Federal Express Corp., 227 Cal.App.3d 425, 277 Cal.Rptr. 807 (1991).

b. Collateral Order Doctrine

1) Appealability of Collateral Orders

The collateral order doctrine is a judicially created exception to the one final judgment rule. To be immediately appealable under this doctrine, an order must:

- involve a matter truly collateral to the merits of the litigation;
- be final as to the collateral matter; and
- direct the payment of money by the appellant or the performance of an act by or against the appellant (as required by many, but not all, state appellate decisions).

Sjoberg v. Hastorf, 33 Cal.2d 116, 199 P.2d 668 (1948). Examples of orders reviewed under the collateral order doctrine are those requiring payment of attorney's or arbitrator's fees, ordering the payment of a creditor's lien, or directing the sealing or unsealing of court filings.

a) Collateral Matter

A matter is collateral if it is distinct from the subject matter or merits of the litigation. It is not considered collateral if it is a "necessary step" in determining the merits of the case. Marriage of Grimes & Mou, 45 Cal.App.5th 406, 419, 258 Cal.Rptr.3d 576, 587 (2020). This requirement is construed narrowly in order to keep the collateral order exception from swallowing the one final judgment rule.

b) Final Order

An order is final if no further adjudication is required on the issues addressed by the order.

c) Payment or Performance

Most California appellate decisions mandate that the collateral order must require the payment of money by the appellant or the performance of an act by or against the appellant. Longobardo v.

Avco Corp., 93 Cal.App.5th 429, 310 Cal.Rptr.3d 877 (2023). A minority of appellate opinions has upheld the application of the collateral order doctrine without imposing a payment or performance requirement. See Meehan v. Hopps, 45 Cal.2d 213, 288 P.2d 267 (1955); and Muller v. Fresno Community Hospital & Medical Center, 172 Cal.App.4th 887, 91 Cal.Rptr.3d 617 (2009).

2) ***Compare Federal Procedure***

The collateral order doctrine is recognized in federal courts, but it is narrowly applied so as to be consistent with 28 USC § 1291, which permits appeal only from "final decisions of the district courts." To qualify for immediate appeal as a collateral order, a district court disposition must be conclusive, must resolve an important issue (one completely distinct from the merits), and must otherwise be unreviewable on appeal from the final judgment. Stolt-Nielsen S.A. v. AnimalFeeds International Corp., 559 U.S. 662, 130 S.Ct. 1758, 176 L.Ed.2d 605 (2010). There is no requirement of payment of money or performance of an act, as there is generally in California procedure.

3) Illustration

Pavel and Dora had a brief but intense relationship in Crescent City, and Dora became pregnant. Dora told Pavel that she wanted to raise the child on her own with no participation from him, but Pavel wanted joint legal and physical custody. Pavel sought custody and visitation orders from the family law court in Del Norte County. The court entered a pretrial interim order spelling out the custody and visitation arrangements until a full trial could be held. The court did not rule on child support or other financial issues. Pavel filed a notice of appeal from the order, contending that it was an appealable collateral order. The order is not appealable under the collateral order doctrine. First, the order is not collateral to the merits of the action, which center exclusively on the custody and visitation arrangements between Dora and Pavel. Second, the order does not direct the payment of money or the performance of an act. It only sets out the terms for custody and visitation. Therefore, Pavel must await entry of a final judgment on custody and

> visitation and then appeal from that judgment. Lester v. Lennane, 84 Cal.App.4th 536, 101 Cal.Rptr.2d 86 (2000).

3. Appealable Interlocutory Judgments and Orders

a. Appealability

There is no general right of appeal from an interlocutory (nonfinal) judgment or order (a ruling disposing of a party's motion or application to the trial court). CCP § 904.1, however, does permit immediate appeal from a limited number of specified interlocutory judgments and orders. Examples include:

- an order made after an appealable judgment has been entered;
- an order granting a motion to quash service of summons;
- an order to stay or dismiss an action on grounds of forum non conveniens;
- an order granting a new trial or denying a motion for judgment notwithstanding the verdict;
- an order granting or refusing to grant an injunction;
- an interlocutory judgment directing a partition;
- an interlocutory judgment or order for payment of monetary sanctions exceeding $5,000; and
- an order granting or denying an anti-SLAPP motion.

b. *Compare Federal Procedure*

The federal courts of appeals have authority to review a narrow range of interlocutory orders and decrees. Examples include: (1) orders granting, continuing, modifying, refusing, or dissolving an injunction; (2) orders appointing receivers; and (3) decrees determining the rights and liabilities of the parties in admiralty cases. 28 USC § 1292(a). In addition, if the district court believes an otherwise nonappealable order involves an uncertain but "controlling question of law," and an immediate appeal will materially advance the litigation, the district judge may certify the order for appeal. The Court of Appeals then may, in its discretion, permit the appeal. 28 USC § 1292(b); and ICTSI Oregon, Inc. v. International Longshore and

Warehouse Union, 22 F.4th 1125 (9th Cir.2022). No similar certification procedure exists under California law.

c. Illustration

Parthy purchased a heavy-duty truck from DieHard Truck Co. for use in her scrap metal business in Los Baños. Soon after purchase, Parthy began to experience serious mechanical problems with the truck, and she eventually had to cease using it. She sued DieHard in Merced County Superior Court for breach of warranty damages. At trial, the jury reached a verdict for Parthy and awarded her damages of $70,000. DieHard brought a motion for judgment notwithstanding the verdict (JNOV) and alternatively for new trial. The trial court denied the JNOV motion and granted the new trial motion. Parthy appealed from the order granting the new trial, but DieHard did not appeal from the order denying the JNOV motion. It instead argued in its responding brief to Parthy's appeal that the trial court improperly denied the JNOV motion. Under CCP § 904.1(a)(4), the Court of Appeal has jurisdiction over Parthy's immediate appeal from the order granting the new trial because it is an appealable interlocutory order. The order denying the JNOV motion is also an appealable interlocutory order under CCP § 904.1(a)(4). DieHard's failure to properly appeal from that JNOV order deprives the court of jurisdiction to review it in conjunction with Parthy's appeal of the new trial order. Berge v. International Harvester Co., 142 Cal.App.3d 152, 190 Cal.Rptr. 815 (1983).

B. Nonappealable Judgments and Orders

If a judgment or order is not immediately appealable under any of the rules and exceptions discussed above, a party ordinarily has two choices: wait until the trial court enters a final or otherwise appealable judgment or order in the action; or file a petition for an extraordinary writ. In some cases, the Court of Appeal may treat an "infirm" appeal as an application for an extraordinary writ, even if the party seeking review has not filed a writ petition. Alternatively, the court might decide to "save" the infirm or premature appeal.

1. Review by Extraordinary Writ

a. Nature of Writ Review

An extraordinary writ is an order from a reviewing court to a trial court requiring it to act or prohibiting it from acting in a particular way. Extraordinary writs provide a vehicle for the Court of Appeal to exercise its discretion to provide immediate review of nonappealable trial court judgments and orders. Because writs are considered an extraordinary remedy, requests for them are frequently summarily denied by reviewing courts. The courts of appeal have original jurisdiction over "common law" writs: mandate, prohibition, and certiorari. In addition, writ review may be authorized by statute for particular trial court rulings, such as an order granting or denying a motion for change of venue (CCP § 400), an order denying a motion for summary judgment (CCP § 437c(m)(1)), and an order denying a motion to quash service of summons (CCP § 418.10(c)).

b. Type of Writs

1) Writ of Mandate

A writ of mandate orders the trial court to take affirmative action. The writ corrects an abuse of discretion or compels the performance of a nondiscretionary duty by the trial court. CCP §§ 1084–1086.

2) Writ of Prohibition

A writ of prohibition is preventive. It is used to restrain threatened judicial action that is without or in excess of jurisdiction. CCP § 1102.

3) Writ of Certiorari

A writ of certiorari (sometimes called writ of review) is used to review completed (as opposed to threatened) judicial acts taken without or in excess of jurisdiction. CCP §§ 1067–1068. Examples of matters reviewable by certiorari include: certain contempt orders; judgments of the appellate division of the superior court; nonappealable probate orders; and decisions of the Public Utilities Commission.

4) Compare: Writ of Supersedeas

A writ of supersedeas is issued by the Court of Appeal to preserve the status quo in the trial court pending appeal. The writ suspends the trial court's power to order execution of the judgment or disposition being appealed. CCP § 923. While supersedeas is a form of common law writ, it is not a means to review action taken by the trial court (as the writs of mandate, prohibition, and certiorari provide).

5) Compare: Writ of Error Coram Vobis

The writ of error coram vobis is issued by the Court of Appeal when, during the pendency of the appeal, the appellant learns of new evidence that might have resulted in a trial court order granting reconsideration or a new trial had it been discovered earlier. The writ compels the trial court to reconsider the appealed judgment or order in light of the newly discovered evidence. The writ is considered a "drastic remedy" and will issue only upon a showing by the appellant that the new evidence was not discovered earlier because of extrinsic fraud that prevented a full hearing on the issue. Chaganti v. Superior Court, 73 Cal.App.5th 237, 288 Cal.Rptr.3d 238 (2021).

c. Alternative and Peremptory Writs

Writs of mandate and prohibition may be issued as alternative or peremptory writs. An alternative writ directs the lower court to act or refrain from acting, or, alternatively, to show why it should not be required to perform or refrain from performing that act. Paul Blanco's Good Car Co. Auto Group v. Superior Court, 56 Cal.App.5th 86, 270 Cal.Rptr.3d 164 (2020). A peremptory writ is a final directive to the lower court to act or refrain from acting. A peremptory writ may be issued either after an alternative writ or in the first instance. Johnny W. v. Superior Court, 9 Cal.App.5th 559, 215 Cal.Rptr.3d 372 (2017). Instead of issuing an alternative writ, the appellate court may issue a "*Palma* notice," in which it informs the parties that the court is considering issuing a peremptory writ in the first instance. Textron, Inc. v. Travelers Casualty & Surety Co., 45 Cal.App.5th 733, 744 n.5, 259 Cal.Rptr.3d 26, 34 n.5 (2020).

d. Requirements for Writ Relief

In order to obtain a writ of mandate, prohibition, or certiorari, the petitioner must establish that there is not a plain, speedy, and adequate appellate remedy, and that the petitioner will suffer irreparable harm if the writ petition is denied. Omaha Indemnity Co. v. Superior Court, 209 Cal.App.3d 1266, 258 Cal.Rptr. 66 (1989).

1) No Adequate Remedy

Usually, obtaining appellate review after a final judgment or order has been entered is considered an adequate remedy. The adequacy, however, depends on the circumstances of the case. The requirement of showing no adequate remedy is often satisfied by demonstrating that the remedy of direct appeal is not available, or that hardship or unusual circumstances make review by direct appeal inadequate. Duke v. Superior Court, 18 Cal.App.5th 490, 226 Cal.Rptr.3d 807 (2017).

2) Irreparable Harm

The petitioner must demonstrate that he will suffer some significant and irremediable damage or injury if the writ is not issued.

e. Treating Infirm Appeal as Extraordinary Writ

If a party attempts to appeal from a nonappealable judgment or order (an "infirm" appeal), the Court of Appeal ordinarily dismisses the appeal. However, if the purported appeal involves unusual circumstances, matters of public importance, and/or issues of first impression, the Court of Appeal may choose to treat the infirm appeal as a petition for extraordinary writ. Van v. LanguageLine Solutions, 8 Cal.App.5th 73, 213 Cal.Rptr.3d 822 (2017). The appellate court may be more inclined to grant this treatment where the issue of appealability is confusing or unclear, and where the merits of the issues already have been briefed in full so that judicial economy would be served by not waiting for the time for appeal. Morehart v. County of Santa Barbara, 7 Cal.4th 725, 29 Cal.Rptr.2d 804, 872 P.2d 143 (1994).

f. *Compare Federal Procedure*

The federal appellate rules authorize the writs of mandamus and prohibition. FRAP 21(a). When deciding whether to issue a writ of mandamus or prohibition, courts balance such factors as whether: (1) other means of relief are available; (2) prejudice or damage exists that cannot be corrected on appeal; (3) the lower tribunal's order was clearly erroneous; (4) the lower tribunal's order was a recurring error; and (5) the lower tribunal's error brings up new and important problems or issues of first impression.

In re Williams-Sonoma, Inc., 947 F.3d 535 (9th Cir.2020). The federal writ of certiorari is commonly requested when a litigant seeks U.S. Supreme Court review of decisions rendered by the courts of appeals. 28 USC § 1254. The writ of certiorari is also used as the Supreme Court's means to review decisions of a state's highest court involving issues of federal law. 28 USC § 1257(a).

g. Illustration

Platt regularly pickets and distributes leaflets outside of the Divisadero Women's Clinic. Platt filed suit in San Francisco County Superior Court against the clinic, alleging that clinic staff obstructed Platt from exercising his First Amendment rights to protest the reproductive services provided at the clinic. During the discovery phase of the lawsuit, Platt propounded interrogatories and document demands seeking identifying information for clinic staff and volunteers who were not parties to the lawsuit. The clinic refused to provide the information on the ground of privacy. Platt filed a motion to compel the disclosure. The trial court granted the motion. The clinic filed a petition for an extraordinary writ with the Court of Appeal. Although discovery orders are typically reviewed upon appeal from a final judgment, the writ petition in this case was proper because: (1) it sought immediate review of an issue of first impression concerning important privacy rights of third parties; and (2) the clinic had no adequate remedy at law because the disclosure of names would have occurred before the matter could be heard on appeal after final judgment. Planned Parenthood Golden Gate v. Superior Court, 83 Cal.App.4th 347, 99 Cal.Rptr.2d 627 (2000).

2. Alternative Means of Review of Nonappealable Orders

a. "Saving" Erroneous or Premature Appeal

An erroneous appeal taken from a nonappealable order may be "saved" by the Court of Appeal. The court may exercise its discretion to wait until a notice of appeal is filed from the final judgment and construe the premature appeal as having been taken from the final judgment. However, some courts of appeal have expressed disapproval of this seeming attempt to bypass the requirements of CCP § 904.1. See Cohen v. Equitable Life Assurance Society, 196 Cal.App.3d 669, 242 Cal.Rptr. 84 (1987).

b. Immediate Review of Nonappealable Orders

If the trial court enters an interlocutory judgment or order made immediately appealable by CCP § 904.1, and that judgment or order is appealed, the Court of Appeal may review any other intermediate nonappealable ruling made by the trial court that "involves the merits or necessarily affects the judgment or order appealed from or which substantially affects the rights of a party." CCP § 906; and Estate of Dayan, 5 Cal.App.5th 29, 209 Cal.Rptr.3d 712 (2016).

IV. OTHER ISSUES AFFECTING APPELLATE REVIEW

In addition to determining the appealability of a judgment or order, issues of standing to appeal and timeliness of the filing of the notice of appeal affect the Court of Appeal's ability to review the matter before it.

A. Standing

Standing to appeal is a jurisdictional requirement. Only a "party aggrieved" has standing to appeal from a judgment or order. CCP § 902.

1. "Party"

To be considered a party, a person or entity generally must be a party of record (named party) to the action in the trial court. A person or entity not named in the trial court action nevertheless might become a party by, for example, successfully moving to intervene in the lawsuit. Hernandez v. Restoration Hardware, Inc., 4 Cal.5th 260, 228 Cal.Rptr.3d 106, 409 P.3d 281 (2018).

2. "Aggrieved"

An aggrieved party "is one whose rights or interests are injuriously affected by the decision in an immediate and substantial way, and not as a nominal or remote consequence of the decision." Doe v. Regents of University of California, 80 Cal.App.5th 282, 293, 295 Cal.Rptr.3d 625, 637 (2022).

3. Aggrieved Nonparties

Nonparties who are aggrieved by a trial court ruling might have standing to appeal from that ruling if: (a) they have an immediate, pecuniary, and substantial interest that is adversely affected by the trial court's ruling; and (b) the ruling has claim-preclusive effect on the nonparties (see Chapter 9(II)(A), below).

Marsh v. Mountain Zephyr, Inc., 43 Cal.App.4th 289, 50 Cal.Rptr.2d 493 (1996).

4. ***Compare Federal Procedure***

Only a party injured by the district court judgment has standing to appeal in the federal appellate courts. Town of Chester v. Laroe Estates, Inc., 581 U.S. 433, 137 S.Ct. 1645, 198 L.Ed.2d 64 (2017).

5. **Illustration**

Preet is among 20 plaintiffs in an action in San Joaquin County Superior Court against the Dragon Scouts youth club in Lathrop. The complaint alleged sexual abuse by three of the club's adult counselors. The individual counselors were not named as parties in Preet's lawsuit. A trial court ruling authorized the public release of sensitive and confidential documents concerning the counselors, despite the counselors' privacy claims. Following entry of judgment for the plaintiffs in the lawsuit, the counselors filed a notice of appeal, seeking review of the trial court's disclosure ruling. Preet argued that the counselors did not have standing to appeal the trial court ruling because they were not parties to the underlying lawsuit. The counselors will be considered aggrieved nonparties with standing to appeal because they have an immediate, pecuniary, and substantial interest that is adversely affected by the trial court's disclosure ruling, and because the ruling has claim-preclusive effect on them. In re The Clergy Cases I, 188 Cal.App.4th 1224, 116 Cal.Rptr.3d 360 (2010).

B. Timeliness of Appeal

1. Filing Notice of Appeal

An aggrieved party triggers the Court of Appeal's jurisdiction by filing a timely notice of appeal in the superior court. CRC 8.100(a)(1). The purpose of the notice of appeal, which is liberally construed, is to "provide notice of who is seeking review of what order or judgment—so as to properly invoke appellate jurisdiction." K.J. v. Los Angeles Unified School District, 8 Cal.5th 875, 883, 257 Cal.Rptr.3d 850, 855, 456 P.3d 988 (2020).

2. Timeliness of Notice of Appeal

CRC 8.104 and 8.108 set out the time limits for filing this notice. These limits are considered jurisdictional—if a party files an untimely notice of appeal, the Court of Appeal has no choice but to dismiss the appeal. CRC 8.104(b); and Meinhardt v. City of

Sunnyvale, 16 Cal.5th 643, 323 Cal.Rptr.3d 354, 552 P.3d 420 (2024). The court may not relieve or excuse a party from the consequences of filing an untimely notice of appeal, even if the party makes a showing of good cause. CRC 8.60(d).

a. Normal Time Limits

A notice of appeal must be filed on or before the earliest of the following times:

- 60 days after the superior court clerk serves a copy of the "Notice of Entry" of judgment or a file-stamped copy of the judgment, showing the date either was served;
- 60 days after appellant serves or is served by a party with a copy of the "Notice of Entry" of judgment or a file-stamped copy of the judgment, accompanied by proof of service; or
- 180 days after entry of judgment.

CRC 8.104(a). "Judgment" includes an appealable order. CRC 8.104(e). The date of entry of a judgment is the date it is filed or entered in the book of judgments. The date of entry of an appealable order is the date it is entered in the minutes. However, if the minute order directs that a written order be prepared, the date of entry is the date the signed order is filed. The date of entry of an order not entered into the minutes is the date the signed order is filed. CRC 8.104(c).

b. Extended Time Limits

1) Post-Order or Post-Judgment Motions

CRC 8.108 extends the normal deadlines in CRC 8.104(a) for filing the notice of appeal in situations where certain post-order or post-judgment motions have been filed in the trial court. These include motions: (a) for new trial; (b) to vacate judgment; (c) for judgment notwithstanding the verdict; and (d) to reconsider an appealable order. These extensions give the would-be appellant additional time to file an appeal following the trial court's ruling on the motion, as long as the motion in the trial court was itself timely.

2) Cross-Appeals

If a party files a notice of appeal after another party has already filed a notice of appeal as to the same judgment or order, the second notice of appeal is treated as a cross-appeal. The timely filing of the first notice of appeal extends the deadline for all cross-appeals for 20 days after the trial court serves notice of the filing of the first appeal. CRC 8.108(g)(1).

c. Premature Appeals

A notice of appeal filed after a judgment is rendered but before the judgment has been entered is a valid notice. The notice is treated as if it had been filed immediately after entry of judgment. CRC 8.104(d)(1). If the notice of appeal was filed before the judgment was actually rendered but after the announcement of the intended ruling, the Court of Appeal may, in its discretion, treat the notice of appeal as having been filed immediately after the entry of judgment. CRC 8.104(d)(2).

3. *Compare Federal Procedure*

Federal appeals are generally subject to shorter time limits than in California. In most cases, a notice of appeal must be filed with the district court clerk within 30 days after entry of the judgment or order being appealed. FRAP 4(a)(1)(A); 28 USC § 2107(a). This time limit may be extended when particular post-judgment motions have been filed. In those cases, the time to file the notice of appeal begins to run for all parties upon the entry of the order disposing of the last remaining motion. FRAP 4(a)(4). In marked contrast to California procedure, the district court may extend the time to file the notice of appeal if a party shows excusable neglect or good cause. FRAP 4(a)(5); 28 USC § 2107(c). The district court may also, upon motion of a party, reopen the time to file a notice of appeal if that party shows that it did not receive notice of the entry of the judgment or order. FRAP 4(a)(6); 28 USC § 2107(c).

4. Illustration

Pack bought a valuable-looking old globe from Dana's secondhand shop in St. Helena. Dana represented that the globe was a rare specimen made in 1880, but Pack later learned (by taking it to a taping of "Antiques Roadshow") that the globe was actually a reproduction made much later and had little monetary value. Pack sued Dana for fraud in Napa County Superior Court. Dana filed a general demurrer to the complaint, which the trial court sustained without leave to amend. The court entered a judgment of dismissal on May 1. On June 1, Dana mailed a notice of entry of judgment, along

> with a proof of service, to Pack's post office box, but Dana had written an incorrect address on the envelope. On September 9, Pack filed a notice of appeal. Dana argued that the appeal should be dismissed as untimely, since Pack filed it more than 60 days after Dana served the notice of entry of judgment and proof of service. However, in the context of the strict construction of CRC 8.104(a), notice sent to an incorrect address is not valid notice, even if the notice is actually received. Thus, the nonconforming notice of entry of judgment did not trigger the time for Pack to file a notice of appeal. Valero Refining Co. v. Bay Area Air Quality Management District Hearing Board, 49 Cal.App.5th 618, 262 Cal.Rotr.3d 885 (2020).

C. Mootness

1. Dismissal of Moot Appeal

Appellate courts may hear only "justiciable" matters. An appeal must "concern a present, concrete, and genuine dispute as to which the court can grant effective relief," which means the "prospect of a remedy that can have a practical, tangible impact on the parties' conduct or legal status." In re I.A., 201 Cal.App.4th 1484, 1489–1490, 134 Cal.Rptr.3d 441, 445–446 (2011). An appeal that does not meet these requirements is moot and must be dismissed. An appeal may become moot by circumstances occurring after the filing of the notice of appeal (such as settlement or performance of an enjoined act).

2. Discretion to Hear Moot Appeal

The Court of Appeal may exercise its discretion to hear a moot appeal if the issue is " 'of broad public interest that is likely to recur,' 'when there may be a recurrence of the controversy between the parties,' or 'when a material question remains for the court's determination.' " In re D.P., 14 Cal.5th 266, 282, 303 Cal.Rptr.3d 388, 400, 522 P.3d 645 (2023).

3. *Compare Federal Procedure*

A federal appeal is moot if there is no longer a "present controversy * * * as to which an appellate court can grant effective relief." Vegas Diamond Properties, LLC v. FDIC, 669 F.3d 933, 936 (9th Cir.2012). A plaintiff who is appealing may avoid a mootness dismissal if she shows that she is likely to again be subject to the same wrongdoing and that no other avenue of review exists. Id.

4. Illustration

Poppy struggled with mental illness for most of her life. Pursuant to a petition filed by the Imperial County Public Guardian, the Imperial County Superior Court found Poppy to be gravely disabled because she was unable to provide for her food, clothing, or housing needs. The court appointed the Public Guardian as her conservator for one year. Prior to the expiration of the conservatorship, the court granted the Public Guardian's petition to reestablish the conservatorship for an additional year, despite Poppy's objection. Poppy appealed from the judgment of reestablishment. Poppy's reestablished conservatorship terminated while her appeal was pending. The Public Guardian sought to dismiss the appeal on the ground of mootness, arguing that the appellate court could no longer grant effective relief as to Poppy since the conservatorship did not remain in place. The Court of Appeal, however, may exercise its discretion to reach the merits of the appeal because the reestablishment of Poppy's conservatorship is an issue of public interest that is likely to recur in other cases and to repeatedly evade review. "Because a conservatorship is relatively brief (one year) in comparison with the appellate process, * * * this issue . . . is one capable of recurring, yet of evading review because of mootness." In re Conservatorship of Joseph W., 199 Cal.App.4th 953, 961, 131 Cal.Rptr.3d 896, 901 (2011).

V. STANDARD OF REVIEW

A. Purpose and Types of Standards of Review

When the appellate court reviews the trial court record for prejudicial error, it must apply the appropriate standard of review. The standard of review affects the degree of deference the appellate court must give to the trial court's ruling. There are three principal standards of review: (1) de novo (independent); (2) abuse of discretion; and (3) substantial evidence. In many cases, the reviewing court will apply more than one standard, depending on the nature of the trial court rulings. Anderson v. County of Santa Barbara, 94 Cal.App.5th 554, 312 Cal.Rptr.3d 43 (2023).

1. De Novo (Independent) Standard

De novo review accords no deference to the trial court's judgment. This standard is applied when the appellate court reviews pure questions of law. Examples include: (a) interpretation of statutes or contracts; (b) determination of whether a duty of care is owed; (c) constitutional issues; and (d) the application of law to undisputed facts. See Make UC a Good Neighbor v. Regents of University of California, 16 Cal.5th 43, 321 Cal.Rptr.3d 409, 548 P.3d 1051 (2024) (statutory interpretation).

2. Abuse of Discretion Standard

If the trial court's ruling was based on the judge's exercise of discretion, the appellate court reviews that ruling under the abuse of discretion standard. The reviewing court will reverse the trial court judgment only if the exercise of discretion resulted in a "miscarriage of justice." The most common formulation of this standard is that the appellate court assesses whether the trial court's ruling exceeded "the bounds of reason." Walker v. Superior Court, 53 Cal.3d 257, 272, 279 Cal.Rptr. 576, 585, 807 P.2d 418 (1991). This standard offers great deference to the trial court's decision. Dozens of trial court rulings are reviewed under the abuse of discretion standard, including discovery rulings, attorney's fee awards, injunctions, sanctions orders, and orders permitting amendment of pleadings. See Du-All Safety, LLC v. Superior Court, 34 Cal.App.5th 485, 246 Cal.Rptr.3d 211 (2019)(discussing what constitutes an abuse of discretion).

3. Substantial Evidence Standard

a. Nature of Standard

The substantial evidence standard applies when the trial court ruling involves the resolution of factual disputes by either the jury or the court. The reviewing court determines, based on the whole record, whether substantial evidence supports the judgment. If so, it will affirm the judgment. This standard accords significant deference to the trial court's ruling.

b. Quality of Evidence

"Substantial evidence" is not a quantitative inquiry. The appellate court does not weigh the evidence. Instead, it focuses on the quality of the evidence in support of the judgment to determine if it is credible, solid, and of a ponderable legal significance. Very little evidence might be considered substantial if it is of a sound and firm nature; conversely, a great deal of weak evidence is not substantial. For example, the testimony of one credible witness may be considered substantial evidence of a fact, even though the testimony of several other less credible witnesses was contradictory. The substantial evidence standard is used to review such matters as the interpretation of a contract where there is conflicting extrinsic evidence, and the underlying factual basis for the trial court's exercise of discretion. Roddenberry v. Roddenberry, 44 Cal.App.4th 634, 51 Cal.Rptr.2d 907 (1996).

B. *Compare Federal Procedure*

The federal circuit courts apply the same three standards of review discussed above. The Ninth Circuit's abuse of discretion standard requires the Court of Appeals "first to consider whether the district court identified the correct legal standard for decision of the issue before it." Then, the court must "determine whether the district court's findings of fact, and its application of those findings of fact to the correct legal standard, were illogical, implausible, or without support in inferences that may be drawn from facts in the record." United States v. Hinkson, 585 F.3d 1247, 1251 (9th Cir.2009). The federal substantial evidence standard is used only to review factual resolutions by a jury. In reviewing a district court's findings of fact in a nonjury case, the federal appeals court applies the "clearly erroneous" standard instead. FRCP 52(a)(6). A ruling will be found clearly erroneous only if "the reviewing court on the entire evidence is left with the definite and firm conviction that a mistake has been committed." United States v. United States Gypsum Co., 333 U.S. 364, 395, 68 S.Ct. 525, 542, 92 L.Ed. 746 (1948).

C. Illustration

Persis sued Dolan in Nevada County Superior Court for selling Persis a defective piano in Rough and Ready. Dolan filed a motion to strike the complaint because it contained irrelevant allegations, but before the court's ruling, Persis filed an amended complaint. Thereafter, Persis was uncooperative in participating in discovery, and the court granted Dolan's request to appoint a special discovery master. Persis filed numerous motions against the special master, the judge, and Dolan's attorney. The court issued an order declaring Persis a vexatious litigant under CCP § 391. (See Chapter 3(VIII)(B).) Persis appealed from the order. The Court of Appeal's review of the order will involve the application of several standards of review. The trial court's exercise of discretion in declaring Persis a vexatious litigant is reviewed for abuse of discretion. The factual findings underlying the court's exercise of its discretion are reviewed under the substantial evidence standard. The trial court's interpretation of the requirements of and legislative intent behind the vexatious litigant statute is subject to de novo (independent) review. Bravo v. Ismaj, 99 Cal.App.4th 211, 120 Cal.Rptr.2d 879 (2002).

VI. PREJUDICIAL VERSUS HARMLESS ERROR

The Court of Appeal, applying the appropriate standard of review, reviews the trial court record for error. Only prejudicial error is sufficient to cause reversal or modification of the trial court judgment. A finding of harmless error results in affirmance of the judgment.

A. Definition of Prejudicial Error

Error must result in a "miscarriage of justice" in order to be deemed prejudicial. Cal. Const., art. VI, § 13. A miscarriage of justice occurs when "it is reasonably probable that a result more favorable to the appealing party would have been reached in the absence of the error." Cassim v. Allstate Insurance Co., 33 Cal.4th 780, 800, 16 Cal.Rptr.3d 374, 388, 94 P.3d 513 (2004). See also CCP § 475; Cal. Evid. Code §§ 353–354. Any error not resulting in a miscarriage of justice is considered harmless. F.P. v. Monier, 3 Cal.5th 1099, 225 Cal.Rptr.3d 504, 405 P.3d 1076 (2017).

1. Actual Error

Because a judgment is generally presumed to be correct, the appellant has the burden to show actual prejudicial error.

2. Exception: Reversible Error Per Se

In a very limited number of cases, error may be considered reversible per se, relieving the appellant of the requirement to prove prejudicial error. See, e.g., Amato v. Downs, 78 Cal.App.5th 435, 293 Cal.Rptr.3d 682 (2022) (erroneous denial of jury trial right is reversible per se). Other examples of errors presumed to be prejudicial include erroneous restriction on the right of cross-examination, and judicial bias.

3. Invited Error

If an appellant has "invited error" by his conduct in the trial court, he may not seek reversal of the judgment based on that error. A deliberate tactical decision may not form the basis for a claim of prejudicial error in the appellate court. Greisman v. FCA US, LLC, 103 Cal.App.5th 1310, 324 Cal.Rptr.3d 182 (2024). For example, an appellant may not seek review of an erroneous jury instruction that she requested be given.

B. *Compare Federal Procedure*

The federal circuit courts may not reverse a district court judgment if the trial court committed only harmless error. FRCP 61; 28 USC § 2111. Under section 2111, the appellate court must exercise its judgment instead of automatically reversing upon the finding of any error. Under the harmless error statute, there is no automatic reversal for "errors that do not affect the essential fairness of a trial." McDonough Power Equipment, Inc. v. Greenwood, 464 U.S. 548, 553, 104 S.Ct. 845, 848, 78 L.Ed.2d 663 (1984).

C. Illustration

Powell sued Dr. Diablo in Mendocino County Superior Court for medical malpractice for leaving a sponge in Powell's chest after coronary bypass surgery at Willits Hospital. Toward the end of the trial, Powell's attorney made a motion to reopen the testimony of Dr. Diablo. In ruling on the motion, the trial judge stated: "Your motion is denied. This trial is going on its third week. I think the jury is getting tired of repeatedly hearing some of the same testimony. I am, too." On objection from Powell, the judge struck the comment she made from the record and admonished the jury to disregard it. The jury rendered a verdict for Dr. Diablo. On appeal from the judgment, Powell asserted that the judge's comment constituted prejudicial error. Except in unusual circumstances, comments of the trial judge do not result in reversible error, especially where the judge admonished the jury to disregard the comment. Aguayo v. Crompton & Knowles Corp., 183 Cal.App.3d 1032, 228 Cal.Rptr. 768 (1986).

VII. APPELLATE SANCTIONS

The appellate courts are authorized to impose sanctions in connection with appeals (CRC 8.276(a)) and writ petitions (CRC 8.492(a)).

A. Frivolous Appeal or Writ

The Court of Appeal may award sanctions to a respondent for an appellant's filing of a frivolous appeal or a petitioner's filing of a frivolous writ petition. CRC 8.276(a); 8.492(a)(1). An appeal is deemed frivolous under a subjective standard when it is pursued for an improper purpose (such as to harass the respondent or delay the effect of an adverse judgment), or under an objective standard when "any reasonable person would agree the grounds for appeal were totally and completely devoid of merit." Workman v. Colichman, 33

Cal.App.5th 1039, 1062, 245 Cal.Rptr.3d 636, 656 (2019). The reviewing court may add to the costs on appeal the attorney's fees and costs respondent incurred in responding to a frivolous appeal. CCP § 907.

B. Violation of Appellate Procedural Rules

CRC 8.276(a) and 8.492(a)(2) authorize sanctions for unreasonable violations of rules of court governing appeals and writs, respectively. Noland v. Land of the Free, L.P., 114 Cal.App.5th 426, 336 Cal.Rptr.3d 897 (2025) ($10,000 monetary sanction appropriate because attorney used artificial intelligence to help prepare appellate briefs, but did not verify the accuracy of the citations and quotations, many of which were AI-generated hallucinations); and In re S.C., 138 Cal.App.4th 396, 41 Cal.Rptr.3d 453 (2006) (sanctioning appellant's counsel for a variety of violations in the preparation of appellant's opening brief, such as failure to cite to authority, to include relevant facts, and to state each point under a separate heading).

C. Disentitlement Doctrine

In addition to sanctions available to the appellate court as authorized by statute or rule, the judicially created disentitlement doctrine permits the appellate court to exercise its inherent discretion to stay or to dismiss the appeal of a party who has refused to obey the superior court's legal orders. Findleton v. Coyote Valley Band of Pomo Indians, 69 Cal.App.5th 736, 285 Cal.Rptr.3d 47 (2021). The doctrine "prevents a party from seeking assistance from the court while that party is in an attitude of contempt to legal orders and processes of the court." In re A.G., 204 Cal.App.4th 1390, 1399, 139 Cal.Rptr.3d 727, 734–735 (2012).

D. *Compare Federal Procedure*

FRAP 38 authorizes the circuit courts of appeals to "award just damages and single or double costs to the appellee" for a frivolous appeal. An "appeal is frivolous if the results are obvious, or the arguments of error are wholly without merit." In re Girardi, 611 F.3d 1027, 1065 (9th Cir.2010). In addition, 28 USC § 1912 permits an award of damages and costs to the prevailing party "for his delay."

E. Illustration

Punch filed a notice of appeal from a judgment of the Fresno County Superior Court. Punch's opening appellate brief violated several appellate rules of court: (1) it did not organize each argument in a separate section with its own heading; (2) it did not summarize key facts restricted to the contents of the trial court record; (3) it did not include specific page cites to the record; and

(4) its appendix included documents irrelevant to the matters on appeal. In addition, Punch's appeal was frivolous because he raised arguments that were "patently disingenuous" and that "distorted the law, the facts, and logic." The Court of Appeal may remand the case to the trial court for determination of the amount of the sanctions to be imposed on Punch. Evans v. CenterStone Development Co., 134 Cal.App.4th 151, 167–168, 35 Cal.Rptr.3d 745, 757 (2005).

SAMPLE EXAM QUESTIONS

OBJECTIVE QUESTIONS

The questions in this section are based on the following hypothetical:

Gail sued Judah in Lassen County Superior Court for breach of contract, negligence, and fraud. Judah filed a general demurrer as to the breach of contract cause of action. The trial court issued an order sustaining Judah's demurrer without leave to amend. The court then conducted a jury trial on only the negligence cause of action. Judgment was entered for Judah on that cause of action. The fraud cause of action remained pending in the trial court.

---

(1) Gail's right of appeal from the judgment comes from:

a. The U.S. Constitution, consistent with U.S. Supreme Court precedent;

b. The California Constitution, consistent with California Supreme Court precedent;

c. California statute;

d. Both b and c.

(2) True or False: The order sustaining Judah's demurrer without leave to amend as to Gail's breach of contract cause of action is not immediately appealable.

(3) True or False: Gail may immediately appeal from the judgment entered for Judah on the negligence cause of action even though the fraud cause of action remains pending.

(4) True or False: Assume final judgment is entered for Judah on all of Gail's causes of action, and Gail appeals from that judgment. If Gail and Judah reach a settlement of all causes of action during the pendency of Gail's appeal, the appeal will be moot.

(5) Which of the following would NOT be immediately appealable under California statute?

a. An order denying Judah's motion to quash service of summons;

b. An order granting Judah's motion for a new trial or denying Judah's motion for judgment notwithstanding the verdict;

c. An interlocutory judgment requiring that Judah pay monetary sanctions exceeding $5000;

d. An order granting or denying Judah's anti-SLAPP motion to strike.

(6) True or False: The Court of Appeal may permit Gail to file a late notice of appeal if she can show good cause.

(7) True or False: The Court of Appeal has discretion to treat Gail's appeal taken from a nonappealable order as a petition for an extraordinary writ.

(8) True or False: If the trial court found that Gail did not have standing to bring her action, Gail also does not have standing to appeal the trial court's finding of lack of standing.

(9) True or False: If the Court of Appeal applies the substantial evidence standard of review to Gail's appeal of the trial court's final judgment, the appellate court must affirm the judgment if the weight of the evidence favors Judah.

(10) True or False: The Court of Appeal will reverse the trial court's judgment in favor of Gail only if the judgment resulted in a miscarriage of justice.

(11) The Court of Appeal may issue sanctions against Gail if:

a. Gail has filed an appeal for an improper purpose;

b. Gail has filed a writ petition that indisputably has no merit;

c. Gail has filed a brief that does not comply with applicable appellate rules;

d. All of the above.

Answers to Objective Questions

(1) **c.** The right of appeal is statutory. Neither the California nor the U.S. Constitution confers a right of appeal.

(2) **True.** An order sustaining a demurrer, with or without leave to amend, is not an immediately appealable order. CCP § 904.1. Nor is it an appealable collateral order. Gail must wait to appeal from the final judgment of dismissal.

(3) **False.** There can only be one final judgment in an action. The California Supreme Court invalidated a former judicial exception allowing an appeal of severed causes of action while others remained pending. Gail must wait to appeal until the trial court enters final judgment on all causes of action.

(4) **True.** Settlement of all issues pending before the Court of Appeal renders the appeal moot, and the Court of Appeal must dismiss it. There are no issues in this action of public importance, or issues that are likely to recur but evade review, that would cause the court to exercise its discretion to retain the appeal.

(5) **a.** CCP § 904.1 sets out appealable orders and judgments. An order *granting* a motion to quash service of summons is appealable under CCP

§ 904.1(a)(3), but not an order *denying* the motion. An order denying a motion to quash may be reviewed upon a petition for writ of mandate under CCP § 418.10(c). The other orders and judgments referred to in this question are expressly made appealable by section 904.1.

(6) **False.** The requirement of filing a timely notice of appeal is considered to be jurisdictional. The appellate court has no discretion to permit a late-filed appeal, even on a showing of good cause. CRC 8.104(b).

(7) **True.** The appellate court may exercise its discretion to treat an appeal from a nonappealable order as an application for an extraordinary writ if the matter involves unusual circumstances, hardship, an issue of public importance, and/or an issue of first impression.

(8) **False.** A party aggrieved by the trial court's ruling has standing to appeal. If the trial court ruled that Gail did not have standing to bring her action, Gail is aggrieved by the trial court decision and has standing to appeal it.

(9) **False.** The appellate court does not weigh the evidence when it applies the substantial evidence standard of review. The court's focus is on the quality of the evidence in support of the judgment, not the quantity.

(10) **True.** Reversal requires a showing of prejudicial error, which is interpreted as a miscarriage of justice. Cal. Const., art. VI, § 13. This case does not fall into the category of error that would be characterized as reversible per se.

(11) **d.** All of the alternatives set out in this question are proper grounds for an award of sanctions. CRC 8.276 & 8.492.

ESSAY QUESTION

One Friday night, Clay and his friends, Tai and Moe, all of whom had recently turned 18 years of age, were sitting in Moe's car outside of Moe's house in Turlock when two police officers approached the car. The officers had received a report from a neighbor that several teenagers had been loading and unloading firearms in a vehicle matching Moe's car's description. The teens said they had no weapons. They told the officers that they had just been talking and that Moe was about to take Tai and Clay home.

The officers ordered all three teens to get out of the car. Tai did not immediately respond, and one of the officers grabbed Tai by the hair and the back of her shirt and pulled her out of the car. Clay became angry and punched the officer and then reached for the officer's gun. The two officers tackled Clay, placed him in a chokehold, and handcuffed him. The officers also handcuffed Tai and Moe and searched the car. Though the officers did not find firearms or other contraband, they took all three teens into custody and detained them overnight. Clay was charged with resisting arrest and assault on a police officer. No charges were ever filed against Tai and Moe.

All three teens have filed a civil rights lawsuit in Stanislaus County Superior Court against the City of Turlock, the city's police department, and the individual police officers. They alleged that the officers engaged in impermissible profiling based on the teens' young age and that the officers used unnecessary force to arrest and detain them. The teens are seeking damages from the City for the alleged mistreatment, and a preliminary injunction preventing the police department and its officers from engaging in such profiling or using extremely dangerous force to detain suspects.

The trial court granted the preliminary injunction for the plaintiffs on March 14. Tai and Moe filed a motion for summary judgment against all defendants on the cause of action for damages. The court granted the motion and entered summary judgment for Tai and Moe on the damages cause of action on June 22. Clay's cause of action for damages remained pending. The police department wishes to appeal the issuance of the preliminary injunction and the summary judgments in favor of Tai and Moe. It filed its notice of appeal on August 31.

(1) Discuss whether the preliminary injunction and the summary judgment are appealable.

(2) Assume for this question that the trial court's rulings are appealable. Discuss:

(a) how much time the police department has to file its notice of appeal from the entry of the preliminary injunction and the summary judgments; and

(b) which standard(s) of review the Court of Appeal is likely to apply to both sets of rulings.

<u>Answer to Essay Question</u>

(1) <u>Appealability</u>

- Appeal from the preliminary injunction:
    - General Rule: parties may appeal from final judgments.
    - CCP § 904.1(a) permits appeal of certain nonfinal orders and judgments. An order granting an injunction is an immediately appealable order. CCP § 904.1(a)(6).
- Appeal from the summary judgment for Tai and Moe:
    - Entry of summary judgment is a final appealable judgment. In contrast, the defendants would not be able to appeal from the order granting summary judgment. Instead, they would have to file a petition for a peremptory writ. CCP § 437c(m)(1).
    - The defendants may appeal from the summary judgment entered for Tai and Moe, even though the action remains

pending against Clay. In actions involving multiple parties, the judgment is considered final if it leaves no issue for further determination as to a particular plaintiff or defendant, even if further proceedings are pending against another party.

(2)(a) Timeliness of Notice of Appeal

- CRC 8.104 governs the timing of the filing of the notice of appeal. There are no circumstances in this case that would extend the filing under CRC 8.108. Under the general rule, the police department must file its notice of appeal by the earliest of the three time limits set out in CRC 8.104(a).
- The time limits are considered to be jurisdictional.
- If either of the two alternative 60-day periods applies, the police department's notice of appeal is filed late. If the 180-day period applies, the notice of appeal is timely.

(2)(b) Standards of Review

- The three main standards of review are de novo (independent), abuse of discretion, and substantial evidence.
- Preliminary Injunction:
    - The court exercises its discretion to issue an injunction. Thus, the issuance is reviewed under the abuse of discretion standard. Any factual determinations underlying the court's exercise of discretion are reviewed under the substantial evidence standard.
- Summary judgment:
    - A grant of summary judgment is a determination that there are no triable issues of material fact and the moving party is entitled to judgment as a matter of law. The judgment is reviewed de novo.

CHAPTER 9

PRIOR ADJUDICATION

I. STARE DECISIS

Stare decisis refers to adherence to legal precedent by the courts. The judicially created stare decisis doctrine promotes certainty and predictability in the application and development of the law. However, "adherence to precedent is the norm but not an inexorable command." Dobbs v. Jackson Women's Health Organization, 597 U.S. 215, 142 S.Ct. 2228, 213 L.Ed.2d 545 (2022).

A. Binding Versus Persuasive Authority

Under the rules of stare decisis, certain court decisions have binding effect on rulings made by other courts. Those court decisions that are not considered binding precedent may nonetheless have persuasive effect on other courts considering the same issues.

1. Decisions on Matters of State Law

When ruling on matters of California law, stare decisis requires that California courts of inferior jurisdiction adhere to decisions of courts of superior jurisdiction. (See California Court System chart, Chapter 1(A)(3)(a).)

a. California Supreme Court Decisions

Decisions of the California Supreme Court are binding on all inferior California courts on issues of state law. Auto Equity Sales, Inc. v. Superior Court, 57 Cal.2d 450, 20 Cal.Rptr. 321, 369 P.2d 937 (1962).

b. United States Supreme Court Decisions

California courts afford "deep deference" to decisions of the U.S. Supreme Court, "even on purely state law questions." Those decisions, however, are not binding; they are of persuasive value only. Piplack v. In-N-Out Burgers, 88 Cal.App.5th 1281, 1285, 305 Cal.Rptr.3d 405, 407 (2023) (California Supreme Court precedent regarding interpretation of state law is binding, whereas United

States Supreme Court decision on same issue of state law is only persuasive.).

c. **California Court of Appeal Decisions**

California Court of Appeal decisions are binding on all California superior courts in the state, even those located outside of the issuing Court of Appeal's district or division. When different panels of the courts of appeal have issued conflicting decisions, the superior courts are free to follow whichever Court of Appeal decision they find more persuasive. California does not follow a "horizontal stare decisis" rule; i.e., one panel of the Court of Appeal does not have to follow any other panel's decision, even if that decision came from the same appellate district or division. In re Marriage of Shaban, 88 Cal.App.4th 398, 105 Cal.Rptr.2d 863 (2001).

2. **Decisions on Matters of Federal Law**

U.S. Supreme Court decisions regarding federal law are binding on all California courts when the state courts are deciding a federal question. Federal circuit and district court decisions addressing federal questions are not binding on California state courts, although such decisions are entitled to significant weight as persuasive authority. When there is a split of authority in the circuit courts, California state courts do not consider Ninth Circuit decisions to be any more persuasive than the decisions of other circuits. Elliot v. Albright, 209 Cal.App.3d 1028, 257 Cal.Rptr. 762 (1989).

3. ***Compare Federal Procedure***

In contrast to the California practice, a federal Court of Appeals decision is binding on only the federal district courts within that circuit. It is also binding on all subsequent panels of the particular circuit under the horizontal stare decisis rule, unless the federal appellate court decision is subsequently reversed by the circuit court en banc or by the U.S. Supreme Court. Agostini v. Felton, 521 U.S. 203, 117 S.Ct. 1997, 138 L.Ed.2d 391 (1997).

4. **Illustration**

California enacted a statute pertaining to bankruptcy filings. On the basis of diversity jurisdiction, a creditor challenged California's statute in federal district court, claiming federal law preempted the state statute. In a 2–1 decision, the Ninth Circuit Court of Appeals ultimately agreed with the creditor that federal bankruptcy law preempted California's statute. In

> a later lawsuit in state court, a California Court of Appeal panel found the reasoning in the dissent from the Ninth Circuit's decision—which concluded that the California statute was not preempted—to be a more persuasive reading of federal law. The state Court of Appeal was not bound by the Ninth Circuit's majority opinion. Credit Managers Association v. Countrywide Home Loans, Inc., 144 Cal.App.4th 590, 50 Cal.Rptr.3d 259 (2006).

B. Overruling Precedent

The stare decisis doctrine requires lower courts to follow appellate court precedent (subject to the limitations discussed above), even if a different panel of appellate justices might have reached another result. Moradi-Shalal v. Fireman's Fund Insurance Co., 46 Cal.3d 287, 250 Cal.Rptr. 116, 758 P.2d 58 (1988). Although the California Supreme Court may overrule its precedent, it will do so only in limited situations.

1. Overruling Court-Created Errors or Unsound Decisions

The California Supreme Court may overrule precedent when the Court created an error that it must correct, especially if the error is of significant concern to the community. In addition, the Court may reconsider its prior decisions if later opinions show that an earlier decision was unsound or is appropriate for reevaluation. The Court is more likely to overrule an earlier decision if "it has generated and will continue to produce inequitable results, costly multiple litigation, and unnecessary confusion." *Moradi-Shalal*, 46 Cal.3d at 297, 250 Cal.Rptr. at 121, 758 P.2d 58.

2. Factors in Court's Consideration to Overrule

In assessing whether it should overrule precedent, the California Supreme Court may consider several factors, including whether: (a) subsequent courts have been reluctant to follow the decision; (b) scholarly analysis has been critical of the decision; and (c) there have been adverse social and economic consequences of the decision.

3. *Compare Federal Procedure*

The U.S. Supreme Court has acknowledged the importance of stare decisis, stating that it will not overrule prior precedent "unless the most convincing of reasons demonstrates that adherence to it puts us on a course that is sure error." Citizens United v. Federal Election Commission, 558 U.S. 310, 362, 130 S.Ct. 876, 911–912, 175 L.Ed.2d 753 (2010). See also Dobbs v. Jackson Women's Health Organization, 597 U.S. 215, 266–267,

142 S.Ct. 2228, 2264, 213 L.Ed.2d 545 (2022) ("[O]verruling a precedent * * * is not a step that should be taken lightly," particularly when the matter involves a constitutional question.). When the Court has overruled prior interpretations of statutes, it typically has done so because changes in legal doctrines or subsequent congressional actions have eroded the reasoning in the previous opinion. Further, the Court has departed from precedent when the decision proved to be unworkable or irreconcilable with other legal goals or was not well reasoned. Additionally, the Court may overrule precedent that is no longer consistent with historical understanding or principles of justice.

4. Illustration

A California Supreme Court opinion held that the Insurance Code contained a private cause of action for noncustomer claimants who were harmed by an insurance company's unfair business practices. After that decision, Plato sued Daggett in San Bernardino County Superior Court for damages caused when Daggett's car collided with Plato's in Rancho Cucamonga. Plato and Daggett settled the dispute with Daggett's insurance company. As permitted under the Supreme Court's previous holding, Plato then sued the insurance company, alleging the company engaged in unfair practices during the settlement. The California Supreme Court reexamined its decision and overruled its interpretation of the Insurance Code on several bases: scholarly criticism; the fact that most other states had refused to adopt such a policy; the inability of lower courts to apply the decision consistently; and the increase in litigation sparked by the old rule. Moradi-Shalal v. Fireman's Fund Insurance Co., 46 Cal.3d 287, 250 Cal.Rptr. 116, 758 P.2d 58 (1988) (reversing Royal Globe Insurance Co. v. Superior Court, 23 Cal.3d 880, 153 Cal.Rptr. 842, 592 P.2d 329 (1979)).

C. Retroactivity

1. Judicial Decisions Versus Legislation

Generally, the California courts consider judicial decisions to apply retroactively and legislation to apply only prospectively. The rule of retroactive application of judicial decisions stems from Blackstone's 18th-century theory that judges "find" the law rather than "create" it. Newman v. Emerson Radio Corp., 48 Cal.3d 973, 258 Cal.Rptr. 592, 772 P.2d 1059 (1989).

a. **Exceptions: Prospectively Applied Judicial Decisions**

Courts need not retroactively apply judicial decisions if: (1) doing so would create significant concerns about the effect of a new rule on the administration of justice; or (2) the parties' reasonable reliance on the existing law would be unjustly undermined.

b. **Exception: Retroactively Applied Legislation**

Legislation that affects substantive rights can apply retroactively only if the Legislature clearly states that intent. Strauss v. Horton, 46 Cal.4th 364, 93 Cal.Rptr.3d 591, 207 P.3d 48 (2009). Moreover, statutes that are silent about their retroactivity may be applied to pending litigation if the statute affects only the litigants' procedural (but not substantive) rights. Californians for Disability Rights v. Mervyn's, LLC, 39 Cal.4th 223, 46 Cal.Rptr.3d 57, 138 P.3d 207 (2006).

2. ***Compare Federal Procedure***

Case law is generally applied retroactively in the federal courts. When deciding whether to deviate from the practice of retroactive application of judicial decisions, federal courts are guided by the following: (a) the decision must either "overrul[e] clear past precedent on which litigants may have relied" or decide "an issue of first impression whose resolution was not clearly foreshadowed," thus establishing a new legal principle; (b) the court must determine whether retroactivity would impede the law's operation, taking into consideration the merits of the specific case and the prior history of the legal principle; and (c) if retroactivity would lead to substantially inequitable results, the court may decline retroactive application. Chevron Oil Co. v. Huson, 404 U.S. 97, 106, 92 S.Ct. 349, 355, 30 L.Ed.2d 296 (1971). As in California, federal statutes generally apply prospectively only, unless Congress clearly indicates a contrary intent. Opati v. Republic of Sudan, 596 U.S. 418, 140 S.Ct. 1601, 206 L.Ed.2d 904 (2020).

3. **Illustration**

In an earlier decision, the California Supreme Court interpreted a provision of California's Fair Employment and Housing Act (FEHA) to apply only to discrimination perpetrated by supervisory workers and not to discrimination perpetrated by nonsupervisory coworkers. The California

> Legislature later amended FEHA to specifically apply the provision to discrimination perpetrated by both supervisory and nonsupervisory coworkers. In the amendment, the Legislature stated that it was merely clarifying the meaning of the existing statute. Because of the strong presumption against the retroactive application of statutes, the California Supreme Court concluded that the Legislature's statement that it was clarifying state law was not sufficient to indicate legislative intent to apply the amendment retroactively. Thus, the statute covered only cases of nonsupervisory discrimination that occurred after the amendment's passage. McClung v. Employment Development Department, 34 Cal.4th 467, 20 Cal.Rptr.3d 428, 99 P.3d 1015 (2004).

D. Law of the Case and Judicial Estoppel

1. Law of the Case

a. Application of Doctrine

The law-of-the-case doctrine applies when cases are tried, appealed, retried, and appealed a second time. Once the appellate court hearing the first appeal states a rule of law essential to the decision and remands the case for further proceedings, subsequent trial and appellate courts must adhere to that rule of law in later proceedings in that case. Leider v. Lewis, 2 Cal.5th 1121, 218 Cal.Rptr.3d 127, 394 P.3d 1055 (2017). This adherence is required even if the rule of law was incorrectly decided or applied in the first appeal. The law-of-the-case doctrine applies until the litigation and appeals are terminated. Compare the doctrines of claim and issue preclusion (see section II, below), which apply to subsequent actions.

b. Exceptions

The law-of-the-case doctrine is a policy, not a strict requirement. As a result, there are several notable exceptions to the doctrine's application:

- Courts need not follow the law of the case when intervening changes in the law have occurred, such that prior precedent was overruled or new controlling precedent was established.
- Courts have declined to adhere to the doctrine when following it would lead to an unjust result.

- The doctrine does not apply if the issue was not addressed during the prior appeal.

2. Judicial Estoppel

Judicial estoppel is an equitable doctrine applied in the court's discretion. It is sometimes referred to as the doctrine of preclusion of inconsistent positions. The court invokes this doctrine when a party's inconsistent positions would result in a miscarriage of justice. Judicial estoppel applies when:

- a party has taken two positions;
- the positions were taken in judicial or quasi-judicial administrative proceedings;
- the party was successful in asserting the first position;
- the two positions are completely inconsistent; and
- the first position was not taken as a result of ignorance, fraud, or mistake.

Vaghashia v. Vaghashia, 106 Cal.App.5th 188, 326 Cal.Rptr.3d 715 (2024).

3. *Compare Federal Procedure*

Federal courts also observe the doctrines of law of the case and judicial estoppel. Those doctrines have essentially the same parameters as California's principles. See Zedner v. United States, 547 U.S. 489, 126 S.Ct. 1976, 164 L.Ed.2d 749 (2006); and Ingle v. Circuit City, 408 F.3d 592 (9th Cir.2005).

4. Illustration

Penne filed suit against Digby in Yuba County Superior Court to reclaim land from Digby located in the Islamic Republic of Iran that Penne alleged she owned. Digby brought a motion to stay or dismiss the action on forum non conveniens grounds, arguing that Iran was a suitable alternative forum. The trial court granted a stay. Penne promptly appealed from the ruling. The Court of Appeal reversed, finding Iran to be an unsuitable forum as a matter of law because it provided "no remedy at all." It remanded the action to the trial court. When the trial court received the case for the second time, Digby renewed his motion to dismiss for forum non conveniens, contending that new evidence that Penne had recently filed a separate action in Iran established that Iran was a suitable alternative forum and compelled the court to grant the motion. Finding no legal support for Digby's argument that Penne's Iran filing proves suitability of that forum, the trial court denied Digby's renewed motion. The determination by the Court of Appeal that Iran is not a suitable alternative forum as a matter of law constitutes the law of the case in all subsequent proceedings and defeats Digby's renewed forum non conveniens motion. Aghaian v. Minassian, 64 Cal.App.5th 603, 279 Cal.Rptr.3d 191, cert. denied, 595 U.S. ___, 142 S.Ct. 715, 211 L.Ed.2d 403 (2021).

II. RES JUDICATA

Res judicata is a common law doctrine barring relitigation of causes of action or issues. Res judicata promotes judicial economy, ensures repose for the parties, and strengthens the court system generally. There is no uniform terminology, in California or elsewhere, regarding the use of the term res judicata. It is here used to include both *claim preclusion* (which is sometimes alone called res judicata) and *issue preclusion* (also known as collateral estoppel).

A. Claim Preclusion

1. Requirements

There are four requirements of claim preclusion:

- a final judgment on the merits in Action #1;
- the same parties or those in privity with a party in Action #2 as in Action #1;
- a judgment in Action #1 that was based on the same cause of action as that brought in Action #2; and
- the cause of action in Action #2 actually was or could have been litigated in Action #1.

Samara v. Matar, 5 Cal.5th 322, 234 Cal.Rptr.3d 446, 419 P.3d 924 (2018).

a. Prior Final Judgment on the Merits

Any final judgment that reaches the legal substance of the claim is considered to be on the merits. Examples include summary judgment, default judgment, and stipulated judgment. A judgment based on procedural matters, such as subject matter jurisdiction, personal jurisdiction, venue, or involuntary dismissal under the diligent prosecution statutes, is not considered a judgment on the merits. A judgment is deemed final for claim purposes upon the conclusion of any appeal taken by a party, or upon the expiration of the time for taking an appeal.

b. Party or in Privity with Party

Claim preclusion applies only against one who was a party to the first action, or against a nonparty who was "in privity" with a party. Privity assumes a relationship between the party and nonparty that is close enough to justify the imposition of claim preclusion principles upon the nonparty. Grande v. Eisenhower Medical Center, 13 Cal.5th 313, 295 Cal.Rptr.3d 126, 512 P.3d 273 (2022). Examples of those in privity include representatives of deceased parties and successors in interest.

c. Same Cause of Action

The definition of "cause of action" is critical in claim preclusion analysis. In marked contrast to most jurisdictions, California subscribes to the "primary rights" theory of the cause of action. "A 'cause of action' is composed of a 'primary right' of the plaintiff, a corresponding 'primary duty' of the defendant, and a wrongful act by the defendant constituting a breach of that duty." Crowley v. Katleman, 8 Cal.4th 666, 681, 34 Cal.Rptr.2d 386, 393, 881 P.2d 1083 (1994). The primary right is the right to be free of the type of harm or injury caused by the defendant. In most other state jurisdictions, claims are considered to be a single cause of action if they arise out of the same transaction or occurrence, as defined by the Restatement (Second) of Judgments (1982).

1) Determining a Primary Right

The identification of a primary right can be challenging, especially in cases involving more than one type of injury. It is a determination with significant impact, since, for claim preclusion purposes, an attempt to litigate the "same" cause of action (i.e., invasion of the same primary right) in a later lawsuit will be barred. However, the same set of facts may yield different primary rights, each of which may be vindicated in separate actions. Each primary right represents a distinct harm suffered. Whether several legal theories are pleaded, or different types of remedies are sought, is irrelevant. What matters is whether the defendant violated the plaintiff's right to be free from the particular sort of injury suffered.

Grisham v. Philip Morris U.S.A., Inc., 40 Cal.4th 623, 54 Cal.Rptr.3d 735, 151 P.3d 1151 (2007).

2) Declaratory Relief

When a party sought purely declaratory relief in Action #1, the resulting judgment does not preclude further litigation of the primary rights involved in Action #2. CCP § 1062. If, however, the party's first action sought declaratory relief mixed with other forms of relief (such as an injunction), any resulting judgment—including the granting of declaratory relief—will preclude further litigation under the doctrine of claim preclusion. Mycogen Corp. v. Monsanto Co., 28 Cal.4th 888, 123 Cal.Rptr.2d 432, 51 P.3d 297 (2002).

3) Causes of Action Based on Both State and Federal Law

If the defendant's conduct violated both California and federal law, the question arises whether there are two primary rights, or one primary right with two legal theories. If the California and federal laws are both intended to address the same injury or harm to the plaintiff, then only one primary right is implicated.

d. Cause of Action Was or Could Have Been Litigated

A final judgment bars relitigation not only of those causes of action that were actually litigated in the first action, but also of those that could have been litigated at the same time. "If the matter was within the scope of the action, related to the subject matter and relevant to the issues, so that it *could* have been raised, the judgment is conclusive on it despite the fact that it was not in fact expressly pleaded or otherwise urged." Sutphin v. Speik, 15 Cal.2d 195, 202, 99 P.2d 652, 655 (1940) (emphasis in original). This requirement causes confusion because it seems at odds with the primary rights doctrine.

2. Claim Preclusion and Compulsory Cross-Complaints

Statutorily, a "related" cause of action that a defendant has against a plaintiff must be brought as a compulsory cross-complaint in the original action or else the defendant will be barred from bringing it as a separate lawsuit. CCP §§ 426.10 & 426.30. (See Chapter 3(V)(A)(1).) The defendant's cause of action is related if it arises out of the same transaction or occurrence as the plaintiff's cause of action. CCP § 426.10(c). This transactional approach to cross-complaints is in stark contrast to the application of the primary rights theory in other claim preclusion situations under California law.

3. *Compare Federal Procedure*

a. Federal Substantive Law

Federal courts applying federal substantive law usually follow the transactional definition of a claim (cause of action), not the primary rights doctrine. If a subsequent claim arises from the same transaction or occurrence as the first claim, its relitigation is barred. This transactional rule is also applied by the majority of states, as recommended by the Restatement (Second) of Judgments (1982).

b. State Substantive Law

In contrast, a state law claim contained in a federal action is subject to the claim preclusion rules of the state in which the federal court sits. Semtek International Inc. v. Lockheed Martin Corp., 531 U.S. 497, 121 S.Ct. 1021, 149 L.Ed.2d 32 (2001). Thus, a California federal court sitting in diversity or exercising supplemental jurisdiction would apply California's primary rights doctrine to claims arising under state law.

4. Illustration

After Phoenix's wife, Wanda, a lifelong cigarette smoker, was diagnosed with lung cancer, Phoenix filed a common law action in Sutter County Superior Court against Donahue Tobacco Co. for loss of consortium. Phoenix subsequently dismissed his action with prejudice. After Wanda's death from lung cancer, Phoenix brought a wrongful death action against Donahue Tobacco, seeking in part damages for his loss of consortium resulting from his wife's death. Donahue Tobacco demurred, arguing that Phoenix's action was barred by the doctrine of claim preclusion because Phoenix's previous loss of consortium action against Donahue Tobacco had involved the same primary right. The court will likely sustain Donahue Tobacco's demurrer. In Phoenix's first action, he had sought compensation for the loss of consortium he suffered and would continue to suffer as a result of his wife's physical condition while she was alive, as well as for the loss of consortium that he anticipated he would suffer as a result of his wife's premature death. Phoenix's second action likewise sought compensation for the loss of consortium that he had suffered and would continue to suffer as a result of his wife's death. The primary right at issue in Phoenix's wrongful death action for loss of consortium was the same as the primary right at issue in his previous action (which resulted in a final judgment of dismissal) for loss of consortium brought while Wanda was still alive. Therefore, the claim preclusion doctrine barred the wrongful death suit based on that cause of action. Boeken v. Philip Morris USA, Inc., 48 Cal.4th 788, 108 Cal.Rptr.3d 806, 230 P.3d 342 (2010).

B. Issue Preclusion

1. Requirements

There are five requirements of issue preclusion:

- an issue of law or fact in Action #2 that is identical to an issue litigated in Action #1;
- the issue was actually litigated in Action #1;
- the issue was necessary to the decision in Action #1;
- the decision in Action #1 was a final judgment on the merits; and
- the party against whom preclusion is sought in Action #2 was a party or in privity with a party in Action #1.

Grande v. Eisenhower Medical Center, 13 Cal.5th 313, 295 Cal.Rptr.3d 126, 512 P.3d 73 (2022); and Restatement (Second) of Judgments § 27 (1982).

a. Identical Issue

A key aspect of issue preclusion involves determining whether the issue litigated in the prior action is identical to an issue raised in the later action, regardless of how the causes of action are framed. A broad definition of the issue can subsume many smaller subissues. A narrow definition of the issue can allow relitigation of many matters that otherwise might appear nearly identical.

b. Actually Litigated

The application of the "actually litigated" requirement by California courts has led to confusion. Some courts appear to have imported the "could have been litigated" standard pertinent to claim preclusion. Torrey Pines Bank v. Superior Court, 216 Cal.App.3d 813, 265 Cal.Rptr. 217 (1989). Other opinions shed doubt on whether the "actually litigated" requirement applies to issues or legal theories. In jurisdictions outside of California that follow the

Restatement (Second) of Judgments § 27 (1982), the requirement that an issue must have been previously litigated is applied strictly. Courts analyze a number of factors in making this determination, including whether the prior proceeding allowed the parties to present their case, and whether the parties had an incentive to vigorously litigate the issue.

c. Necessary to the Decision

An issue must not only have been actually litigated, but resolution of that issue also must have been "necessary" to the judgment. If the ultimate disposition of the prior action was not based on the determination of the issue, it was not necessary to the judgment, and further litigation of that issue is not precluded. Four Star Electric, Inc. v. F & H Construction, 7 Cal.App.4th 1375, 10 Cal.Rptr.2d 1 (1992). The issue will be deemed "necessary" as long as it was not "entirely unnecessary" to the prior judgment. Lucido v. Superior Court, 51 Cal.3d 335, 342, 272 Cal.Rptr. 767, 770, 795 P.2d 1223 (1990). If the prior judgment is based on alternative grounds, California follows the rule in the Restatement (Second) of Judgments § 27, comment *i* (1982), which provides that if either alternative ground is sufficient standing alone to support the judgment, the judgment is not conclusive as to either issue by itself. If the reviewing court affirms on only one of the alternative grounds, the second ground is not considered conclusively established. Samara v. Matar, 5 Cal.5th 322, 234 Cal.Rptr.3d 446, 419 P.3d 924 (2018).

d. Final Judgment on the Merits

The judgment in the prior action must be final and on the merits. Factors in favor of finality include whether: (1) the parties were heard on the matter; (2) the court issued a reasoned opinion; and (3) any potential appeal has been resolved. Sandoval v. Superior Court, 140 Cal.App.3d 932, 190 Cal.Rptr. 29 (1983). Default judgments are considered final for issue preclusion purposes. If an appeal is pending, or the time for bringing an appeal has not yet expired, the judgment is not yet final.

e. Party or In Privity with Party

For issue preclusion to apply, a party in a subsequent action must have been the same party in the previous litigation, or that party must have been so closely related in interest that the party can fairly be said to have had its day in court.

Grande v. Eisenhower Medical Center, 13 Cal.5th 313, 295 Cal.Rptr.3d 126, 512 P.3d 73 (2022).

2. Nonmutual Issue Preclusion

a. Defensive Use

Issue preclusion in California may be raised defensively (i.e., by a defendant in Action #2 against a plaintiff who litigated and lost on that issue against a different party in Action #1). Bernhard v. Bank of America, 19 Cal.2d 807, 122 P.2d 892 (1942).

b. Offensive Use

The doctrine may also be asserted offensively (i.e., by a plaintiff in Action #2 against a defendant who litigated and lost on that issue against a different party in Action #1). Imen v. Glassford, 201 Cal.App.3d 898, 247 Cal.Rptr. 514 (1988). The court will scrutinize the application of offensive issue preclusion for fairness to ensure that:

- the party against whom it is asserted had a full and fair opportunity to litigate;
- the party against whom it is asserted could foresee multiple suits;
- the party asserting it could not easily have been joined in the first action; and
- there are no inconsistent judgments on the record.

Id. at 906, 247 Cal.Rptr. at 518 (citing Parklane Hosiery Co. v. Shore, 439 U.S. 322, 99 S.Ct. 645, 58 L.Ed.2d 552 (1979)).

c. Preclusive Effect as to Third Parties

In the contractual arbitration context, determination of an issue in arbitration proceedings is not issue preclusive as to persons who were not signatories to the arbitration agreement, unless the parties to the arbitration agreement expressly agree to permit third parties to assert issue preclusion. Vandenberg v. Superior Court, 21 Cal.4th 815, 88 Cal.Rptr.2d 366, 982 P.2d 229 (1999). Similarly, issues that are stipulated to or are settled in Action #1 are not preclusive as to third parties in Action #2.

3. *Compare Federal Procedure*

Federal courts strictly apply the requirement that an issue must have been "actually litigated." Arizona v. California, 530 U.S. 392, 120 S.Ct. 2304, 147 L.Ed.2d 374 (2000). The fundamental elements of issue preclusion in federal practice are otherwise virtually identical to those in California, and both defensive and offensive uses of issue preclusion are allowed. Unlike California, however, a final federal judgment has issue-preclusive effect even if an appeal is pending. Moreover, default judgments rendered in federal court are not issue preclusive.

4. Illustration

Pop's son, Sonny, who was fleeing arrest, was shot and killed by officers employed by the City of Delano Police Department. Pop filed a complaint against the City of Delano in U.S. District Court for the Eastern District of California. The federal civil rights complaint alleged violations of Sonny's Fourth and Fourteenth Amendment rights and claims for wrongful death under California law. The federal court bifurcated the state and federal claims and tried only the federal claims, which resulted in a judgment of dismissal of the federal causes of action with prejudice. The district court dismissed Pop's state law claims without prejudice. Pop then filed a wrongful death (negligence) lawsuit against the City of Delano in Kern County Superior Court, based on the same allegations as those raised in the federal action. The City of Delano demurred to the complaint, arguing that issue preclusion barred the California state court action because the issue of the Police Department's alleged excessive and unreasonable force had already been determined in the City of Delano's favor in the federal action. Pop asserted that the standard of reasonableness applicable in a Fourth Amendment action was not the same as the standard of reasonableness in a California negligence action. Because the same objective consideration of the totality of the circumstances was required for the determination of reasonableness in both actions, the doctrine of issue preclusion prevented Pop from relitigating the excessive force matter in his state court wrongful death action. Hernandez v. City of Pomona, 46 Cal.4th 501, 94 Cal.Rptr.3d 1, 207 P.3d 506 (2009).

CHAPTER 9

SAMPLE EXAM QUESTIONS

OBJECTIVE QUESTIONS

(1) Which of the following represent(s) binding precedent on the California Court of Appeal for the First District?

a. A prior decision of the California Supreme Court;

b. A prior decision of the U.S. Court of Appeals for the Ninth Circuit;

c. A prior decision of the California Court of Appeal for the First District;

d. Both a and c.

(2) The California Supreme Court may overrule its own precedent:

a. When the Court created an error that must be corrected;

b. When the precedent is unsound;

c. Never—only the United States Supreme Court can overrule California Supreme Court precedent;

d. Both a and b.

(3) True or False: In California, legislation is generally applied prospectively and judicial decisions retroactively, absent a judicial or legislative requirement to do otherwise.

(4) True or False: The law-of-the-case doctrine applies to both legal and factual rulings made by an appellate court.

(5) True or False: The doctrine of judicial estoppel applies in California courts as well as in federal courts.

(6) True or False: For both claim and issue preclusion purposes in California, a judgment is considered final as soon as it is entered by the superior court.

(7) In California, claim preclusion bars a party from filing a lawsuit if:

a. The current cause of action arises from the same transaction, occurrence, or series of transactions or occurrences as a previously litigated cause of action;

b. The plaintiff seeks to vindicate in a subsequent action the same primary right as was previously litigated;

c. A court previously issued solely a declaratory judgment on the matter to be litigated in the subsequent action;

d. Both b and c.

(8) Under California's issue preclusion principles, a party will be unable to relitigate an issue raised in a subsequent proceeding when which of the following conditions exist(s)?

a. The issue to be litigated is identical to that actually litigated and necessarily decided in the former proceeding;

b. The decision on the issue in the former proceeding is final and on the merits;

c. Issue preclusion is sought against a person who was a party or in privity with a party to the former proceeding;

d. All of the above.

(9) True or False: California permits defensive use of issue preclusion but not offensive use of issue preclusion.

<u>Answers to Objective Questions</u>

(1) **a.** The decisions of California courts of superior jurisdiction are binding on courts of inferior jurisdiction. Therefore, decisions of the California Supreme Court are binding on all California courts of appeal. Answer (b) is incorrect because federal circuit court decisions (regardless of circuit) are not treated as binding authority by the California state courts. Answer (c) is incorrect because a ruling issued by a California Court of Appeal panel is not binding on any subsequent appellate panel, regardless of which district issued the ruling.

(2) **d.** Both (a) and (b) are correct bases for the California Supreme Court to overrule its precedent.

(3) **True.** Generally, California applies judicial decisions retroactively and legislation prospectively, unless the court or Legislature requires otherwise.

(4) **False.** Law of the case applies to rules of law, not factual determinations.

(5) **True.** The judicial estoppel doctrine is recognized in both California and federal courts.

(6) **False.** A judgment is considered final for claim and issue preclusion purposes when the appeal from the judgment is completed or the time to appeal has expired.

(7) **b.** California is in the minority of states that recognizes the primary rights doctrine, in contrast to the transactional standard used by federal courts and in many state jurisdictions (see Answer (a)). A single cause of action under the transactional standard might be considered two causes of action under the primary rights doctrine. Answer (c) is incorrect because a prior judgment that granted only declaratory relief does not have claim-preclusive effect in a subsequent action.

(8) **d.** This question sets out the requirements for issue preclusion in California.

(9) **False.** California permits both defensive and offensive use of issue preclusion.

ESSAY QUESTION

Ruby experienced severe abdominal pains and saw Dr. Nan in Yreka. After conducting an examination, Dr. Nan concluded that Ruby's pains were a mild digestive ailment and nothing to worry about. As it turned out, Ruby's pains were caused by a dangerous ectopic pregnancy. As a result of the harmful pregnancy, Ruby had to have a hysterectomy. Ruby was hospitalized for two weeks. In addition to her physical injuries, Ruby has suffered emotional distress.

Ruby sued Dr. Nan in Siskiyou County Superior Court for professional negligence. Ruby prevailed. The jury awarded Ruby damages based on both her physical injuries and emotional distress, and the court entered judgment. One year later, Ruby and her husband, Tim, decided that they wanted to have a baby. Because of Ruby's condition, the couple retained a gestational surrogate to carry the pregnancy, for which they paid roughly $150,000. Ruby and Tim filed a new suit in Siskiyou County Superior Court against Dr. Nan and Sycamore Hospital, where Dr. Nan worked at the time of Ruby's initial injury, to recover the expenses associated with the surrogacy. (Sycamore Hospital was not a party to the first lawsuit.)

Analyze the potential claim and issue preclusion defenses Dr. Nan and Sycamore Hospital might raise in response to Ruby's and Tim's lawsuit. Discuss whether Ruby and Tim might successfully assert issue preclusion against Dr. Nan and/or Sycamore Hospital.

Answer to Essay Question

- Claim Preclusion
    - Dr. Nan and Sycamore Hospital will contend that Ruby and Tim's causes of action are barred by claim preclusion and had already been decided in the earlier lawsuit.
    - Elements of claim preclusion:
        - Final judgment on the merits in the first action;
        - Same plaintiffs and same defendants (or those in privity) in both first and second actions;
        - Both causes of action are based on the invasion of the same primary right; and
        - The cause of action in the second action actually was or could have been litigated in the first action.

- Final judgment on the merits of the first case:
  - There was a judgment on the merits of Ruby's personal injury and emotional distress causes of action.
  - It is probable that the time for appeal has expired.
- Same parties or privies:
  - Ruby was the plaintiff in both actions. Tim became a plaintiff in the second action. His relationship as Ruby's husband is probably one of privity.
  - Only Dr. Nan was a defendant in the first case. Thus, Sycamore Hospital may not assert claim preclusion, but it may be asserted by Dr. Nan.
  - Sycamore Hospital might argue that Dr. Nan litigated in privity with the Hospital in the first case, because she was employed there at the time. However, since the Hospital was not involved in the original trial, this argument is not likely to be successful.
- Same cause of action:
  - The contrast between the causes of action in the two lawsuits is the difference in the damages sought. The underlying theory of recovery—negligence—is the same in both cases. Both suits involve recovery for injuries that Ruby sustained to her body. As such, both claims arguably involve the invasion of the same "primary right" to be free of the kind of reproductive injury that Ruby suffered, making claim preclusion appropriate, at least with regard to Dr. Nan. However, some courts could reasonably interpret Ruby's claims as arising from different primary rights.
  - Under the transactional standard used in other jurisdictions, the plaintiffs' causes of action may be regarded as one.

- Issue Preclusion
  - Ruby and Tim will probably contend that the negligence issue has already been litigated and decided in the first action against Dr. Nan, and the jury's finding of negligence should be conclusive.
  - Requirements for issue preclusion:
    - Valid final judgment on the merits of the first action;
    - Same issue was actually litigated and necessarily determined in the first action.

    - Issue preclusion may only be asserted against person who was a party or in privity with a party in the first action.
    - Issue preclusion may be asserted by someone not a party in the first action:
    - Nonmutual defensive issue preclusion: permissible provided the person against whom it is asserted had a full and fair opportunity to litigate the issue.
    - Nonmutual offensive issue preclusion: permissible provided it is not unfair and:
        - The party against whom it is asserted had a full and fair opportunity to litigate;
        - The party against whom it is asserted could foresee multiple suits;
        - The party asserting it could not easily have been joined in the first action; and
        - There are no inconsistent judgments on the record.
- Valid, final judgment:
    - The judgment for Ruby in the first action was on the merits of her personal injury and emotional distress causes of action.
    - It is probable that the time for appeal has expired.
- Same issues actually litigated and necessarily determined:
    - The issue litigated in the first action was the negligence of Dr. Nan, not the negligence of Sycamore Hospital. However, under a theory of vicarious liability, Dr. Nan's negligence might be attributed to the Hospital. The Hospital might be considered to be in privity with Dr. Nan.
    - The issue of negligence was essential to the judgment in the first action because it was the basis for the judgment. Dr. Nan had full motivation to litigate it vigorously the first time.
- Preclusion asserted against a person who was a party:
    - Dr. Nan was a party in the first action, so Ruby and Tim could assert issue preclusion against her. However, Sycamore Hospital was not a party in the first action. Unless the Hospital is considered to be in

privity with Dr. Nan, issue preclusion against it may not be proper.

- Nonmutual application:
    - Tim was not a party to the first suit, but he might be able to assert issue preclusion against Dr. Nan because she had a full and fair opportunity to litigate in the first action. Tim could not have been joined in the first action because he had no cause of action to plead at that time.

TABLE OF CASES

INDEX

References are to Pages